THE CRUCIFIED GOD

THE
CRUCIFIED GOD

*The Cross of Christ as the Foundation
and Criticism of Christian Theology*

JÜRGEN MOLTMANN

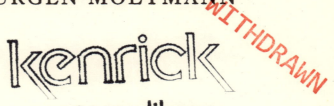

HARPER & ROW, PUBLISHERS
NEW YORK, EVANSTON, SAN FRANCISCO, LONDON

Illustrissimae
Dukianae universitati
in civitate Carolina septentrionali
ob summum in Sancta Theologia
honorem sibi oblatum
hunc librum
grato devotoque animo
dedicat

Jürgen Moltmann
a.d. III. Id. Mai.
anno p.Chr.n. MCLXXIII.

Translated by R. A. Wilson and John Bowden from the German
Der gekreuzigte Gott
published by Christian Kaiser Verlag, Munich,
second edition 1973

FIRST U.S. EDITION

ISBN: 0-06-065901-7

LIBRARY OF CONGRESS CATALOG CARD NUMBER: 73-18694

CONTENTS

IN EXPLANATION OF THE THEME

*The cross is not and cannot be loved. Yet only the crucified Christ can bring the freedom which changes the world because it is no longer afraid of death. In his time the crucified Christ was regarded as a scandal and as foolishness. Today, too, it is considered old-fashioned to put him in the centre of Christian faith and of theology. Yet only when men are reminded of him, however untimely this may be, can they be set free from the power of the facts of the present time, and from the laws and compulsions of history, and be offered a future which will never grow dark again. Today the church and theology must turn to the crucified Christ in order to show the world the freedom he offers. This is essential if they wish to become what they assert they are: the church of Christ, and Christian theology.

Since I first studied theology, I have been concerned with the theology of the cross. This may not have been so clear to those who liked *Theology of Hope*, which I published in 1964, as it was to its critics; yet I believe that it has been the guiding light of my theological thought. This no doubt goes back to the period of my first concern with questions of Christian faith and theology in actual life, as a prisoner of war behind barbed wire. I certainly owe it to the unforgettable lectures on Reformation theology which I heard from Hans Joachim Iwand, Ernst Wolf and Otto Weber in 1948/49 in Göttingen. Shattered and broken, the survivors of my generation were then returning from camps and hospitals to the lecture room. A theology which did not speak of God in the sight of the one who was abandoned and crucified would have had nothing to say to us then. One cannot say, of course, whether as the result of our experiences we understood the crucified Christ better than anyone else. Experiences cannot

I

be repeated. Moreover, one speaks of personal experiences only to explain why one is fascinated by what one is trying to communicate. It is not the experiences which are important, but the one who has been experienced in them. The theology of the cross which was meaningful to us then, and gave us firm ground beneath our feet, came to my mind again when the movements of hope in the 1960s met stiffer resistance and stronger opponents than they could stand, and many abandoned their hope, either to adapt themselves, half resigned, to the usual course of events, or to withdraw into themselves in total resignation. I can only speak for myself, but on my disappointment at the end of 'socialism with a human face' in Czechoslovakia and the end of the Civil Rights movement in the USA, and at what I hope is only a temporary halt in the reforms in the ecumenical movement and the Catholic church which began so confidently with the Second Vatican Council and the Uppsala Conference in 1968, the centre of my hope and resistance once again became that which, after all, is the driving force of all attempts to open up new horizons in society and the church: the cross of Christ.

The criticism of the church and theology which we have been fortunate enough to experience, and which is justified on sociological, psychological and ideological grounds, can only be accepted and made radical by a critical theology of the cross. There is an inner criterion of all theology, and of every church which claims to be Christian, and this criterion goes far beyond all political, ideological and psychological criticism from outside. It is the crucified Christ himself. When churches, theologians and forms of belief appeal to him—which they must, if they are to be Christian—then they are appealing to the one who judges them most severely and liberates them most radically from lies and vanity, from the struggle for power and from fear. The churches, believers and theologians must be taken at their word. And this word is 'the word of the cross'. It is the criterion of their truth, and therefore the criticism of their untruth. The crisis of the church in present-day society is not merely the critical choice between assimilation or retreat into the ghetto, but the crisis of its own existence as the church of the crucified Christ. Any outside criticism which really hits the mark is merely an indication of its inner christological crisis. The question of ecclesiology, however unpleasant it may be for conservatives and progressives, is no more than a short prelude to its internal crisis, for only by Christ is it possible to tell what is a Christian church and what is not. Whether or not Christianity, in an alienated, divided and oppressive society, itself becomes alienated, divided and an accomplice of oppression, is ultimately decided only by whether the crucified Christ is a stranger to it or the Lord who determines the form of its existence. The objection has been made that it is still too early to raise this question in the churches and ecclesial communities, that the churches have not yet achieved the openness to the world which society has achieved, that in their ideology and practice they have not even admitted the justification of secular freedom movements and the criticisms which they make—and now their very basis is being questioned. I admit that this tactical question is justified, but do not believe that it leads any further than to the adaptation of antiquated forms of the church to newer forms. As far as I am concerned, the Christian church and Christian theology become relevant to the problems of the modern world only when they reveal the 'hard core' of their identity in the crucified Christ and through it are called into question, together with the society in which they live. Ideological and political criticism from outside can only force theology and the church to reveal their true identity and no longer to hide behind an alien mask drawn from history and the present time. Faith, the church and theology must demonstrate what they really believe and hope about the man from Nazareth who was crucified under Pontius Pilate, and what practical consequences they wish to draw from this. The crucified Christ himself is a challenge to Christian theology and the Christian church, which dare to call themselves by his name.

But what kind of theology of the cross does him justice, and is necessary today? There is a good deal of support in tradition for the theology of the cross, but it was never much loved. It begins with Paul, to whom its foundation is rightly attributed, and then leaps forward to Luther, in whom it is given explicit expression, and is present today in the persecuted churches of the poor and the oppressed. It returned to life in a distinctive way in Zinzendorf. It left its mark on the better side of early dialectical theology and on the Luther renaissance of the 1920s. In a famous lecture in 1912, Martin Kähler described the cross of Christ as the 'basis and standard of christology', but unfortunately did not cling to this principle himself. In all the cases we have mentioned, the theology of the cross was relevant only within the framework of human misery and of salvation, even though attempts have been made to take it further.

To return today to the theology of the cross means avoiding one-sided presentations of it in tradition, and comprehending the crucified Christ in the light and context of his resurrection, and therefore of freedom and hope.

To take up the theology of the cross today is to go beyond the limits of the doctrine of salvation and to inquire into the revolution needed in the concept of God. Who is God in the cross of the Christ who is abandoned by God?

To take the theology of the cross further at the present day means to go beyond a concern for personal salvation, and to inquire about the liberation of man and his new relationship to the reality of the demonic crisis in his society. Who is the true man in the sight of the Son of Man who was rejected and rose again in the freedom of God?

Finally, to realize the theology of the cross at the present day is to take seriously the claims of Reformation theology to criticize and reform, and to develop it beyond a criticism of the church into a criticism of society. What does it mean to recall the God who was crucified in a society whose official creed is optimism, and which is knee-deep in blood?

The final issue, however, is that of the radical orientation of theology and the church on Christ. Jesus died crying out to God, 'My God, why hast thou forsaken me?' All Christian theology and all Christian life is basically an answer to the question which Jesus asked as he died. The atheism of protests and of metaphysical rebellions against God are also answers to this question. Either Jesus who was abandoned by God is the end of all theology or he is the beginning of a specifically Christian, and therefore critical and liberating, theology and life. The more the 'cross of reality' is taken seriously, the more the crucified Christ becomes the general criterion of theology. The issue is not that of an abstract theology of the cross and of suffering, but of a theology of the crucified Christ.

I may be asked why I have turned from 'theology of hope' to the theology of the cross. I have given some reasons for this. But is it in itself a step backwards? 'Why,' asked Wolf-Dieter Marsch with approval, 'has Moltmann come back from the all too strident music of Bloch, step by step to the more subdued *eschatologia crucis?*' For me, however, this is not a step back from the trumpets of Easter to the lamentations of Good Friday. As I intend to show, the theology of the cross is none other than the reverse side of the Christian theology of hope, if the starting point of the latter lies in the resurrection of the *crucified* Christ. As I said in *Theology of Hope*, that theology was itself worked out as an *eschatologia crucis*. This book, then, cannot be regarded as a step back. *Theology of Hope* began with the *resurrection* of the crucified Christ, and I am now turning to look at the *cross* of the risen Christ. I was concerned then with the remembrance of Christ in the form of the *hope* of his future, and now I am concerned with hope in the form of the *remembrance* of his death. The dominant theme then was that of *anticipations* of the future of God in the form of promises and hopes; here it is the understanding of the *incarnation* of that future, by way of the sufferings of Christ, in the world's sufferings. Moving away from Ernest Bloch's philosophy of hope, I now turn to the questions of 'negative dialectic' and the 'critical theory' of T. W. Adorno and M. Horkheimer, together with the experiences and insights of early dialectical theology and existentialist philosophy. Unless it apprehends the pain of the negative, Christian hope cannot be realistic and liberating. In no sense does this theology of the cross 'go back step by step'; it is intended to make the theology of hope more concrete, and to add the necessary power of resistance to the power of its visions to inspire to action. In giving a more profound dimension to the theology of hope, I am aware that I am following the same course as Johann Baptist Metz, who for several years has been associating his politically critical eschatology more and more closely with the 'dangerous remembrance' of the suffering and death of Christ. Ernst Bloch too is becoming more and more disturbed by the problem of evil, and the failure of both philosophy and theology to give it conceptual form. Nor need anyone feel comforted that the theme of the 'theology of revolution' is no longer to be found in the chapter headings. The revolution of all religious, cultural and political values which proceeds from the crucified Christ will come in due time.

I have presented individual ideas and parts of this book in lectures in various European and American universities. I have discussed them with my students in lectures and seminars in the

University of Tübingen. I would like to thank all who have taken part in these dialogues for their critical stimulation. I would like to thank, too, my assistants, who have encouraged me to work out a theology of the cross: Dr Karl-Adolf Bauer, Dr Reiner Strunk, Dr Rudolf Weth and Gerhard M. Martin. I thank Douglas Meeks, Daniel Louw, E. P. van de Beek, Rafael Severa, Herwig Arts and Martin Tripole, who have written theses upon my theology and have obliged me to give fresh thought to my arguments. Michael Welker has constantly criticized and corrected this manuscript. I owe him special thanks.

In front of me hangs Marc Chagall's picture 'Crucifixion in Yellow'. It shows the figure of the crucified Christ in an apocalyptic situation: people sinking into the sea, people homeless and in flight, and yellow fire blazing in the background. And with the crucified Christ there appears the angel with the trumpet and the open roll of the book of life. This picture has accompanied me for a long time. It symbolizes the cross on the horizon of the world, and can be thought of as a symbolic expression of the studies which follow. A symbol invites thought (P. Ricoeur). The symbol of the cross invites rethinking. And this book is not meant to bring the discussion to a dogmatic conclusion, but to be, like a symbol, an invitation to thought and rethinking.

Tübingen

6

I

THE IDENTITY AND RELEVANCE OF FAITH

If it is true that the inner criterion of whether or not Christian theology is *Christian* lies in the crucified Christ, we come back to Luther's lapidary statement: *Crux probat omnia.*[1] In Christianity the cross is the test of everything which deserves to be called Christian. One may add that the cross alone, and nothing else, is its test, since the cross refutes everything, and excludes the syncretistic elements in Christianity. This is a hard saying. To many it sounds unattractive and unmodern, and to others rigid and orthodox. I will try to disappoint both.

We may want to make Christian theology reveal that it is Christian, but this cannot be done in abstract and timeless terms, or from the mere desire for self-assertion. It has a definable and circumscribed place amongst modern problems. The Christian life of theologians, churches and human beings is faced more than ever today with a double crisis: the *crisis of relevance* and the *crisis of identity*. These two crises are complementary. The more theology and the church attempt to become relevant to the problems of the present day, the more deeply they are drawn into the crisis of their own Christian identity. The more they attempt to assert their identity in traditional dogmas, rights and moral notions, the more irrelevant and unbelievable they become. This double crisis can be more accurately described as the *identity-involvement dilemma*. We shall see how far, in these specific experiences of a double crisis, reflection upon the cross leads to the clarification of what can be called Christian identity and what can be called Christian relevance, in critical solidarity with our contemporaries.

7

1. *The Crisis of Relevance in Christian Life*

The struggle for a renewal of theology and the churches began with the realization, which has become widespread and irrefutable, that Christianity faced a growing crisis of relevance and credibility. After a certain period in the post-war years in Western society, the churches and theology fed undisturbed upon their own resources. It then dawned upon many, and especially upon those on whom the church depended for its continuance, the students of theology, that a church which simply continued its previous form and ideology was in process of losing contact with the scientific, social and political reality of the world around it, and in many respects had already lost it. Its credibility, which in Germany it had to some extent gained by many acts of resistance during the period of National Socialism and 'German Christians', and of which it had given proof by surviving the collapse of most public institutions at the end of the war, was irresistibly disappearing. This lack of contact and blindness to reality makes theologians and churches increasingly obsolete. Many abandon the study of theology or their ministry as priests and pastors, and their religious orders, and study sociology, psychology or revolution, or work amongst the wretched of our society, because they feel that in this way they can contribute more to solving the conflicts of this fragmented society.[2] The old theology which they have learnt seems to them like a fossil surviving from a previous age. Fundamentalism fossilizes the Bible into an unquestionable authority. Dogmatism freezes living Christian tradition solid. The habitual conservatism of religion makes the liturgy inflexible, and Christian morality—often against its better knowledge and conscience—becomes a deadening legalism. What began as a theoretical discussion about the demythologization of the Bible, the secularizing of tradition and the 'opening of the church towards the world' (*aggiornamento*), consequently led, in many places, to the practice of ecclesiastical disobedience, withdrawal from the ministry, abandonment of the church, rebellion and even weary indifference. Critical theology produced 'critical Catholicism' and the 'critical church', and all three rapidly went on to a criticism of theology and the church as a whole. The attention of many was drawn by the gospel and the frequently suppressed revolutionary traditions in Christianity, to the sufferings of the oppressed and

8

abandoned in the world; and they began to have a passionate social and political commitment. When they followed this course, they quite often felt obliged to abandon the churches as they now exist, because they found in their institutions no possibility of realizing this commitment, and indeed often had to commit themselves in opposition to the church as a society. For them, their total questioning of the church and theology arose from their apprehension of the 'cross of the present time' in the situation of those who in this society live in the shadow of the cross, and from the wish to take this cross of reality upon themselves and to live in solidarity with and for these others. This exodus from a blinded society, which has psychologically and socially repressed its pain at the suffering in the world, and pushes people who suffer to the fringes of society, in order to withdraw undisturbed into its own small groups, consequently led to an exodus from a church which did not dissociate itself with sufficient determination from these inner and outward defence-mechanisms of its social environment, but enjoyed the religious tolerance of a frigid society, and which, in order to maintain itself in being, has made a dishonourable peace with society and become sterile.

All attempts to reform the church into a more credible form of life came to a halt at the point where the intimate links between this kind of church and this kind of society could be perceived, and when it was realized that church reform without social reform would hardly achieve its purpose. Thus the critics of the church became social critics, and saw the churches as no more than fragments, offering no hope, of a society divided and in conflict. The question of the sources of the renewal of the world in society and in its churches then took a new form. Will the fatal problems of mankind at the end of this century be apprehended and solved in continuity with the critical and liberating tradition of the gospel, or will this and the coming generations, through the default of churches and theologians enclosed within their own sects, nourish their hopes of life and justice from other sources which seem to them less corrupt and more accessible?[3]

Although humanist Marxism is fundamentally discredited by its Stalinist and post-Stalinist practice, and has recently attracted more obloquy by the destruction of 'socialism with a human face' in Czechoslovakia in 1968, its uninterrupted activity is astonishing. Its vitality in face of all the factual evidence seems to lie in the analytical power of its criticism and even more in the mobilizing power of its 'dream of the future'. The 'homelessness' of the Left in both West and East is only the reverse side of its certainty for the future. Much the same could probably be said of authentic Christian faith. The best of its content seems to be refuted by the vagaries and confusions of church history down to the present day. And yet it displays its vitality in permanent reformations, and in spite of all proof to the contrary, lives by the experience of inextinguishable hope. It is this inner homelessness which enables it to perpetuate its institutions, even when they become an established part of society.

Under the pressure to give a public demonstration of the relevance of theology to the problems of society and of individuals in it, and to manifest in a new form its relationship to a changed world, a long series of theological structures of great integrity were created. All of them provided Christian theology with the characteristics of a relationship to the surrounding world which was to make it relevant. There was existentialist theology, hermeneutic, ontological, cultural, social, indigenous, religious and political theology, and also the theology of secularization, of revolution, of liberation, etc. Because the relevance of Christian theology had become uncertain, there was and is an attempt to supply Christian theology with new categories of fundamental theology in the spirit and the circumstances of the present day. It is clear that theology can no longer find a permanent basis in the general thinking, feeling and action of contemporary society. The reason for this lies less in theology than in the fact that in a pluralist society, what concerns everyone absolutely, and what society must absolutely desire, is more difficult to identify than in earlier and more homogeneous societies. Since Hegel, it has been regarded as the task of the metaphysics of history, which 'apprehends its own time in thought', to present a 'theory of the present age', but such a theory is in practice hard to draw up, because no outline which seeks to comprehend all possible points of view can claim to be more than provisional itself.[4] The longing for a society with a unified ideology, or for a unified Catholic or Christian state, continues to grow, as it becomes more difficult for men to endure the plurality of different patterns of life and to use their differences for productive and fertile developments. Thus every theology must include reflections upon its own point of view in these conflicts and on its own place in the social and political situation.[5] An attempt to adopt an absolute point of view would be equivalent to having no point of view at all. To make one's own point of view absolute would be stupidity. This does not amount to relativism. Anyone who understands the relativity of relativity, will see himself as relative to others; but this does not mean giving up one's own position. To see one's own point of view as relative to that of others means to live in concrete relationships and to think out one's own ideas in relationship to the thought of others. To have no relationship would be death. This 'relationality' can transcend the absolutism of a single ideology and the totalitarian aspect of relativism. In this sense the recent 'political theology' has attempted to transfer the old verification model of 'natural theology', which in practice was always the prevailing religion of society, from orthodoxy into a new verification model of theology in social and political 'orthopraxy'.[6] Verification may mean that a particular insight can be demonstrated by what everyone can experience and check by repeating the experience. In that case it is only a matter of right *doxa* (orthodoxy). But verification can also mean to translate into act and experience, through *verum facere*, what everyone is not yet assumed to be able to experience. This is the way of 'orthopraxy'.

To translate something into action and experience, however, is possible and meaningful only in living relationships with others. Thus if Christian theology is relational, it can find a meaningful way between absolutist theocracy and unproductive tolerance, and replace the previously assumed unity of a society. Theologies which are drawn up in order to achieve a connection with the surrounding world, to which they wish to make Christian life relevant, must give serious attention to the necessity to be relational. Otherwise the value of the ready-made attributes applied to these theologies is rightly called into question. What is Christian in these new theological perspectives, which are meant to characterize some particular relationship of theology to the surrounding world? Does not theology lose its Christian identity if it is still determined to do nothing more than to adapt itself to the constantly changing 'spirit of the time'? Does it not become a chameleon, always taking on the colours of its environment, in order to adapt itself to it and remain unnoticed?

Similar movements to those in theology have come into being

in the churches themselves. The more the perceptive members of the church feel themselves threatened by the increasing social isolation of their churches and a withdrawal into the ghetto, the more they seek in practice the relevance of Christian life 'for the world', 'for others', and solidarity with man in his threatened and betrayed humanity. A church which cannot change in order to exist for the humanity of man in changed circumstances becomes ossified and dies. It becomes an insignificant sect on the margin of a society undergoing rapid social change. People ask themselves what difference it makes to belong to this church or not. Only old, tired and resigned people who no longer understand the world find in such a church a repository of unchanging ideas, the affectionately remembered past and religious folk-lore. Thus the ancient religious commitment of the church, that of arousing, strengthening and maintaining faith, has been supplemented since as early as the nineteenth century and even more at the present day by charitable work, social commitment in racial and class struggles, involvement in development aid and revolts against economic and racist tyranny. 'If anyone wants to become a Christian, don't send him into the churches, but into the slums. There he will find Christ.' So people say. In the present century, the ecumenical movement has brought to an end the denominational age of divided Christianity. But this breakthrough has achieved its most widespread effects less as a result of dogmatic agreement on the traditional controversial doctrines, and much more in ethical matters and in relationship to the world, in secular ecumenical action or in the 'indirect ecumenism' which results from co-operation on new social and ideological problems, for which none of the different traditions has the correct answer to hand.[7] The idea of a critical political theology has made a reality of the older ideas of the 'church for the world' and the 'church for others'. In the face of world problems, there has come into being in the world-wide ecumenical movement the idea of offering a unified Christianity as the future religion for a mankind which is to be united and for its universal society. On the local level, it has been suggested that the churches should be subjected to a thoroughgoing efficiency control from the point of view of social therapy, in order to maximize the aid they can give to the socially disadvantaged, and to give more effective form to the assistance they can offer in the socializing of the individual, the task of giving meaning to his life and the humanization of society.

'But if the church adopts this course—where is it leading the church?' asked R. Augstein in *Der Spiegel* in 1968.[8] Does not the departure made by the church from the traditional and established forms into social and psychotherapeutic commitment not mean bidding farewell to the church itself? Will the so-called progressives found a new church, perhaps 'the coming church', or are they moving into no man's land, to be taken over in the course of time by other groups and parties, who alone can give rational and institutional and effective organizational form to that necessary commitment? But the same question can be asked of the so-called conservatives. If, with their anxious concern for their own identity, they cling to the form of the church received from the past, opt for religion against politics and associate themselves with the forces of social and political conservatism, then they have chosen a particular form of relevance, of which similarly no one can say whether it is Christian or not. The church of the old religion is as much subject to the prevailing social concern for self-justification and self-assertion as is the new alliance of those who are critical of the churches with the forces critical of society. By the way in which they assert their relevance, both are led into a *crisis of identity*.

If social and political commitment is necessary, what is 'Christian' about it? If religious commitment is necessary for fulfilling the religious needs in a society, what is 'Christian' about that? In the critical theological thought in which a theologian uses and applies the critical scholarship developed since the Enlightenment, as a historical critic in exegesis, as an ideological critic in dogmatics, as a social critic with regard to the church, and in the political commitment which brings a Christian into solidarity with a non-Christian—why is one a Christian, why does one believe? Or is one no longer Christian, so that belief or unbelief make no difference here? It is not criticism that makes one a Christian, because others practise it. It is not social commitment on behalf of the poor and wretched, for this is fortunately found amongst others. It is not rebellion against injustice that makes one a Christian, for others rebel, and they often protest with more determination against injustice and discrimination than Christians. Is it necessary to give a Christian justification for these actions at all, or is it sufficient to do what is reasonable and humane? But what is reasonable and humane?

The *Evangelische Studentengemeinde* (the German Protestant Student Association) and the World Student Christian Federation are in a particular sense experimental areas in Christian existential life, in one of the most disturbed points in our society, the universities. What is true of the churches in general, in a way that is not always visible, is here attempted and suffered in a radical way. A Christian student community or group forms an outstanding example of what we have called the identity-involvement dilemma. The tension that is inherent in all Christian life, between identity in faith and public solidarity in living and struggling alongside others, has led here to polarizations and divisions which have had a paralysing effect upon many student communities. Since the world-wide student protest movement reached Germany—and this clearly dates from the day the student Ohnesorg was shot in Berlin in 1967—many student communities have identified themselves with this political movement. They understood themselves as part of this protest movement, and abandoned the traditional assertion of their Christian identity. 'On the basis of its democratic principles, the Protestant Student Association believes that it may legitimately use the power at its disposal to bring about the changes which a critical analysis of the present situation shows to be necessary.' This raises the problem of political association with others: 'The bid for power naturally assumes that one associates with others for certain purposes, for it is usually only such an association which gives the power to bring about what one desires. Fundamental changes in the university field can only be achieved in co-operation with other groups.' This use of power, albeit limited, is necessarily also applied against those from whom the Protestant Student Association receives the means of exercising power: 'A change in political institutions remains a question of power, because it can never be carried out except against the will and the power of those to whose advantage they work.'[9]

Even more dramatic was the symbolic action of the Christian student task force at the Meiji-Gakuin University in Japan. The first barricade in the university was erected in the university church, and sparked off a general conflict. The students wrote:

So we have put our own faith at risk in protest against the university authorities and have barricaded the church, although we ourselves suffer

as a result. By making our church a refuse dump we want to *proclaim* to
the university authorities and our fellow students that Christianity and
worship can become symbols of the absence of humanity and contempt
for it. We want to create true Christianity in the midst of this stormy
struggle within the university by common action with all our fellow-
students . . . God does not exist in this church, but rather in the living
deeds of a man involved in human relationships. We want our actions to
be understood as a question, as a request, for which we have *risked our
whole life*. For us Christians studying at Meiji Gakuin, this is *our cross*.[10]

Theoretical and practical solidarity with the general student
protest movement has in fact brought these Christian student
communities and groups to the point of effective action in a
situation of political conflict. They have carried out their theological theory in practice and have taken their faith to the point
of an existential testimony which is ready for sacrifice. But by
doing so they have inevitably fallen into a crisis of identity, and
have consciously risked this, as is shown by the symbolic action
of the Japanese students in destroying the Christian chapel and
'taking the cross upon themselves', in a specific act of resistance.

This crisis of identity exists at several levels. The question
whether Christianity is abandoned by solidarity with others in a
particular political situation can be the question of those who
stand on what they suppose is the firm ground of the Bible,
tradition and the church, and bewail the abandonment by revolutionary youth of everything that is sacred to themselves. Here the
question of 'what is specifically Christian', to which an appeal is
so often made, is posed in Pharisaic terms, and would not in fact
have been acceptable to Jesus. It is much more the question of a
man's own personal identity and integrity, for every self-emptying
in historical action is a venture, and a way into non-identity. A
man abandons himself as he was and as he knew himself to be,
and, by emptying himself, finds a new self. Jesus's eschatological
saying tells us that 'Whoever seeks to gain his life will lose it, but
whoever loses his life will preserve it.' Modern anthropology has
made this the basic principle by which man becomes human, in
accordance with the couplet in Schiller's *Reiterlied*:

> 'Unless you place your life at stake,
> your life you will never win.'

Gehlen has called this 'the birth of freedom out of alienation' and he regards idealism as an error, which holds that the ideal possibilities which he admits to be present in man can be the object of direct subjective experience.[11] Only by self-emptying in encounter with what is alien, unknown and different does man achieve selfhood. If Christians empty themselves in this way in a situation of political conflict, then in fact they abandon the traditions, institutions and opinions, accepted in faith, in which they previously found their identity. But this includes what Christoph Blumhardt once called 'the ceaseless prayer for the spirit of persistence'. That is, trust in the hidden and guaranteed identity with Christ in God (Col. 3.3) makes possible the self-abandonment, the road into non-identity and unidentifiability, which neither clings to ancient forms of identity, nor anxiously reaches out for the forms of identity of those one is fighting in common. This, as the Japanese students said—whether rightly or wrongly in their case does not matter for the moment—is really 'to take one's cross upon oneself' in imitation of the one who abandoned his divine identity and found his true identity in the cross (Phil. 2).

That in following his Lord a Christian should place his own identity at stake without reservation when it is a matter of helping his fellow men in distress, is not disputed. But what limits a Christian community must draw if it is to be associated with other groups to work in common with them to help men in distress, is another matter. Here it is not the identity of the individual Christian which is at stake, but that of the Christian community, its faith and its ethical values.[12]

This would be better expressed by saying that what is at stake is their strangeness and difference with regard to their old and new allies. Solidarity with others in meaningful actions loses its creative character if one no longer wishes to be anything different from the others. Bonhoeffer's 'existence for others', to which so much appeal has been made, becomes meaningless if one is no longer any different from the others, but merely a hanger on. Only someone who finds the courage to be different from others can ultimately exist for 'others', for otherwise he exists only with those who are like him. And this is not much help to them. Thus we must say that, 'as the result of the debate about [political] organization, these communities are faced with the theological question of their Christian identity as churches'.[13] Because this question is posed not merely by the ancient traditions and institutions from which they have separated themselves, but also by those others with whom they have associated themselves in solidarity, it must be taken seriously and answered. The identity in question here is the identity of the object of faith, for the sake of which individuals and whole groups have accepted self-emptying and non-identity and a solidarity which allows no distinction. When a Christian community feels obliged to empty itself in certain social and political actions, it must take care that its traditional religious and political identity is not exchanged for a new religious and political identity, but must sustain its non-identity. Otherwise a church which, seeking for an identity and not preserving its distinctiveness, plunges into a social and political movement, once again becomes the 'religion of society'. It is of course no longer a conservative religion of society, but the progressive religion of what may perhaps be a better future society. It then follows those who criticize the old religion from a political point of view, only to make a religion of their new politics.[14] But can a Christian community or church ever become the 'political religion' of its existing or future society, without forgetting the man from Nazareth who was crucified, and losing the identity it has in his cross? Moreover, true Christian existence can only be present in the best of all possible societies, or, in symbolic terms, can only 'stand under the cross', and its identity with the crucified Christian can be demonstrated only by a witnessing non-identification with the demands and interests of society. Thus even in the 'classless society' Christians will be aliens and homeless. Where solidarity is achieved, this distinction must still be observed. It is a criticism of the traditional solidarity of the established churches with authority, law and order in society. But it is also a criticism of the more recent attempts to establish solidarity with democratic and socialist forces. Not of course in the same way, because the cross does not make the world equal by bringing down the night in which everything looks alike, but by enabling people to criticize and stand back from the partial historical realities and movements which they have idolized and made absolute.

It follows from these reflections upon the concrete political problems of Christian life, that the question of identity comes to a head only in the context of non-identity, self-emptying for the sake of others and solidarity with others. It cannot be established in isolation, but only revealed in contact with others. In exile one seeks home. In alienation one seeks identity. Love is revealed in hatred and peace in conflict. Thus the place where the question of identity can meaningfully be asked is the situation of the crisis of identity, brought about by meaningful self-emptying and solidarity. 'Temptation teaches us to pay heed to the Word,' said Luther. These temptations can be suffered passively, where, as in Luther's hymn, sin, hell and death swallow man up and human existence is called into question. But temptations are much more often actively suffered. A man's mettle is tried only in the front line, not back at base, even supposing that the sufferings of others do not leave him in peace there. But in the front line, he is put to the test because he is struggling to do his utmost; the more he tries, the more he is tried. Anyone who does not put himself to the test is hardly tried or tested at all. Only when, with all the understanding and consistency he possesses, a man follows Christ along the way of self-emptying into non-identity, does he encounter contradiction, resistance and opposition. Only when he leaves behind the circle of those who share and reinforce his opinions in the church, to go out into the anonymity of slums and peace movements, in a society 'where the absence of peace is organized', is he tempted and tested, inwardly and outwardly. Then the crisis inevitably comes, in which the identity of that for which he involves and commits himself comes into question, and a decision has to be made about it. It is these active trials and temptations which at the present day teach us to pay attention to the word of the cross.

2. *The Crisis of Identity for Christian Faith*

While the question of identity comes to a head only in the context of non-identity, the question of relevance arises only where identity is a matter of experience and belief. When something can be identified, it is possible to ask whether it is relevant to anything else and whether it has any connection with anything else. Where the Christian identity of faith is abandoned, this question no longer arises. One is simply a fellow human or a contemporary or an adherent of other institutions and groups, and they supply one's identity. But where the Christian identity of faith is asserted, the question of its relevance arises.

Where does the identity of Christian faith lie? Its outward mark is church membership. This, however, takes us no further, but merely moves the problem on. For the Christian identity of the church is itself questionable, when the form it takes is affected by so many other interests. One can point to the creed. But to repeat the formula of the Apostles' Creed is no guarantee of Christian identity, but simply of loyalty to the fathers and to tradition. One can point to particular experiences of vocation, conversion and grace in one's own life. But even they do not guarantee one's identity as a Christian; at best, they point to what one has begun to believe in such experiences. Ultimately, one's belief is not in one's own faith; within one's experiences in faith and one's decisions, one believes in someone else who is more than one's own faith. Christian identity can be understood only as an act of identification with the crucified Christ, to the extent to which one has accepted the proclamation that in him God has identified himself with the godless and those abandoned by God, to whom one belongs oneself. If Christian identity comes into being by this double process of identification, then it is clear that it cannot be described in terms of that faith alone, nor can it be protected against decay by correct doctrinal formulae, repeatable rituals and set patterns of moral behaviour.

The decay of faith and its identity, through a decline into unbelief and a different identity, forms an exact parallel to their decay through a decline into a fearful and defensive faith. Faith is fearful and defensive when it begins to die inwardly, struggling to maintain itself and reaching out for security and guarantees. In so doing, it removes itself from the hand of the one who has promised to maintain it, and its own manipulations bring it to ruin. This pusillanimous faith usually occurs in the form of an orthodoxy which feels threatened and is therefore more rigid than ever. It occurs wherever, in the face of the immorality of the present age, the gospel of creative love for the abandoned is replaced by the law of what is supposed to be Christian morality, and by penal law. He who is of little faith looks for support and protection for his faith, because it is preyed upon by fear. Such a faith tries to protect its 'most sacred things', God, Christ, doctrine and morality, because it clearly no longer believes that these are sufficiently powerful to maintain themselves. When the 'religion of fear' finds its way into the Christian church, those who regard themselves as the most vigilant guardians of the faith do violence to faith and smother it. Instead of confidence and freedom, fearfulness and apathy are found everywhere. This has considerable consequences for the attitudes of the church, faith and theology to the new problems posed by history. 'Why did the church cut itself off from cultural development?' asks R. Rothe, whose messianic passion in the face of the modern age can speak for itself here:

> I blush to write it down: because it is afraid for faith in Christ. To me, it is not faith in Christ if it can be afraid for itself and for its Christ! To me, this is not to have faith, but to be of little faith. This, however, is the consequence of a lack of faith that the Saviour is the real and effective ruler of the world; and only when this faith is lacking is such fear psychologically possible.[15]

Christians, churches and theologians who passionately defend true belief, pure doctrine and distinctive Christian morality are at the present day in danger of lapsing into this pusillanimous faith. Then they build a defensive wall round their own little group, and in apocalyptic terms call themselves the 'little flock' or the 'faithful remnant', and abandon the world outside to the godlessness and immorality which they themselves lament. They lament the assimilation of Christianity to the secularized society which has declined since the 'good old days', and bewail the loss of identity of those who in theology and in practice involve themselves in the conflicts of this society and work with others to resolve them. But by this reaction, they themselves are running the risk of a loss of identity by passive assimilation. They accept the increasing isolation of the church as an insignificant sect on the margin of society, and encourage it by their sectarian withdrawal. The symptoms of the increase of this kind of sectarian mentality at the present day include the preservation of tradition without the attempt to found new tradition; biblicism without liberating preaching; increasing unwillingness to undergo new experience with the gospel and faith, and the language of zealotry and militant behaviour in disputes within the church.[16] People boast of their own growing meaninglessness, and the failure of the world to understand, as the 'cross' which they have to bear, and they regard their own obstinate lack of courage as bearing the cross. Because the situation has become so obscure and their own identity so uncertain, they seek to cut the Gordian knot with the sword of a decision taken in isolation. This leads to the fragmentation of the church into the true 'church of Jesus' and the evil, political 'church of Barabbas'; or the true 'church of Mary' which alone hears the word of the Lord, and the 'church of Martha' preoccupied with useless social activity. Friends and enemies are clearly distinguished, if possible with the aid of the godless communists, so that a final decision can be made and the situation can be clarified once again. The missionary situation of the 'open church' is left behind in a retreat into the apocalyptic situation of the 'closed church'. People grow tired of maintaining the open situation of dialogue and co-operation with others, in which the boundaries are always fluid, and look for the final hour, in which the only possible response is yes or no.

In this post-Christian, legalistic apocalyptic, the present time becomes the moment of the great decision: the world is lapsing into the spiritual death of atheism, atomic catastrophe, the death of the young from drugs or ecological self-destruction. At the same time, it is the hour in which the true church has to rise up as the visible place of refuge in the disaster: 'Rise up for the final struggle.' It cannot be denied that such visions of the future exist in the New Testament, and that the crises of history may come to such a critical end. But nowhere in the New Testament does the 'end of the world' bring about the second coming of Christ. The New Testament looks forward to the very reverse, that the second coming of Christ will bring the end of destruction and persecution in the world. Anyone who reads the 'signs of the time' with the eyes of his own existential anxiety reads them falsely. If they can be read at all, they can be read by Christians only with the eyes of hope in the future of Christ. Otherwise the apocalyptic interpretations of the age will be like the nihilistic attempt of the 'devils' of Dostoevsky, who want to destroy the world in order to force God to intervene, and who for romantic reasons regard chaos itself as creative. But this no longer has anything to do with the cross as the horizon of the world, for this cross is the sign of the unity of love for God and the love with which, according to the Gospel of John (3.16), God 'so loved the world, that he gave his only Son'.

For Christian faith to bring about its own decay by withdrawal into the ghetto without self-criticism, is a parallel to its decay through uncritical assimilation. And the decline into pusillanimous faith and superstition is a parallel to the decline into unbelief. How close this parallel is, is shown by the way debates within

Christianity become polarized in false alternatives. The more student communities become absorbed in political Christianity and in liberation struggles, and understand themselves as a part of this movement, the more they surrender the area of personal devotion and existential sensitivity to the meaning of life to political conservatives or unpolitical student mission groups. The tension between identity in faith and solidarity in action can no longer be tolerated by either side. Polarizations come into being, which break down this productive Christian tension. Devout students and religious people no longer protest. As a result, they are thought well of by politically conservative forces. Protesting students and people committed to political criticism usually no longer want anything more to do with faith and Christian religion. In many Christian churches, similar polarizations have come into being between those who see the essence of the church in evangelization and the salvation of souls, and those who see it in social action for the salvation and liberation of real life. But in Christian terms evangelization and humanization are not alternatives. Nor are inner repentance and a change in situations and circumstances. Nor are the 'vertical dimension' of faith and the 'horizontal dimension' of love for one's neighbour and political change. Nor are 'Jesuology' and christology, the humanity and the divinity of Jesus. Both coincide in his death on the cross. Anyone who makes a distinction here, enforces alternatives and calls for a parting of the ways, in dividing the unity of God and man in the person, the imitation and the future of Christ.

These alternatives are equally absurd from the point of view of practice. Evangelization would lead either to a crisis of relevance or to an inevitable involvement in the social and political problems of society. Beginning with preaching, one is then faced with questions of community organization, the education of children and work for the sick and poor. The humanization of social circumstances leads either to a crisis of identity, or inevitably to evangelization or pastoral care. Beginning with the improvement of social conditions in the poverty-stricken areas and liberation from political oppression, one is then faced with the question how the wretched and oppressed can be removed from their inner apathy and given new self-confidence, that is, with the question how to arouse faith and conquer the structure of servility in their minds. Of course one person cannot do everything, but at least everyone must recognize the other charismata in the body of Christ and the necessity for other work by other people to relieve misery.

'Change yourself,' some say, 'and then your circumstances will also change.' The kingdom of God and of freedom is supposed to have to do only with persons. Unfortunately the circumstances will not oblige. Capitalism, racism and inhuman technocracy quietly develop in their own way. The causes of misery are no longer to be found in the inner attitudes of men, but have long been institutionalized.

'Change the circumstances,' others say, 'and men will change with them.' The kingdom of God and of freedom is supposed to be a matter only of circumstances and structures. Unfortunately, however, men will not oblige. Breakdowns in marriage, drug addiction, suicide and alcoholism continue undisturbed. Structures which make people unhappy can be broken down, but no guarantee is attached that men will be happy.

Thus both must be done at the same time. Personal, inner change without a change in circumstances and structures is an idealist illusion, as though man were only a soul and not a body as well. But a change in external circumstances without inner renewal is a materialist illusion, as though man were only a product of his social circumstances and nothing else. The discussion of Christian practice cannot fall below the level of Karl Marx's third thesis on Feuerbach:

> The materialist doctrine that men are the products of circumstances and upbringing, and that, therefore, changed men are the product of other circumstances and changed upbringing, forgets that it is men who change circumstances and that the educator himself needs educating . . . The coincidence of the changing of circumstances and of human activity can be conceived and rationally understood only as *revolutionary practice*.

This is true of all practical action in history which is aimed at liberation. If the title 'Christ' refers to the redeemer and liberator, then practical 'Christian' action can only be directed towards the liberation of man from his inhumanity. Consequently the 'coincidence' of the change in circumstances and of human activity as a change in man himself applies to Christian practice to an eminent degree. The alternative between arousing faith in the heart and the changing of the godless circumstances of dehumanized man is a false one, as is the other alternative, which hinders by paralysing. The true front on which the liberation of Christ takes place does not run between soul and body or between persons and structures, but between the powers of the world as it decays and collapses into ruin, and the powers of the Spirit and of the future. In inner experience of the Spirit in the liberty of faith, certainty and prayer are just as much anticipations of the future of Christ and of the liberating of creation as the opening of a ghetto, the healing of a sick person, a new right to social justice or a successful revolution for independence. There is no vertical dimension of faith opposed to a horizontal dimension of political love, for in every sphere of life the powers of the coming new creation are in conflict with the powers of a world structure which leads to death. In Christ, God and our neighbour are a unity, and what God has joined together, man shall not put apart, least of all the theologian.[17]

Christian theology finds its identity as such in the cross of Christ. Christian life is identified as Christian in a double process of identification with the crucified. His cross distinguishes belief from unbelief and even more from superstition. Identification with the crucified Christ alienates the believer from the religions and ideologies of alienation, from the 'religion of fear' and the ideologies of revenge. Christian theology finds its relevance in hope, thought out in depth and put into practice, in the kingdom of the crucified Christ, by suffering in 'the sufferings of this present time', and makes the groaning of the creation in travail its own cry for God and for freedom.[18] Jesus was folly to the wise, a scandal to the devout and a disturber of the peace in the eyes of the mighty. That is why he was crucified. If anyone identifies with him, this world is 'crucified' to him, as Paul said. He becomes alienated from the wisdom, religion and power politics of his society. The crucified Christ became the brother of the despised, abandoned and oppressed. And this is why brotherhood with the 'least of his brethren' is a necessary part of brotherhood with Christ and identification with him. Thus Christian theology must be worked out amongst these people and with them. It is 'contemporary' theology when its thought is conducted in the sufferings of the present time, and this means in concrete terms, amongst and with those who suffer in this society. The 'identity-involvement dilemma' of Christian life at the present day is consequently not a dilemma, but the inevitable tension of Christian faith. Christian identification with the crucified Christ means solidarity with the sufferings of the poor and the misery both of the oppressed and the oppressors. On the one hand, if this solidarity is seriously accepted, selflessly and without reserve, it is in itself an identification with the one who was crucified and 'became poor, so that by his poverty you might become rich' (II Cor. 8.9). By alienating the believer from the compulsions and automatic assumptions of an alienated world, Christian identification with the crucified necessarily brings him into solidarity with the alienated of this world, with the dehumanized and the inhuman. But this solidarity becomes radical only if it imitates the identification of the crucified Christ with the abandoned, accepts the suffering of creative love, and is not led astray by its own dreams of omnipotence in an illusory future.

We have said that the crisis of relevance and the crisis of identity are complementary to each other. Where identity is found, relevance is called into question. Where relevance is achieved, identity is called into question. We can now define this double crisis more closely with regard to Christian faith, by saying that each of these crises is simply a reflection of the other; and that both crises can be reduced to a common denominator. Christian theology must be theology of the cross, if it is to be identified as Christian theology through Christ. But the theology of the cross is a critical and liberating theory of God and man. Christian life is a form of practice which consists in following the crucified Christ, and it changes both man himself and the circumstances in which he lives. To this extent, a theology of the cross is a practical theory.

3. *Revelation in Contradiction and Dialectic Knowledge*

One of the basic difficulties of Christian life in the world today is clearly the inability to identify with what is other, alien and contradictory. This inability leads to assimilation on the one hand and a sectarian mentality on the other. From the psychological point of view, a lack of sensitivity to others and an inability to see ourselves in others and as others see us is presumably a sign of ego-weakness. One's own strangeness with regard to others can no longer be tolerated, and the result is a withdrawal into the circle of those who think the same as oneself; or else one abandons Christian life and assimilates oneself to those from whom it is hoped to receive recognition and status. As long as the church lived in a 'Christian world', it could rely upon the presence of corresponding ideas and purposes in culture, society and politics, and by fulfilling a social purpose itself could bring about this identity of aims and activities. The church and society lived as it were in 'concentric circles', overlapping, complementing and affirming each other.[19] The generally accepted principle of society was 'like seeks after like', as Aristotle puts it in the *Nicomachean Ethics*. Things which are like or similar understand each other on the basis of what they have in common, and affirm each other. Christian communities in practice live by this principle. When the Christian church represents the religion of a society, it also represents in a symbolic and ritual way the functions tending to integration and homogeneity in this society. But if the Christian life of an individual or of a church is identified with the crucified Christ, it becomes alienated from this principle of likeness and similarity in society. Again, the more this domain of external similarity, the 'Christian world', collapses and society becomes 'different', the more this analogical thinking and action loses its force. For both reasons, there then has to be a move towards dialectical thought and dialectical existence, and one's own identity has to be recognized and set forth in what is different and alien.

The social principle 'like seeks after like' corresponds on the epistemological level to the Platonic principle, 'like is known only by like' (*similis a simili cognoscitur*).[20] The process of knowing takes place under the guidance of analogy, and in these circumstances is always recognition. If likeness is taken in the strict sense, knowing is a matter of *anamnesis* within a closed circle. If it is extended to similarities in what differs, the process of knowing can become an open circle of learning, in which new apprehensions are made and progress is possible. Christian theology very early adopted the epistemological principle of the Platonic school and introduced the principle of analogy into its doctrine of the knowledge of God. Either the invisible God is known in the analogies to him in the order of creation or in acts of history which point to him, or else he is known in his self-revelation, or only in the Holy Spirit of God. If the principle of likeness is applied strictly, God is only known by God. But if like is known only by like in this way, then revelation in something else which is not God, and in what is alien and not of God, is in fact impossible. Here God can only rule over what is similar, over other gods, but not over men and animals. If like is known only by like, then the Son of God would have had to remain in heaven, because he would be unrecognizable by anything earthly.

This analogical principle of knowledge is one-sided if it is not supplemented by the dialectic principle of knowledge. This principle derives from medicine, going back to Hippocrates, and states that *contraria contrariis curantur*,[21] or, in Schelling's words: 'Every being can be revealed only in its opposite. Love only in hatred, unity only in conflict.'[22] Applied to Christian theology, this means that God is only revealed as 'God' in his opposite: godlessness and abandonment by God. In concrete terms, God is revealed in the cross of Christ who was abandoned by God. His grace is revealed in sinners. His righteousness is revealed in the unrighteous and in those without rights, and his gracious election in the damned. The epistemological principle of the theology of the cross can only be this dialectic principle: the deity of God is revealed in the paradox of the cross. This makes it easier to understand what Jesus did: it was not the devout, but the sinners, and not the righteous but the unrighteous who recognized him, because in them he revealed the divine righteousness of grace, and the kingdom. He revealed his identity amongst those who had lost their identity, amongst the lepers, sick, rejected and despised, and was recognized as the Son of Man amongst those who had been deprived of their humanity.[23] And this makes it easier to understand Paul's theology of the cross in his doctrine of justification: in his revelation in the cross God justifies the godless, and always justifies them alone (E. Käsemann). One must become godless oneself and abandon every kind of self-deification or likeness to God, in order to recognize the God who reveals himself in the crucified Christ. One must abandon every self-justification if one is to recognize the revelation of the righteousness of God amongst the unrighteous, to whom basically one belongs oneself. The dialectical principle of 'revelation in the opposite' does not replace the analogical principle of 'like is known only by like', but alone makes it possible. In so far as God is revealed in his opposite, he can be known by the godless and those who are abandoned by God, and it is this knowledge which brings them into correspondence with God and, as I John 3.2 says, enables them even to have the hope of being like God. But the basis and starting point of analogy is this dialectic. Without revelation in the opposite, the contradictions cannot be brought into correspondence. If the principle of analogy alone is followed, the result would be a *theologia gloriae*, applicable to heaven alone. It is the dialectical knowledge of God in his opposite which first brings heaven down to the earth of those who are abandoned by God, and opens heaven to the godless.

Thus the theology of the cross must begin with contradiction and cannot be built upon premature correspondences. The dialectic of this theology in the knowledge of God has far-reaching critical consequences for the conventional religious theism which is found in Christianity. It has critical consequences for the constituent elements of the Christian community. If a being is revealed only in its opposite, then the church which is the church of the crucified Christ cannot consist of an assembly of like persons who mutually affirm each other, but must be constituted of unlike persons. 'Like seeks after like,' as Aristotle says in his discussion of friendship (*Ethics*, Book VIII). But for the crucified Christ, the principle of fellowship is fellowship with those who are different, and solidarity with those who have become alien and have been made different. Its power is not friendship, the love for what is similar and beautiful (*philia*), but creative love for what is different, alien and ugly (*agape*). Its principle of justification is not similarity, but the justification of the other (Hegel), the creative making righteous of the unrighteous and the attribution of rights to those who are without rights. Consequently, the church of the crucified Christ cannot be assimilated to what is different and alien to it. Nor can it shut itself away from what is alien in a social ghetto, but for the sake of its identity in the crucified Christ, must reveal him and itself, by following him, in what is different and alien. Otherwise, it does justice neither to the one to whom it appeals nor to those to whom he revealed himself. Only in the practical form of fellowship with others can it bear witness to the crucified Christ and live out in life the justification of the godless in which it believes, and from which it derives its own life. Bonhoeffer once said that it is often difficult to mention God by name to religious people, but to people with no religion it can be done quite calmly and as a matter of course.

NOTES

1. Luther, WA 179, 31.
2. Cf. the 'Candid Foreword' in H. Küng, *Infallible? An Enquiry*, Fontana Books 1972, p. 22; R. P. McBrien, *Do We Need the Church?*, New York 1969.
3. C.-D. Schulze, 'Reformation oder Performation der Kirche? Versuch einer Typologie von Kirchenreform-Bestrebungen', *MPTh* 58, 1969, 106–22. Here Schulze gives an apt description of the ideas of the 'traditionalists', the 'avant-garde', the 'progressives' and the 'new left' in the field of German Protestantism.
4. Cf. D. Rössler, 'Positionelle und kritische Theologie', *ZThK* 67, 1970, 215–31.
5. J. Moltmann, 'Theologische Kritik der politischen Religion', in J. B. Metz, J. Moltmann and W. Oelmüller, *Kirche im Prozess der Aufklärung*, 1970, 14ff. So too D. Sölle, *Politische Theologie. Auseinandersetzung mit Rudolf Bultmann*, 1971, 85ff.
6. J. B. Metz, *Theology of the World*, Burns and Oates 1969, 107ff.
7. J. B. Metz, *Reform und Gegenreformation heute*, 1969, 33.
8. R. Augstein, 'Das grosse Schisma', *Der Spiegel* 18, 1969, 166.
9. *ESG-Material*, NF, vol. 3. I take these three quotations from the essay by W. Kratz, 'Wege und Grenzen christlicher Solidarität. Beitrag zu einer aktuellen Diskussion in den Evangelischen Studentengemeinden', in *Christliche Freiheit im Dienst am Menschen. Festschrift für M. Niemöller zum 80. Geburtstag*, 1972, 199, 202. The world-wide questionnaire conducted by the World Student Christian Federation concerning this polarization is summarized only briefly by R. Lehtonen, 'The Story of a Storm. An Ecumenical Case Study', *Study Encounter* 18, vol. VIII, 1, 1972. For the whole problem see also L. Gilkey, *How the Church can Minister to the World without Losing Itself*, New York 1964; R. Ruether, *The Church against Itself*, New York 1967.
10. Cf. Toshikazu Takao, 'An Alliance of Egoists', *Japan Christian Quarterly*, Fall 1969, 225, and U. Luz, 'Japanische Studenten und christlicher Glaube', *EvTh* 32, 1972, 70ff. The view of P. Beyerhaus, 'Die gegenwärtige Krise von Kirche und Theologie in Japan', *EMZ* 29, 1972, vol. 11, 13: 'This is in fact the disappearance of theology in thoroughgoing humanism', is not true. Rather, it is a prophetic symbolic action.
11. A. Gehlen, 'Über die Geburt der Freiheit aus der Entfremdung', *Studien zur Anthropologie und Soziologie*, 1963, 232ff., esp. 244.
12. W. Kratz, op. cit., 197.
13. R. Thoma, quoted in W. Kratz, op. cit., 200.
14. Thus L. Feuerbach, *Die Notwendigkeit einer Reform der Philosophie*, 1842, Werke II, ed. Bolin and Jodl, 1969, 219: 'For we must once again become religious—politics must become our religion . . .'
15. R. Rothe, *Vorträge*, 1886, 21.
16. J. B. Metz, 'Gefährliche und befreiende Erinnerung. Zur Präsenz der Kirche in der Gesellschaft', *Publik* no. 41, 1970, 23.

17. This thesis does not mean that God is our neighbour and our fellow-man God. The assertion of unthinking Protestant Ritschlianism, that in Christianity the love of one's neighbour has replaced the love of God, and morality religion, is the ruin of both private and political morality, and makes it illiberal, tortured and embittered. If E. Käsemann, 'Worship and Everyday Life', *New Testament Questions of Today*, SCM Press 1969, 191, is right to say that for Paul 'the doctrines of worship and Christian "ethics" necessarily converge', this does not merely mean that the worship of God becomes ethical, but also the reverse, that ethics becomes the festival of life. A wedding feast is Jesus' symbol for the imminence of the kingdom of God, and the 'liberty of the children of God' is Paul's symbol for discipleship of the cross. If the gap between relationship with God and relationship with our neighbour really has been bridged, then ethics cannot become religion. In the eschatological festival of new life, even the ethical approach of Kant and Ritschl represents an unbalanced regression. If in the prophets God is displeased at the clamour of singing and the smell of sacrifices, he is no doubt even more displeased at the bad conscience spread by Christian moralists and strained love of one's neighbour. Without joy in one's neighbour and rejoicing with one's neighbour in God, the love of one's neighbour is a poor thing. See my *Theology and Joy*, SCM Press 1973.

18. Cf. E. Käsemann, 'The Cry for Liberty in the Worship of the Church', *Perspectives on Paul*, SCM Press 1971, 122–37, and *Jesus Means Freedom*, SCM Press 1969.

19. So too Karl Barth, 'Church and Culture' (1926), in *Theology and the Church*, SCM Press 1962, 334–54; id., 'The Christian Community and the Civil Community', in *Against the Stream. Shorter Post-War Writings 1946–52*, SCM Press 1954.

20. This principle goes back to Empedocles: 'Sweet seized sweet and bitter rose to meet bitter, sour went to sour, hot quickly caught up hot' (quoted in Plutarch, *Quaestiones Convivales*, in *Moralia* VIII, LCL, Heinemann 1969, 311); '[. . . whole matured forms]. These the fire sent forth, desiring to reach its like' (K. E. Kirk and C. Raven, *The Presocratic Philosophers*, Cambridge University Press 1957, 338). According to Theophrastus, *On Sensation* I, 'Parmenides, Empedocles and Plato . . . attribute sensation to the principle of likeness': 'For with earth do we see earth, with air bright air, with fire consuming fire; with Love do we see Love, Strife with dread Strife' (Kirk and Raven, op. cit. 343). Aristotle, *Metaphysics* III 4, 1000 b5: 'Knowledge is of like by like' (ἡ δὲ γνῶσις τοῦ ὁμοίου τῷ ὁμοίῳ). Goethe set this principle out in the following epigram: 'Were not the eye like the sun/ how could it look at the sun?/ Were not God's own power within us,/ how could the divine delight us?' Cf. also A. Schneider, 'Der Gedanke der Erkenntnis des Gleichen durch Gleiches in antiker und patristischer Zeit', *Abhandlungen zur Geschichte der Philosophie des Mittelalters, Festschrift für C. Baeumker*, 1923, 65–76.

21. ΠΑΡΟΙΜΙΩΝ ΣΥΜΟΓΗ, *Gilberto Cognato collectore et interprete, quas Erasmus in suas Chiliadas non retulit*, in: *Des. Erasmi Roterodami Adagiorum chiliades quatuor. Basileae, ex officina episcopiana, per Eusebium Episco-*

pum et Nicolai Fr. haeredes, 1574, 431 B: '*CONTRARIA CONTRARIIS PELLUNTUR: Gregorius Theologus lib. 2 Sententiarum: id est: Contrariis nam pellitur contrarium. Hominum deinde sermone vulgatum. Blasius Hollerius in Hippocratis librum De natura hominis, in fine: Sic enim curationem optime praescribet et adhibebit, iis videlicet auxiliorum generibus, quae per contrarium morbis (id enim axioma est medicorum universale) facultatem vincant. Hieremias Triverus in primum Hippocratis aphorismum: Nam quod contrarium curetur contrario, antiquum est et apud omnes in confesso. Hinc Gallis est in proverbiis: Contre pechie est vertu medicine. Id enim prius traditum est Hippocrate de flatibus: Contraria contrariis remedio esse. Therapeuticae autem medicinae communissimus scopus est:* τὰ ἐναντία τῶν ἐναντίων ἰάματα: *Contraria contrariorum medicamenta.* I am grateful to Dr W. Werbeck, Tübingen, for this reference.

22. F. W. J. Schelling, *Über das Wesen der menschlichen Freiheit* (1809), Reclam 8913–15, 89. Also E. Bloch, *Tübinger Einleitung in die Philosophie* II, 1964, 16, asks, 'Can only like apprehend like, or, on the contrary, would the unlike be more appropriate?'

23. E. Peterson, 'Was ist der Mensch?', in *Theologische Traktate*, 1951 227ff., esp. 236: 'Christ calls himself "Son of Man" because he has transcended man. The "Son of Man" is the one who understands himself in the sicknesses of man by taking them on himself.'

2

THE RESISTANCE OF THE CROSS AGAINST ITS INTERPRETATIONS

1. *The Unreligious Cross in the Church*

When archaeologists dig up a place of worship in the desert sand and find in it the sign of the cross, they can be virtually certain that it is a Christian church. Today, too, we find the cross in Christian churches as the central symbol. The worshippers gaze upon the crucifix. The word of the cross is preached to the congregation. They are blessed and sent from the church with the sign of the cross. Many make the sign of the cross as the Holy Trinity is named. In Passiontide, in many churches, devout Christians follow the course of Jesus' passion in the stations of the cross, and meditate on the reasons for his sufferings and the redeeming effects of his death. In other churches, even today, Good Friday is the central Christian festival of the church year. There is little that expresses Christian fellowship with God better than passion hymns. Even in the world of Islam, Christianity is represented by the symbol of the cross:

What keeps the Copt a Copt is the cross of Jesus, *al salib*, in other words, his inward, unutterable and ineffable faith in Jesus who died on the cross to redeem mankind.[1]

Thus Christianity has rightly been described as 'the religion of the cross': 'Thou alone, religion of the cross, dost join in one wreath the double palm of humility and power' (Schiller). Goethe describes Christianity as the 'ultimate religion', because it was the ultimate and final thing which mankind could and had to achieve; for not until Christianity was the 'divine depth of suffering' revealed to us.[2] But what does this actually mean? It is often better recongized by non-Christians and atheists than by

32

religious Christians, because it astonishes and offends them. They see the profane horror and godlessness of the cross, because they do not believe the religious interpretations which have given a meaning to the senselessness of this death. All they find in it is 'the image of irreconcilability'.[3] To restore Good Friday in all its horror and godlessness (Hegel) it is necessary for Christian faith first of all to abandon the traditional theories of salvation which have made the way the cross is spoken of in Christianity a mere habit. From the very first the Christian faith was distinguished from the religions which surrounded it by its worship of the crucified Christ.

In Israelite understanding, someone executed in this way was rejected by his people, cursed amongst the people of God by the God of the law, and excluded from the covenant of life. 'Cursed be everyone that hangs on a tree' (Gal. 3.13; Deut. 21.23). Anyone who, condemned by the law as a blasphemer, suffers such a death is cursed and excluded from the circle of the living and from the fellowship of God. 'We have a law, and by that law he ought to die, because he has made himself the Son of God' (John 19.7). One can only turn one's back on him. Of course when Israel was occupied by the Romans, there were many freedom fighters during the revolts who died on the cross. But they were martyrs for the righteous cause of the God of Israel, and not rejected blasphemers.

To the humanism of antiquity the crucified Christ and the veneration of him were also an embarrassment. Crucifixion, as the punishment of escaped slaves or rebels against the Roman empire, was regarded as 'the most degrading kind of punishment'.[4] Thus Roman humanism always felt the 'religion of the Cross' to be unaesthetic, unrespectable and perverse. 'Let even the name of the cross be kept away not only from the bodies of the citizens of Rome, but also from their thought, sight and hearing,' declared Cicero.[5] It was regarded as an offence against good manners to speak of this hideous death for slaves in the presence of respectable people.[6] In the human search for the good, the true and the beautiful, the crucified Christ was not a valuable aesthetic symbol. He possessed 'no form or comeliness' (Isa. 53.2). The idea of a 'crucified God' to whom veneration and worship were due was regarded in the ancient world as totally inappropriate to God, just as for Israel the assertion that a condemned blasphemer had risen from the dead was bound to conflict with the righteousness of God revealed in the law. Thus Christian belief in the crucified Christ was bound to produce on Jews and Romans the effect of continued blasphemy. The early Christians had constantly to defend themselves against the charge of *irreligiositas* and *sacrilegium*. In so far as they refused to make the obligatory sacrifices to the gods of the Roman state they drew on themselves the charge of 'atheism'. This was not meant merely as an abusive description of Christians, but was a formal accusation which resulted in exclusion from society as 'enemies of the human race'. Justin readily admitted his Christian atheism, which consisted of a denial of the gods of the state, and with regard to these 'so-called gods' confessed himself to be an 'atheist'.[7] Amongst the educated despisers of Christianity, this belief in a crucified Christ was merely bad taste, which was met with mockery. There is a graffito on the Palatine which represents a crucified figure with a donkey's head, and bears the inscription: 'Alexamenos worships his god.'[8] At that time, the cross was not the sign in which one conquered, a sign of triumph on churches, or an adornment on the Imperial Throne, nor was it the sign of orders and honours; it was a sign of contradiction and scandal, which quite often brought expulsion and death.

Modern, post-Christian humanism has done a great service by bringing to the fore once again this original and natural dislike of the cross. In this way it has reminded Christianity, which has made itself so much at home in European civilization, of its original and fundamental alienation. When Hegel received from his pupils on his sixtieth birthday a medal which showed an owl and a cross, Goethe reacted angrily: 'Who can demand that I love the cross if with that I am forced to share its burden?'[9] For him, its harshness and nakedness was in conflict with the 'humane and rational', which was indispensable.[10] Hegel's symbolic link between philosophy and the theology of the cross in the well-known statement in the introduction to the *Philosophy of Right* that reason is 'the rose in the cross of the present', was offensive to him. 'An airy, decorative cross is always a cheerful object: the loathsome wood of the martyrs, the most repugnant object under the sun, no man in his right mind should be concerned to excavate and erect.'[11] The symbol under which the cross was discussed at this period was the Rosy Cross. K. Löwith has described the various interpretations of this symbol on Luther's coat of arms, amongst the Rosicrucians, in Hegel and in Goethe. For Goethe the roses add gentleness to 'the rough wood' and make Good Friday a humane Good Friday. Although he regarded the roses as of more value for his humanity and religion than the cross which they surrounded, Goethe nevertheless challenged Christianity with the mystery of this cross:

> There the cross stands, thickly wreathed in roses.
> Who put the roses on the cross?
> The wreath grows bigger, so that on every side
> The harsh cross is surrounded by gentleness.[12]

At the end of the last century, the 'roses' of humanity from the Western Christian tradition were no longer visible to Nietzsche on the cross of Christianity. He saw Christianity as standing alone beside the crucified Christ, and therefore decried it in *The Antichrist* as a 'religion of decadence', as a religious hatred for everything proud, for freedom, for sensual joy, and as the hostility of the weak and lowly against the lords of the earth and the noble.

Modern men, with their obtuseness as regards all Christian nomenclature, no longer have the sense for the terribly superlative conception which was implied to an antique taste by the paradox of the formula, 'God on the cross'. Hitherto there had never and nowhere been such boldness in inversion, nor anything at once so dreadful, questioning and questionable as this formula: it promised a transformation of all ancient values (*Beyond Good and Evil*, III, 46).

He called its morality the pitiful 'morality of a child made to stand in the corner', which had made the morbid virtue of compassion out of the necessity of suffering. He treated Christianity as a nihilist religion which had developed from Judaism. One statement which sums up his criticism is: 'Basically there was only one Christian, and he died on the cross.'[13] Down to the present day, everything else was morality for slaves. Karl Marx also directs his criticism of Christianity to the 'roses' in the 'cross of reality':

Criticism has plucked the imaginary flowers from the chain, not so that man should wear an unimaginative, comfortless chain, but so that he might throw away the chain and break the live flowers.[14]

The more post-Christian humanism breaks away from the religious and humanist 'roses' of the cross, the more Christian faith today is forced back upon the naked cross without all the roses of tradition. It can no longer be a traditional faith in the roses which make the cross of Christ pleasant and wholesome for it. It is drawn into the full, undisguised bitterness and abandonment of Good Friday, where it can become true faith.

The cross is the utterly incommensurable factor in the revelation of God. We have become far too used to it. We have surrounded the scandal of the cross with roses. We have made a theory of salvation out of it. But that is not the cross. That is not the bleakness inherent in it, placed in it by God. Hegel defined the cross: 'God is dead'—and he no doubt rightly saw that here we are faced by the night of the real, ultimate and inexplicable absence of God, and that before the 'Word of the cross' we are dependent upon the principle *sola fide*; dependent upon it as nowhere else. Here we have not the *opera Dei*, which point to him as the eternal creator, and to his wisdom. Here the faith in creation, the source of all paganism, breaks down. Here this whole philosophy and wisdom is abandoned to folly. Here God is non-God. Here is the triumph of death, the enemy, the non-church, the lawless state, the blasphemer, the soldiers. Here Satan triumphs over God. Our faith begins at the point where atheists suppose that it must be at an end. Our faith begins with the bleakness and power which is the night of the cross, abandonment, temptation and doubt about everything that exists! Our faith must be born where it is abandoned by all tangible reality; it must be born of nothingness, it must taste this nothingness and be given it to taste in a way that no philosophy of nihilism can imagine.[15]

For Christian faith this means that it can no longer understand itself only in the context of its place in world history, and of the history and success of Christianity, but must recall the event in which it originated. 'The primary existent for faith, revealed only to faith, and, as revelation, the first thing to bring faith into being, is, as far as "Christian" faith is concerned, Christ, the crucified God.'[16] If any one of the historical forms in which it has expressed itself grows out of date, as its educational process is completed, it is not sufficient simply to distil out the idea inherent in that form of Christianity. Instead, the Christian faith which once 'conquered the world' must also learn to conquer its own forms when they have become worldly. It can do so only when it breaks down the idols of the Christian West, and, in a reforming and revolutionary way, remembers the 'crucified God'. 'For how should the Christian pilgrimage *in hoc saeculo* ever become homeless in the land where it has never been at home?'[17] A radical return to the origin of Christian faith in the night of the cross makes this faith homeless not only in an alien, religious world, but also in the syncretistic world of present-day bourgeois Christianity. The task of theology is then no longer that of presenting itself as the self-awareness of Christianity as one of the phenomena of world history, but that of committing itself radically to the event which is the origin of faith in the cross; that is, of becoming a theology of the cross. If it were to be satisfied with a theory of present-day Christianity, it would be like the owl of Minerva which spreads its wings only with the falling of the dusk, and the philosophy which 'paints its grey in grey' when a form of life has grown old. 'With . . . grey in grey, it cannot be rejuvenated but only understood,' said Hegel.[18] A rejuvenation of Christianity when it has grown old and grey is only possible on the basis of its own origin, and becomes a dangerous and liberating reality when faith becomes aware of the incommensurability of the cross of Christ with the revelation of God, and realizing this, becomes aware too of its own strangeness and homelessness in its own Christian world. If faith in the crucified Christ is in contradiction to all conceptions of the righteousness, beauty and morality of man, faith in the 'crucified God' is also a contradiction of everything men have ever conceived, desired and sought to be assured of by the term 'God'. That 'God', the 'supreme being' and the 'supreme good', should be revealed and present in the abandonment of Jesus by God on the cross, is something that it is difficult to desire. What interest can the religious longing for fellowship with God have in the crucifixion of its God, and his powerlessness and abandonment in absolute death?[19] In spite of all the 'roses' which the needs of religion and theological interpretation have draped round the cross, the cross is the really irreligious thing in Christian faith. It is the suffering of God in Christ, rejected and killed in the absence of God, which qualifies Christian faith as faith, and as something different from the projection of man's desire. The modern criticism of religion can attack the whole world of religious Christianity, but not this unreligious cross. There is no pattern for religious projections in the cross. For he who was crucified represents the fundamental and total crucifixion of all religion: the deification of the human heart, the sacralization of certain localities in nature and certain sacred dates and times, the worship of those who hold political power, and their power politics. Even the disciples of Jesus all fled from their master's cross. Christians who do not have the feeling that they must flee the crucified Christ have probably not yet understood him in a sufficiently radical way. The fatal and liberating contradiction which man experiences in his most sacred religious feelings when faced with the crucified Christ can then be applied to the tacit religious assumptions of his modern criticism of religion, with which he legitimizes his flight and his contempt: to the self-deification of atheist movements of liberation; to the post-Christian idolization of the laws of history and historical success; and to post-Christian confidence in an eternally productive nature. The historical cross of Christ, believed in as revelation and calling true faith into being, is the crux of the criticism of religion in Feuerbach and Freud. The cross, as the negation of everything which is religious in their sense, of all deifications, all assurances, all images and analogies and every established holy place which promises permanence, remains outside the conflict between religion and the criticism of religion, between theism and atheism. The faith that it arouses is something quite different from either.

Faith in the cross distinguishes Christian faith from the world of religions and from secular ideologies and utopias, in so far as they seek to replace these religions or to inherit their legacy and bring them to realization. But faith in the cross also distinguishes Christian faith from its own superstitious manifestions. The recollection of the crucified Christ obliges Christian faith permanently to distinguish itself from its own religious and secular forms. In Western civilization, this means, in concrete terms, distinguishing itself from the 'Christian-bourgeois world' and from Christianity as the 'religion of contemporary society'.

A Christianity which does not measures itself in theology and practice by this criterion loses its identity and becomes confused with the surrounding world; it becomes the religious fulfilment of the prevailing social interests, or of the interests of those who dominate society. It becomes a chameleon which can no longer be distinguished from the leaves of the tree in which it sits.

But a Christianity which applies to its theology and practice the criterion of its own fundamental origin cannot remain what it is at the present moment in social, political and psychological terms. It experiences an outward crisis of identity, in which its inherited identification with the desires and interests of the world around it is broken down. It becomes something other than what it imagined itself to be, and what was expected of it.[20]

To be radical, of course, means to seize a matter at its roots. More radical Christian faith can only mean committing oneself without reserve to the 'crucified God'. This is dangerous. It does not promise the confirmation of one's own conceptions, hopes and good intentions. It promises first of all the pain of repentance and fundamental change. It offers no recipe for success. But it brings a confrontation with the truth. It is not positive and constructive, but is in the first instance critical and destructive. It does not bring man into a better harmony with himself and his environment, but into contradiction with himself and his environment. It does not create a home for him and integrate him into society, but makes him 'homeless' and 'rootless', and liberates him in following Christ who was homeless and rootless. The 'religion of the cross', if faith on this basis can ever be so called, does not elevate and edify in the usual sense, but scandalizes; and most of all it scandalizes one's 'co-religionists' in one's own circle. But by this scandal, it brings liberation into a world which is not free. For ultimately, in a civilization which is constructed on the principle of achievement and enjoyment, and therefore makes pain and death a private matter, excluded from its public life, so that in the final issue the world must no longer be experienced as offering resistance, there is nothing so unpopular as for the crucified God to be made a present reality through faith. It alienates alienated men, who have come to terms with alienation. And yet this faith, with its consequences, is capable of setting men free from their cultural illusions, releasing them from the involvements which blind them, and confronting them with the truth of their existence and their society. Before there can be correspondence and agreements between faith and the surrounding world, there must first be the painful demonstration of truth in the midst of untruth. In this pain we experience reality outside ourselves, which we have not made or thought out for ourselves. The pain arouses a love which can no longer be indifferent, but seeks out its opposite, what is ugly and unworthy of love, in order to love it. This pain breaks down the apathy in which everything is a matter of indifference, because everything one meets is always the same and familiar.

Thus the cross in the church is not just what Christian custom

would have imagined. The cross in the church symbolizes the
contradiction which comes into the church from the God who was
crucified 'outside'. Every symbol points beyond itself to something else. Every symbol invites thought. The symbol of the
cross in the church points to the God who was crucified not
between two candles on an altar, but between two thieves in the
place of the skull, where the outcasts belong, outside the gates of
the city. It does not invite thought but a change of mind. It is
a symbol which therefore leads out of the church and out of
religious longing into the fellowship of the oppressed and abandoned. On the other hand, it is a symbol which calls the oppressed
and godless into the church and through the church into the
fellowship of the crucified God. Where this contradiction in the
cross, and its revolution in religious values, is forgotten, the cross
ceases to be a symbol and becomes an idol, and no longer invites a
revolution in thought, but the end of thought in self-affirmation.

The 'religion of the cross' is a contradiction in itself, for the
crucified God is a contradiction in this religion. To endure this
contradiction is to take leave of one's religious traditions; to be
free of one's religious needs; to abandon one's previous identity
as known to others, and to gain the identity of Christ in faith; to
become anonymous and unknown in one's environment and
obtain citizenship in the new creation of God. To make the cross
a present reality in our civilization means to put into practice the
experience one has received of being liberated from fear for oneself; no longer to adapt oneself to this society, its idols and taboos,
its imaginary enemies and fetishes; and in the name of him who
was once the victim of religion, society and the state to enter into
solidarity with the victims of religion, society and the state at the
present day, in the same way as he who was crucified became their
brother and their liberator.

The religions and humanist world which surrounded Christianity from the very first despised the cross, because this dehumanized Christ represented a contradiction to all ideas of God,
and of man as divine. Yet even in historic Christianity the bitterness of the cross was not maintained in the recollection of believers
or in the reality presented by the church. There were times of
persecution and times of reformation, in which the crucified
Christ was to some extent experienced as directly present. In
historic Christianity there was also the 'religion of the suppressed'

(Laternari), who knew that their faith brought them into spontaneous fellowship with the suffering Christ. But the more the church of the crucified Christ became the prevailing religion of society, and set about satisfying the personal and public needs of this society, the more it left the cross behind it, and gilded the cross with the expectations and ideas of salvation.

We have made the bitterness of the cross, the revelation of God in the cross of Jesus Christ, tolerable to ourselves by learning to understand it as a necessity for the process of salvation . . . As a result the cross loses its arbitrary and incomprehensible character.[21]

This is to maintain the significance which the cross has come to have in the context of the process of one's own salvation, one's own faith, and one's own theory of reality, and to suppress and destroy the unique, the particular and the scandalous in it. We shall now describe this process of the absorption of the cross in Christianity, in the double sense of its maintenance and its destruction, in the various forms under which the crucified Christ has been realized: in the cult of the cross, the mysticism of the cross, the ethics of the cross and the theology of the cross, in order to restore faith in the crucified Christ to its truth, the truth of him who was crucified.

2. *The Cult of the Cross*

By the cult of the cross we understand the unbloody repetition of the event that took place on Golgotha on the altar of the church; that is, the making present of Christ in the sacrifice of the mass.

We can begin with the finding of general anthropology and comparative religion, that from a very early stage men understood their existence as a gift from a transcendental power. The response which they made in their lives to this existence, experienced as a gift of grace, was that of self-sacrifice, in which they devoted themselves to this transcendental power. In the sacrificial cults of religion, this self-offering of man was celebrated through real symbols as a *pars pro toto*. The basic form of all sacrifice was the sacrifice of first fruits. Through them, the whole flock or the whole harvest was consecrated to the gods and so sanctified. It was also thought of as a sacrifice of praise and thanksgiving, expressing the recognition of the deity's right of ownership. The representative nature of these sacrifices brought them, like all representative action, into the ambiguous region between the relief of a burden and alienation. The offering of the part for the whole can never mean more than the part instead of the whole. In comparative religion it is not a tenable view that the sacrificial gifts of men were calculated to bring the favour of the gods. This *do ut des* formula does recur in many late forms of religion, and especially in Rome, but is a departure from the original situation in which all sacrificial gifts unite the giver and the receiver and bring them into a solemn and fundamental fellowship. All the societies of antiquity into which Christianity came were at heart religious, and at the heart of their social religions were the cults; and at the heart of the cults were the sacrifices to the gods of the state and the fellowship with them established at festivals. The more the Christian church obtained public recognition, the more it was also obliged to fulfil this public need for cult and sacrifice. The church did suppress pagan sacrificial actions and cultic drama, but replaced them by its own cult. It radically altered the meaning of cultic sacrifice. The gods no longer had to be reconciled by men's sacrifices. Nor was life any longer regarded as a gift from the ultimate realities of existence in nature, society and politics, a gift of grace which had to be acknowledged and consequently sanctified. It was the one God himself who by the sacrifice in the self-offering of Christ had reconciled sinful men to himself and provided the basis of their life by his grace, so that it was to him that thanks had to be offered for it, and to him it had to be consecrated. But the unbloody repetition of the self-offering of Christ took place at that integral point in public life and private devotion at which the ancient sacrificial religions had been celebrated and had become effective. As a result, the Christian cult of the sacrifice of Christ retained and still retains a manifold significance, and has been at the disposal of more than one interest.

The dogmatic problem of the concept of sacrifice lies in the development of a concept of sacrifice which on the one hand does justice to the data of comparative religion in general (however varied these may be), and at the same time is applicable both to the 'sacrifice' of Christ on the cross, and also to the celebration of the mass as a 'sacrifice', without doing violence to both these New Testament sacrifices.[22]

In so far as it is true that the meaning of 'sacrifice' in the case of the cross and the mass can be known from themselves alone, to understand them as 'sacrifices' would be tautological, if it were not possible to assume an independent concept of sacrifice applicable to them at least in an analogous and modified way.[23] But this makes the sacrifice of the mass and the eucharist particularly ambiguous. On the one hand, the understanding of the mass as a sacrifice is based on biblical tradition, according to which it is the symbolic actual presence by anamnesis of the unique atoning sacrifice of Christ. 'The cross remains the absolute sacrifice, and the mass the relative. Christ himself is the true priest in the mass, and the earthly priest acts *in persona ejus*.'[24] But on the other hand the sacrificial death of Christ is thereby recognized as a divine, transcendent background for the cultic practice of the church, and as a result the unique, historical and eschatological event of the self-offering of Christ is absorbed into the cultic repetitions of the church, which are celebrated in a modified analogy to sacrifice in religions in general. From the point of view of the relative sacrifice of the eucharist, dependent upon this basis, all that is visible of Christ's death on the cross is his absolute self-sacrifice which provides the basis for it. What is maintained and made a present reality by the continuous and repeated cult is that which in the cross on Golgotha seems to be of eternal significance: the divine value of the self-sacrifice of Christ for the relationship of God to man and of man to God, for grace and thanksgiving. What was unique, particular and scandalous in the death of Christ is not retained, but suppressed and destroyed. How did this come about, and how should it be regarded?

His cross is not found in the intimacy of the individual, personal heart, nor in the sanctuary of a purely religious devotion. It is erected beyond these protected and separated precincts, 'outside', as the theology of the Epistle to the Hebrews tells us. The curtain of the temple is torn forever.[25]

But this means that basically the crucified Christ represents the end of the cult. He has died 'once for all', as Paul emphasizes. His death is not a sacrifice which can be repeated or transferred. He has finally risen from the death which he died once for all, as Paul emphasizes again, and 'will never die again' (Rom. 6.9), in either a bloody or an unbloody way. He cannot be turned into an eternally dying and rising cultic god. He is not drawn into the cycle of the 'eternal return of the like' (M. Eliade), but breaks

43

The Crucified God

out of the compulsive repetition of the cult. It is true that the eucharist or the celebration of the Lord's supper recalls and makes present the death of Christ 'until he comes' (I Cor. 11.26), but in the form of 'proclamation', not in the form of the 'repetition' of Christ's death on the cross. Thus one must distinguish between the death of Christ on the cross on Golgotha, which happened once for all, and the constantly repeated celebration of the hope which remembers him, to the point of using different terms. The unique historical nature of his death on the cross, outside religion and the temple, makes the identification of the crucified Christ with the cult impossible. The eschatological finality which associates the preaching of the resurrection with the one who was executed at a particular time and place makes it impossible for him to be part of cultic repetition, and both ultimately make the separation of cultic and profane in Christianity impossible, and demand that Christians should break down this separation.

Thus it is not enough simply to Christianize the cults of religious societies. It is not enough simply to 'do justice' in the theology of the cross to the sacrificial concept of comparative religion by accepting it in an analogical and modified way. Cultic religion must be replaced by the spreading of the word of the cross, the celebration of faith and the practical following of Jesus. The cultic division between the religious and the profane is potentially abolished in faith in the Christ who was profaned by crucifixion. Thus the eucharist, like the meals held by Jesus with 'sinners and publicans', must also be celebrated with the unrighteous, those who have no rights and the godless from the 'highways and hedges' of society, in all their profanity, and should no longer be limited, as a religious sacrifice, to the inner circle of the devout, to those who are members of the same denomination. The Christian church can re-introduce the divisions between the religious and the profane and between those who are within and those who are without, only at the price of losing its own identity as the church of the crucified Christ. But because even a cultic religious church, if it is Christian, however splendid a form it may have taken on, still retains the memory of the crucified Christ, it constantly bears with it its own crisis. This crisis becomes a reality when faith encounters the total truth of the crucified Christ, and when the whole truth of the crucified Christ encounters unbelief. Then the arbitrary aspect of his death on the cross, with which the cult

44

cannot deal, reappears from beneath its representations in the cult and makes the *memoria passionis Domini* a dangerous matter even for the established cultic churches. And it is the godless, forced out by the church, who recognize the inner distinction between the reality of the cross on Golgotha and its cultic representation within the church. Thus for the faith which believes in and celebrates the representation of the crucified Christ as a reality in the 'sacrifice of the mass', it is also indispensable to be aware once again of this inner distinction.

3. *The Mysticism of the Cross*

In historic Christianity, the passion of Christ has also been understood and relived in the sense of the mysticism of suffering. Here the crucified Christ was seen less as the sacrifice which God creates to reconcile the world to himself, and more as the exemplary path trodden by a righteous man suffering unjustly, leading to salvation. Fellowship with God is not attained by outward sacrifice and presence in the church's cult; the way to glory leads through personal suffering. Thus by meditation and adoration people have drawn closer to the sufferings of Christ, participated in them and felt them as their own sufferings. And again, in their own sufferings, people have discovered a fellowship with the 'sacred head sore wounded'. This spiritual absorption into the sufferings of Christ led, as late medieval mysticism said, to a conformity of the soul with the crucified Christ. And this *conformitas crucis* indirectly brought an assurance of salvation and of glorification. One did not achieve fellowship with Christ by sacrifice and good works, but by mystical suffering and resignation. In fellowship with the sufferings of Christ, one received in a very personal way a more inward fellowship with Christ in belonging to the organized church and in taking part in the Christian cult. The *via negativa* of mystical theology internalized or even replaced the *via analogiae* laid down as a positive requirement by the church.

It is impossible to overlook how much this passion mysticism was and is the devotion of the laity in Christianity. It is demonstrably the devotion of the poor and sick, the oppressed and crushed. The 'God' of the poor, the peasant and the slave has always been the poor, suffering, unprotected Christ, whereas the

God of empires and rulers has usually been the Pantocrator, Christ enthroned in heaven.[26] In the later Middle Ages, the Christian people of Europe were seized by this devotion to the passion. The Byzantine portraits of Christ, the divine lord of heaven, and the imperial images of Christ, the judge of the world, were supplemented in churches by images of the crucified Christ of the poor, in which no realistic detail of pain and torture was omitted. The 'man of sorrows' spoke to those who were wasting away in pain, and to whom no one else spoke, because no one could help them. In representations of the crucified Christ, the emphasis moved away from sacramental devotion to his victory on the cross to inward devotion to his sacrificial death on the cross. These images of the crucifixion, such as that upon the Isenheim altar, were not merely the artistic expression of a new form of devotion, but at that time were regarded as miracle-working images. The sick, the cripples and the incurable were brought before these images, and in their worship there they experienced relief from their sufferings and healings. We shall not discuss here the medical question whether such miraculous healings can exist or not. What is theologically more important is the faith that they express. It derives its vitality not from Christ healing as a superhuman, divine miracle-worker, but on the contrary from the fact that he brings help through his wounds and through what from the human point of view is his impotent suffering. 'When my heart is most fearful, help me out of my fears, through thy fear and pain,' says a hymn by Paul Gerhardt. This mysticism of the passion has discovered a truth about Christ which ought not to be suppressed by being understood in a superficial way. It can
• be summed up by saying that suffering is overcome by suffering, and wounds are healed by wounds. For the suffering in suffering is the lack of love, and the wounds in wounds are the abandonment, and the powerlessness in pain is unbelief. And therefore the suffering of abandonment is overcome by the suffering of love, which is not afraid of what is sick and ugly, but accepts it and takes it to itself in order to heal it. Through his own abandonment by God, the crucified Christ brings God to those who are abandoned by God. Through his suffering he brings salvation to those who suffer. Through his death he brings eternal life to those who are dying. And therefore the tempted, rejected, suffering and dying Christ came to be the centre of the religion of the

oppressed and the piety of the lost. And it is here, in the theology of the mysticism of the cross in the late Middle Ages, that we first hear the monstrous phrase 'the crucified God', which Luther then took up.[27]

In our own time, this understanding has taken on new vitality in Protestant theology. Dietrich Bonhoeffer wrote from prison, shortly before his execution:

God lets himself be pushed out of the world on to the cross. He is weak and powerless in the world, and that is precisely the way, the only way, in which he is with us and helps us. Matt. 8.17 makes it quite clear that Christ helps us, not by virtue of his omnipotence, but by virtue of his weakness and suffering . . . Only the suffering God can help . . . That is a reversal of what the religious man expects from God. Man is summoned to share in God's sufferings at the hands of a godless world.[28]

At about the same time, and in a similar political situation in his country, the Japanese Lutheran theologian Kazoh Kitamori was writing his book *Theology of the Pain of God*,[29] in which he developed a similar theology of the cross: the pain of God heals our pains. In the suffering of Christ God himself suffers. These suggestions must be taken further.

Why and in what way did the suffering, crucified God become the God of the poor and abandoned? What is the significance of the mysticism of the cross in popular devotion? These people in their wretchedness clearly understood him better because of their own concrete situation than the rich and their masters. They understood him better, because they rightly had the impression that he understood them better than their masters.

In Europe, Christmas and Easter are the high points of the church year, in custom and folklore and popular piety. This is not so in Latin America. The Christian 'feasts of life and hope' mean nothing to Indians and Mestizos. Their feast is Holy Week. The suffering and death of Jesus, the pain and mourning is something in which they can share. There they are at home. That is their life. The submission to fate and ability to suffer of the original inhabitants of Latin America has long been assisted by particular devotional forms. These include the stations of the cross, intercessory processions around representations of the fourteen biblical and legendary stations of Jesus during his passion.[30]

Here, of course, the dominant church has from earliest times so formulated the texts of the stations of the cross that the believers are made aware only of the pains caused to Christ by their individual sins and their private immorality. But the poor no doubt recognized all their suffering in the crucified Christ: what they suffered from society and what they suffered from their fate.

Similarly, the piety of the Negro spirituals sung by black slaves in the southern states of the USA concentrates upon the crucifixion and resurrection of Jesus. For them his sufferings and death were a symbol of their own sufferings, their despised condition and their temptations in an unfriendly and inhuman world. They saw their fate in his sufferings. On the other hand, they could say that when Jesus was nailed to the cross and the Roman soldiers stabbed him in the side, he was not alone. The black slaves suffered with him and died with him.

'Were you there, when they crucified my Lord?' begins one of their songs. And the answer is: 'We, the black slaves, were there with him in his agony.'

In Jesus' death black slaves saw themselves, and they unleashed their imagination in describing what they felt and saw ... His death was a symbol of their suffering, trials and tribulations in an unfriendly world. They knew the agony of rejection and the pain of hanging from a tree ... Because black slaves knew the significance of the pain and shame of Jesus' death on the cross, they found themselves by his side.[31]

By his suffering and death, Jesus identified himself with those who were enslaved, and took their pain upon himself. And if he was not alone in his suffering, nor were they abandoned in the pains of their slavery. Jesus was with them. And there too lay their hope of freedom, by virtue of his resurrection into the freedom of God. Jesus was their identity with God in a world which had taken all hope from them and destroyed their human identity until it was unrecognizable.

One can perhaps apply to this mysticism of the cross of the poor, the sick and the slaves the saying of Karl Marx: 'Religion is the groaning of oppressed creation, the heart of a heartless world, as it is the spirit of situations where there is no spirit.'[32] The point of this mysticism of the cross is missed if it is seen as only the 'opium of the people', given to them by their masters to keep them quiet, as is suggested by the other expression of Lenin, that religion is 'opium for the people'. Of course the mysticism of suffering can easily be peverted into a justification of suffering itself. The mysticism of the cross can of course praise submission to fate as a virtue and be perverted into melancholy apathy. To suffer with the crucified Christ can also lead to self-pity. But faith is then dissociated from the suffering Christ, seeing him as no more than a replaceable pattern for one's own sufferings, as the patient sufferer who provides the example for one's own endurance of an alien destiny. His suffering is then no longer of special significance for one's own acceptance of suffering. It does not change anything in it, nor does it change the human being who suffers. The church has much abused the theology of the cross and the mysticism of the passion in the interest of those who cause the suffering. Too often, peasants, Indians and black slaves have been called upon by the representatives of the dominant religion to accept their sufferings as 'their cross' and not to rebel against them. Luther need not have recommended the peasants to accept their suffering as their cross. They already bore the burdens their masters imposed upon them. Instead, a sermon on the cross would have done the princes and the bourgeoisie who ruled them a great deal of good, if it was aimed at setting them free from their pride and moving them to an attitude of solidarity with their victims.[33] Thus it makes a difference who speaks of this mysticism of the cross, to whom he speaks and in whose interests he speaks. In a world of domination and oppression one must pay close attention to the concrete function of any preaching and any devotion. As 'opium for the people', produced by those who caused the suffering, this mysticism of suffering is a blasphemy, a kind of monstrous product of inhumanity.

But this does not explain the strange fact that the Christ of the poor has always been the crucified Christ. What do they themselves see in him? They clearly do not find in his passion another 'poor devil' who had no better luck than they. Rather, they find in him the brother who put off his divine form and took on the form of a slave (Phil. 2), to be with them and to love them. They find in him a God who does not torture them, as their masters do, but becomes their brother and companion. Where their own lives have been deprived of freedom, dignity and humanity, they find in fellowship with him respect, recognition, human dignity and hope. They find this, their true identity, hidden and guaranteed in the Christ who suffers with them, so that no one can deprive them of this identity (Col. 3.3). They find open to them in the crucified Christ the heaven from which, as a negro spiritual says, 'No one can throw me out', as from a white bus. As a result, this mysticism of the cross on the part of the oppressed is in fact an 'expression of misery', and is already implicitly a 'protest against misery', as Marx said. In essence, however, it is something more, and something quite different, which was not recognized by Marx: the expression of human dignity and self-respect in the experience that God counts them worthy and the belief that Christ loves them. For in the hymns of this mysticism of the cross a new experience of identity is concealed. Anyone who in these hymns encounters the passion of Christ, and experiences in them the pain of the love of God for himself, knows that he himself is something different from what sorrow and the fear of death, the yoke of slavery and his masters have made and seek to make of him. He finds an identity in the fellowship of the cross, which contradicts the definitions of suffering and slavery, and in which the definitions made by his masters find their limit. This is a foothold and a freedom in faith which prevents those who suffer from abandoning themselves involuntarily to suffering and abandoning themselves in it, from coming to terms with slavery and from feeling themselves to be nothing more than slaves or units of labour, complete nobodies. The faith which is obtained by gazing upon the suffering and crucified God in this mysticism of the cross prevents them from sinking back into misery, from giving themselves up for lost and often enough from committing suicide out of despair. Thus we can describe this intangible experience of identity in faith in the cross as the enduring element in the mysticism of the cross, and as the inner reason for the outward expression of misery and the ever recurring protest against it.

With this account of the inner significance of the mysticism of the cross, our trend of thought is leading beyond the mere *conformitas crucis*. When the poor and oppressed look upon the poor and humiliated Christ they do not see only their own poverty and humiliation repeated in another human being. He shows them their misery in someone who is different from them. He therefore basically shows them a different misery and a different suffering. If those who practise the mysticism of the passion were to regard the crucified Christ only as the archetype of their own pain and humiliation, they would indeed be maintaining the memory of the features of his humanity and abasement, and would be making it a present reality in their own consciousness of abasement. But they would then be destroying what is distinctive about the person of Jesus and what is special about his suffering and dying. They

would then be understanding his cross only in the general sense
of 'cross and misery', as the passive suffering of an uncomprehended fate, like a miscarriage, an illness, a plague, a premature
death, or suffering from the deep rooted evil of other people, as
social suffering, and suffering from the society which humiliates
them. But these sufferings would not be the sufferings of Christ.
There is no mention in the gospels of his suffering from nature
and fate, and his economic sufferings as a 'carpenter's son'.
Rather, his sufferings and humiliation came from his actions,
from his preaching of the imminence of the kingdom as a kingdom
of unconditional grace, from his freedom towards the law, and
from his table-fellowship with 'sinners and tax-collectors'. Jesus
did not suffer passively from the world in which he lived, but
incited it against himself by his message and the life he lived. Nor
did his crucifixion in Jerusalem come upon him as the act of an
evil destiny, so that one could speak of a heroic failure, as heroes
have often failed and yet remained heroes to posterity. According
to the gospels, Jesus himself set out for Jerusalem and actively
took the expected suffering upon himself. By proclaiming the
righteousness of God as the right of those who were rejected and
without grace to receive grace, he provoked the hostility of the
guardians of the law. By becoming a 'friend of sinners and tax-
collectors', he made their enemies his enemies. By claiming that
God himself was on the side of the godless, he incited the devout
against him and was cast out into the godlessness of Golgotha.
The more the mysticism of the cross recognizes this, the less it
can accept Jesus as an example of patience and submission to fate.
The more it recognizes his active suffering, the less it can make
him the archetype of its own weakness. To the extent that men in
misery feel his solidarity with them, their solidarity with his
sufferings brings them out of their situation. If they understand
him as their brother in their sufferings, they in turn do not become
imitators of his sufferings until they accept his mission and actively
follow him. He suffered on account of the liberating word of God,
and died on account of his liberating fellowship with those who
were not free. Consequently, his sufferings and death are the
messianic sufferings and death of the 'Christ of God'. His death
is the death of the one who redeems men from death, which is
evil. In other words, they are the pains of love for abandoned men,
which the mysticism of the cross apprehends when it identifies

men with the sufferings of Christ. And the traditional Christian praise of poverty cannot be Christian if it simply gives a religious blessing to the situation of the poor, promising them compensation in heaven, so that on earth the poor become poorer and the rich become richer. As Jesus understood it, poverty is 'to become poor', to empty oneself and devote everything that one is and has to the liberation of the poor. 'Though he was rich, yet for your sake he became poor, so that by his poverty you might become rich,' said Paul (II Cor. 8.9), demonstrating this by the life he lived as an apostle, 'always carrying in the body the death of Jesus, so that the life of Jesus may also be manifested in our bodies . . . so death is at work in us, but life in you' (II Cor. 4.10, 12). This apostolic suffering and death cannot be attributed in an equivocal fashion to the suffering and death of men in general, as Christian tradition has unfortunately often done, even in Luther. The poverty and sufferings of Christ are experienced and understood only by participation in his mission and in imitating the task he carried out. Thus the more the poor understand the cross, in the mysticism of the cross, as the cross of *Christ*, the more they are liberated from their submission to fate and apathy in suffering. Thus the potential contained in the devotion of the poor to the cross is different from what has been attributed to it by the dominating religion. For the crucified Messiah to become a present reality amongst slaves is therefore as dangerous to their masters as their reading of the Bible in general.

The church of the crucified was at first, and basically remains, the church of the oppressed and insulted, the poor and wretched, the church of the people. On the other hand, it is also the church of those who have turned away from their inward and external forms of domination and oppression. But it is not the church of those who inwardly are self-righteous and outwardly exercise domination. If it truly remembers the crucified Christ, it cannot allow a bland, religious indifference to prevail towards everyone. As the crucified Messiah, it is the church of liberation for all men, whether Jews or Gentiles, Greeks or barbarians, masters or servants, men or women, but not for everyone in the same way. As the people of the crucified Christ, the church originated in the particular earthly events of the oppression and liberation of Jesus, and exists in the midst of a divided and mutually hostile world of inhuman people on one side and dehumanized people on the other. Its concrete language must therefore take this difference into account, and its action must be that of commitment. The liberation of the poor from the vicious circle of poverty is different in form from the liberation of the rich from the vicious circle of riches, although both vicious circles are interlinked. The justification of godless sinners is different from that of the sinful devout. The liberation of slaves who have been deprived of human life is different from the liberation of the slave owners, who in a double sense of the word themselves 'take life'. Thus to save all men, and in accordance with the contradiction of the cross, the church of the crucified Christ must take sides in the concrete social and political conflicts going on about it and in which it is involved, and must be prepared to join and form parties. It must not ally itself with the existing parties, but in a partisan fashion intervene on behalf of betrayed humanity and suppressed freedom. The sole legitimate starting point for this is the apprehension of the liberating cross of Christ in the concrete situations in which it is involved with others. To give an example of how the passive criticism of the cross can become an active and politically relevant imitation, let us quote an attempt made in Latin America:

Today the favourite cultic practice of Latin America, the stations of the cross, has come to be fruitful for the inculcation of a social conscience. The central point is the guilt of society, and the leading idea is that Christ is our suffering fellow-man, oppressed, exploited and defenceless. That is, the following statement of Christ is taken literally: 'As you did it to one of the least of these my brethren, you did it to me.' The 'twentieth century stations of the cross' from Central America are a classic example of this new form of the stations of the cross, and its social and political relevance . . . They have often been put on the stage and broadcast, but in 1964 were forbidden by the military government.[34]

4. Following the Cross

In the previous chapter we went on from the mysticism of the cross in passive suffering, by way of the recognition of the active sufferings of Christ, in the direction of active imitation of the crucified Christ. We must now describe in outline the forms in which the crucified Christ becomes a present reality in the experience of fellowship with Christ, on the part of those who follow him. We shall then ask once more how much of his cross on Golgotha is to be found in the cross of those who follow him, and how much is exclusively his own cross. The idea of following Christ has been neglected by bourgeois Protestantism, because it no longer recognized or wished to recognize the suffering church, the church of the martyrs, but established itself in a situation of apparent harmony with the 'Christian world'. Not until the period of conflict between the church and society did anyone have the experience of consciously following Christ, did anyone come forward as a martyr and understand once again what it means to be crucified with him.

7   The gospels intentionally direct the gaze of Christians away from the experiences of the risen Christ and the Holy Spirit back to the earthly Jesus and his way to the cross. They represent faith as a call to follow Jesus. The call to follow him (Mark 8.31–38 par.) is associated with Jesus' proclamation of suffering. To follow Jesus always means to deny oneself and to take 'his cross' on oneself. Let us first of all summarize the basic features of his call to follow Jesus. He gathers about himself a circle of disciples who follow him (Mark 1.29; Matt. 8.1; 14.13; Luke 7.9; 9.11; John 6.2, etc.). Outwardly, there is no distinction between this and the picture presented by the scribes and their disciples. But the relationship was of a different kind. The disciples of Jesus did not request to be accepted into his 'school', but were called by him. Presumably calling and following were originally concerned with God alone. Thus for Jesus to call people to follow him was an unparalleled claim to authority on his part. His disciples did not follow him in order to become rabbis themselves one day. They were to call each other brother, rather than rabbi (Matt. 10.24). For Jesus did not found a new rabbinic school, but proclaimed the imminence of the kingdom. His call to discipleship was made under the sign of the kingdom of God which was beginning, and this sign was Jesus himself in person. Consequently, the call to follow him was absolute, and no motive was given at the time or later. Instead, there was a direct appeal: 'Follow me!' (Mark 1.17 par.; 2.14 par.). Those who followed this call abandoned everything, and others refused and remained what they were. To follow Jesus was to break all links with one's family, job, etc., and indeed to break the link with oneself, to deny and hate oneself, in order to gain the kingdom: 'Whoever would save his life will lose it; and whoever loses his life for my sake and the gospel's will save it' (Mark 8.35).

Thus the motivation for the call to follow Jesus is eschatological, and must not be understood in a moral sense. It is a call into the future of God which is now beginning in Jesus, and for the sake of this future it is not only necessary but possible to break one's links with the world which is now passing away and abandon a concern for one's own life. The call to follow Jesus is the commandment of the eschatological moment. But as a call to follow Jesus, it is also a call to share his suffering and to stand beneath his cross. What is this suffering? Bonhoeffer has rightly pointed out that according to the proclamations of his suffering in the context of which the call to follow him occurs, Jesus has to suffer and to be rejected.[35] To suffer and to be rejected are not identical. Suffering can be celebrated and admired. It can arouse compassion. But to be rejected takes away the dignity from suffering and makes it dishonourable suffering. To suffer and be rejected signify the cross. To die on the cross means to suffer and to die as one who is an outcast and rejected. If those who follow Jesus are to take 'their cross' on themselves, they are taking on not only suffering and a bitter fate, but the suffering of rejection. According to their own experience, the greatest Christian saints were also the most profoundly abandoned by God. The expression 'cross' for the sufferings undergone in following Jesus takes its meaning solely from the cross of Christ, not from natural or social sufferings. 'The cross . . . is not the sort of suffering which is inseparable from this mortal life, but the suffering which is an essential part of the specifically Christian life.'[36] And the cross of Christ, in the context of his life, is explained in the first instance by his mission, which provoked hostility. But in addition to the hostility of the law and society, it also contains the element of abandonment by God, expressed in Mark 15.34. His cross includes acceptance of rejection by the Father, in which, in the context of his resurrection, election and atonement are revealed. We must ask whether this cross of absolute abandonment by God is not exclusively his cross alone, and is endured in the cross of those who share in his sufferings only in a watered-down form. The cross of Christ cannot be reduced to an example for the cross of those who follow him. His suffering from abandonment by God is not merely a blueprint for Christian existence in the abandonment by God of a world which is passing away. And therefore Mark 8.35 reads, no doubt intentionally, not that the disciple should take up 'his', that is Christ's cross, but 'your' cross. There is no question of their being on the same level, as is shown by the story of Gethsemane. Jesus suffered and died alone. But those who follow him suffer and die in fellowship with him. For all that they have in common, there is a difference. 'Hence while it is still true that suffering means being cut off from God, yet within the fellowship of Christ's suffering, suffering is overcome by suffering, and becomes the way to communion with God.'[37] And therefore to follow Jesus is joyful.

In the exhortatory passages in his epistles, Paul translated his well-known proclamation of the 'word of the cross' (I Cor. 1.18) into the ethics of the cross, and tells the members of the churches to crucify their flesh and to make the dying of Jesus visible in their bodies.[38] Crucifixion with Jesus was creatively symbolized in baptism and practised in the new obedience which is no longer conformed to this world (Rom. 12.2). He who has died with Christ (Rom. 6.4) is crucified to the world and the world to him (Gal. 6.14). The 'world' here does not mean the essence of experienced reality, but the world of the law, of sin, of the powers and of death. He is 'dead' to this world, so that he no longer has any rights and any claims upon it. But he lives in the life-giving spirit of the new creation, is governed by it, and walks in a renewed life. Paul no longer uses the expression 'following', but he can sometimes speak of 'imitating' (I Cor. 11.1; I Thess. 1.6). In the disagreement about his legitimation as an apostle he counters ideas of following in the sense of succession by the visible signs of the cross in his life and his body (II Cor. 4; II Cor. 6; II Cor. 11.22ff.).[39] These are the very tangible experiences of suffering, of persecution and rejection, to which his apostolate had led him. If as an apostle Paul follows the mission of Christ, by its outward and inward temptations it leads him into the following of the cross. He bears the dying of Jesus in his body, so that the life of Jesus may be revealed. 'So death is at work in us, but life in you' (II Cor. 4.12). These were not sufferings he had chosen himself. Nor is there an attempt to achieve a deeper fellowship with Christ through suffering. Nor is there any imitation of the sufferings of Christ. They are apostolic sufferings and the cross of one who bears witness. The authentication of his apostolate is given by Christ himself, who reveals himself in his apostle's cross. Because he follows the mission of Christ, Paul takes 'his' cross upon him and reveals the power of Christ through his weakness and the life of the risen Christ through his daily dying.

In church history, the closest form of following the crucified Christ was to be a *martyr*. E. Peterson has shown that the apostles were a limited group, whereas the idea of a martyr was not limited to that of an apostle. 'The apostolic church, based upon apostles who were martyrs, is also the suffering church, the church of the martyrs.'[40] The sufferings of an apostle could be renewed in a martyr, who in a juridical sense was not a successor of the apostles. The apostolate of the eye-witnesses of the risen Christ could not be passed on to anyone else. But the ministry of preaching and of being crucified with Christ is passed on to the whole church (A. Schlatter). In the ancient church of the time of persecution, martyrdom was regarded as a special charisma. Those who were put to death were considered to have undergone the 'baptism of blood' and to have fellowship with Jesus in death. Their testimony was consummated in the giving of their lives, and the giving of their lives was understood as sharing in the victory of the crucified Christ. Thus a martyr did not suffer only *for Christ*, his lord, as a soldier goes to his death for his king. His martyrdom was understood as a suffering *with Christ*, and therefore also as the suffering of Christ in him and with him. And because Christ himself suffered in the martyrs, it can be said with Col. 1.24 that the martyrs 'in their body complete what is lacking in Christ's afflictions for the sake of the church'. Thus they do not merely imitate the sufferings of Christ and bear witness to it by doing the same, but take part in and fulfil the continuing sufferings of Christ. They are drawn into the mystery of the suffering of Christ and come to participate in him. This led later to the idea that the altars of the church must be built over the graves or relics of apostles and martyrs, and that the sufferings of the martyrs, by participating is the sufferings of Christ, could be counted as good works. But the imitative participation and co-operation of the martyrs in the agony of Christ must not be understood in this sense. They also make clear the connection between the sufferings of Christ and the sufferings of the final age, which pervade the whole of enslaved creation (Rom. 8.19). 'Suffering in this cosmos is universal, because it is a suffering with the suffering of Christ, who came into this cosmos and yet has burst the bounds of this cosmos, when he rose from the dead and ascended into heaven.'

This is the interpretation of E. Peterson,[41] who thereby makes
clear the universal and public character of the cross of Christ in
its significance for the unrecognized sufferings of the final age
undergone by a world which is godless and abandoned by God.
Thus between Golgotha and the eschatological end of the world,
the death of a martyr is a public testimony. The suffering and
rejection of Christ on the cross is understood as eschatological
suffering and rejection, and is brought by the martyrs into the
eschatological public arena, where they are cast out, rejected and
publicly executed. Kierkegaard's 'attack on Christianity', in the
midst of the liberal bourgeois-Protestant world of the nineteenth
century, made impressively clear that the rejection of the concept
of martyrdom had brought with it the abandonment of the
church's understanding of suffering, and meant that the gospel of
the cross had lost its meaning and ultimately that established
Christianity was bound to lose its eschatological hope. The
assimilation of Christianity to bourgeois society always means
that the cross is forgotten and hope is lost.

A third manner of following Christ came into being later than
the period of the martyrs, in the special form of *monasticism*.
The concept of following was changed here to that of imitation
(*imitatio Christi*). The humiliations which the apostles and martyrs
experienced became the Christian virtue of humility. The per-
secutions undergone by the apostles and martyrs in their proclamation of the truth of Christ became the exercise of the
self-abnegation of the soul. Concrete martyrdom became 'spiritual
death' in the form of self-mortification. Jesus' eschatological calls
to follow him became spiritual and moral maxims. The process
of transformation and spiritualization can no doubt be described
this way. Yet in this form, too, the recollection of the sufferings
of Christ was maintained in a vital form. The foundations and
reforms of monastic orders were constantly inspired by the idea
of the imitation of Christ. The Celtic monks were to be homeless,
as Jesus had been homeless. The unmarried state was based upon
the fact that Jesus was not married, and poverty, upon Jesus'
poverty. In the Franciscans, the mendicant orders and the *devotio
moderna*, the reforming protest against the riches, political power
and secularization of the church appealed time and again to the
example of Jesus. The Christian movements which set out to
follow Christ but did not succeed in remaining within the church,

like the Waldensians, Albigensians, Luddites and Hussites, were suppressed and persecuted. The following of Christ was then spiritualized in the form of mystical exercises, which often supplemented and replaced scholastic theology. The issue here was the unity of theory and practice in Christian life. Belief without following Christ became a matter of merely giving credence to doctrines and carrying out ceremonies. From an Augustinian and Franciscan legacy, Bonaventure introduced a voluntarist and affective element into theology.[42] Theology is not pure theory, but a synthesis of theory and practical wisdom, that is, a *theologia affectiva*. It is a unity of intellectual reflection and spiritual experience. But the spiritual experiences which belong to the knowledge of God are made in the form of the *meditatio crucis*. Here the *via crucis* becomes a third factor, parallel to the *via activa* of good works pleasing to God and the *via contemplativa*, the eternal adoration of mystical, negative theology.[43] The *itinerarium in Deum* begins with a mental absorption in the sufferings and death of Christ, until his sufferings are experienced as one's own sufferings and his temptations as one's own temptations. This assimilation of the soul to Christ through suffering was called by Eckhardt and Tauler the *via compendii*, the shortest way to the mystical divine birth of the soul. By the aid of the *meditatio crucis*, the soul returns to the darkness of its uncreated ground. By conformity to the cross, the soul conforms to God. The way of salvation in mystical crucifixions with Jesus leads through suffering to glory, by way of abandonment for damnation to election, and through the cross to the crown. It is described in this way by Thomas à Kempis in his *Imitation of Christ*, which still influences Christian piety at the present day.[44] The primary virtue in following Christ is humility (*humilitas*). This is displayed in obedience, contempt for the world and silence. Jesus is the pattern of this humility. His way of humility leads through the cross to eternal life. To follow him is to give up love for the world and self-love, and to be seized by the *amor crucis*. On the *via regia sanctae crucis* one passes through severe temptations, the withdrawal of grace and inner annihilation (*annihilatio*), arriving at complete calm in God. The *conformitas crucis* leads to the *contemplatio Dei* in the mystical *excessus mentis*. The *Spiritual Exercises* of Ignatius of Loyola, in the third week, contemplate the sufferings of Christ:

The special grace to ask for in the passion is sorrow with Christ in His sorrow, a broken heart with Christ heart-broken, tears and interior suffering for the great suffering Christ endured for me.

The intention is for the soul to participate in the very moment of Christ's suffering and crucifixion. And Luther's theology of the cross is not conceivable without this mystical imitation of the cross and its *conformitas* christology.[45] By way of the spiritual exercises of the cross, the believer becomes an 'imitator of Christ' in a spiritual and internalized way, and by so doing continues the experiences of the apostles and martyrs, without himself becoming an apostle and martyr. Faith in the crucified Christ leads to an existence which is in conformity with the cross and with Christ. The cross of Christ is taken up existentially as one's own cross. This 'mysticism of introversion', an internalization of the following of Christ, can be considered a departure from the practical, physical following of Christ. But it must also be realized that his mysticism of the inner light can be and has been transformed into the 'consuming flame, which turns outward'.[46] The transformation of mysticism into millenarianism and of religion into revolution can be seen both in the Reformation Anabaptists and also in Thomas Münzer's mysticism of the cross.[47] But to follow Jesus is not to imitate him, for following him does not mean becoming a Jesus oneself. Nor does it mean admiration of a hero and a mystical contemporaneity with him.[48] One follows Christ in one's own response to the mission of Christ at the present day and in taking up one's own cross.

To follow Christ means to have faith, and faith is in fact an existential unity of theory and practice, as can be seen in the life of the apostles, in the life of the martyrs, and to a certain extent also in the mystical theology of inner experience.

But two things must be considered: 1. What are the suffering and cross of Christ, and what are the sufferings and the cross of those who follow him? 2. When the mission and cross of Christ become a present reality today, what form do they take, if they are to be anything more than a private imitation?

The significance of the first question can be seen from Rudolf Bultmann's understanding of the cross.

By giving up Jesus to be crucified, God has set up the cross for us. To believe in the cross of Christ does not mean to concern ourselves with a mythical process wrought outside of us and our world, or with an objective event turned by God to our advantage, but rather to make the cross of Christ our own, to undergo crucifixion with him.

For Bultmann the cross is an 'eschatological event':

In other words, the cross is not just an event of the past which can be contemplated in detachment, but the eschatological event in and beyond time, for as far as its meaning—that is, its meaning for faith—is concerned, it is an ever-present reality.

Bultmann gives as an example Paul's apostolic theology of the cross, and continues:

In its redemptive aspect the cross of Christ is no mere mythical event, but a permanent historical fact originating in the past historical event which is the crucifixion of Jesus. The abiding significance of the cross is that it is the judgement of the world, the judgement and the deliverance of man . . . The preaching of the cross as the event of redemption challenges all who hear it to appropriate this significance for themselves, to be willing to be crucified with Christ.[49]

Bultmann is rightly resisting the mythical objectivization of the cross of Christ, and the historicizing of the cross of Jesus until it is completely meaningless. Yet here the cross of Jesus Christ seems to have been deprived of any significance of its own, and to obtain historical significance only in the existential process of being crucified with Christ. To believe in the cross of Christ certainly also means to let oneself be crucified with him, to justify the justifying judgment of God. But it is so only in a secondary sense. Paul tells us that 'while we were yet helpless, at the right time Christ died for the ungodly' (Rom. 5.6), 'while we were yet sinners' (v.8). His death on the cross 'for us', the godless, the sinners, is certainly not a vividly portrayed mythical action. Nor is it sufficient to give it mere doctrinal acknowledgment. But neither is it an event of eschatological history in the sense that it originates in the crucifixion of Jesus, is continued in the crucifixion of the believer with him, and is 'always present'. The inner basis and continual assumption of Paul's 'we with Christ' is found in 'Christ for us'. That we are crucified with Christ, as it were simultaneously and in conformity with him, is something which comes about in faith, and is possible and effective only on the basis of the revelation of God in his counterpart, in the one who was abandoned by God, and in the death of Christ for his enemies, the godless and the sinners. The significance of the cross of Christ does not derive from the crucifixion of the believer with him. The reverse is true; the crucifixion of the believer with Christ takes its meaning from Christ's death on the cross for the godless. If this 'meaning' is to be understood as nothing more than 'interpreted history', and this 'historical interpretation' is nothing more than existential repetition, then in the cross with which we follow Christ we find his cross rather than the reverse. But in the first instance the preaching of the cross does not ask the hearer whether he will allow himself to be crucified with Christ; it proclaims to him Christ abandoned by God and crucified for him who is godless. It is the revelation of God in abandonment by God, the acceptance of the godless by Christ himself taking on his abandonment, which brings him into fellowship with the crucified Christ and makes it possible for him to follow Christ. Not until Christ has taken on our cross as his own is it meaningful to take up our cross in order to follow him. As a result of his distinctions between mythical and historical, and between historical in the sense of hard fact and historical in the sense of an event in its meaning for us, and his exclusively existential understanding of this latter, interpreted history, Bultmann is in danger of being able to understand the cross of Christ only as an example for the *conformitas* of Christian existential life by following him. There is a good deal of support for this in Luther's early theology of the cross, which is still mystical in form, but it easily leads to the impossibility of regarding Jesus as the Christ except in so far as this event of eschatological history, this liberating judgment, had its historical origin in his crucifixion, and in so far as he was the first person in time to have borne the eternally present cross of eternity.

This danger is even greater, when the creative following of Jesus through a personal response seeks its own example in him, or even accepts only those elements in the 'course followed by Jesus' which a person can follow himself, and which seem meaningful at the present day.[50] It is true that in a technocratic society all human relationships are reduced to the level of things, and general apathy is spreading on an epidemic scale. It is true that in a world of high consumption, where anything and everything is possible, nothing is so humanizing as love, and a conscious interest in the life of others, particularly in the life of the oppressed. For love leaves us open to wounding and disappointment. It makes us ready to suffer. It leads us out of isolation into a fellowship with others, with people different from ourselves, and this fellow-ship is always associated with suffering. It changes the world, in so far as it puts life into a static situation and overcomes the death urge which turns everything into a possession or an instrument of power. It is also true that in Jesus' preaching of the imminence of the kingdom of God's prevenient grace, and in his life for and with the lepers, the outcasts, the sinners and the tax-collectors, such love can be seen personified. Moreover, it is right to follow Jesus at the present time in the specific activities of love, suffering and revolt. This does not mean that in following Christ, faith is reduced to ethics, as the orthodox fear; orthodoxy is fulfilled in the unity of theory and practice, in 'orthopraxy'. This leads in the end beyond the narrow circle in which Christ is understood in the categories of the historicity of an individual's life, into the domains of economic, social and political life, in which men in fact have to carry out their struggle for 'existence'. This means that to be crucified with Christ is no longer a purely private and spiritualized matter, but develops into a political theology of the following of the crucified Christ. But it is not sufficient for the ethics of following Christ to begin only with the 'portrait and testimony of the man Jesus' and 'to live on the pattern of Jesus'.[51] It is right to extend the understanding of the following of Christ and to give concrete meaning to our taking up the cross, for this does not take place only in the inner life of faith, any more than concrete martyrdom is exhausted in the mystical *conformitas crucis*. But this imagery obscures the unique and un-repeatable nature of the course taken by Christ and of his cross. His suffering contains more than merely the necessary suffering of love which becomes a reality in following him, the ability of love to be wounded and disappointed. When the pains of love are accepted, they deepen love. But Christ's suffering on the cross does not consist merely in the ethical suffering of love, even if 'ethics' is not used here in any disparaging or limited sense. Bonhoeffer rightly says: 'In the passion Jesus is a rejected Messiah. His rejection robs the passion of its halo of glory.'[52] Jesus was also rejected by inhuman persons because of his love for those whom they had dehumanized. But this was not all; he was also, and most completely of all, abandoned by his Father, whose immediate presence he proclaimed and experienced in his life. This rejection in suffering, this judgment in the cross, goes far beyond the suffering involved in the love of one's neighbour or enemy. But it leads beyond it not into metaphysics, but into the universal, cosmic eschatology of the end, into the abandonment by God of the godless and the destruction of all that exists. Seen in this light, the cross of Christ comes to have a significance for the testimony of faith, of perseverance when there is no support at all, and of fellowship with Christ in abandonment, which goes beyond the sufferings of love. Nor can the significance of being crucified with Christ as Paul describes it be reduced to that of an example or archetype of the sufferings of love. The list of afflictions endured in II Cor. 4 is not a paradoxical ethic of love regardless of suffering, but must be read in the apocalyptic context of the destruction of the world and the new creation. Nor was the crucifixion of the martyrs with Christ simply a matter of suffering for love; it was more than this—it was a testimony of the truth against the lords of the lie. The suffering of love for forgotten, despised and betrayed human beings wherever they are oppressed is concrete suffering in imitation of Christ, and in practice can be called taking 'one's cross' upon oneself. But it should not be isolated, and for all the existential understanding of Jesus that in fact is achieved in it, the qualitative difference between Christ's own cross and the cross of those who follow him should not be ignored. The cross of Christ is the basis on which the apostle, the martyrs and those who show selfless love are crucified with him. This basis can be recognized only through what it underlies, but it is more than that. When faith and love take up the cross and follow Christ, his cross becomes the object of existential experience; but in time, in content and in its eschatological significance for the godless, the cross of Christ is prior to the taking up of the cross by others.

It would be a good thing if, after speaking of the cross of Christ who died for the godless, the theology of the cross were to distinguish between:

1. The apostolic cross of the establishment of the obedience of faith in a world full of idols, demons, fetishes and superstition.
2. The cross of the martyrs, who bore bodily witness to the lordship of the crucified Christ before the rulers of the world.
3. The suffering of love for abandoned, despised and betrayed human beings.

4. The 'sufferings of this age', the groaning of the enslaved creation, the apocalyptic sorrow of the godless world.

The theology of the cross must make these distinctions in order to perceive and put into effect the connections between them with realism, and, in the sense of the eschatological liberation of the world with hope. A Christian stands at the intersection of these four different points of suffering, and must give a theoretical and practical account of the significance of the cross of Christ in them, if he is to do justice to the cross on Golgotha in the context of the world. The theology of the cross cannot permit itself any equivocation here, as unfortunately it has constantly done in history.

5. *The Theology of the Cross*

Christian faith stands and falls with the knowledge of the crucified Christ, that is, with the knowledge of God *in* the crucified Christ, or, to use Luther's even bolder phrase, with the knowledge of the 'crucified God'. What does this mean for the *theology* of Christian faith? Let us look once again at basic forms of Christian theology, and ask what their attitude is to the cross as their inner criterion.

In Greek usage, 'theology' is talking about God, the gods, or divine things.[53] Plato called the poets' stories of the gods 'theologies' (*Republic*, 379a). He regarded them as *mythical theology*, as the Stoics later called it. The myths and rites of the state religion could also be called theological. The later Stoics called this field *political theology*. Plato himself, in considering the 'theology' of the poets and the statesmen, looks for the *typoi peri theologias*, i.e. the standards for the admissibility of such stories of the gods; and he found them in his theory of ideas and in morality. Aristotle speaks in the same terms of the 'theologizing' poets of myth such as Hesiod and Homer (*Metaphysics* III, iv, 1000a); yet we should note that he calls his own metaphysical doctrine of the 'unmoved mover' *theological philosophy* (*Metaphysics* VI, i, 1026a). The Stoics later distinguished between three forms of theology: the *mythical theology* of the poets, the *political theology* of the legislators and the *natural theology* (study of being) of the philosophers.[54]

The expression 'theology' does not occur in the New Testament. This explains why the ancient church in the Greek-speaking area found the philosophical concept of theology most readily accessible and adopted it. By 'theology' the Alexandrians meant the 'knowledge of the eternally existent *logos*', by contrast to the mythical conceptual world of simple faith. In the following period the expression 'theo-logy' was also reserved for the special knowledge of God, the *doctrine of God*, the *vision of God*, and was associated in Christian practice with the *praise of God* in hymns, in the liturgy. The 'economy of salvation' in which the incarnation of the *logos*, the cross and the resurrection, the church and the sacraments were described, was distinguished from this.[55] Thus there was doxological theology and economic theology, or in other words, theology as 'pure theory' and theology as 'practical theory', concerned with the history of salvation.

The first forms of *theological science* did not arise until the Middle Ages. They included not only the special doctrine of God, but the whole complex, drawn from specifically Christian tradition, of *sacra doctrina*, and more generally of the philosophical theology which included the knowledge of the time. *Unde theologia, quae ad sacram doctrinam pertinet, differt secundum genus ab illa theologia, quae pars philosophiae ponitur*, said Aquinas (S.Th. I, q I, a I). Thus he distinguished between *philosophical theology* and *theological theology*, and yet used the same word 'theology' for both.[56] Here, theology as a science means giving public account of Christian faith with all the intellectual means generally available at a particular time, and at the same time the use made of contemporary knowledge by Christian faith. The claim tacitly made is that Christian theology is 'true philosophy', and not a branch of specifically religious knowledge, or a private matter.

Both forms of theology exist at the present day. But they proceed from a strict understanding of the concept 'theology', and by the *logos* of theology they understand theology as the word of God.[57] In this 'word' God is not only the object of human discourse; for God is not an object of experience like the objects in the world which human understanding can know, define and control. If God himself is taken seriously as the Lord, he must be perceived and thought of as the subject who utters his word. Thus theology as *speaking about God* is possible only on the basis of *what God himself says*. Theology as the reflection of faith upon the word received assumes the event of the word spoken by God himself. Faith can claim to be in accord with rational understanding only in so far as it understands what God says. And this understanding consists of considering the word of God in constant awareness that God is the subject of everything which theology considers, and in attentiveness to the word of God as it is uttered.[58] The *theology of faith* presupposes the *theology of God*, which is found in the word of God which has been and which is uttered.[59] Thus it is *church theology*. The weakness of this starting point is that it comes very close to the distinction made by the early church between theology as the doctrine of God and economy as the doctrine of salvation, and can therefore lose contact with the reality of unredeemed humanity. It does not always begin by taking seriously that both are united in the cross of Christ, and that therefore, as Paul states, the λόγος τοῦ θεοῦ (II Cor. 2.17) cannot in Christian terms be anything other than the λόγος τοῦ σταυροῦ (I Cor. 1.18).[60]

On the other hand, one can conduct *theology as a science* under the conditions of the modern age, appealing to Schleiermacher and Hegel. Here theology is a 'positive science', the parts of which are drawn together into a whole by their common relationship to a particular form of belief. Here Christian theology is the science of Christianity.[61]

One can then go further than Schleiermacher in affirming that in Christian countries in the modern age this 'Christianity' is by no means to be found solely in the organized church, but has become involved in numerous material and personal ways in general culture. This sociological insight is often expressed in the thesis which R. Rothe put forward with messianic and millenarian emotion, that after its ecclesiastical stage, Christianity has for the time being moved into the epoch in which it is part of secular history.[62] This assertion, which states not merely a fact, but a myth, confronts theology with the overwhelming task of developing a 'theory of present-day Christianity' as a whole. And this includes the medieval claim that Christian theology must be in a position to present the *true philosophy*, by developing a Christian theory of the present time. In the circumstances of present-day history, this means that the 'theory of Christianity' undertakes the task of a philosophy of world history which Hegel saw as the task of philosophy, as the knowledge of being, to 'apprehend its own time in thoughts'.[63] But if such a philosophy is only possible when what is real is rational, so such a theory of Christianity in terms of world history is possible only when what is real is

Christian. But what is 'real'? And even if this theory were ever to prevail, its price would have to be paid: that of ignoring the 'dialectic of the Enlightenment' (M. Horkheimer, T. Adorno) in the modern world, the misery of the modern age characterized by the names of Auschwitz and Hiroshima, and the conflicts which modern capitalism and the white man have produced.[64] The credibility structure of modern society is often enough, in more than one respect, one of delusion. And it would be necessary, within the inner identity of Christianity, to reduce the contradiction and foolishness of the cross to the 'wisdom' of Christianity. Yet even a theory of world-accepting Christianity, which saw Christianity as religious culture, would not be able totally to conceal the alien nature of the crucified Christ in a 'Christian' culture. Outsiders and atheists would remind the Christians of it.[65]

A Christian theology which sees its problem and its task in knowing God in the crucified Christ, cannot be *pure theory*. It cannot lead to a pure theory of God, as in the vision of God in the early church. Pure contemplation of this kind abandons the realm of the transitory, of mere appearance and uncertain opinion, and finds true, eternal being in the *logos*. The pure, self-forgetting contemplation of God transforms him who contemplates into that which he contemplates, and enables him to participate in God himself, making him divine through *mimesis* and *methexis*. He who loves wisdom, through the *eros* for wisdom which has taken hold of him, himself becomes wise. Thus pure contemplation indirectly bestows participation in, and likeness to, what is contemplated. The steps by which it is imported can here only be the likenesses of God in nature, history and tradition, which indirectly reflect and reveal something of God himself—e.g., his works in creation and history, in men and ideas which have been conformed to God. The principle of knowledge prevailing here is that of analogy, as in Parmenides, Empedocles and Aristotle.[66]

But in the crucified Christ, abandoned by God and cursed, faith can find no equivalents of this kind which provide it with an indirect, analogical knowledge of God, but encounters the very contrary. In the crucified Christ the contrary is found on several levels: in the contrary to the God who has revealed his will in the law and is in practice known in the works of the law. For Jesus was sentenced to death by the law as a blasphemer. Faith finds in

68

him the contrary to, and liberation from, the so-called gods, who are venerated in the political theology of political religions. For Jesus died, whether rightly or wrongly, a political death as a rebel, on the cross. Finally, faith finds in him the contrary to a God who reveals himself indirectly in the creation and in history. For Jesus died abandoned by God. But if this is the point at which *faith* comes into being, this means first of all that Christian theology cannot be a pure theory of God, but must become a *critical theory of God*. This criticism is directed from the crucified Christ to man in his attempt to know God, and destroys the concern which guides him to knowledge. For man seeks God in the law, and attempts to conform to him through the works of the law, in order to bring himself into the righteousness of God. If he sees and believes in God in the person of Christ, condemned by the law, he is set free from the legalist concern to justify himself. Man seeks God in the will for political power and world domination. If he sees and believes God in Christ who was powerless and crucified, he is set free from this desire to have power and domination over others. Man seeks to know God in the works and ordinances of the cosmos or the course of world history, in order to become divine himself through knowledge. If he sees and believes God in the suffering and dying Christ, he is set free from the concern for self-deification which guides him towards knowledge. Thus the knowledge of God in the crucified Christ takes seriously the situation of man in pursuit of his own interests, man who in reality is inhuman, because he is under the compulsion of self-justification, dominating self-assertion and illusionary self-deification. 'For this reason, the *crucified* Jesus is the "image of the invisible God".'[67] Thus because of its subject, the theology of the cross, right down to its method and practice, can only be polemical, dialectical, antithetical and critical theory. This theology is 'itself crucified theology and speaks only of the cross' (K. Rahner). It is also crucifying theology, and is thereby liberating theology.

We can see this clearly in the theological tradition which is called the *theology of the cross* in the special sense. In this sense, the theology of the cross was founded by Paul. Just as in Rom. 1.17ff. Paul develops justification by faith in a critical direction against justification by the works of the law, so that it leads to liberation from the compulsion for self-justification by works, so in I Cor. 1.18ff., he developed the word of the cross against wisdom and the knowledge of God from the world, so that the knowledge of the cross would bring about liberation from the powers of the cosmos. What is a stumbling block to the Jews and folly to the Greeks, becomes for believers the power of God for freedom. The question here is not whether in his polemic Paul gives a just account of historic Judaism, faithful to the law, or of historic Hellenism, with its wisdom piety. For his polemic is aimed at the deeper issue of the situation of dehumanized man as one who pursues his own interest, and who, whether he is a Jew or a Greek, cannot let God be God, but must make himself the unhappy and proud God of his own self, his fellow men, and his world. At this level the word of the cross liberates dehumanized man from the fatal concern for deification, and it is no accident that in the first chapter of the First Epistle to the Corinthians, Paul draws attention to the concrete social consequences, in order to demonstrate the power which is contained in the weakness and folly of the crucified God:

For the foolishness of God is wiser than men, and the weakness of God is stronger than men. For consider your call, brethren; not many of you were wise according to worldly standards, not many were powerful, not many were of noble birth; but God chose what is foolish in the world to shame the wise, God chose what is weak in the world to shame the strong, God chose what is low and despised in the world, even things that are not, to bring to nothing things that are, so that no human being might boast in the presence of God ... Let him who boasts, boast of the Lord (I Cor. 1.25–31).

The theology of the cross leads to criticism of the self-glorification of dehumanized man and to his liberation, and is directly associated with the human way of life and practice chosen by this congregation of weak, lowly and despised persons, a way of life which takes away the power of the social circumstances which bring about the aggression of dehumanized man, and endeavours to overcome it.

The 'theology of the cross' is the explicit formulation which Luther used in 1518 in the Heidelberg Disputation, in order to find words for the Reformation insight of the liberating gospel of the crucified Christ, by contrast to the *theologia gloriae* of the medieval institutional church.[68]

Appealing constantly to Paul, Luther in his polemic contrasts the knowledge of God through his sufferings and cross with the knowledge of God through his works in creation and history. He does not deny that man in himself can have an indirect knowledge of God from creation, history and the soul. But man is no longer in himself, but in practice is outside himself. He is in practice a sinner, although he is created in the image of God. Thus dehumanized man, who must exalt himself, because he cannot ensure himself as he is, in practice uses these religious insights only in the interest of his own self-deification. As a result, they do not help him to achieve humanity, but only give greater force to his inhumanity. The knowledge of the cross is the knowledge of God in the suffering caused to him by dehumanized man, that is, in the contrary of everything which dehumanized man seeks and tries to attain as the deity in him. Consequently, this knowledge does not confirm him as what he is, but destroys him. It destroys the god, miserable in his pride, which we would like to be, and restores to us our abandoned and despised humanity. The knowledge of the cross brings a conflict of interest between God who has become man and man who wishes to become God. It destroys the destruction of man. It alienates alienated man. And in this way it restores the humanity of dehumanized man. Just as Paul contrasted the wisdom of this world and the folly of the cross, and in parallel with this, contrasted righteousness by the works of the law and the scandal of the cross, so Luther brought together the religious way to knowledge through the contemplation of the works of God, and the moral way of self-affirmation through one's own works, and directed the *theologia crucis* polemically against both. 'Religious speculation and sanctification by works are only two manifestations of the same desire in man, the desire for unbroken, direct dealings with God.'[69] In fact ethics and metaphysics never run parallel, without contact with each other, but influence each other in accordance with the needs and concerns of man. Moreover, the metaphysics and ethics of Aristotle, which lie behind medieval theology as a science and as church practice, are both based upon achievement and works.[70]

The historical question, whether Luther's portrait of the 'theology of glory' which he opposed was a correct description of medieval catholic theology, is a superficial one. His *theologia crucis* is not an attack on medieval catholic theology as such, but what he recognized in it, man's inhuman concern for self-deification through knowledge and works. The knowledge of God in the suffering of the cross of Christ destroys man who abandons his humanity, for it destroys his gods and destroys his supposed divinity. It sets him free from his inhuman hybris, to restore his true human nature. It makes the *homo incurvatus in se* once again open to God and his neighbour, and gives Narcissus the power to love someone else.

Luther developed his *theologia crucis* as the programme of critical and Reformation theology. *Theologia crucis* is not a single chapter in theology, but the key signature for all Christian theology. It is a completely distinctive kind of theology. It is the point from which all theological statements which seek to be Christian are viewed (W. von Löwenich). And yet it only remains *theologia crucis* in the context of critical and liberating practice in preaching and life. The theology of the cross is a practical doctrine for battle, and can therefore become neither a theory of Christianity as it is now, nor the Christian theory of world history. It is a dialectic and historical theology, and not a theology of world history. It does not state what exists, but sets out to liberate men from their inhuman definitions and their idolized assertions, in which they have become set, and in which society has ensnared them.

The limit of Luther's *theologia crucis* in its historical form lay in the fact that it was impossible for him to oppose Aristotle's philosophy of works with its aid so effectively that a *philosophia crucis* could arise from it. Although in his polemic against Erasmus in 1525 he once again put forward his theology of the cross against the rising humanism of the modern age, the humanism of Erasmus, with the aid of Melanchthon, found its way into Protestantism and encouraged the Protestant ethic of achievement.

In political terms, its limit lay in the fact that while as a reformer Luther formulated the *theologia crucis* in theoretical and practical terms against the medieval institutional church, he did not formulate it as social criticism against feudal society in the Peasant Wars of 1524 and 1525.[71] What he wrote to the peasants did not express the critical and liberating force of the cross, the choosing of the lowly which puts the mighty to shame, nor the polemic of the crucified God against pride and subjection, domination and slavery, but instead a non-Protestant mysticism of suffering and humble submission.[72] The task therefore remained of developing the theology of the cross in the direction of an understanding of the world and of history. The theology of the cross had to be worked out not merely for the reform of the church but as social criticism, is association with practical actions to set free both the wretched and their rulers. A thoroughgoing theology of the cross must apprehend the crucified God in all the three areas in which the ancient world used the term theology, and in which even today men are inescapably religious: in mythical theology, in the form of demythologization; in political theology, in the form of liberation; and in philosophical theology, in the form of understanding the universe as creation.

We must once again ask a critical question: Is this theology of the cross in accordance with Jesus who was historically crucified? Does the word of the cross, as Paul calls the gospel, absorb the person of Jesus and the event of the crucifixion into language? The crucified Jesus is dead, and dead men do not speak. Death is dumb and deprives one of speech. Is the 'word of the cross' as Paul and Luther understood it simply one more of many possible interpretations to which the dead Jesus has had to submit? Paul understood the gospel as the 'revelation' of the gracious righteousness of God and as the imparting of the liberating power of God in Christ. The word of the cross enables one to participate in the divine event of the cross, and faith allows the godless to participate in this in fellowship with Christ. This is something more than merely conveying a piece of information or an arbitrary interpretation. For Paul the 'word of the cross' is *based* in the event of the resurrection of the crucified Christ; but it is a message about the cross of Christ. He did not understand the resurrection of Christ as an event which simply followed his death, but as the eschatological event which characterized the earthly Jesus, crucified under Pontius Pilate, as the *Kyrios*. On the basis of the resurrection of the crucified Christ, he spoke in his gospel of the '*cross* of the risen Christ' and worked out its significance for the godless, whether Jews or Gentiles. His gospel, which he expresses in his theology of the cross, is not meant to be one possible interpretation, which the dead must accept, but claims to be the one revelation of the crucified Christ in the light of his resurrection from the dead. A dead man cannot forgive sins. The gospel, as the present forgiveness of sins, assumes the new, divine, eschatological life of the crucified Christ, and is itself the 'Spirit' and the present 'power of the resurrection'. Thus according to Paul's understanding, in the 'word of the cross' the crucified Christ himself speaks. Consequently, the event of revelation consists not only of the event of the cross and resurrection of Christ, but also the preaching of the gospel.[73] The modern distinction between fact and interpretation, which we assume in natural science and history, is inappropriate to the understanding of the 'word of the cross'. This distinction is essential to modern knowledge, which dominates, which defines in order to affirm and to control what has been affirmed, and which isolates facts in order to take possession of them. But does this mean that the 'word of the cross' is beyond all criticism? It claims that the crucified Christ himself speaks and is revealed in it. But if one accepts this claim, one must ask whether this word reveals the one whom it intends to reveal and is in conformity with the one whose voice it intends to make heard: and again, whether the crucified Christ is to be found in this word, so that it can take his place and be his representative (II Cor. 5.20). It is important for the history of the primitive Christian tradition to realize that after the theology of the resurrection and the enthusiasm of the Spirit, faith once again returned and reached back to the earthly and crucified Jesus of Nazareth. Students of Paul have emphasized this astonishing fact and its significance.[74] It was this which gave rise to the new literary category of a gospel, in the synoptic sense. This raises the further question of the relationship of the gospel as the 'word of the cross' in Paul's sense to the gospel in the sense of the passion narrative. Does the 'word of the cross' really make superfluous the synoptic gospels, which Kähler rightly called 'passion narratives with an extended introduction', in the sense that faith no longer knows Christ 'from a human point of view' (II Cor. 5.16, RSV; literally: 'according to the flesh')? Or do they point to historical features in Jesus' crucifixion on Golgotha which are not taken into account by Paul's preaching? Alternatively, is the 'word of the cross' possible without a recollection of the historic cross on Golgotha? We shall return to this in greater detail in the next section. In this context, the intrinsic difference between the cross on Golgotha and the 'word of the cross' should always be kept in mind, even when it is maintained that the crucified Christ, by virtue of his resurrection, is present himself in the preaching of the cross and speaks in the profession of faith and the promise of freedom. The crucified Christ speaks in the 'word of the cross', but he is reduced wholly to this preaching. 'The crucifixion was more than a speech event.'[75] Although this preaching reveals him to the godless and brings them to faith, when Christ rose, he did not turn into words. The crucified Christ is more than the preaching of the cross. For the very reason that this preaching is the only adequate access which the godless have to God who was crucified, this intrinsic distinction must not be removed. Precisely because the person must be apprehended in the word, the word cannot be taken for the person himself. There is a reality in the crucified Christ which cannot be identified with any Logos in such a way that it is replaced. The cross signifies that in Jesus which makes him the object of preaching and every subsequent theological interpretation, an object which is in contrast to them, and with which hearer and interpreter are brought face to face. The crucified Christ therefore remains the inner criterion of all preaching which appeals to him. So far as it points to him, it is tested by him; so far as it reveals him, it is authorized by him.

NOTES

1. Pater Ayraut, in *Kirche im Islam* I, 50.

2. Goethe, *Wilhelm Meisters Wanderjahre* II, 1: 'But we must now speak of the third religion, based on reverence for that which is below us; we call it the Christian one, because this disposition of mind is chiefly revealed in it; it is the last one which humanity could and was bound to attain. Yet what was not demanded for it? Not merely to leave earth below, and claim a higher origin, but to recognize as divine even humility and poverty, scorn and contempt, shame and misery, suffering and death; nay, to revere and make lovable even sin and crime, not as hindrances but as furtherances of holiness! Of this there are indeed found traces throughout all time; but a track is not a goal, and this having once been reached, humanity cannot turn backwards; and it may be maintained, that the Christian religion having once appeared, can never disappear again; having once been divinely embodied, cannot again be dissolved.' English text from Goethe, *William Meister's Travels*, Bell 1882, p. 156.

3. The phrase comes from T. Storm, *Crucifixus*, 1865:

> There hung on the cross his tortured limbs,
> sweaty with blood and put to shame;
> the virgin-pure nature vanished from sight,
> under the picture of terror.
> But those who called themselves his disciples,
> formed it in bronze and stone,
> and set it within the temple's gloom
> and on the sunlit meadow.

So to every eye a horror
is present in our days;
maintaining the ancient crime,
the enmity unassuaged.

4. J. Schneider, *TDNT* VII, 573. On this see W. Schrage, 'Das Verständnis des Todes Jesu Christi im Neuen Testament', in *Das Kreuz Jesu Christi als Grund des Heils*, ed. F. Viering, 1967, 61 n. 34.

5. Cicero, *Pro Rabirico* 5.16: '*Nomen ipsum crucis absit non modo a corpore civium Romanorum, sed etiam a cogitatione, oculis, auribus.*'

6. H. Schelkle, quoted by W. Schrage, op. cit.

7. Cf. A. von Harnack, *Der Vorwurf des Atheismus in den drei ersten Jahrhunderten*, TU NF XIII, 4, 1905, 12. In *Apol.* I 6, 13, Justin attempted to repel the charge by attesting Christian belief in the Father of all, the Son, the angel host and the Holy Spirit in the philosophical emperors. However, the masses, who raised the charge of atheism against the Christians, thought that they were blaspheming and denying the state gods. Justin readily accepted this charge: ὁμολογοῦμεν τῶν τοιούτων νομιζομένων θεῶν ἄθεον εἶναι.

8. However, possibly this may be a reference to a Gnostic.

9. Quoted following K. Löwith, *From Hegel to Nietzsche*, Constable 1965, p. 15. See the whole section on 'The Rose and the Cross', pp. 14–29.

10. Ibid., 16.

11. Ibid., 16.

12. Goethe, *Die Geheimnisse. Ein Fragment.*

13. F. Nietzsche, *Werke* VII, 265. On this see K. Jaspers, *Nietzsche und das Christentum* (1938), 1948.

14. K. Marx, *Frühschriften*, ed. S. Landshut, 1953, 208.

15. H. J. Iwand, *Christologievorlesung* (unpublished). Quoted following B. Klappert, *Diskussion um Kreuz und Auferstehung*, 1967, 288f. Similarly K. Jaspers, *Die Frage der Entmythologisierung*, 1954, 88: '. . . I would count the scandal of the claim of faith to justification and redemption from sin to be small compared with the scandal that Jesus, the one sent by God, suffered the most shameful and grievous death. This scandal, in the union of the historical reality of the death of a man . . . with the myth of the God who sacrifices himself in it, is tremendous . . . The crucified Christ . . . is at the same time both reality and myth.'

16. M. Heidegger, *Phänomenologie und Theologie* (1928), 1970, 18. Cf. the whole section on the 'positivity of theology', 17–21, which clearly defines Christian theology as a theology of the cross and theology as a knowledge of the 'crucified God', and shies away from theology as a theory of the phenomenon of Christianity in the world.

17. K. Löwith, op. cit., 418, ends his book with this sentence after describing the 'revolutionary abyss in the thought of the nineteenth century' and the collapse of the 'bourgeois-Christian' world.

18. G. W. F. Hegel, *Philosophy of Right*, Oxford University Press 1952, p. 13.

19. Note the difficulties which Feuerbach had with Luther's theology of the cross. *Das Wesen des Glaubens im Sinne Luthers* (1844),

The Resistance of the Cross against its Interpretations

1970, 40: 'Of course you do not produce God in your sense from yourself; a crucified God is as ludicrous a contradiction as a painfully punished notion.'

20. This has been felt by M. Polanyi, *Personal Knowledge. Towards a Post-Critical Philosophy*, Routledge 1962, 199: 'Christian worship sustains, as it were, an eternal, never to be consummated hunch: a heuristic vision which is accepted for the sake of its unresolvable tension. It is like an obsession with a problem known to be insoluble, which yet follows, against reason, unswervingly, the heuristic command: "Look at the unknown!" Christianity sedulously fosters, and in a sense permanently satisfies, man's craving for mental dissatisfaction by offering him the comfort of a *crucified God*.'

21. H. J. Iwand, op. cit., 289.

22. K. Rahner, 'Opfer', *LThK* VII, 1174. Cf. also *Die vielen Messen und das eine Opfer*, 1951.

23. K. Rahner, ibid.

24. J. Betz, 'Messopfer', *LThK* VII, 348.

25. J. B. Metz, *Theology of the World*, 113.

26. K. A. Keller, *Geschichte der Kreuzwegandachten von den Anfängen bis zur völligen Ausbildung*, 1908; N. Gorodetsky, *The Humiliated Christ in Modern Russian Thought*, SPCK 1938; J. H. Cone, *The Spirituals and the Blues*, New York 1972; H. Lüning, *Mit Maschinengewehr und Kreuz— oder wie kann das Christentum überleben?*, 1971.

27. Luther, WA I, 614, 17.

28. D. Bonhoeffer, *Letters and Papers from Prison. The Enlarged Edition*, SCM Press 1971, 360f.

29. *Theology of the Pain of God*, SCM Press 1965.

30. H. Lüning, op. cit., 82.

31. J. H. Cone, op. cit., 52ff. Cf. also T. Lehmann, *Negro Spirituals, Geschichte und Theologie*, 1965.

32. K. Marx, op. cit., 208.

33. E. Bloch, *Atheismus im Christentum*, 1968, 44 etc.

34. H. Lüning, op. cit., 82ff.

35. D. Bonhoeffer, *The Cost of Discipleship*, SCM Press 1959, 76ff.: 'Discipleship and the Cross'.

36. Ibid., 78.

37. Ibid., 81.

38. E. Käsemann, *Perspectives on Paul*, SCM Press 1971, 32ff.; id., *Jesus Means Freedom*, SCM Press 1969, 36ff.

39. E. Käsemann, *Die Legitimität des Apostels*, 1942; E. Guttgemanns, *Der leidende Apostel und sein Herr*, 1966.

40. E. Peterson, 'Zeuge der Wahrheit', *Theologische Traktate*, 1951, 173. For Kierkegaard's understanding of discipleship see V. Eller, *Kierkegaard and Radical Discipleship*, Princeton 1968.

41. Ibid., 187f., 199: 'We always have the same notion, that all suffering is eschatological suffering, suffering which is endured in the same form as the suffering of Christ, and that therefore the glory of Christ, too, is certain to the one who has suffered with Christ.' Cf. also *Apostel*

und Zeuge Christi, 1952. P. Stuhlmacher, *Gerechtigkeit Gottes bei Paulus*, 1965, 232, also sees a parallel between the παθήματα Χριστοῦ (Phil. 3.10) and the παθήματα τοῦ νῦν καιροῦ (Rom. 8.18): 'The suffering which anonymously enslaves the world can be seen for (and in!) Christians as the struggle of the creator with the powers of the world for his rights in his creation, introduced by Christ.' For Col. 1.24 cf. I. Kremer, *Was an den Leiden noch mangelt ...* , 1956; E. Lohse, *Märtyrer und Gottesknecht*, 1963, 202ff.; E. Guttgemanns, op. cit., 323–8, who rightly establishes gradations in suffering with the crucified Christ.

42. Bonaventura, *Itinerarium mentis in Deum*, 1961.

43. Thus W. von Loewenich, *Luthers Theologia crucis*, ⁵1967, 169ff.

44. Cf. also Ignatius, *Spiritual Exercises*, no. 97, and on it J. Sudbrack, *Existentielles Christentum*, 1964.

45. Cf. E. Wolf, *Staupitz und Luther*, 1927; E. Vogelsang, *Der angefochtene Christus bei Luther*, 1932; H. J. Iwand, *Glaubensgerechtigkeit nach Luthers Lehre*, ²1951.

46. K. Marx, *Frühschriften*, op. cit., 17.

47. K. Mannheim, *Ideology and Utopia*, Routledge and Kegan Paul 1936, 192ff.

48. M. Heidegger, *Being and Time*, SCM Press 1962, 436: 'The authentic repetition of a possibility of existence that has been—the possibility that Dasein may choose its hero—is grounded existentially in anticipatory resoluteness.' However, the discipleship of Christ is by no means the choosing of a hero.

49. R. Bultmann, 'New Testament and Mythology', in H. W. Bartsch (ed.), *Kerygma and Myth*, SPCK 1953, 36f.

50. The following pages consider D. Sölle's understanding of discipleship. Cf. *Christ the Representative*, SCM Press 1967; *Atheistisch an Gott glauben*, 1968, 37ff.; *Das Recht ein anderer zu sein*, 1971; *Politische Theologie. Auseinandersetzung mit R. Bultmann*, 1971. I gladly follow her theology as it is related to practice, but I cannot share her undifferentiated charge that theology and faith are metaphysics. Her ethics of discipleship comes very near to popular Ritschlianism and easily becomes legalistic. Her criticism of the 'mythology of apocalyptic promise', which is how she describes my *Theology of Hope* (*Politische Theologie*, 67), is probably to be ascribed to her horizon, which is formed by Gogarten and Bultmann, in which one says of everything which transcends the existentialist horizon within which heroes are chosen and of which 'nothing practical can be made' (Kant), 'I don't understand it.'

51. E.g. *Atheistisch an Gott glauben*, 86, and often in other writings.

52. D. Bonhoeffer, op. cit., 76.

53. Thus Lutheran orthodoxy also says '*Theologia est*' or '*Sermo de Deo et rebus divinis*'. For the history of its origin see F. Kattenbusch, *Die Enstehung einer christlichen Theologie. Zur Geschichte der Ausdrücke* θεολογία, θεολογεῖν, θεολόγος (1930), 1962.

54. M. Pohlenz, *Die Stoa* I, ³1964, 198: 'Panaitius distinguished three classes of divine figures: natural forces conceived of as persons, the gods of the state religion and those of myth (*genus physikon, politikon,*

mythikon), and in this way laid the foundations for *tripertita theologia*, which continued in the rationalistic theology of Rome.'

55. For what follows see G. Ebeling, 'Theologie', *RGG*³ VI, 754–69.

56. G. Söhngen, *Philosophische Einleitung in die Theologie*, ²1964.

57. Thus E. Brunner, 'Die Offenbarung als Grund und Gegenstand der Theologie' (1925) in: *Anfänge dialektischer Theologie* I, 1962, 298ff.; K. Barth, 'Das Wort Gottes als Aufgabe der Theologie' (1922), ibid., 197ff.; id., *Die Christliche Dogmatik im Entwurf*, 1927, 18ff.

58. The best example of this is K. Barth, *Anselm: Fides Quaerens Intellectum*, SCM Press 1960.

59. In this sense early Protestant dogmatics distinguished between the *theologia archetypos* as *cognitio quam Deus ipse de ipso habet* and *theologia ektypos* as *scientia de Deo et rebus divinis cum creaturis intelligentibus a Deo ad imitationem theologiae suae communicata*.

60. Although Barth seeks to think strictly of the unity, he continually returns to the inner difference between God in his 'own impassibility in face of the whole world' and his satisfaction with himself 'and with the impassible glory and blessedness of his own inner life' and God in his self-determination in Jesus Christ (cf. *Church Dogmatics* II, 2, 163, 166 etc.).

61. F. D. E. Schleiermacher, *Kurze Darstellung des theologischen Studiums*, ed. H. Scholz, 1961 §1: 'In the sense in which the word is always taken here, theology is a positive science whose parts are only joined together as a whole through their common relationship to a particular form of the consciousness of God; thus the Christian by its relationship to Christianity.'

62. R. Rothe, *Theologische Ethik* III, 1848, 477, 1010: 'A necessary prerequisite for finding one's bearings in the present state of Christianity is to recognize that the church stage of the historical development of Christianity is past, and that the Christian spirit has already entered its moral, i.e. political age. If the church is the essential form in which Christianity has its existence, then—and this must be conceded in all honesty—in our days, and indeed for some time past, it is in a lamentable state, and one cannot see how matters can ever improve it. But Christianity in its innermost nature tends beyond the church; it seeks to have nothing less than the total organism of human life as its own organism, and that means the state. It is essentially concerned to become increasingly more secular, that is, to put off the garb of the church which it must necessarily assume on its entry into the world, and take upon itself the general form of human life, morality.' For the context in Rothe see H. J Birkner, *Spekulation und Heilsgeschichte, Die Geschichtsauffassung Richard Rothes*, 1959. T. Rendtorff has recently taken up this idea again in a modified form. Cf. *Christentum ausserhalb der Kirche. Konkretionen der Aufklärung*, 1969. 'The transition of Christianity to its world-historical era sets the scene for the problems of modern theology' (Introduction to E. Troeltsch, *Die Absolutheit des Christentums*, Siebenstern-Taschenbücher 138, 1969, 7). The reversal of the much discussed secularization thesis in the sense that the secularization of the church is or can be called

the realization of Christianity, is one-sided, because the interests in secularization are manifold. It is beyond question that an integral theory of the history of modern Christianity would be desirable, but it replaces neither theology nor dogmatic work. The old and new chiliasm of modern times and the modern secularization of the church was and is blind to the blinding of a compulsively optimistic society.

63. J. Ritter, *Hegel und die französische Revolution*, 1957, 13. R. Bubner, 'Philosophie ist ihre Zeit, in Gedanken erfasst', in *Hermeneutik und Dialektik* I, 1970, 317–42, makes critical comments on this.

64. G. Rohrmoser, 'Zum Atheismusproblem im Denken von Pascal bis Nietzsche', *Internationale Dialog-Zeitschrift* 1, 1968, vol. 2, 143, asks: 'How can I understand and accept as being shaped and formed by the God of the Bible a social and societal form of human practice in which all the horrors are possible which take place in the twentieth century, and which Nietzsche foresaw with astounding clarity as a necessary consequence of the practical rule of atheism?'

65. E.g. A. Camus, *The Rebel*, Penguin Books 1962.

66. On this see ch. 1, p. 26.

67. Karl Barth, *Church Dogmatics* II 2, 123.

68. Luther, WA V, 162, 21: by virtue of his *humanitas* Christ makes himself like us and crucifies us, *'faciens ex infoelicibus et superbis diis homines veros, idest miseros et peccatores. Quia enim ascendimus in Adam ad similitudinem dei, ideo descendit ille in similitudinem nostram, ut reduceret nos ad nostri cognitionem. Hoc est regnum fidei.'* On this see E. Wolf, 'Menschwerdung des Menschen?', *EvTh* 6, 1946, 4ff. (*Peregrinatio* II, 1965, 119ff.).

69. W. von Loewenich, op. cit., 21.

70. E. Jüngel, 'Die Welt als Möglichkeit und Wirklichkeit', *EvTh* 29, 1969, 417ff.

71. This is grounded in Luther's own understanding of the Reformation. It is usually pointed out that in contrast to the attempts at a 'reform of the head and members of the church' in the fifteenth century, the Reformation began from the newly-discovered Word of God and therefore was more theological and fundamental than the former reform movements and attempts. It should not, however, be overlooked that for its humanistic and Protestant followers, the Reformation was often an apocalyptic phenomenon. Mathesius and Bugenhagen already regarded the discovery of the 'Word of God' as a fulfilment of Rev. 14.6 and the angel with the 'eternal gospel'. There are even signs of such an apocalyptic understanding of the Reformation in Luther himself (Antichrist, conversion of the Jews). Soon after Luther, the 'reformation of doctrine' was regarded as being incomplete. Thus in the Pfalz in 1563 there arose the 'Second Reformation' (Reformed movement in Germany) which aimed at a complete purification of the churches from the 'court colours and standards of the Pope', and after that the 'reformation of life' in the Puritans and the pietistic movement. For J. Böhme and A. Comenius, 'Reformation' was fundamentally the *reformatio mundi*, again an apocalyptic theme. The internal and external disaster of the German Peasant War

shows one problem overhang of the Reformation, which soon turned into a German dream. In a theological and Christian sense, 'Reformation' has an anticipatory claim to totality and therefore points beyond the history of its attempts and failures.

72. On this see P. Althaus, *Luthers Stellung im Bauernkrieg*, 1952.

73. E. Käsemann, 'The Problem of the Historical Jesus', *Essays on New Testament Themes*, SCM Press 1964, 15–47.

74. Thus rightly R. Bultmann, 'The Concept of Revelation in the New Testament', in *Existence and Faith: Shorter Writings of Rudolf Bultmann*, ed. Schubert M. Ogden, Fontana Books 1962, 58ff.

75. H. Jonas, 'Heidegger und die Theologie', *EvTh* 24, 1964, 629.

3

QUESTIONS ABOUT JESUS

In spite of all the cultural, philosophical and spiritual riches of historic Christianity, Christian faith basically lives only as a profession of faith in Jesus. On the other hand, when critics of Christianity trace its cultural and humane traditions to non-Christian origins in antiquity or the present time, they come up against an irreducible core in the profession of faith in Jesus. Wherever Jesus is acknowledged as the Christ of God, Christian faith is to be found. Wherever this is doubted, obscured or denied, there is no longer Christian faith, and the riches of historic Christianity disappear with it. Christianity is alive as long as there are people who, as the disciples once did, profess their faith in him and, following him, spread his liberating rule in words, deeds and new fellowship. For this reason, it is right that christology should once again have become the centre of Christian theology.

Adolf von Harnack began his lectures on *What is Christianity?* in 1899/1900 with the observation:

John Stuart Mill has somewhere observed that mankind cannot be too often reminded that there was once a man of the name of Socrates. That is true; but still more important is it to remind mankind again and again that a man of the name of Jesus Christ once stood in their midst.[1]

But who was Jesus of Nazareth, and what is his significance for Christianity? Was he a prophet, who uttered the will of God for men? Was he a redeemer, bringing the salvation for which all men thirst and long? Did he embody God in the world, or true humanity in the sight of God? With what questions should one approach his person and history?[2] What question was he answering by manifesting himself? What question does his appearance not answer? Historical phenomena, and persons above all, give no answer to alien and improper questions. Stupid questions usually produce only the answer that one wants to hear. 'What you call the spirit of the time, is usually, gentlemen, basically your own spirit', is the mocking comment of Faust in his dialogue with Wagner about historians' portraits of the past. And Christians and non-Christians have quite often produced an image of Jesus which suits their own desires. They have idolized Jesus, and then have taken away the idolizations of believers and humanized him again. He has become the archetype of the divine authority and glory which men have longed for. He has become the teacher of a new morality to mankind. He has become the resistance fighter from Galilee. An analysis of the changing ideas of Christ and portraits of Jesus in history shows that they correspond so much to the needs of their age, place of origin and intended purpose that one cannot avoid the suspicion that they are illusory and artificial. The question then arises: Who was Jesus himself, and what does he himself signify at the present day? Do we know Jesus, and who is he in fact for us at the present day?

These questions about Jesus must be seen in a twofold context:

1. There have been disagreements about Jesus since the very beginning of Christian faith. They arose first of all between Christians and Jews in the dispute about his resurrection and enthronement as Christ, the Messiah; then between Christians and pagans in the dispute about his divinity and incarnation; at the beginning of the modern age between Christians and humanists, in the dispute about his humanity and sinlessness; and at the present day, in our own civilization, between Christians and post-Christian atheists in the dispute about the liberation of man and the righteousness of the world. It is important to take into account the whole of this broad context in which the disagreements about Jesus have occurred, for when Jesus is put on trial before the world in this way, Christians cannot regard themselves as judges, but only as witnesses.[3]

2. Since the beginning of Christian faith, however, Jesus has also been the subject of disagreement within Christianity itself. Where is his truth to be found? In the earthly Jesus, who appeared in Palestine in the time of the Emperor Tiberius and was crucified under the Procurator Pontius Pilate—or in the risen Christ whom his church proclaimed and in whom it believed? Although faith has always acknowledged that Jesus is the Christ, this dispute between 'Jesuology' and christology runs throughout the history of the

church and has become particularly acute in recent times. That the confession that Jesus is the Christ is true, and not a pious illusion, is the issue on which faith stands or falls. This confronts Christian theology with a twofold task:

1. It must show what is really meant by the profession of faith that 'Jesus is the Christ'. It must demonstrate the intrinsic basis and justification of christology in the person and history of Jesus.[4] Does one have to speak in christological terms of Jesus and his history? Do Jesus and his history demand a christology? How far is it true, as faith believes, that Jesus is the Christ of God? This is the question of the intrinsic truth and rightness of the appeal of faith and the church to the one in whose name they believe and speak. This is not a question posed from outside, but arises from within faith itself, which hungers for knowledge and understanding: *fides quaerens intellectum*. Is the preaching of Christ appropriate to Jesus, or does it replace him by something else? Does faith in Christ arise with intrinsic necessity from the apprehension of the person and history of Jesus, or are the statements it makes about him the arbitrary affirmations of believers, and personal value judgments?

2. Christian theology must show how far the Christian confession of faith in Jesus is true as seen from outside, and must demonstrate that it is relevant to the present-day understanding of reality and the present-day dispute about the truth of God and the righteousness of man and the world. For the title 'Christ' has never been used by faith only to say who Jesus was in his own person, but to express his dominion, future and significance with regard to God, men and the world.[5]

Thus the first task of christology is the critical verification of the Christian faith in its origin in Jesus and his history. The second task is a critical verification of Christian faith in its consequences for the present and the future. The former can be called the hermeneutics of its origin, and the second the hermeneutics of its effects and consequences. If one were to limit oneself to the hermeneutics of the origin of christology in Jesus, the resultant account, however true it was to scripture, could easily become sterile and would be condemned to ineffectiveness. If one were to limit oneself to the hermeneutics of the effects of christology in Christianity and world history, the inward justification and authority of faith would rapidly disappear. Thus the one must

constantly be related to the other. This tension is itself a characteristic of Christian faith, for the confession of Christian faith
always has two aspects: the earthly and the eternal, the particular
and the universal, the temporal and the eschatological. The name
of Jesus covers the earthly, particular and temporal side of his
origin, and the titles attributed to him cover the eternal, universal
and eschatological side. The confession that he is the Christ
associates a proper name, 'Jesus', with titles implying a dignity
and a function, such as 'Christ', 'Son of Man', 'Son of God',
'Lord' or 'Logos'. The purpose of these 'titles of office' is to state
what Jesus is. In them, faith states what Jesus means for it, and
what it believes, receives, expects and hopes about and from him.
Even in the earliest Christian times they were interchangeable and
replaceable.[6] As Christianity passed from one linguistic world to
another, a title often became incomprehensible or was understood
as a proper name. The ancient Jewish-Christian title 'Christ' soon
lost its functional meaning and became a name, and was then
extended: 'Jesus Christ is the Lord.' The same happened to the
title 'Son of man', which as early as Ignatius is no longer understood in an apocalyptic sense, but as a description of Jesus' human
nature, and is supplemented by the title 'Son of God'. Other
titles disappeared, like 'Son of David', and new titles appeared,
such as 'Logos'. Thus the titles changed as faith came to be
expressed in new languages and in new historical situations. Just
as they were formulated to express Jewish or Greek reasons for
faith in Jesus, it is possible on principle to formulate new titles to
express, say, Hindu reasons or even Marxist reasons for faith in
Jesus. This historical openness and variability of the titles for
Jesus, to which the history of Christian tradition bears witness,
has, however, a point of reference and a criterion. This is provided
by his personal name, Jesus, and the history which concluded with
his crucifixion and resurrection. If one wishes to say who the Christ,
the Son of Man, the Son of God, the Logos, etc. actually is, then
one must use the name of Jesus and recount his history. The name
of Jesus can neither be translated into other languages nor be
replaced by other names, or by the names of other people. His
history cannot be replaced by other histories, or by the histories of
other people. To say what Jesus is, means and does, one must go
to the ancient and modern titles for his office and function, ex-
pound them and supplement them anew. The constant in the

changes brought about by time, and in the transformations in the concrete form of faith, love and hope, is the name of Jesus, and the essential reference to him and his history in every Christian state-ment about God, the world and man. But the variables are to be found in the titles and predicates which can always be altered, and which are meant to state what Jesus is for us today.[7] The name says *who* is meant. The titles and predicates say *what* is meant. And just as in a sentence the subject governs the predicate, so in christology Jesus must govern the christological predicates. 'Every christological title represents a particular interpretation of reality, and this means in concrete terms a particular understanding of the way in which man is claimed, questioned, threatened and given hope.' But 'the meaning of χριστός, κύριος, υἱὸς τοῦ θεοῦ etc., when applied to Jesus, is not immediately obvious from the then existing use of these terms—which is by no means to suggest that the existing use is of no consequence for the interpretation. Rather, they only receive a definite meaning when they are applied to Jesus';[8] as G. Ebeling rightly says.

If this tension between the name and the titles of Jesus, between his historical particularity and the universality attributed to his rule by faith, is characteristic of Christian belief, then we can go a step further. The problem intrinsic to every christology is not merely its reference to the person called by the name Jesus, but also the reference to his history, and within his history, to his death on the cross. All christological titles presumably express what faith receives, what love gives and what one may hope. But the critical point for them comes when, faced with the 'double conclusion of the life' of Jesus (M. Kähler),[9] they have to state what it means for the Christ, the Son of God, the Logos, the true man or the representative to have been crucified. The process of the reinterpretation of Jesus' titles begins not merely with his historical person, but in a radical sense with the historical end of his life. His cross requires christology, as Kähler said,[10] but it is also the mystery behind all christologies, for it calls them into question and makes them in constant need of revision. This is the starting point for the real work of language and thought on behalf of Christian faith. It is not the changes brought by time which in the first instance require faith constantly to ask new questions about Jesus and his meaning for the present day. Historical and social changes do in fact cause old world-views and religious conceptions to become outdated, and lead to the construction of new ones. But this is only one side of christological revisionism.[11] It is he, the crucified Jesus himself, who is the driving force, the joy and the suffering of all theology which is Christian. Since the time of the apostles, the history of faith and theology has been concerned with the mystery of the crucified Jesus himself; and it has been a history of permanent revisions, reformations and revolts, aimed at recognizing him for the person he really is and conforming to him by changing one's own life and thinking. Christologies rise and are broken down in reference to him. Even if historical life were to be ossified and history were to be brought to an end by people in 'post-history',[12] the crucified Christ would still be the spur to Christian faith and would mean that for it at least history could not be concluded. To speak metaphorically, the cross of Christ is the source of a permanent iconoclasm of the christological icons of the church and the portraits of Jesus in Christianity; and the theology of the cross is a kind of iconoclasm of the christological images and titles of the church. It is iconoclasm for Jesus' sake and is justified and regulated by the recollection of his cross.[13]

1. *Is Jesus true God?*

Every question presupposes a context in which the question arises. It excludes other questions as irrelevant, and establishes the level of significance on which meaningful conclusions are sought. Which questions provide the basis for understanding Jesus as the person he was, so that for us today he may be revealed as the one who he truly is? In this chapter we discuss the four most important questions which typify the dispute between faith and unbelief about Jesus.

One possible starting point, constantly adopted since the days of the early church, is the fact that man, like every transitory being in the finite world, is concerned with the question of God. Everything that exists and yet does not endure raises the question of a being which exists and endures eternally, and which can give it endurance in the midst of impermanence. Where is this being which is called 'divine' revealed, and how is its permanence and immortality imparted to that which every day rushes into decay? 'God' here is the answer to the question implied in man's finitude.[14]

This presupposes that being itself, the divine being in its unity, indivisibility and unchangeableness, exists. By contrast, man in his impermanence and the transitory world are questionable. And the question which they pose is that of their participation in the eternal, divine being. In antiquity the divine being was not a problem. Its existence was rarely doubted. It was man in his relationship to God which was the problem. The next step was from the general question of God to the mystery of Jesus. Was the eternal, unchangeable God revealed in Jesus? And the answer was, the one God whom all men seek in their finitude and transitoriness became man in Jesus. 'He is the image of the invisible God' (Col. 1.15). 'In him all the fullness of God was pleased to dwell' (Col. 1.19). He is of one substance with God, begotten, not created, God of God, light of light, etc., as the Nicene Creed says in the style of a hymn. The mystery of Jesus here is the incarnation of God, the incarnation of eternal, original, unchangeable being in the sphere of temporal, decaying, transitory existence, in which men live and die. If the mystery of Jesus is the eternal presence of God amongst men, then the salvation of the world is also to be found in him. God became man, so that men could partake of God. He took on transitory, mortal being, for that which is transitory and mortal to become intransitory and immortal.[15]

But because of its origin in the experience of finitude and its context in the hope of immortality, the general question of God which was taken as a starting point assumes a particular concept of God. The divine being is intransitory, immortal, unchangeable and impassible. If these attributes of God are applied to the mystery of Jesus and his death on the cross, they raise the very problems which preoccupied the christology of the early church. How can the intransitory God be in a transitory human being? How can the universal God be in an individual? How can the unchangeable God 'become' flesh? How can the immortal God suffer and die on a cross?

Thus in antiquity the general question of God, and the expectation of salvation implicit in it, also provided reasons for not believing in 'God in Christ'. The access it offered to the mystery of Jesus was at the same time an obstacle to belief in Jesus as the Son of God. The Alexandrian philosopher Celsus clearly formulated this unbelief on the basis of the question about God which it implied:

Everyone saw his suffering, but only a disciple and a half crazed woman saw him risen. His followers then made a God of him, like Antinous . . . The Christian idea of the coming down of God is senseless. Why did God come down for justification of all things? Does not this make God changeable? Why does he send his Son into one corner of the world and not make him appear in many bodies at once?[16]

The christology of the early church had to come to grips with these and similar objections derived from the concept of God assumed in antiquity. The more it emphasized the divinity of Christ, making use of this concept of God, the more difficult it became to demonstrate that the Son of God who was of one substance with God was Jesus of Nazareth, crucified under Pontius Pilate. Consequently, a mild docetism runs through the christology of the ancient church.[17] Anyone who began with the question about what was 'above' in terms of the question of God and salvation, as posed in antiquity, found it hard in any real sense to find an answer 'below', in the history of Jesus of Nazareth, and even harder to find an answer in the abandonment by God of the crucified Jesus.

But it is not right to call these kinds of christology 'christology from above'.[18] It is true that the christological answer starts 'above' and presents the mystery of Jesus on the pattern of the incarnation and resurrection, the humiliation and exaltation of the eternal Son of God. But the question about God which it assumes is that of finite being seeking the infinite being of God which imparts permanence. Thus it is not necessary 'to stand in the position of God [oneself] in order to follow the way of God's Son into the world'.[19] Rather, one must accept the openness of one's own finite existence in order to recognize its fulfilment of one's own openness.[20]

The problem of the modern speculative christology of German idealism is somewhat different. After Kant's criticism of the cosmological proofs of the existence of God, there remained not only the moral proof of God's existence, but also the ontological proof. Speculative christology made the reformulation of this proof its starting point. But it took seriously the idea that no way leads to God which does not begin in God himself.[21] The question about God is only the subjective side of the objectively prior question of God about man. The knowledge of God presupposes the self-revelation of God. Consequently, God must not only be thought of as substance, but also as subject.[22] For if God is thought of as subject, he is not thought of as the basis of something else, but for his own sake. Man must not think of God in order to provide a basis for the world or for human existence. But if one thinks of God, one must necessarily think of his existence and his subjectivity, otherwise one has not thought of God. This was the origin of the idea of the self-revelation of God, which since Fichte and Hegel has determined the course of speculative christology. It led to a 'reversal of thought' from thinking to being thought of, from apprehending to being apprehended, from knowing to being known.[23] If man really thinks of God, then God is thinking of himself in man, otherwise man would not have thought of God, but only of the image of his own thought.[24] If Christ knows himself as the Son of God, then God must know himself in him. If Jesus speaks of God, it is only about God if God speaks of himself in him.[25] According to the view of the speculative christologians of the nineteenth century, the divinity of Jesus could only be concluded *a posteriori* at the end of his history, as the gospels tell us; but the prologue to the Gospel of John supplies the corresponding *a priori* of his being and his origin in God. From Fichte on, they interpreted this prologue as the metaphysics of the gospel history. This 'reversal of thought' occurs in Fichte:

The originally divine idea of a particular standpoint in time cannot for the most part be asserted, until the man inspired by God comes and carries it out. What the divine man does is divine.

But then follows the typical statement:

In this action it is not man that acts, it is God himself in his original inner being and essence who acts in him and does his work through man.[26]

Schelling similarly gave a speculative basis to christology with the aid of this 'reversal of thought', and spoke of the 'finitization of the divine in Jesus'.[27] Finally, in Hegel, who makes this reversal comprehensible with the aid of mystical theology, the history of Jesus of Nazareth belongs in the whole context of truth, and must accordingly be understood in a speculative way, for 'truth is the whole'. The 'history of God' includes his self-emptying in what is different and alien to him, and the return which he himself has realized.[28] In the words of I. A. Dorner:

Through the philosophy of Schelling and Hegel the idea of the incarnation . . . came to be acknowledged: it is essential to the idea [of the God-head] to enter into finitude, to descend into it as its contrary being, but also eternally to elevate itself out of it and to restore itself; and this comes about by the eternal spirit attaining to consciousness, consciously apprehending itself in its absolute essence or its absolute unity with God, and therefore knowing itself as God-man.[29]

But in Hegel not only was the idea of the incarnation thought necessary to God, for the sake of the subjectivity of God, but also the idea of the 'death of God'. Here the human, finite, imperfect, weak and negative becomes itself a divine element, in God himself.[30] Here again, christology is worked out on the pattern of incarnation and resurrection, humiliation and exaltation. But we cannot describe it as a 'christology from above', completely beyond the power of our mind to comprehend. Rather, its basis lies in the wholly meaningful 'reversal of thought'. It considers itself the metaphysics of the particular, gospel history of Jesus of Nazareth. According to ancient theological doctrine, the order of knowing (*ratio cognoscendi*) works in the opposite direction from the order of being (*ratio essendi*). What is the last thing for human knowledge is first with regard to being. Whereas Jesus is not recognizable as the Son of God until his death on the cross and his resurrection, in the order of being he is the Son of God before this history takes place. All knowledge begins inductively 'from below' and is *a posteriori*, and all historical knowledge is *post factum*; but that which is to be known precedes it. The difference between a 'christology from below' and a 'christology from above' is only apparent. They are no more alternatives than the famous question: 'Does Jesus help me because he is the Son of God, or is he the Son of God because he helps me?'[31] It is only when the inverse relationship of the order of knowledge to the order of being is ignored that such questions are asked.

But the criticism that can be made of speculative christology is the same as that which can be made of the christology of the early church. The pattern of incarnation and resurrection, humiliation and exaltation associates the mystery of Jesus with the mystery of God himself. But it makes the particular features of the real, historical human being Jesus of Nazareth and the arbitrary occurrences of his life inessential. The idea of the incarnation of God and even the 'fearful thought' of the death of God can be thought necessary for the sake of God, for the sake of his self-realization;

91

but it is difficult to deduce and not particularly easy to reconstruct his incarnation in Jesus of Nazareth and his death in the death of Jesus on Golgotha.[32] The sublimation of history in the spirit always endeavours to apprehend what has happened in its necessity. But the sublimation of history as it has happened into history as it is apprehended of course does not merely preserve it, but also destroys it. In the crucified Jesus on Golgotha there remains something which still resists its sublimation into the concept of atonement. Only a new creation which is based upon the crucified Christ can sublimate the scandal of his cross into a pure hymn of praise. Since C. H. Weisse, therefore, the lack of eschatology in the speculative christology of the atonement has repeatedly been criticized.[33] But this criticism is Christian only if it begins with the elements of the cross of Christ which are not integrated into the system.[34]

2. Is Jesus true Man?

Since the Renaissance, the Enlightenment and the rise of modern technology, the relationship between man and nature in most fields has been reversed. Man is no longer dependent upon uncomprehended forces in nature and history, recognizing in this dependence his total reliance on the gods or on God. Instead, nature and history have become increasingly dependent upon man. The problem of modern man is no longer so much how he can live with gods and demons, but how he can survive with the bomb, revolution and the destruction of the balance of nature. He usurps more and more of nature and takes it under his control. The vital question for him, therefore, is how this world which he has usurped can be humanized.[35] His main problem is no longer the universal finitude which he experiences in solidarity with all other creatures, but the humanity of his own world.

Thus the christological question is no longer, 'Is the eternal God in Christ?', but, 'Can Jesus be called God, and in what respect and how far is he divine?' Thus from the time of Lessing to the present day the vital question of humanity has for many become the main question about Christ. Thus J. G. Herder said: 'Humanity is both the nature and the work of Christ. The divine in our race is education for humanity.'[36] Whereas in the ancient church the dispute about the relationship of the two natures in the person of

Christ was always a dispute about physical redemption as well, and the idea of the real incarnation of God was always associated with the deification of man (*theosis*) which it made possible, the dispute at the present time about the true humanity of Jesus, his awareness of God, his 'inner life' and his freedom finds its basis in the demand for true humanity, authentic life, inner identity and liberation. The point of reference and the purpose of the questions have changed, and Jesus is accordingly manifested in a different way and must supply a different answer. Jesus is no longer understood against the background of discourse about God as 'God-man', but as it were in the anthropological foreground as the exemplary and archetypal 'man of God'. The virgin birth as the sign of his incarnation and the resurrection as the sign of his exaltation have become incomprehensible, as 'physical miracles of divine power', in the world view of modern man and give the impression of being purely mythologoumena. On the other hand, the personal sinlessness of Jesus is now explained as a 'miracle of the love of God' in the moral world.[37] This sinlessness becomes a moral demonstration of his awareness of God, which is always intense. This brings with it a change in the question of salvation. Salvation no longer envisages the whole world, tormented by its transitory nature. Salvation loses its cosmological breadth and ontological depth and is sought in the context of man's existential problem, in the form of a quiet conscience, an inner experience of identity or as pure personality.[38] Finally, there is a further change associated with this. If man, driven on by the problem of his existence, is basically aware of everything only within the horizon of his own subjectivity, he also cannot understand anything which is not important to himself and which is not involved in what he does in practice and in his own understanding of himself. Consequently, objective doxological statements about the person of Christ seem to him to be outdated metaphysics. Modern thought is scarcely any longer a thought which wonders and contemplates, but is operational thought. Thus for many theologians since Kant, ethics in the broader sense of the word has replaced metaphysics as the fundamental category for christology.

For Kant practical reason provided the framework of categories for theology and also for christology. Anything 'which is of no practical use' does not concern us. 'Scripture texts which contain certain theoretical doctrines stated to be sacred, but surpassing every conception of reason (even of moral reason) may be expounded for the benefit of the practical reason, while those which conflict with practical reason must be so expounded.' The doctrine of the Trinity 'offers absolutely nothing of practical use ... And the same is true of the doctrine of the incarnation of one divine person.' Something similar can be said of the stories of the resurrection and ascension. For 'articles of faith do not mean what ought to be believed ... but what for practical (moral) purposes it is practical and useful to accept, even though it may not be possible to prove it, but only to believe it.' Thus the revelation of God can only be what is in agreement with what reason understands to be 'appropriate to God'. 'In this way all expositions of scripture, in so far as they concern religion, must be made in accordance with the principle of morality intended in revelation, and without this are either in practice empty or even hindrances to good.' For we understand only him who speaks with us through our own understanding and our own reason. Therefore 'the God in us', i.e. the free conscience, is 'himself the interpreter'.[39]

Within this context of practical reason, Jesus becomes the 'personified idea of the good principle'. The final purpose of creation, the 'man alone pleasing to God', is in God from eternity in the form of the idea. Because we are not the originator of this idea, it can be said that it has come down to us from heaven, that it has taken on humanity.

> We can represent to ourselves this ideal of a humanity pleasing to God ... only as the idea of a person who would be willing not only to discharge all human duties himself ... but even, though tempted by the greatest allurements to take upon himself every affliction, up to the most ignominious death, for the good of the world and even for his enemies ...

As far as he can, Kant avoids the name of Jesus in these discussions, in order to present the idea of mankind pleasing to God as a pure example of practical faith; for the personification of the idea has only a mediating character. 'Even the Holy One of the gospel must first be compared with our ideal of moral perfection before we can recognize him to be such.'[40]

Schleiermacher, on the other hand, considered that the mediating factor between the ideal and the real, between theoretical and practical reason, being and consciousness, lay in direct awareness, in 'feeling'. By this he meant the basic characteristic of human existence. Here is the seat of the religious factor, in the emotional nature of the whole of life, before human activities are extended into knowledge and practice. Consequently, Schleiermacher did not attempt to discuss Christ in terms of theological metaphysics, yet did not restrict himself to a christology of moral example. In the context of the basic characteristic of existential life, he developed a christology of the personal relationship of faith to Jesus.

The Redeemer, then, is like all men in virtue of the identity of human nature, but distinguished from them all by the constant potency of his God-consciousness, which was a veritable existence of God in him.

In negative terms, the Redeemer was distinguished from all men by his essential sinlessness. In the context of the rule of the consciousness of God over knowledge and action how is Jesus manifested? The personal development of Jesus must be thought of as quite free from everything which can be described only as struggle. The purity of Jesus is without the traces and the scars of a struggle. This archetypal potency of his consciousness of God must have been, from the beginning to the end, perfect in him, and perfectly historical. Its redeeming effect therefore consists in Jesus empowering our weak and efficient consciousness of God, and in his drawing us into the constant potency of his own consciousness of God.[41] Here Jesus is not only a moral example, but a productive archetype of redeemed being.

For productivity belongs only to the concept of the ideal and not to that of the exemplary. We must conclude, then, that ideality is the only appropriate expression for the exclusive personal dignity of Christ.[42]

Just as for Kant practical reason became the hermeneutic criterion for christology, so since the time of Schleiermacher the criterion for many has been the present experience of redemption in the empowering of our consciousness of God. But this also sets limits to this empowering.

The facts of the Resurrection and the Ascension of Christ, and the prediction of His return to Judgment cannot be laid down as properly constituent parts of the doctrine of His Person . . . The disciples recognized in Him the Son of God without having the faintest premonition of His Resurrection and Ascension.[43]

Nor does his death on the cross add anything new or special to the redeeming effects which derive from his sinless life.

For the subsequent Jesuology of Protestantism, the examples of

Kant and Schleiermacher made clear how a starting point in moral practice, the consciousness of God, one's own personal existence or the identity of the self had power both to provide and obstruct insight. It showed Jesus as true man to those who had lost or not yet found their humanity, and were seeking it. As the perfect Man of God, Jesus is the fulfilment of our destiny as the image of God which we have not fulfilled. Wherever he is manifested in this problematic situation, his truth and our truth is experienced. 'If he (i.e. man) finds the revelation which most successfully resolves the discord in his innermost being, then for him this is the true revelation', said A. Tholuck.[44] Thus the metaphysical problems of the eternal being are replaced by the existential problems of man in his world. An '*a priori* theory based on anthropological needs' replaces the cosmological *a priori*.[45] When this is realized, the gap between modern Protestant christology and that of the early church seems less, as indeed the former has always asserted. It has only altered the context and purpose of the question about Jesus. The problems are very similar. Both ways of posing the question proceed from a universal in order to assert its truth and to verify it in the concrete form of the person and history of Jesus. The unresolved problems for both are first, the individuality of Jesus of Nazareth and, secondly, his abandonment by God on the cross.

For questions about Jesus to start from the existential problem of man hinders an answer based upon him as he is as, much as did the question about God posed in antiquity by finite being. Why should Jesus of Nazareth, of all people, be the moral example or the redeeming archetype of true humanity? Why cannot the desire for humanity, for freedom from the world and a quiet conscience pay equal attention to Moses, Socrates, Buddha and the others? Jesus may be obliged to give an answer to the general question of humanity, but he can only represent a relative answer as one amongst many, for tolerance and a plurality of patterns of true humanity have been one of the requirements for humanity since long before the Enlightenment. What is left of the 'absolute claim' of Christianity? The answer given is often that in the whole history of human thought no one better has been found, or else that by chance of fate we are heirs of the Christian tradition. But if we give this answer, we are only adding to the price to be paid for the early Christian certainties of faith, which regarded Jesus as the final revelation of the one God, and therefore made the world Christian in the way which it has continued to be with some degree of permanence down to the present day. This absolute claim, which is no longer asserted, but seems to be accepted as tradition, and in institutional form, is of course the central problem of modern Protestant Jesuology. Like Celsus in the past, D.F. Strauss said: 'It is not [the mode of idea] to lavish all its fullness on one exemplar . . . it rather loves to distribute its riches among a multiplicity of exemplars which reciprocally complete each other.'[46] The general existential question of the idea of moral humanity pleasing to God can lead to following the moral example of Jesus, but can also lead to determined unbelief in Jesus or to the tolerant placing of Jesus in the long series of heroes and helpers of mankind. The absolute claim of Christianity, which could no longer be defended, made E. Troeltsch a philosopher, but made the 'philosophical faith' of K. Jaspers intolerant of it. It is possible to interpret Jesus as the perfect man to those who by tradition are already Christians, but hardly to pagans and post-Christian atheists. Jesus *can* be understood in this way, but why *must* one necessarily go to the trouble of doing so? Thus modern christology always assumes faith, and states that Jesus can be understood in this way in faith. But it rarely says why one should have faith, and have faith in Jesus in particular. Thus it becomes a modern christology which is accepted within its own circle, but has virtually nothing to say to non-believers, unbelievers or those who hold a different faith.

The whole Jesuology of modern times, which for the reasons given is derived from the life of Jesus, is faced in the double conclusion of the life of Jesus with the same unresolved difficulties as the christology of the early church and that of speculative idealism. Since his resurrection from the dead is filed away as a miracle which cannot be posited by the physical world, and therefore as a mythologoumenon from the past, it becomes intolerable to take into account his abandonment by God to his death on the cross in all its severity. Thus the attention is turned away from his death and concentrated upon his life and preaching. His death on the cross is seen only as the consummation of the life he lived, of his obedience or of his freedom. And yet basically, in the light of his preceding life, no adequate interpretation of his death on the cross can be found. The crucified Christ no longer has any place in the context of questions about practical action, the consciousness of God, personal identity or the certainty of faith. A criticism of modern Protestant Jesuology ought not to be based upon an extra-historical point of view, or on a previously assumed concept of God, but upon the point of view of the crucified Christ, who in his own way is outside history, outside society and outside the question of the humanity of living men. The transcendence of the crucified Christ is not metaphysical, but the transcendence of concrete rejection. It also cuts across the anthropological needs and existential questions to which the presentation and discussion of Jesus in modern Jesuology relates him, and radically alters the examples and archetypes which are found in Jesus.

3. *'Are you he who is to come?'*

We can come closer to the person and history of Jesus by doing today what the disciples did, entering into dialogue with Jews and taking their questions seriously. The expectations and language which formed the background to Jesus' life, against which the disciples saw and listened to him, do not simply belong to the past, but in substance are still a living reality alongside Christianity in Judaism and atheistic messianism. Here the questions asked about Christ are not: 'Is the eternal God man in Jesus?' or, 'Can the man Jesus be called divine?' but, 'Are you he who is to come, or shall we look for another?' This was the question put by the Baptist to Jesus, and in the Gospel of Matthew Jesus replies, 'Go and tell John what you see and hear: the blind receive their sight and the lame walk, lepers are cleansed and the deaf hear, and the dead are raised up, and the poor have good news preached to them. And blessed is he who takes no offence at me' (11.2ff.). This is an indirect answer. The events which took place around Jesus and at his word speak on his behalf, for they are the signs of the messianic age. The gospel which comes in the miracles to those without hope, and to the poor in his preaching, upholds and authenticates Jesus. His office is upheld not by the incarnation of the eternal Son of God nor by the archetype of true humanity, but by the future of the kingdom which is inaugurated in and around him. Here the question is that of the future of the history revealed by the Old Testament promises, the messianic expectation of the kingdom. It manifests Jesus, with his preaching and his signs, as 'he who is to come'. The divine world above does not descend to earth in him, nor does man, seeking his identity, find himself in him. A new future for God, man and the world in their history together is being inaugurated. In terms of the open questions of the Old Testament and the apocalyptic promises, and the existential experience of Israel in exile and alienation, Jesus is revealed as the one who fulfils these promises. This of course can be described superficially as a proof from prophecy. But what is meant is that the person and history of Jesus have been manifested and understood as open to the future of God in the way which was characteristic of the distinctive existence of Israel amongst all the nations. This is a different openness from the general, metaphysical question of finitude, and raises questions different from the general anthropological questions about man's humanity. Properly understood, the question of the redeeming future of the history shared by God, man and the world includes these questions about God and about man's humanity, and is not narrower, but broader than both. If we start from this point, it is no longer a matter of indifference or chance that Jesus was a Jew, appeared in Israel, came into conflict with the guardians of his people's law, and was condemned and handed over to the Romans to be crucified, and that, because he appeared to the disciples, they proclaimed him as 'raised from the dead'. The messianic question, 'Are you he who is to come?' seems to have been the earliest question about Christ. It is the context in which the earliest witnesses of Christianity spoke the language which was most natural to them and to Jesus himself. Whenever this question is ignored as peculiar to its own time, it is harder to understand Jesus.

But can a pagan ask this question without first having become a Jew? Does the return to the messianic question not make prophecy and apocalyptic a precondition of Christian faith, as the law and circumcision were in their time? Is this not a re-Judaizing of Christianity? I do not think so. As a result of the continuous influence of Judaism and Christianity upon the societies in which they were and are present, the experience of reality as history open to the future, and with it messianism, has become universal. The effect of the Bible was to bring an eschatological awareness into the world (E. Bloch), and the universal longing for redemption became a future hope. Without this orientation towards the future, the experience of reality as history is hard to maintain. This is clear from present-day attempts, now that these hopes have been abandoned, to suppress history or bring its study to an end, and to bring it under bureaucratic control. It is also shown by the attempts, after the loss of these hopes, to embed the experience of history in a new confidence in nature, in order to rid history of its terrors.

But the messianic question not only points to its answer in Jesus, but also hinders that answer. It is the complex of messianic problems which raises the essential conflict between Judaism and Christianity. Their dispute about Jesus is conducted on the basis of their common question about the future. This dispute is between an atonement, which is already believed to be present, and a real redemption which lies in the future. It is also continued in the dispute over Hegel between Christianity and messianic atheism.

The Jew is profoundly conscious of the unredeemed nature of the world, and in the midst of this unredeemed condition he recognizes no enclaves of redemption. The conception of a redeemed soul in the midst of an unredeemed world is of its very nature totally alien to him, it is inaccessible by virtue of the very foundation of his existence. This is the basic reason for Israel's rejection of Jesus, not a purely external or national conception of messianism,

explains Shalom Ben-Chorin.[47] But does anyone who believes in Jesus really regard himself as a redeemed soul in the midst of an unredeemed world?

In all its forms and manifestations, Judaism has always held firmly to a concept of redemption which understood it as a process which takes place under the public gaze, on the stage of history and in the medium of society, that is, which definitely takes place in the visible world . . . By contrast, the view of Christianity is one in which redemption is a process in the intellectual sphere and in the invisible, which takes place in the world, in the world of every individual, and brings about a hidden transformation, to which nothing external in the world need correspond . . . The reinterpretation of the prophetic promises of the Bible to apply to the realm of the inner life . . . has always seemed to the religious thinkers of Judaism an illegitimate anticipation of what could be manifested at best as the inward aspect of a process which essentially takes place in the external world—and which could not be manifested without this process,

said Gershom Sholem.[48] But does Christian faith really represent such an interiorization of salvation? It is true that in historic Christianity there has in fact been both an abandonment of the real and universal hope of redemption, and at the same time a cessation of suffering over the unredeemed state of the world.

There are two sides to this. On the one hand, one can say that the imminent expectation of early Christianity was disappointed, and was then replaced by cult, morality and metaphysics.[49] On the other hand—and historically there seems to me to be much better historical evidence for this—one enthusiastic certainty of fulfilment followed another in Christianity. The kingdom of redemption was seen as already present in the church, or in the Constantinian state, in one's own exclusive denomination or in the Christianized secular world. Historical Christianity has lived not so much under the shadow of its original disappointment, as by the anticipation of the kingdom. This gave rise to the triumphalism of the theocratic state or the state church, which regularly led to the persecution of the Jews and other representatives of unfulfilled messianic hope. A faith which worships Christ as God without his future, a church which understands itself as the kingdom and a consciousness of atonement which no longer suffers from the continued unredeemed condition of the world, a Christian state which regards itself as God here present upon earth, cannot tolerate any Jewish hope beside itself. But is this still authentic Christian faith?

It is true that faith lives by the anticipation of the kingdom through and in Jesus. But this is not a spiritualization or individualization of real salvation. Nor is it an enclave of redemption in an unredeemed world. Nor is faith a redeemed soul which still regards the unredeemed world with indifference. It is the eschatological anticipation of redemption, an anticipation through and in one who was an outcast, rejected and crucified. The memory of the crucified anticipator of the kingdom makes impossible for a Christian any spiritualization or individualization of salvation, and any resigned acceptance of participation in an unredeemed world. Did not Paul develop from the 'sufferings of this present time' and the 'groaning' of the enslaved creation, and from Israel (Rom. 9–11), an eschatological christology of the crucified Jesus? Did he not understand the gospel for the godless, the Spirit and faith, baptism and the eucharist as anticipations of the redemption of the whole longing creation? Did he not regard the crucified Christ as the representative and central figure of the universal future in which God is 'everything to everyone' (I Cor. 15.28)? Even for Christians, Jesus, the crucified, cannot be understood without suffering for the unredeemed condition of the world, or without the hope of the kingdom which he has revealed to all the godless. In view of the misery of the creation, the fact that the atonement is already accomplished, although its struggle continues, is incomprehensible without the future of the redemption of the body and of the peace which brings the struggle to an end. 'For Jesus is he who is to come. Everyone who truly encounters him, encounters him from the future, as the life to come, as the Lord of the world to come. Otherwise he cannot be our Lord ... Only as he who is to come is he the one who came. As he who is to come, who reveals a new future to the godless, he is present.'[50] Israel and the church have drawn further apart in the course of the dispute about Jesus. 'For the Jews the Messiah has tended to disappear behind the kingdom of God. For the Christian church the kingdom of God has tended to disappear behind the figure of the Messiah' (Shalom Ben-Chorin). Since the beginning of Christianity, what Israel had to say about the one man tended increasingly to be overshadowed by what it had to say about the one time, and its message about the Messiah was replaced by its message about the messianic age to come. Christian christology made the hope of the Messiah suspect in Judaism. On the other hand, the Jewish expectation of the kingdom, with its realism, made realist and futurist eschatology suspect amongst Christians. On this level, after the long history of divergence, a history of convergence is wholly conceivable. But the more profound difference lies in the kind of life which each lives. The life of a Jew takes place within himself, in the sight of God. The life of a Christian takes place in the sight of God and Christ. What does this mean for the redemption of the world, which both feel to be unredeemed? Does redemption depend upon the repentance of man? If it does, redemption will never come. If it does not, it seems to be irrelevant to men. The Jewish answer could be described by saying that God forces Israel to repent through suffering.[51] The Christian answer is that God brings the sinner, whether a Jew or a Gentile, to repentance through his own suffering in the cross of Jesus. The ultimate difference between Jews and Christians lies in the attitude to the crucified Christ. For Christians, this must also bring about a breakthrough in the direction of messianic expectations and questions, and provide a new basis for hope in an unredeemed world.

4. *'Who do you say that I am?'*

So far, we have dealt with the question of Christ in its various forms as the assumption and preliminary to the understanding of the person and history of Jesus. Our conclusion was that a starting point in a universal can both reveal and obscure the concrete element of his person and history, so that in the framework of any universal question, both faith and unbelief are possible. It also became clear that the tentative answer implied in the questions had to be corrected, reinterpreted and radically changed in the light of Jesus' individuality and his concrete historical death upon the cross, if it was to do justice to Jesus and his history. A universally relevant christological conception of the incarnate Son of God, of the redeemer or of the exemplary human being cannot be Christian, without an indispensable reference to his unique person and history. If the question of Christ, whatever form it takes, is to do justice to Jesus himself, its relationship to him must not be one of questioning, but of being questioned; must not be one of demanding an answer but of giving an answer. It cannot simply manifest him as its object, but must be aware of its object as a subject. Otherwise it would never be in contact with Jesus himself, but only with that in him which was originally implicit in the question.

Thus we cannot conclude our discussion of questions about Christ without pointing to the remarkable circumstance that in the synoptic gospels the question of Christ is not only posed to Jesus by others, but is also asked by Jesus himself.[52] Jesus is presented not only as the answer to the question which man asks, but as himself asking the disciples who he is. 'Who do men say that the Son of Man is?' They reply, 'Some say John the Baptist, others say Elijah, and others Jeremiah or one of the prophets.' The follows the question 'Who do you say that I am?' Peter replies, 'You are the Christ, the Son of the living God.' And Jesus replies: 'Blessed are you, Simon Bar-Jona! For flesh and blood has not revealed this to you, but my Father who is in heaven' (Matt. 16.13ff.). The passage shows how contemporaries thought of Jesus, on the pattern of great figures of the salvation history of the past, as *prophetus redivivus*. Jesus' question about himself to his disciples was not, as his answer to Peter's confession of faith shows, a curious test question, but an open question. Thus the Jesus of the synoptic gospels is speaking indirectly of himself.

The claim he made could obviously not be comprehended in one of the titles of Israel's tradition of salvation history, or one of the titles in the history of the hope of a later Israel. It is as though he wanted first of all to draw out a recognition of himself, as if he depended upon the revelation of himself through God and those who believed in him. The question of his historical self-consciousness or self-understanding, whether he called himself 'Son of Man' or 'Christ', is never answered unambiguously. It is more important to realize that according to the synoptic gospels the earthly Jesus lived in a way which was singularly open to the one from whom he awaited his revelation, and that he spoke in relation to the future which his identity would bring about. It is also important that it is he himself who calls his disciples to answer him. 'He existed for the one who he was to be,' O. Weber rightly says.[53] Here, however, he is actually pointing beyond his own earthly reality into a future the freedom of which he respects . . . (he is) in the totality of his being an enigma, a question, a promise, demanding fulfilment and response,' says E. Käsemann.[54] The life, words and actions of the Jesus of the synoptic gospels are centred not upon himself, but on the future which is called the 'kingdom of God'. His God and Father is to reveal him as the one who he truly is. The kingdom of God, which he proclaimed to be imminent and realized in practice, shows him as the one who he is in truth. What Matthew explicitly presents as a question about Christ put by Jesus himself to the disciples, was, as far as we can tell historically, a basic feature in Jesus' actual life.

No customary or current conception, no title or office which Jewish tradition and expectation held in readiness, serves to authenticate his mission, or exhausts the secret of his being . . . We thus learn to understand that the secret of his being could only reveal itself to his disciples in his resurrection.[55]

It is above all in the exceptional claim of Jesus, which goes beyond all traditional and contemporary titles, that the starting point for the formation of christology is to be found.[56] If Jesus had appeared as a rabbi or a prophet in the succession of Moses, he would have raised no questions. Only the fact that he is, and acts as though he were, someone different from the figures which his age remembered and hoped for raises a question about him. Thus it is he, he himself, who first raises the specific question of Christ. In his words and in his life, Jesus is open and dependent upon what is to come from God. The question about himself which according to Matthew he asks of the disciples, derives from the fact that he is open to the future and that his centre is outside himself. By the answer of faith the disciples place themselves within this openness to the future, accept his truth by their confession of faith, and hope at the same time to be revealed with him in his future.

What are these answers of faith to the open question presented by Jesus? They begin by recalling the memory of similar figures in the past, Moses, the prophets and the Baptist. They then recollect the hope of Israel, the Messiah, the Son of Man, the Son of David. Thus the staggering novelty of Jesus is first of all conceived by their recollection of the past, or of what has previously been promised. Consequently, the expectation of the renewal of Israel, the return of its earliest days and the restitution of Zion came to be associated with him. But the future for which Jesus lived and of which he spoke presents a different appearance. It is no longer the righteousness of God glorified in the law, but that righteousness revealing itself in prevenient grace. This departure from the continuum of Israel's salvation history and the development of its hopes also made the novelty in Jesus a scandal, and led to his rejection and crucifixion. When the disciples proclaimed the resurrection of the crucified Jesus, they were proclaiming the future of the crucified Christ, a novelty which is determined by the very difference of Jesus, to which his crucifixion bears witness. And therefore the novelty represented by Jesus can no longer be described by recalling anything similar in history or in the future hope, and becomes an open question, which demands answers which are a confession of faith. The titles from history and the future hope are changed, applied to the novelty which is Jesus and, as we say, are reinterpreted. But basically the novelty in Jesus cannot be contained in the category of repetition, and recollection itself is changed. What 'Son of Man' or 'Christ' now mean can no longer be rooted in the reality of the sufferings and expectations of Israel, but must find their realization in the person and the history of Jesus. This made the way open for a degree of creativity in Christian faith. It was set free by the novelty in Jesus and by the question which he represented. The question of Christ in the form 'Who do you say that I am?' is posed by Jesus himself and by the twofold conclusion of his life, from life into death and from death into new life. The fact that the centre of his existence is outside himself, and that the end of his life is open in two directions, has determined the scope of this question. If he exists for the sake of the one who is to be, then his question and his openness to the future are greater than all the answers which believers and non-believers can give. This question of Christ can only be answered by a new creation, in which the novelty which is Jesus is no longer a novelty, and his cross is no longer a scandal, and in which they have become the basis and the light of the kingdom. By confessing Jesus as the Christ, faith also confesses that this future of his is real. Its confession of Jesus does him justice when it also anticipates the future for the sake of which he existed, died and was raised. Consequently, when faith confesses Christ, this cannot be a final ontological or factual judgment, which could only ever relate to a closed reality. Nor can it be an arbitrary subjective value-judgment on the basis of devout experience. If it is in accordance with Jesus himself, it is an anticipatory judgment of trust and confidence, and therefore, for all its certainty with regard to the person and mission of Jesus, is nevertheless provisional in an eschatological sense. For it anticipates the future in which, as the Revelation of John (5.12) says, 'Worthy is the Lamb who was slain, to receive power and wealth and wisdom and might and honour and glory and blessing!' and 'God will wipe away every tear from their eyes' (7.17). The confession of faith takes the form of an anticipatory doxology. In the 'unredeemed world' it is already a demonstrative expression of the rejoicing of the redemption, and by this very fact makes suffering because of the 'unredeemed world' a conscious pain. For faith too, then, the question of Christ which is raised by the novelty in Jesus and his history is greater than all the titles attributed to him which describe him as 'the eschatological event'. For the openness of the person and history of Jesus is open, beyond the believer's confession of faith, to the new creation and the liberation of the whole longing creation. It is therefore not closed either by faith or by the church, but only by the redemption itself, that is, by new and liberated being. Thus it is profoundly significant that the name of Jesus and his history remain fixed, as fixed as his death, whereas the titles of Christ which are a response to his openness are historically changeable with the passing of time, and in fact change history.

Thus christology is essentially unconcluded and permanently

in need of revision. In its very concentration upon Jesus and his history, Christianity is in the fullest sense *pro-visio* and *promissus*, for it points forward to the new age and new creation, in which the crucified Christ can no longer be a scandal and foolishness, because he has become the basis of the proclamation 'I make all things new' (Rev. 21.5). And therefore the confession of faith in Jesus concludes with the future hope, 'Amen. Come, Lord Jesus!' (22.20), and thereby places the true starting point at the end.

NOTES

1. A. von Harnack, *What is Christianity?*, reprinted New York 1957, 1.
2. The expression 'person and history of Jesus' which will be used in this chapter is meant to denote Jesus himself in his history with his God and 'Father' and with man, as it is integrally presented in the twofold ending of his life: cross and resurrection. History comes about in a person, and a person comes into being in his history. Thus history is an interaction between partners. In the case of Jesus, his history is determined by his relationship to the God whom he called 'my Father' and whose kingdom he proclaimed, and at the same time through his relationship with his contemporaries, Pharisees and publicans, rich and poor, enemies and disciples, to mention the main representatives. We sum up these circumstances of his life, death and resurrection in the term 'history'.
3. The expression 'witness' is a juristic term in the New Testament. The believers understood themselves to be witnesses in the trial between God and his world over his creation. The expression has nothing to do with testimonies to the feelings of a splendid soul. On this see O. Michel, 'Zeuge und Zeugnis. Zur neutestamentlichen Traditionsgeschichte', in *Festschrift für O. Cullmann*, 1971.
4. This 'new quest' of the historical Jesus arose with criticism of Bultmann's kerygma theology in his school by E. Käsemann, 'The Problem of the Historical Jesus', in *Essays on New Testament Themes*, SCM Press 1964, 15–47; E. Fuchs, 'The Quest of the Historical Jesus', in *Studies of the Historical Jesus*, SCM Press 1964, 11–31; G. Ebeling, 'Kerygma and the Historical Jesus', in *Theology and Proclamation*, Collins 1966, 32–81. Cf. James M. Robinson, *A New Quest of the Historical Jesus*, SCM Press 1959, and H. Ristow and K. Matthiae, *Der historische Jesus und der kerygmatische Christus*, [2]1961; also R. Bultmann, 'The Primitive Christian Kerygma and the Historical Jesus', in Carl E. Braaten and Roy A. Harrisville (eds.), *The Historical Jesus and the Kerygmatic Christ*, New York and Nashville 1964. I do not believe Bultmann's rejection of the inner legitimation of the message of Christ by Jesus himself and his history to be justified; it is determined by a dogmatic concept of the kerygma.
5. This question has been taken up in particular by W. Pannenberg, *Jesus—God and Man*, SCM Press 1968. I agree with him about the

unreliability of this information, but differ from him in the conclusions I draw.

6. On this see F. Hahn, *Christologische Hoheitstitel. Ihre Geschichte im frühen Christentum*, 1962.

7. Here I challenge the thesis of H. Braun, 'Der Sinn der neutestamentlichen Christologie', *ZThK* 54, 1957, 341ff. and 'Die Problematik einer Theologie des Neuen Testaments', *ZThK* 57, 1961, Beiheft 2, 3ff., according to which the self-understanding of the believer is the constant and christology is the variable.

8. G. Ebeling, op. cit., 50f.

9. M. Kähler, *Zur Lehre von der Versöhnung*, 1898, 258; otherwise often 'the two-sided conclusion of the life of Jesus'.

10. M. Kähler, 'Das Kreuz. Grund und Mass der Christologie', in *Schriften zur Christologie und Mission*, ThB 42, 1971, 328: 'The cross with its universal claim, with its universal appeal and its universal effect . . . this cross, as it reveals the living God in the incomparable, demands his worship, demands christology.'

11. Critical demythologizing of scripture and tradition can be understood as such revisionism. According to Bultmann, its criteria lie in the transformation of the world picture and in the cross of Christ. Unfortunately he has not always made a clear enough distinction between the two criteria.

12. See K. Homann, 'Geschichtlosigkeit', *Historisches Wörterbuch der Philosophie*, ed. J. Ritter, vol. 2, and R. Seidenberg, *Posthistoric Man*, 1950; A. Gehlen, *Studien zur Anthropologie und Soziologie*, 1963; C. Lévi-Strauss, *The Savage Mind*, Weidenfeld and Nicolson 1966. Technocracy, conservatism and structuralism here combine in a common attempt 'to end' history.

13. I am not in favour of an anarchistic iconoclasm, since I do not follow Novalis and Bakunin in believing in the fruitfulness of chaos. I am arguing for an iconoclasm of the crucified Christ, because in him, not only the first but also the second commandment seem to me to be fulfilled. G. Vahanian has initiated investigations into the iconoclastic elements in Christian faith. Cf. *The Death of God. The Culture in our Post-Christian Era*, New York 1957.

14. This starting-point for theology recurs in a different form in P. Tillich and R. Bultmann: 'God is the answer to the question which lies in the finitude of man' (*Systematic Theology* I, Nisbet 1953, 234; 'The Idea of God and Modern Man', *Journal for Theology and the Church*, vol. 2, New York 1965, 89 n.27).

15. Athanasius, *De incarnatione* 54: 'For he was made man that we might be made God; and he manifested himself by a body that we might receive the idea of the unseen Father; and he endured the insolence of men that we might inherit immortality.'

16. R. Seeberg, *Lehrbuch der Dogmengeschichte* I (1922), 1965, 333.

17. So too G. Ebeling, op. cit., 35.

18. As does W. Pannenberg with an uncritical acceptance of terminology from K. Barth and O. Weber, op. cit., 33ff. Similarly P. Hodgson,

Jesus—Word and Presence. An Essay in Christology, New York 1971, 6off.

19. W. Pannenberg, op. cit., 35.

20. This openness-fulfilment pattern was continually used for the verification of revelation. Cf. J. Moltmann, 'Gottesoffenbarung und die Wahrheitsfrage', in *Perspektiven der Theologie*, 1968, 13ff.

21. See D. Henrich, *Der ontologische Gottesbeweis. Sein Problem und seine Geschichte in der Neuzeit*, 1960.

22. G. W. F. Hegel, *Phenomenology of Mind*, rev. ed. Allen and Unwin 1931, 80: 'In my view . . . everything depends on grasping and expressing the ultimate truth not as substance but as subject as well.' See D. Henrich, *Hegel im Kontext*, 1971, 95.

23. F. von Baader, *Über den Zwiespalt des religiosen Glaubens und Wissens* . . . (1833), 1957, 61: 'In the same way Descartes paved the way for atheism with his *"Cogito ergo sum"*, by presupposing that creation reflects on God's primal thought, against which man can and should not say other than "I am seen, looked through, known, thought, understood and therefore see, know, think, understand. I am willed, desired, loved, therefore I will, desire, love or hate. I am made, and therefore I make."'

24. G. W. F. Hegel, *Philosophy of Religion*, Routledge and Kegan Paul, reprinted 1968, vol. 3, p. 303: 'Man knows God only in so far as God Himself knows Himself in Man. This knowledge is God's self-consciousness, but it is at the same time a knowledge of God on the part of Man, and this knowledge of God by Man is a knowledge of Man by God.' Cf. also Vol. III, 45.

25. E. Jüngel, *Paulus und Jesus*, 1962, 82ff. attempts a similar reversal in respect of the historical objectivity and subjectivity of Jesus himself. It is important 'to do historical work as theological work. In that case by "historical Jesus" we would have to understand Jesus himself as the one to be investigated, in that as subject he becomes the object of historical investigation which has to correspond to his claim as a historical phenomenon (subject) in its objectivation.'

26. J. G. Fichte, *Die Anweisung zum seligen Leben oder auch die Religionslehre* (1806), 1962, 90; *Über die Bestimmung des Gelehrten* (1805), 1959.

27. F. W. J. Schelling, *Werke* I, 5, 292, 452.

28. G. W. F. Hegel, op. cit., 98.

29. I. A. Dorner, *Entwicklungsgeschichte der Lehre von der Person Christi* II, ²1851, 374.

30. On this see the detailed account by H. Küng, *Menschwerdung Gottes*, 1970, 207ff.

31. R. Bultmann, *Essays*, SCM Press 1955, 286. Cf. also F. Gogarten, *Gericht oder Skepsis*, 1937, 122 (against Karl Barth): 'Does faith know the eternal Son of God by knowing the man Jesus Christ, or does it know the man Jesus Christ by knowing the eternal Son of God?' F. Schleiermacher did not pose any alternatives here, but merely saw a question of method. 'We could treat the whole doctrine of Christ either as that of His activity, for then the dignity must naturally follow from that, or as that of His

dignity, for the activity must then result of itself' (*The Christian Faith*, T. & T. Clark 1928, §92, 3).

32. Paul had already inserted the phrase 'even to death on the cross' as the most concrete fact about Jesus in the pattern of humiliation and exaltation of the early Christian hymns in Phil. 2.8. Cf. E. Käsemann, 'Kritische Analyse von Phil. 2.5–11', in *Exegetische Versuche und Besinnungen* I, 51ff. H. Küng, op. cit., 375, rightly asks of the christology of Hegel: 'The only question is whether a basic christological conception can be convincing without the concrete Christ . . .'

33. Cf. T. Koch, *Differenz und Versöhnung. Eine Interpretation der Theologie G. W. F. Hegels nach seiner Wissenschaft der Logik*, 1967, 21ff.

34. This should distinguish a Christian theological critique of Hegel from the atheistic-messianic criticism of the lack of hope for redemption in Hegel's philosophy of reconciliation, as has become customary through E. Bloch. On the other hand, it is not possible to exploit Hegel's idea of reconciliation against the 'theology of hope', which is what happens with P. Cornehl, *Die Zukunft der Versöhnung*, 1971, unless one changes the reconciliation of the world through God, which has taken place in the crucified Christ, into a reality of reconciliation which is claimed to be present in modern Christianity. See M. Theunissen, 'Die Verwirklichung der Vernunft', *Philosophische Rundschau*, Beiheft 6, 1970, 89: 'The Jew believes in the coming of a salvation which is completely lacking in the present; the Christian in the objective anticipation of salvation in the event of redemption. Unlike the former, the latter is in constant danger of projecting the reconciliation which has already been made on to the objects in the world which surround him.'

35. I have taken over this apt distinction from J. B. Metz, *Theology of the World*, 56ff.

36. J. G. Herder, *Werke*, ed. Suphan, 13, 290.

37. On this see E. Günther, *Die Entwicklung der Lehre von der Person Christi im 19. Jahrhundert*, 1911.

38. W. Pannenberg, op. cit., 45, rightly speaks of a 'modesty of soteriological interest'.

39. I. Kant, *Der Streit der Fakultäten*, A50, 51, 57, 70.

40. I. Kant, *Religion with the Limits of Reason Alone*, reprinted New York 1960, 54f.; *Grundlegung der Metaphysik der Sitten*, Akademieausgabe, 408.

41. F. Schleiermacher, *The Christian Faith*, T. & T. Clark 1928, §94, cf. §11, §93.4, §100, p. 385.

42. Ibid., §93.2, p. 379.

43. Ibid., §99, §99.1, pp. 417f.

44. A. Tholuck, *Guido und Julius. Die Lehre von der Sünde und dem Versöhner*, 1823, 296. Similarly M. Kähler: 'When the human situation and historical Christianity come together in a man to form a living experience, we have the decisive basis for the origin of faith' (quoted by J. Wirsching, *Gott in der Geschichte. Studien zur theologiegeschichtlichen Stellung und systematischen Grundlegung der Theologie M. Kählers*, 1963, 64, n.84).

45. J. Wirsching rightly criticizes Kähler's theology with this expression.

46. D. F. Strauss, *The Life of Jesus Critically Examined*, reprinted SCM Press 1973, 779f.; on this Kähler remarked with some irony: 'Certainly not; for this is nothing but the general concept stripped of all special life, the empty canvas on which pictures may be painted. One looks in vain even for the ideal in the tradition of Jesus of Nazareth' (op. cit., 342).

47. Shalom Ben-Chorin, *Die Antwort des Jona*, 1956, 99.

48. Gershom Sholem, 'Zum Verständnis der messianischen Idee im Judentum', in *Judaica* I, 1963, 7f. Cf. also F. Rosenzweig, *Der Stern der Erlösung*, [2]1954, 97ff., 178f.

49. R. Bultmann, *History and Eschatology*, Edinburgh University Press 1957, 38ff. stresses only this side.

50. H. J. Iwand, *Die Gegenwart des Kommenden*, 1955, 37.

51. This has been described very impressively by E. Fackenheim, 'The Commandment to Hope. A Response to Contemporary Jewish Experience', in *The Future of Hope*, ed. W. Capps, Philadelphia 1970, 68ff.

52. H. Vogel, *Christologie* I, 1949, has drawn attention to this.

53. O. Weber, *Grundlagen der Dogmatik* II, 1962, 75.

54. E. Käsemann, *New Testament Questions of Today*, SCM Press 1969, 123f.

55. G. Bornkamm, *Jesus of Nazareth*, Hodder and Stoughton 1960, 178; similarly E. Schweizer, *Jesus*, SCM Press 1971, 22.

56. P. Vielhauer, *Aufsätze zum Neuen Testament* ,ThB 31, 1965, 90.

4

THE HISTORICAL TRIAL OF JESUS

The two following chapters deal with the historical and the eschatological trial of Jesus. We shall attempt to achieve an understanding of the crucified Christ, first of all in the light of his life and ministry, which led to his crucifixion, and then in the light of the eschatological faith which proclaims his resurrection from the dead, and in so doing proclaims him as the Christ. The understanding of the death of Jesus depends upon the point of view from which one attempts to understand his death: 'Whether from the point of view of the life Jesus lived, or from that of the relationship of God to the life which he lived and which was ended in this way.'[1] But these must not be one-sided alternatives. To understand his death solely in the light of his resurrection would rapidly lead to a Christ-myth in which the death of the bringer of salvation was an important fact, but not Jesus himself and what brought him to the cross. If his death were considered only in the light of the life he lived, ultimately neither the death nor the life of Jesus would have any special importance beyond that of the comparable life and death of great prophets or demagogues. If it is *the same* Jesus who was crucified and rose from the dead—and this must be the starting point of Christian faith—then only an integral consideration from both points of view, constantly relating to the two aspects to each other, can do him justice.

The modern dilemma lies in the fact that the two sides can no longer be reduced to a common denominator. The choice is made between *Jesuology*, referring to the earthly Jesus, accessible to historical investigation and capable of human imitation, and *christology*, referring to the Christ whom faith and the church proclaim. But this leads to fatal divisions in theology and in the life of Christianity.[2]

Jesuology had occupied the foreground since the early days of the historical Enlightenment, but the development of radical historical scepticism and historical positivism brought a new and different emphasis upon christology.[3]

The very title of the book by M. Kähler, *The So-Called Historical Jesus and the Historic, Biblical Christ* is characteristic of this.[4] R. Bultmann's books *Jesus and the Word, Primitive Christianity in its Historical Setting* and more recently 'The Primitive Christian Kerygma and the Historical Jesus' have only made this dilemma more intense.[5]

The problem has been produced by the inevitable task of critical historical scholarship. This has made it increasingly difficult to reduce to a common denominator the historical and the theological, history and eschatology, as they relate to Jesus Christ. The understanding of the death of Jesus in the light of the life which he lived seems to be a purely historical task. The interpretation of the Christian Easter faith seems to be a purely theological task. In the pages which follow, however, we will attempt to treat *the historical task* of describing the death of Jesus within the framework of his life as a *theological task*; for his life, preaching and ministry, and his death too, were in his own mind theologically determined. We shall then approach the *theological task* of setting forth and interpreting the Easter faith as a *historical task*, in so far as all statements of faith concerning his resurrection and exaltation by God and his functions as Christ, Kyrios and Son of God are related to his life and his death. Our starting point here will be a reciprocal relationship between historical and eschatological method. In the historical account, birth precedes life, and life precedes death. The past can be narrated, and every narration, like enumeration, begins at the beginning and proceeds to the end. But in the direction of eschatological anticipation, the last must come first, the future precedes the past, the end reveals the beginning and objective time-relationships are reversed. 'History as recollection' and 'history as hope', within the 'hope in the form of recollections' which is the determining element of Christian faith, are not contradictory, but must be complementary.[6]

The expression 'trial' is used in the following chapters in its broadest sense, and refers both to a legal trial concerning the truth and also a historical trial. Thus the 'trial of Jesus' does not mean, in the narrow sense, his trial before the Sanhedrin or Pilate, but the struggle for the truth of God in which he came forward as a witness; while from the other point of view it refers to the 'trial about Jesus' in the judgment of God, in which his witnesses speak up on his behalf. The expression moves from one significance to another, but this makes it more fertile. Behind its use lies the view that history is better understood in the categories of a legal trial and of a struggle for righteousness, life and freedom than in naturalistic categories.

1. *The Question of the Origin of Christology*

M. Kähler, as a previous quotation shows, regarded the cross of Christ as the origin of christology: 'Without the cross there is no christology, nor is there any feature in christology which can escape justifying itself by the cross.'[7] He was not attempting here to reduce christology to a single theme, but to draw christology, and with it the whole of Christian theology, within the range defined by the cross. The crucified Christ, in his view, was to be the key for all the divine secrets of Christian theology. His theses are sometimes still advanced at the present day. But even when they are repeated with approval, they still do not sound as though they have been 'decoded'.[8] They do not deal with the issues of the christological task of present-day theology. If his theses, and those of Luther, which are similar, are not to remain credal acclamations, they must be tested in the form of historical and theological debate about the origin of christology.

The question of the *origin* of christology unites a historical and an exegetical interest in the *early stages* of christology and an interest on the part of systematic theology in the permanent *basis* of christology. Here we are touching on the question of the intrinsic basis of the christology of faith, in Jesus and his history. Do Jesus and his history themselves legitimize the preaching of Jesus as the Christ? Is the preaching of the church in continuity and harmony with Jesus and his history?

This is a *historical question*, in so far as the exegesis of primitive Christian proclamations does not confine itself to elucidating what they express in terms of their formal categories and as religious phenomena, but goes on to test these statements continually against what they state; and this it must do if it is to do the work of historical criticism. It is not enough to identify what these testimonies say about how the believer understands his existence. Critical scholarship must also ask what the testimonies have to say about those to whom they bear witness, and what faith has to say about the one who is the object of faith, and whether it is in accordance with him.[9] Thus the central question about the origin of christology is this: How did Jesus who preached become Jesus Christ who was preached? Why and in what way did the 'witness of faith' become the 'basis of faith'?[10] What is the relationship between the primitive Christian gospel of Christ and the historical Jesus? What justification was there for the church to proclaim Jesus as the Christ after his public execution on the cross?

This is also a *theological question*; for every Christian must ask whether his faith in Jesus Christ is true and is in accordance with Jesus himself, or whether Christian tradition offers him or itself something different instead, an idea, a spirit or a phantom.[11] The way in which faith turns back to Jesus and his history in self-criticism derives from faith itself. The task of theological reflection is to carry out this questioning in a methodical fashion and to help faith to distinguish itself from its own superstition and its own unbelief and to seek the truth of Jesus himself.

It can carry out this task only if it conducts theological work on historical lines, without losing sight of its own ends.

The questioning which works back from the christological traditions of the church to the truth of Jesus may be impelled by a number of different concerns. But it is always a contemporary problem.

Let us outline three ways in which this questioning can take place.

1. In the New Testament itself, the truth of Jesus Christ is put on trial in the debate between different churches and traditions. This trial gave rise to the Christian creeds. In the earliest days, the Easter faith gave rise to different forms of Christian Judaism and enthusiastic Christian gnosis; then, as the gospels were written, the experiences of Christ and the Spirit at the present moment were subjected to criticism and linked to the history of Jesus himself. The danger that the veneration of a being of the spirit or heavenly world might replace the recollection of Jesus was recognized by Paul in the Corinthian church, and his answer was the preaching of Jesus crucified. In this way he intensified the identification of the exalted Lord with Jesus who was crucified

on Golgotha, but did not contrast the earthly crucified Jesus with
the risen Christ.

For if primitive Christianity identifies the humiliated with the exalted
Lord, in so doing it is confessing that, in its presentation of his story, it is
incapable of abstracting from its faith. At the same time, however, it is
also making it clear that it is not minded to allow myth to take the place of
history nor a heavenly being to take the place of the Man of Nazareth.[12]

This process of looking back critically and recalling the earthly
Jesus assumed a faith in the exalted Christ and the hope of his
coming again, and kept faith and hope located in the identity of
Jesus Christ; this is expressed in the couplet 'crucified-risen'
(Rom. 10.6). This questioning of the past did not take the form
here of explicit historical criticism, but in accordance with its
purpose introduced into the christological traditions of primitive
Christianity, as their criterion, the indispensable association of all
statements about Christ with the *name of Jesus*. The trial undertaken by primitive Christianity concerning the truth of Christ
derived its unifying factor from this. One might say that in the
disputes of early Christianity, the name of Jesus became the
primary mark of what could be called Christian and regarded as
proper to the church. It became the basis and standard of the
early christologies.

2. In the Reformation, the trial in which the truth of Christ was
sought was conducted on the basis of the conflict between scripture
and tradition. The Reformation principle *sola scriptura* took the
place of the basic principle *solus Christus*. 'The scriptures' became
the criterion of the true preaching and church of Christ against the
false church which, in addition to him and beyond him, believed
that it had the duty of teaching, demanding and propagating a
great deal else. Thus for Protestantism the basis and standard of
church doctrines came to be that they should be *in accordance
with scripture*.[13] And in its turn, the standard of what was in
accordance with scripture was for Luther the justifying gospel,
or 'what is about Christ', as he put it. Any theology which by this
criterion is in accordance with scripture and critical of tradition
can be called 'Reformation theology', not because it goes back to a
Reformation in the sixteenth century, but because it makes and
must make continual reforming claims concerning preaching, the
church and life. In the light of scripture and the Christ who was

crucified to justify sinners, the church who bears witness to him becomes *ecclesia reformata et semper reformunda*.

3. The quest for the 'historical Jesus' as a criterion appeared only in association with the historical and critical thought of the modern age; but it makes similar claims. The motive of the quest for the historical Jesus was the attempt to set free the portrait of the historical Jesus from the accretions of church christologies and, behind them, the accretions of the post-Easter kerygma of primitive Christianity, in order to encounter *Jesus himself* without what those who venerated and followed him had made of him. The 'historical Jesus' was to be 'Jesus himself'. This quest of the historical Jesus was not merely a 'noble act of truthfulness on the part of the German spirit', as A. Schweitzer and P. Tillich said,[14] but is a direct successor of the continuing christological revisionism set in motion by the critical theology of the Reformation. But historical criticism in the name of the historical Jesus not only directed ideological criticism against church doctrines, but also criticized the testimonies of the primitive Christian faith in Christ which are gathered together in the scriptures. The standard by which a doctrine could be judged to be in accordance with scripture, that of the apostolicity, sufficiency and unambiguity of scripture, collapsed in the face of the disagreements and errors which historians unearthed in scripture. It was replaced by the general scientific standard of knowledge firmly based on historical criticism. It made faith a matter of arbitrary choice and located the basis of faith in man's free subjectivity.

The result of the enquiry of historical criticism into the Jesus behind the traditions can be summed up from two points of view. It stumbled upon the discontinuity in time and the difference in content between Jesus' preaching of the kingdom and the preaching of Christ by primitive Christianity. At the same time, it stumbled upon a multitude of continuities in the tradition and analogies in content. This is not surprising, since historical knowledge can perceive differences only in the framework of common factors, and common factors only amongst differences. Discontinuity is recognizable in history only within continuity, a fact to which the terminology itself bears witness. And continuity becomes an issue and gives rise to utterance only when there is a perception of discontinuity.[15] Discontinuity cannot signify a complete lack of connection, because it is impossible either to perceive or to express such a thing. Continuity cannot signify direct and unmediated identity, because no history within time can contain such a thing. In history identity and difference belong together in a dialectic, just as analogy and novelty belong together in historical knowledge. It is impossible to give expression to a novelty without a parallel, as Marcion already felt obliged to assert with regard to Jesus. A historical novelty is never totally new. Some dream or promise always comes first.[16] On the other hand, analogies lose their illuminative power if they assume that everything that happens is essentially the same.[17] Exclusive alternatives are impossible. But when particular *concerns* are associated with the twofold possibilities of historical knowledge, then alternatives arise. Historical criticism may emphasize that the church's faith in Christ has very little to do with Jesus of Nazareth. In this case, historical criticism is associating itself with man's concern to be emancipated from tradition, the church and authority: 'The historical consciousness breaks the last chains which philosophy and natural science could not tear off. Now man is completely free.'[18] Here the concern of the historical consciousness is to set the subjectivity of man free from the prejudices and guardians of the institutional traditions of Christianity, which also sets it free with regard to Jesus. But the historical consciousness can also elucidate the humanity of Jesus of Nazareth. Here its concern is to educate present-day man to be more human. The authority of the heavenly Christ within the churches is replaced by a Jesus who is stylized as a teacher of morality and the brother of all men, and who is made comprehensible, as a human being, to other human beings. Here the aim of the historical consciousness is no longer the emancipation of man from traditions and history, but an understanding of human existence in the past for the purpose of one's own human life within history. The first aim of its interpretation is to make the tradition a present reality. But this assumes that there is a continuous factor within the traditions and something which men share throughout history. Here it is possible for the long-standing question of humanity to be completely re-expressed within the programme of an existentialist interpretation: 'Man's quest for meaningful existence is his highest stimulus to scholarly enquiry: consequently a serious quest of the historical Jesus must have meaning in terms of man's quest for meaningful existence.'[19] If this quest on the part of man for existence, a quest given its theme by death, is taken as a continuous factor throughout history, with all its differences and fresh starts, and if the historicity of existence is taken as a fundamental category for history altogether, then this concern encounters analogies between Jesus' understanding of himself and believers' understanding of themselves, between the preaching of Jesus and the preaching of Christ in the primitive church; for both face man, in a similar way, with the eschatological decision about his existence. But analogies are not genealogies. The ultimate legitimation of the Christian kerygma in Jesus himself and in his history is no longer called into question. The essential common factor which goes beyond the differences of time and circumstance is found here in a claim, a desire or an understanding of existence. Then a questionable anthropology really is providing the constants, and the christology which is being questioned the variables.

The disagreements between R. Bultmann and his pupils who have undertaken the new quest of the historical Jesus show that the common factors cannot remove 'the fundamental difference between his (i.e. Jesus') preaching and the kerygma of Christ', as Bultmann emphasizes; nor can this difference remove the common factors, as his pupils emphasize.[20] Thus the quest must begin at a more profound level than hitherto, in order to avoid the 'dead ends in the dispute about the historical Jesus' (E. Käsemann).

If theological study is to be carried out as historical study, there is no way of avoiding the possibilities of the historical knowledge of dialectic historical connections. Therefore the opposite task must be attempted, of regarding historical study as theological study;[21] i.e., in this case the relationship of the primitive Christian gospel to the historical Jesus must be understood as the theme of christology. But this means in the first instance that the intimate link between Jesus' preaching and his person must be taken seriously, and attention must be paid to the significance of his death on the cross for his preaching and for the primitive Christian kerygma. For his death is not simply a turning-point in history which can be compared with others, or one amongst many discontinuities in history. The true critique of the kerygma of Christ is to be found in the history of Jesus, which had its earthly end when he died, abandoned by God, on the cross.

The approach from the point of view of the history of ideas has increasingly shown the differences between the preaching of Jesus and the kerygma of Christ. 'The point which was everything to Paul was nothing to Jesus.'[22] 'For Paul, Jesus himself is the object not only of faith, but of religious veneration . . . this is something completely new by comparison with the preaching of Jesus . . . I see here a gap which no theological skill can bridge.'[23] 'Jesus' teaching is—to all intents and purposes—irrelevant for Paul.'[24] If we go beyond the approach of the history of ideas and look for the substance which was recognized and given utterance in these 'ideas', the picture changes. We owe this more profound understanding to Rudolf Bultmann.[25] The preaching of Jesus, like that of Paul, is eschatological preaching; in the case of Jesus, the preaching of the kingdom of God; in the case of Paul, of the righteousness of God. The difference between them is not the superficial one of changed ideas, but is determined by their different theological situation. For Paul, that which for Jesus was the future is the present or the future of God inaugurated in the history of Jesus. The differences arose not from the further development of the teaching of Jesus, but from an apprehension of the changed situation of the essential substance itself. Jesus speaks and acts with respect to the dominion of God which is to come and is now coming into being. Paul speaks and acts with regard to the dominion of God which has already been inaugurated in the crucifixion and the resurrection of Jesus, and the righteousness of God which has already been revealed. Thus their situations are determined by an event which they understand theologically. The difference in their theological situations is determined by a shift in the *eschaton* itself, from that of a future which is just beginning to a future which has already begun. Thus the eschatological event as it were lies behind the preaching of Paul, in which it is proclaimed as the Christ event. Apart from this intrinsic assumption, his preaching is incomprehensible. But according to Bultmann, this is also true of Jesus himself. He understands his preaching eschatologically. The true novelty was not *what* he preached. John the Baptist had already preached the imminence of the kingdom. But *the fact that* Jesus preached it, that it was *he* who preached it, and *the way* in which he preached—all this was new. What Jesus preached, on the level of the history of language and concept, can largely be reduced to the traditions of contemporary Judaism. According to Bultmann, the content of his preaching is pure prophetism or radicalized *Torah*.[26] But the fact that he now announces the kingdom of God which was yet to come, the fact that he says this and the way in which he says it, were so novel that they led to his crucifixion. For him to announce his hour as 'the last hour' and to characterize a decision for his person and his message as the eschatological decision is novel. Thus Bultmann emphasized that it is not the content but the fact of his preaching which is decisive. One must not overlook the fact that by contrast with prophets, Pharisees and Zealots, the content of his preaching also changed and became new. Beyond the radicalization of the *Torah* which was revealed in Jesus' claim, he proclaimed the righteousness of God as the law of grace, as is shown by the parables and his forgiveness of sins.[27] It was this, in the first instance, which separated Jesus from the circle associated with John the Baptist. In this respect Jesus was also someone other than a pure prophet. Yet Bultmann and Ernst Fuchs are right in pointing to the distinctive nature of the 'announcement of the eschatological moment' in the sayings of Jesus. The verification of the announcement of an eschatological moment does not lie in its harmony with what has been regarded as true 'from of old', but in the *kairos* of the actual time. The announcement of a time can come too early, too late or 'at the right time'. The guarantee of the 'right time' of his proclamation is the time itself, the kingdom proclaimed and the promised forgiveness of sin by God. If we are to understand Jesus' preaching 'kairologically' in this way, the following becomes clear:

1. His preaching is tied to his person, and cannot be transferred to anyone else: 'But *I* say to you . . .', and 'Blessed is he who takes no offence at me.'

2. His preaching is particularly linked with his hour, and his hour with the hour of the kingdom: '*Today* this scripture has been fulfilled in your hearing' (Luke 4.21).

3. It is a concrete promise to concrete human beings to whom he presents himself and his preaching, and thereby, the God who is to come.

As I see it, Bultmann has clearly understood the identification of Jesus with his preaching. He saw this identification as follows: '. . . the person of Jesus is merged in his words. This means also that his Word is event.'[28] It is often only the first part of this identification which is stressed, even by Bultmann himself. But the other side remains: 'His word becomes event (in him).' Not only is the person of Jesus wholly taken up into his word, but his word in its turn is wholly taken up into his person, and becomes event in it. Only when the other side of this identification is understood can we see what it was in his preaching which gave offence: that someone from Nazareth ('Can anything good come out of Nazareth?'), someone who was one of the poor, should proclaim the kingdom and the justification of God to the poor and the sinners. Julius Schniewind always laid particular emphasis upon this.[29] But if the person of Jesus is not only taken up into his word, but his word is also taken up into his person, so that it can no longer be separated from his person, then it cannot be transferred to anyone else. If this other side of the issue is not taken seriously, then it is possible to trace direct continuities in the history of the word of Jesus down to the primitive church; or else to point to the way in which the kerygmatic challenge to faith is firmly maintained; or else there is stress on the maintenance of the 'coming to utterance of God' in the history of Jesus down to the primitive church. Here Jesus and Paul are understood only as different phenomena of the history of faith or of the history of God's coming to utterance. But if we follow Schniewind in taking the other aspect seriously, we are faced with the scandalous fact that the death of Jesus is also the death of his eschatological message through which he brought God to utterance and made the kingdom of God imminent. This means that for Jesus there cannot be disciples of his teaching as there were in the case of Socrates, and after the death of Socrates. His preaching then as it were goes down with him into the grave. And 'the cause of Jesus' cannot 'continue' without having regard to Jesus and his death.[30] If it is true that Jesus' proclamation of the kingdom is associated essentially with his person, and not merely by chance, then no continuities in the field of history, the philosophy of history, the history of language or the history of existential life can bridge the discontinuity which lies in his death. The 'great enigma of New Testament theology, how the proclaimer became the proclaimed',[31] becomes no longer a problem of general history or the philosophy of history, but is the essential problem of Jesus himself, and can only be understood in christological terms. From the point of view of the end to which he came, the historical Jesus is the crucified and dead Jesus. If his preaching is inseparable from his person, then his preaching dies with him on the cross, and there can be no disciples to carry on his teaching or his cause. The true critique of the preaching of Jesus is the outcome of his life and his end upon the cross.[32]

The historical gap introduced by his death, a death as one rejected on the cross, is a radical one in view of the intimate association between his person and his preaching. It cannot be compared with the dialectic association between continuity and discontinuity, likeness and difference in other historical upheavals.

Here, then, the problem of the origin of christology is reduced to the question whether his death on the cross was and still is a refutation of his preaching, or whether behind the preaching of the resurrection of the crucified Jesus there lies the refutation of this refutation by his death. The claim of the preaching of Christ after Easter is consequently directed not merely against unbelief or superstition, but against the reality of death, against this very fact, which is as sure as death. The true criticism of history is then the proclamation that the crucified Jesus has risen. The purpose of this claim is not merely to achieve a new understanding of one-self, but at a more profound level, to bring new being out of non-being. Jesus associated his eschatological word with his human person and his vulnerability, and therefore with the fate which overtook him. This means either that his death represented the end of his eschatological message, or that his message must be proclaimed, on a 'wholly other' basis, as the 'word of the cross'. The preaching of Christ by the primitive church is therefore the apostolic form of Jesus' preaching of the kingdom. Because the preaching of the church, as a result of the fate that overtook Jesus himself, has taken on the form of the crucified one, the church proclaims his message by proclaiming the crucified and risen Christ. 'For Jesus' preaching of the kingdom *could not* be handed on unaltered, since it had an essential link with his person and could never be separated from it; and it *had to be* transformed, since with the death and resurrection of Jesus the *eschaton* had begun, and no disciple could ignore this event, when he spoke of Jesus.'[33] The historical and hermeneutic question, how Jesus who preached became Christ who is preached, is therefore basically the christological question, how the dead Jesus became the living, the crucified the resurrected and the humiliated the exalted. This transcends the other questions and is basically the theological question within christology; for this is the point at which it is necessary to speak of God. Faith in God is faith in the resurrection. The identity of the historical Jesus and the Christ in whom one believes, of the crucified and of the risen Jesus, is the eschatological mystery and lies in the faithfulness of God, who manifests himself to be the same in the abandonment and in the resurrection of Jesus.[34]

Historically and hermeneutically, continuities and differences can be located and described at several levels. There are correspondences between the love shown by faith and the attitude and behaviour of Jesus. There are correspondences between the preaching of Jesus and the kerygma of the church. There are correspondences between the meals which Jesus took with his disciples and the Lord's supper of the church, between the meals which Jesus took with sinners and tax collectors and the *agape* feasts of the church. There are correspondences between the suffering of Jesus and the suffering of the apostles and martyrs. But the legitimation of these analogies is found only in the identity of the person of Christ in the crucifixion and the resurrection, which is determined by theological considerations.

This argument compels the conclusion that the understanding of the crucified Jesus must be the origin of all christology, for otherwise his death on the cross would mean the end of all christology. The crucifixion of Jesus either refuted his preaching in view of his person, or his person in view of his preaching, and so refuted both together; or else his preaching was drawn into his person to the very point of his death, so that on the basis of his resurrection from the dead it had to continue to be preached as the 'word of the cross'. But in that case it can continue to be preached only together with and in the form of the proclamation of his person, that is, in the kerygma of Christ. Either the cross makes every Jesuology and every christology impossible, or else, in association with his resurrection, it makes Jesuology possible as christology, and christology possible as Jesuology.

Let us check this by working out the alternative. Let us accept that sayings of Jesus were received and handed on in isolation from his person after his death. They would then be sayings which, like the truth of the *Torah* or of proverbs, spoke for themselves. Their truth would then have to be demonstrable, even without Jesus, in regard to something else, whether this was the moral law, man's existential questions, or the general experience of life.

But this is not possible for sayings which are directly associated with the person of Jesus and his personal claim. The expression from the antitheses of the Sermon on the Mount: 'But I say to you . . .' cannot be transferred to any other 'I'. Nor can it be handed on as a saying of his, if this 'I' has in the meantime been crucified and is dead. It would then have to read 'But he said to them . . .', and by his death would be inescapably condemned to the past. The preaching of Jesus would therefore have to be depersonalized and transformed into a moral or religious teaching, if anyone were to hand it on after the general recognition of his death. But this would no longer be in accordance with his preaching. Moreover, if the exceptional claim of Jesus lay in his forgiveness of sins, the attempt might be made at least to go on forgiving sins in his name.

But it is impossible to forgive sins in the name of a dead man, particularly if he has died the death of a blasphemer. One could also continue to arouse faith in his name by the kerygma, as Jesus did through his preaching. But what faith can one call for in the name of a dead person? Finally, just as Jesus once anticipated the future kingdom, so it would be possible to stir up hope through eschatological preaching. But how can one arouse hope in the name and in the following of a preacher whose hope was cut off by his death? How can one base hope on good reasons, if the basis of this hope fell prey to death and has long ago decayed in the grave?

Thus ultimately it is not historical criticism which calls into question every church christology and every humanist Jesuology, but the cross. He who proclaimed that the kingdom was near died abandoned by God. He who anticipated the future of God in miracles and in casting out demons died helpless on the cross. He who revealed the righteousness of God with an authority greater than Moses died according to the provision of the law as a blasphemer. He who spread the love of God in his fellowship with the poor and the sinners met his end between two criminals on the cross. Thus in the end the basic problem and the starting point of christology is the scandal and the folly of the cross. In this sense M. Kähler is right: without the cross there is no christology, and there is no christology which does not have to demonstrate its legitimation in the cross.

2. *Jesus' Way to the Cross*

Scarcely any historian now seriously doubts that Jesus of
Nazareth lived at the beginning of our era. By the standards of
historical certainty, his death on the cross can also be regarded
as an assured 'nuclear fact'.[35] But the question of the meaning of
his death on the cross remains open. Death makes one dumb, and
is dumb itself. But this does not mean that any arbitrary religious
or secular interpretation can be put upon his death, for it was 'his
death'. No interpretation of his death can ignore his person and
his ministry. The life and death of Jesus are accessible to us in the
sources only in the context of the interpretations in which his
death was understood and recounted. These are almost exclusively
Christian testimonies. In them the experiences of the Easter faith
have become so intermingled with the *recollections* of the history
of Jesus that it is difficult to separate out the historical kernel.[36]
But as we have seen in the previous section, there are two possible
ways of understanding his death on the cross: we can understand
his violent end in the context of his life, and we can understand it
in the context of the primitive Christian belief in the resurrection.
The retrospective historical understanding and the reflective
understanding of theology must be constantly related to each
other, in so far as they relate to the same person and the same
events which happened to this person. Thus in the three sections
which follow, we shall try to understand the end to which Jesus
came, in the context of his life, by relating it to *his way to the
cross*; then in the four subsequent sections of the next chapter we
shall try to understand his death in the context of his resurrection
by God and of eschatological faith. The first process looks at the
trial of Jesus in the narrower sense, while the second is concerned
with the recapitulation of the trial of Jesus by God and faith in the
resurrection. This brings into an eschatological light not only his
death on the cross, but also his life and his way to the cross, since
the resurrection affects not only his death or his cross in itself,
but his whole person and therefore also his life, preaching and
ministry. It is not his death which is lifted up into the divine life;
it is not his cross which is transfigured; it is the crucified Jesus
who, according to the Easter testimony, is raised and exalted to
become the lord of the future of God. Thus we must understand Jesus' way to the cross not only for the sake of historical

understanding, but even more for the sake of eschatological faith.

Since Jesus was condemned and executed on the cross, he did not die a natural or accidental death, neither of which have much connection with the kind of life one has led, but died because of the action taken against him by his Jewish and Roman contemporaries, provoked by the actions of his own life. Thus his death is also a 'consequence of his ministry'.[37] But because Jesus did not kill himself, his death must be understood in the context of the conflicts between him and the world around him. The *causae crucis* also belong to his crucifixion. His death on the cross was not a fact without any reason, which could be interpreted afterwards in any way. The concepts in which his death is described in the setting of his resurrection and of eschatological faith are not only able to call upon the fact of his death. They must also be able to draw upon the *causae crucis*, in recapitulating the trial and testing of Jesus and going back to the crucified Jesus himself. Without going back to the history of Jesus which led to the cross, no post-Easter interpretations are possible. This must not lead to a biographical description of the life of Jesus, nor to psychological conjectures about his personal evaluation of his suffering and death. The history of Jesus which led to his crucifixion was rather a *theological history* in itself, and was dominated by the conflict between God and the gods; that is, between the God whom Jesus preached as his Father, and the God of the law as he was understood by the guardians of the law, together with the political gods of the Roman occupying power. In biographical terms we have very little interpretation of Jesus' death by himself; such an interpretation occurs at best in the tentative form of the passion prophecies, if they are themselves historical. But his death cannot be understood without his life, and his life cannot be understood without the one for whom he lived, his God and Father, and that for which he lived, the gospel of the kingdom for the poor. A historical understanding of the history of Jesus must understand his history as a theological history defined in this way; otherwise it understands nothing. His death on the cross, however, cannot be understood solely from the more immediate circumstances of his ministry, but only through the interaction between Jesus, the Jews and the Romans. An interpretation of his death in the context of his life therefore goes beyond his life as a private person and must understand the life of Jesus as that of a public person. Consequently, a retroactive interpretation in the light of his resurrection by God must consider the death of Jesus as the consequence of his ministry and as the consequence of the reactions of the Jews and Romans to his ministry. Not until this is done is the testimony to the resurrection by God brought back into the public sphere in which he was crucified and Christian faith made a public testimony in the legitimation of God with regard to Jesus.

(a) Jesus and the law: 'The blasphemer'

Doubts have been expressed whether Jesus was really condemned and executed because of a declared claim to be the Messiah. The cleansing of the temple and the prophecy of the destruction of the temple can also be advanced as the direct reason for his death.[38] But that he was regarded and condemned as a 'blasphemer', as a demagogic false Messiah, is difficult to dispute in view of the whole of his scandalous message. The career of Jesus from Galilee to Jerusalem was unusual and unparalleled.[39] With arrogant authority Jesus proclaimed God as the one who in his eschatological condescension towards lost men is free from the human observance of the prescriptions of the law, and in prevenient love shows gracious mercy towards men. By so doing, Jesus placed his preaching of God, and therefore himself, above the authority of Moses and the *Torah*. This freedom of God is unmistakably manifested in the attitude and behaviour of Jesus, in the antitheses of the Sermon on the Mount, in the call to follow him and in his sovereign transgression of the sabbath commandment. But anyone claiming authority beside and above Moses in fact places himself above Moses and the law, and ceases to be a rabbi, who never possesses any authority other than that derived from Moses.[40] He has also ceased to be a prophet in the succession of Moses. In his ministry Jesus placed himself with sovereign authority above the limits of the contemporary understanding of the law, and demonstrated God's eschatological law of grace towards those without the law and the transgressors of the law, through his forgiveness of sins. By so doing he abolished the legal distinction between religious and secular, righteous and unrighteous, devout and sinful. He revealed God in a different way from that in which he was understood in the law and the tradition and was perceived by the guardians of the law. The acts of forgiveness of sin represent the very culmination of his freedom from the law, for the right of showing mercy belongs to the judge alone. When a man who cannot but be under the law arrogates to himself this exclusive right of a judge, and puts himself in the judge's place, he reaches out his arm towards God and blasphemes the Holy One. This is not the blasphemy of cursing God, according to the law, but the blasphemy of self-deification.[41]

Not only with regard to the law and the tradition of the law, but also with regard to the figures represented in the hopes of prophecy and apocalyptic, the appearance and activity of Jesus was a novelty which was bound to arouse resistance. 'Whereas according to the expectation of the Jews the Son of Man was to appear at the last judgment only as the judge of sinners and the redeemer of the righteous, Jesus actually turned towards the sinners and the lost.'[42] But anyone preaching and acting in this way was abandoning the role attributed to the figures of the messianic hope. They all represented the victory of the righteousness of God according to the law with the exaltation of the righteous who suffer injustice on earth, and the putting to shame of the lawless and godless. The splendour of all their hopes was merely a reflection of the mighty and glorified *Torah* at the end of history. Anyone who preaches the imminent kingdom of God not as judgment, but as the gospel of the justification of sinners by grace, and demonstrates it as such through his life with sinners and tax-collectors, contradicts the hope based upon the law, is deceiving the sinners and tax-collectors and is blaspheming the God of hope. Clearly this drastic novelty and contradiction formed part of the preaching and the ministry of Jesus from the first. It was probably for this reason that he withdrew from the circle of John the Baptist in which he himself had received the baptism of repentance.[43] His preaching was literally the same as that of John: 'The kingdom of God is at hand', but the content of his preaching of this imminent kingdom was different. The kingdom does not come as judgment, so that one must anticipate it in one's self through repentance in order to endure. Rather, anticipated by the word of the gospel which Jesus preached and his living offering of himself to the poor, the sinners and the tax-collectors, it comes as the unconditional and free grace of God, by which the lost are sought out and those without rights, and the unrighteous, are accepted. It is this different and new righteousness of God promised and demonstrated by Jesus which separates him from John the Baptist and his repentance movement in Israel.

Thus Jesus' claim of authority had no legitimizing basis in the traditions of Israel, either in the traditions of the rabbis and Pharisees, or in those of the prophets and of apocalyptic, for all of which the law comes at the beginning and will triumph in its righteousness at the end. Consequently Jesus had to reject the self-characterizations of the rabbis and prophetic apocalyptic. To lay claim to the righteousness of God on behalf of those outside the law, and the transgressors of the law, was in contradiction to the traditions of his people. His authoritative claim to the righteousness of God through grace had, in the light of the traditions which drew on the memory and hope of the history of salvation, no authority at all: that is, his claim was derived directly, and by himself alone, from the God whom he called 'My Father'. In this sense, Jesus was someone anonymous, whose true name derived solely from his authentification by his God and Father, and could be revealed only when the grace which he proclaimed should come.

Anyone who proclaimed the coming of the kingdom and the closeness of God as prevenient and unconditional grace to those who according to the law were rightly rejected and could have no hope, and who demonstrated this coming grace by giving himself to those outside the law and the transgressors of the law, who placed himself above the authority of Moses, and who was all the time no more than 'a carpenter's son from Nazareth', was inevitably bound to come into conflict with the devout and the ruling class and their laws, and from the human point of view was bound to lose this conflict. The conflict was provoked not by his incomprehensible claim to authority as such, but by the discrepancy between a claim which arrogated to itself the righteousness of God and his unprotected and therefore vulnerable humanity. For one 'without office or dignities' to abandon the tradition and lay claim to the office and dignity of God himself, and to reveal divine righteousness in a 'wholly other' way by the forgiveness of sins, was a provocation of the guardians of the law.

We must make a close distinction here between the anticipatory structure of Jesus' preaching and its new content. From the formal point of view, Jesus' gospel of the kingdom was wholly proleptic in nature.[44] But in its content it goes far beyond apocalyptic conceptions of the righteousness of God, because it does not anticipate the kingdom for the righteous and judgment for the unrighteous, but paradoxically promises the kingdom to the unrighteous as a gift of grace, and leaves the supposedly righteous outside it. The scandal lay not just in its anticipation of the kingdom and its openness to the future, nor just in its proclamation of the eschatological age. In the structures of the anticipation of the future of God, the preaching of Jesus is in fact similar to that of John the Baptist, of the apocalyptists and the Zealots. The source of the contradiction is that he, a human being who was powerless, should anticipate the power of God as grace amongst the rejected and the powerless. Through its association with his lowliness, his preaching was open to rejection. Through its association with his claim for authority, his humanity could be refuted by casting him out and killing him. The inner contradiction between his claim and his poverty is characteristic of his whole appearance. Such a claim associated with such poverty was bound to be understood as a contradiction. The preaching of the kingdom by the poor man Jesus of Nazareth was open to refutation by crucifixion; but by that very fact it was also wholly dependent upon the God whom he proclaimed and demonstrated in this way, and not in any other. This inner contradiction, as it was bound to appear to any outside onlooker, is resolved only in the light of the resurrection of the crucified Jesus by his God and Father, in that through his very poverty, lowliness and abandonment the kingdom, the righteousness and the grace of God come to the poor, lowly and abandoned and are imparted to them. This is the message of the 'word of the cross' on the basis of his resurrection into the future of his God, through his progress to the cross and through Jesus crucified.

The sources show that from the very first Jesus received not merely support, but also hostility and opposition. The conflict which ultimately led to his death was inherent from the first in his life because of his opposition. Thus his death on the cross cannot be understood without the conflict between his life on the one hand and the law and its representatives on the other. If this is true, then through his death the prevailing law calls him into question, as one who by his freedom in life and preaching had called into question this understanding of the law.

But if Jesus was nailed to the cross in the name of the God who was regarded as the guarantor of the religious and cultic legal ordinance with which Jesus had come into collision, then his life ended, leaving open the question whether he had rightly associated with sinners and placed himself above Moses, and whether God's eschatological action had truly been inaugurated in his preaching and actions.[45]

It is necessary to add that his life ended with this question only in the light of his resurrection and in the testimony of the Easter faith. For in the first instance his death on the cross dealt with the 'open question' of his trial before the law concerning the true righteousness of God, with an unequivocal rejection. His execution must be seen as a necessary consequence of his conflict with the law. His trial by the guardians of the law was in the broader sense of the term a trial about the will of God, which the law claimed to have codified once for all. Here the conflict between Jesus and the law was not a dispute about a different will, or the will of a different God, but about the true will of God, which for Jesus was hidden and not revealed by the human concept of the law. Jesus' claim to fulfil the law of the righteousness of God, the claim made in the Sermon on the Mount, and his freedom from the law should not be understood as contradictory. For Jesus the 'radicalization of the *Torah*' and the 'transgression of the *Torah*' basically both amount to the same thing, the freedom of God to show grace. Thus the right which he claimed to forgive sins goes beyond the *Torah* and reveals a new righteousness of God in judgment, which could not be expected according to the traditions of the law.

Jesus' uncomplaining suffering and his powerless death were a visible demonstration to everyone of the power and the right of the law and its guardians. Consequently the disciples left him in the hour of the crucifixion and 'all fled' (Mark 14.50). One cannot but flee from someone who has been so visibly rejected, even and indeed above all when one has believed and followed him. Thus the flight of the disciples can be regarded as historical, because it conflicts with any kind of veneration for a hero and forbear. It is a record not of cowardice, but of a faith contradicted by the fact of a contemptible death.[46] For the disciples who had followed Jesus to Jerusalem, his shameful death was not the consummation of his obedience to God nor a demonstration of martyrdom for his truth, but the rejection of his claim. It did not confirm their hopes in him, but permanently destroyed them. Nor had they any examples from the tradition which might have suggested to them a 'dying Messiah', or a bringer of salvation condemned by the law as a 'blasphemer', to explain to them the fate of Jesus and to give them comfort. In view of their flight from the cross, there can be no suggestion that the disciples in any way maintained their faith; someone who believes does not flee.

From this point of view, the life of Jesus was a theological clash between him and the prevailing understanding of the law. From this clash arose the legal trial concerning the righteousness of God in which his gospel and the law were opponents. He did not die through chance or misfortune, but died by the law as one who was 'reckoned with transgressors' (Luke 22.37), because he was condemned as a 'blasphemer' by the guardians of the law and of faith. As they understood it, his death was the carrying out of the curse of the law. Of course this is not a necessary and inevitable explanation of the way in which the guardians of the law reacted, the historical circumstances of his betrayal by Judas and the political situation which led to his crucifixion. There remains a sufficient element of historical chance in his trial before the Sanhedrin and Pilate. Yet his conflict with the law displays a certain intrinsic necessity which was bound to lead to his rejection and cursing as a 'blasphemer'. The understanding of the causes of Jesus' conflict with the law and of this *causa crucis* do not make clear every feature of his historical death, but make clear why he was drawn into the trial which led to his death. Ultimately the understanding of the matter in dispute and the substance of the trial can make the continuation of the dispute and trial comprehensible when they come to be recapitulated. The primitive Christian interpretations of the crucified Jesus in the light of his resurrection by God and within the testimony of eschatological faith set out to recapitulate the trial in which Jesus and the law are opposed, and to draw upon it in the name of God. Paul did this with complete clarity: since the law had brought Jesus to his death upon the cross, so the risen and exalted Jesus becomes 'the end of the law, that everyone who has faith may be justified' (Rom. 10.4).

Thus the theological trial concerning Jesus after Easter turns on the question of righteousness: *Aut Christus—aut traditio legis.* It is a contest between the gospel and the law, between the righteousness of faith and the righteousness of works, between the justification of the godless and the justification of the righteous. The theology of the cross understands Christian faith as bearing testimony to the righteousness of Jesus Christ in this judicial trial of God. It therefore forms a parallel to Jesus himself with regard to his gospel and the theological conflict in his life and death. In so far as Jews and Gentiles are involved in the crucifixion of Jesus, faith in the righteousness of the crucified Jesus regards itself as bearing public witness in the universal trial concerning the righteousness of God, a trial which is the ultimate motive force of human history. The cross does not divide Christians from Jews, but brings them into the most profound solidarity with them, as Paul put it in Rom. 9.3. It is a universal triumph for a further reason: because it embraces both the question of human guilt and man's liberation from it, and also the question of human suffering and man's redemption from it.

Here we shall break off, and in the following chapter we shall recapitulate the trial of Jesus before this understanding of the law, in the eschatological context of his resurrection.

By way of an appendix to this discussion of Jesus and the law we must deal with certain misunderstandings which arose in the dialogue between Christ and the Jews and continue to be found. Jews and Christians are divided by their attitude to the crucified Jesus, equally as they are drawn by it into a history which they share. Christians are drawn into an inescapable solidarity with Israel—not only with the Israel of the Old Testament, but also with the Israel which rightfully exists alongside the church and which in consequence cannot be abolished. Israel demonstrates this to the church which lives through the reconciliation of the (Gentile) world in the crucified Christ, that the redemption of the world is still to come. The church of Christ is not yet perfect and the kingdom of God has not achieved full revelation as long as these two communities of hope, Israel and the church, exist side by side. Thus one cannot conclude from the above discussion that Israel is the old 'religion of the law' which since the death and resurrection of Christ has been inherited and replaced by the Christian 'religion of love'. Anyone who speaks here of an inheritance by way of the history of salvation is basically declaring that the testator is dead. The struggle between the gospel of Jesus and the understanding of the law which prevailed at this time cannot lead to any division, for it turned upon something held in common, the freedom of God in his faithfulness to his promises. I have therefore related the conflict between law and gospel to the promise to Abraham, the promise of life, and have argued that through the gospel this promise was liberated from the shadow of a legalist understanding of the law and given universal force for everyone who believes, whether Jew or Gentile.[47] The gospel assumes this promise and leads the believer out of the uncertainties of a legalist understanding to the point of trust in the faithfulness of God, 'who gives life to the dead and calls into existence the things that do not exist' (Rom. 4.17). The conflict of Jesus with this contemporary understanding of the law and the conflict of the kerygma of Christ with the nomist understanding of the law in Paul in the following period consequently invalidate neither the promises of Israel nor the election of Israel; rather, they give force to the latter and make it universal. I am convinced that Christian faith understood in this way can be a profitable partner in dialogue for a convinced Jew, for with the crucified Jesus it reminds him of his best traditions, and indeed of the very basis of his existence, which lies prior to the law in election and promise. An openness on the part of Christians to the existential basis of Judaism automatically follows from this. Thus when we have spoken of the conflict into which Jesus came with the 'law', this does not refer to the Old Testament *Torah* as instruction in the covenant of promise. The more the understanding of the *Torah* became remote from the promise, the more violent became the conflict with the gospel. The closer the understanding of the *Torah* draws to the original promise and election of Israel, the greater the possibility of an understanding for the law of grace of the gospel and for the hope which it gives to the hopeless and to the Gentiles. For a Christian there can be no question of any guilt on the part of the Jews for the crucifixion of Jesus—for his history is a theological history; there can only be a question of an offer of God's law of grace, and therefore only a question of hope for Israel. I regard the declarations of the second Vatican Council on the attitude of the church to the Jews to be weak, since here Judaism is still included amongst the 'non-Christian religions', while the church is described as a successor organization in the history of salvation to Israel, which she cannot be. Much better is Article 17 of the confession of faith of the Dutch Reformed Church, *Fundamenten en Perspektieven van Belijden* ('Confessional Fundamentals and Perspectives'), 1949, which speaks of the 'present and future of Israel' and expresses the eschatological dependence of the church upon Israel.[48]

(b) *Jesus and authority: 'The rebel'*

The theological conflict between Jesus and the contemporary understanding of the law can explain his rejection as a 'blasphemer', and in some circumstances his condemnation by the Sanhedrin, if such a trial is historical, but does not explain his execution by crucifixion. Jesus did not undergo the punishment for blasphemy, which in Israel at his time, as can be seen from the death of Stephen, was always that of stoning. Jesus was crucified by the Roman occupying power.

According to Roman law, crucifixion was a punishment for escaped slaves, as we know from the revolt of Spartacus and the crucifixion of more than 7,000 slaves on the *Via Appia*.[49] It was also a punishment for rebels against the *Imperium Romanum*, as is shown by the many crucified resistance fighters after the revolts in Israel had been crushed. Crucifixion was a punishment for crimes against the state, and not part of general criminal jurisdiction. To this extent, one can say that crucifixion at that time was a political punishment for rebellion against the social and political order of the *Imperium Romanum*.[50]

The spread of the *Imperium Romanum* was associated with the idea of the *Pax Romana*, and the *Pax Romana* in its turn was associated, in spite of all the religious tolerance which we know the Romans to have exercised, with the compulsory recognition of the Roman emperor cult. The *Imperium Romanum* was a religious and political ordinance in the world of that time. In Israel the resultant setting up of Roman standards in the temple and the placing of the head of Caesar on the currency in circulation was consequently regarded by the 'zealots for the law' as a breach of the first commandment and therefore as an offence against religion which had to be resisted. It can be said, then, that Jesus was crucified by the Romans not merely for tactical and immediate political reasons of peace and good order in Jerusalem, but basically in the name of the state gods of Rome who assured the *Pax Romana*. In the societies of that time there was no politics without religion, any more than there was religion without politics. 'Jesus was condemned by Pilate as a political rebel, as a Zealot.'[51] If we follow the historical conjectures of Oscar Cullmann, the Roman cohorts whose duty was to protect the temple captured Jesus in Gethsemane. He was consequently from the first a prisoner of the Romans who, as the result of his appearances in

Jerusalem, feared *stasis*, revolt. In this case, the hearing before the High Priest would rather have been a moral consultation which Pilate desired, in order to be certain that as a result of the execution of the supposed Zealot leader Jesus of Nazareth, the Jewish authorities and the Jewish people would not rise against him. The true trial, then, was a trial before Pilate, a political trial, made possible by the collusion of the Sanhedrin and Pilate. The inscription over the cross, the *titulus*, followed the practice of antiquity in naming the crime for which the punishment was given. It read: INRI—'Jesus of Nazareth, King of the Jews'. As this *titulus* is recorded in the gospels, it can hardly be an invention of the Christian church, for it was too dangerous, and came into conflict with the terms which the Christian churches later sought with the *Imperium Romanum* in order to survive.[52]

How can we explain the political fact that Jesus was crucified as a 'rebel' against the Roman Empire and as 'King of the Jews'? R. Bultmann states:

What is certain is merely that he was crucified by the Romans, and thus suffered the death of a political criminal. This death can scarcely be understood as an inherent and necessary consequence of his activity; rather it took place because his activity was misconstrued as a political activity. In that case it would have been—historically speaking—a meaningless fate.[53]

But was he really no more than the victim of a misunderstanding and a meaningless fate? And if it was a misunderstanding, what brought it about? Was it merely a chance misunderstanding or an intrinsically necessary and inevitable misunderstanding? How otherwise could the Romans, afraid of revolt and anxious to maintain order, have understood Jesus? Is not their 'misunderstanding' on the same level as the 'misunderstanding' of him by the Pharisees? Did not even his own disciples 'misunderstand' him, as is shown by their flight from the cross? The simple distinction between religion and politics which Bultmann introduces when he speaks of his activity 'being misconstrued as a political activity' is nothing less than the projection back of the separation of religion and politics—'religion is a private matter'—from the bourgeois world of the nineteenth century, a separation which was sought only after a thousand years of conflicts between church and emperor, but has never yet been reached, even at the present day.

The first question is, was Jesus a Zealot? Or had he in fact nothing to do with the Zealots?[54] These are the specific historical questions raised by the theological history of Jesus, and they must not be overshadowed by prejudice. One cannot begin by assuming that whatever the motivation of Jesus' ministry, it was 'un-political'. This is to beg the question. How could a public ministry in so tense a political situation between the Roman occupying forces and popular uprisings, such as existed in Palestine at that time, have remained without political effects? In the Judaism of that period, the political and the religious situations were inseparable. The ministry of Jesus could have been non-political only if it had been concerned with ineffective inner dispositions. But it was effective, and produced reactions which took effect themselves. Any such activity takes place within a network of interactions. To speak of the effects of the ministry of Jesus without mentioning these concrete interactions is deliberate abstraction. For Pilate, the case of Jesus of Nazareth was clearly on the same level as that of Barabbas, who was probably a Zealot; we read of him as a 'rebel' captured 'in the insurrection' (Mark 15.7). Such an 'error of justice' would probably not have been possible on the part of the Romans if the effect of the ministry of Jesus had not created at least the danger of a new popular revolt. Nor could the Jewish authorities have accused Jesus to the Romans as a Zealot leader seeking to be king of Israel if his ministry had not included a claim which it was possible to misrepresent as a Zealot claim.[55] Let us begin, then, by listing the features which could have led to the association of Jesus with the Zealots:

1. Like the Zealots, Jesus preached that the kingdom of God was at hand.

2. Like them, he understood his ministry and his gospel as a mission to bring about the kingdom, i.e. as an anticipation of the kingdom of God.

3. The sources record Jesus' polemic against the Pharisees, but scarcely any polemic against the Zealots.

4. He adopted Zealot criticism in calling Herod a 'fox' (Luke 13.32). In the face of the established political and social ruling class he formulated the fundamental alternative for himself and his disciples: 'The kings of the Gentiles exercise lordship over them; and those in authority over them are called benefactors. But not so with you; rather let the greatest among you become as the youngest and the leader as one who serves' (Luke 22.25–27; Mark 10.42–45).

5. Jesus actually attracted Zealots to himself. Amongst the Twelve there was at least one, Simon Zelotes, who had previously belonged to the Zealots; and it is possible that Peter Bar-Jonah had been a Zealot.[56] It is very probable that Judas Iscariot belonged to the Zealot group know as the *sicarii*. Moreover, amongst the motley crew of his disciples there were some who carried weapons. This is in accordance with the Jewish practice of going armed on journeys as a protection against wild animals and robbers.[57] The farewell saying, which is certainly a post-resurrection utterance, in Luke 22.35–38, warns the disciples to go well armed: 'And let him who has no sword sell his mantle and buy one.' In the garden at Gethsemane some of the disciples carried swords. This is not evidence for a planned Zealot revolt by Jesus in Jerusalem; nor is it evidence that from the first Jesus imposed upon his disciples the duty of absolute non-violence and disarmed them.

6. The entry into Jerusalem and the cleansing of the temple could perfectly well have been understood by the disciples, the Jewish inhabitants and the Romans as Zealot symbolical actions.

Let us now list the features that distinguished Jesus from the Zealots:

1. The Zealots anticipated the coming Messianic kingdom by the struggle for liberation from Rome. To use an expression of the time, they sought to 'bring in the kingdom by violence'. Jesus may have been referring to them by his saying: 'Until now the kingdom of heaven has suffered violence, and men of violence take it by force' (Matt. 11.12). It is significant that it is not clear whether this passage expresses praise or blame. For the Zealots, the occupation of Israel by the heathen Romans was a usurpation by men of violence. The violent imposition of Roman imperial rule was an offence against religion: 'Caesar demands what belongs to God.' By his statues he was setting himself up in the place of the Holy One. In these circumstances, the 'holy war', understood in an apocalyptic sense, was appropriate. Militant resistance against the godless, lawless Romans was the political worship of the Zealots: 'Anyone who sheds the blood of a godless man is like one who offers a sacrifice.'[58] They let themselves be tortured to death rather than call the Roman Caesar *Kyrios*, for to them this title was the Old Testament attribute of God. Thus for the Zealots the eschatological 'holy war' was the apocalyptic commandment of the moment. But the purpose of this 'holy war' was solely to establish the law

of God, and above all the first and second commandments. Thus those who broke the law had to be killed, those without the law driven out and Israel purified, in order for it to rise again out of its shame.

In Jesus' case, the anticipation of the kingdom of God through his gospel to the poor was brought about not by this kind of legalism, but by the divine principle of free grace. What distinguishes Jesus from the Zealots is not the anticipation of the future of God as such, nor the principle of non-violence, but his freedom from the legalism which led the Zealots to carry out here and now the final judgment upon the enemies of God and Israel. The often-quoted saying of Jesus, 'My kingdom is not of this world' (John 18.36), does not signify that his kingdom is elsewhere, but that it is of a different pattern from this world. Yet, different as it is, it is in the midst of this world through Jesus himself. Thus it is not in accordance with Jesus' preaching to call the kingdom 'unpolitical' and to banish it into another sphere, that of heaven or of the heart. The kingdom is political in a quite different way, and politically, it is quite different from the systems and rules of the struggle for world domination and revenge.

2. It is clear from the accounts by Josephus that the Zealots were a kind of 'radically legalist' Pharisee party. Thus Jesus' polemic against the Pharisees' concept of the law was also aimed at the Zealot enthusiasts for the law. Jesus did not attack the thoroughgoing moral obedience of the Pharisees towards God, so he did not attack the thoroughgoing political obedience of the Zealots either. He made a fundamental attack upon the legalism of both. The main theme of his polemic was not the practical question whether resistance should be non-violent or violent, but the fundamental question of the righteousness which was demanded by God. As we have shown, Jesus anticipated the divine righteousness of grace, which makes both lawbreaker and lawless righteous. Here he was in conflict with the central issue of Zealot faith, that the coming righteousness of God could be anticipated by the judgment and punishment of the godless.

3. The disciples of Jesus included not only the Zealots, but also their deadly enemies, the tax collectors. These were people who, because of their collaboration with the Roman occupying forces, were particularly hated by the Pharisees and Zealots. Jesus did not dismiss these collaborators as beyond redemption. The notorious

'friend of tax collectors and sinners' thereby broke down the strictly regulated pattern of friend and enemy prescribed by Pharisees and Zealots, just as he broke down the traditional pattern of friend and enemy which divided Jews and Samaritans. This is a further sign of the completely different righteousness of God which he proclaimed and revealed by his behaviour. Finally, Jesus did not demand any 'social-revolutionary rejection of consumption', as M. Hengel describes the mourning of that period for Israel's lost freedom and the penance carried out to purify the abomination of desolation. Pharisees and Zealots mocked him as a 'glutton and drunkard' (Luke 7.34) who, in the midst of the misery of Israel, did not fast with his disciples, but feasted. This too points to a different understanding on his part of the imminent righteousness of the kingdom of God. In spite of the economic distress, political servitude and religious oppression of his people, for Jesus the kingdom of God was like a marriage feast. In the Zealots' eyes, this must have been the very substance of his folly. The God of Israel could not be like this in the face of the distress of his people. This was contradictory to their understanding of the law. They must have understood Jesus' thoroughly festive way of life as a mockery of their serious purpose.

4. In a similar way to the political and social criticism of the Zealots, Jesus also pilloried the offence against religion committed by rulers who divinized themselves, and sharply distinguished what they confounded. 'Render to Caesar the things that are Caesar's, and to God the things that are God's' (Luke 20.25). Like them, he perceived the superstition and godlessness of Mammon, and considered it difficult for a rich man to enter the kingdom of heaven. Like them, he condemned social injustice. His beatitudes for the poor are paralleled by woes concerning the rich (Luke 6.24; Luke 12.16ff.). But he did not call upon the poor to revenge themselves upon their exploiters nor the oppressed to opress their oppressors. Theologically, this would have been no more than the anticipation of the last judgment according to the law, but not the new righteousness of God which Jesus revealed in the law of grace. Instead, its consequence is: 'Love your enemies and pray for those that persecute you.' This is the beatitude upon the peacemakers, the new men who break the pattern of oppression and are not concerned to gain power. 'This Magna Charta of *agape* is, if you please, that which is actually revolutionary in

the message of Jesus.'[59] It cannot be called 'revolutionary' in the context of the revolutionary strategy and tactics of the self-liberation of the enslaved righteous from oppression by the rich and the Romans, with the aim of restoring the ancient righteousness of God in the land of their fathers. But it can be called 'revolutionary' in contrast to the legalism with which the righteous hoped to establish the righteousness of God in place of the Roman *nomos*. Finally, it is 'revolutionary' in an eschatological context: in the final judgment God replaces his sovereign righteousness by his law of grace. In this way, the future hope is free from visions of revenge and dreams of omnipotence on the part of the oppressed and the weak. Everything that can be categorized as 'non-violence' in the sayings and actions of Jesus can ultimately be derived from this 'revolution in the concept of God' which he set forth: God comes not to carry out just revenge upon the evil, but to justify by grace sinners, whether they are Zealots or tax collectors, Pharisees or sinners, Jews or Samaritans, and therefore, also, whether they are Jews or Gentiles. This liberation from legalism, which was bound and is always bound to lead to retribution, by means of a disarming delight in God's law of grace, can indeed be called the 'humane revolt' of Jesus—if one is to use the modern terminology of revolution at all, something which is possible only with caution.

5. The danger of losing this freedom from the vicious circle of legalism, of violence and counter-violence, of guilt or retribution, and of falling victim to it once again, can clearly be seen from the experiences of the church and its recollections of Jesus to have been faced several times by him and his disciples. According to the temptation narrative, this danger was seen as the particular temptation of Jesus. Satan shows Jesus the kingdoms of the world and promises to give them to him. Here he is proposing the ideal of the Zealots to Jesus.[60] Something similar may have faced Jesus in the dialogue on the road to Caesarea Philippi (Mark 8.27–33) in Peter's rejection of his Master's suffering. According to the tradition Jesus reacted sharply: 'Get behind me, Satan!' In spite of the general rejection of the Zealot ideal in the tradition, this indicates that it would have been dangerously easy for Jesus to have followed this course.

To sum up, we can make the following comments on this question, which is so hotly disputed at the present day:

1. Like the Zealots, Jesus broke with the *status quo* and those who maintained it in being. Like them, he provoked tangible political unrest (*stasis*). He was therefore crucified by the Romans as a 'Zealot leader'. But in fact he was breaking with a quite different *status quo* from the Zealots. Unlike them, he was breaking not merely with a compromising transgression of the law and Gentile lawlessness, in order to restore the law, but was breaking with legalism—in so far as it concentrated upon the *jus talionis*—in order to proclaim the kingdom of freedom through joy in God's righteousness of grace, and to anticipate it by demonstrating it.

2. He therefore propagated the coming righteousness of God as the law of grace amongst the righteous and the unrighteous in order to liberate Zealots and tax collectors from their legalistic relationship of hostility.

3. He denied that human beings, Zealots and Romans, had the right to pass judgment and execute vengeance in their own cause: 'Let him who is without sin among you be the first to throw a stone' (John 8.7). He revealed God not as a righteous avenger in judgment, but as an incomprehensibly gracious and thereby righteous God. Consequently, his preaching set men free from the legalism with which they sought to bring themselves into accordance with the God of vengeance.

4. His opponents clearly understood this. They were well aware of the attack upon their religious and political principles implied in his preaching and in his familiarity with both friend and enemy. For the Pharisees and Zealots he was a 'traitor' to the sacred cause of Israel. For the Romans, he was, like the leaders of the Zealots, one more instigator of unrest. Jesus' ministry and the reactions it provoked led logically to his being handed over to the Romans, and therefore to his crucifixion.

5. Even though Pilate was merely removing one more agitator and demagogue, and from his point of view could not have distinguished between an anti-Roman Zealot leader and the non-Zealot agitator Jesus, his condemnation of Jesus as a 'rebel' against the imperial *Pax Romana* does not merely imply a 'misunderstanding' of Jesus inevitable in the circumstances. The freedom of Jesus and his proclamation of God's law of grace affected not only the Pharisees and Zealots, but equally the cultic and political religious foundations of the *Pax Romana* and the archaic conceptions of righteousness held by all men. By regarding him as a Zealot rebel,

Pilate certainly misunderstood Jesus, and because of his fear of a popular revolt was bound so to misunderstand him. But in the deeper sense of a challenge to the *Pax Romana* and its gods and laws, we can look back and realize that Pilate understood him aright. This is shown by the effect that the crucified man from Nazareth ultimately had upon the Roman Empire in the life of early Christianity. The worship of such a 'crucified God' contained a strictly political significance which cannot be sublimated into the religious sphere. The Christians' open rejection of emperor worship brought them martyrdom in a sense which was both religious and political. 'Since demons rule in the world, anyone who wishes to live there must show them veneration and submit to their ordinances. And therefore one must also submit to rulers, even if they demand that one takes an oath in their name. Through this belief Rome grew great, and it is not right to reject their gods and accept a god who is not even able to give his followers a patch of earth or a home, so that they have to slink about secretly in constant fear,' says Celsus.[61] He accused the followers of the crucified Christ of rebellion (*stasis*). By their irreligiousness they were introducing revolt into the heavenly world amongst the gods and were therefore bringing revolt into the religious and political world on earth which corresponded to those gods.[62] In an age in which politics and religion were one and, apart from domestic cults, could not be separated, it was scarcely possible for the activity of Jesus to be 'misconstrued as a political activity', as R. Bultmann supposes. The gospel of Jesus and his public behaviour were political in the extreme. He was bound to be understood as both religious and political, even if this did not mean that he himself was not understood as an object of faith. Consequently, he alienated both the anti-Roman Zealots and the anti-Jewish Romans. Both knew their business, the use of armed force as divine judgment, as was the custom in the world of that time. But Jesus interfered in this religious and political business to challenge and disrupt its rules, and 'had to be' removed.

Thus as a second theological dimension to the history of Jesus which led to his crucifixion as a 'rebel', we can definitely add the political dimension of the gospel of Jesus within a world in which religion and politics were inseparable.

If the one who was crucified in this way was raised up and vindicated by God, as eschatological faith affirms, then this aspect too of the trial of Jesus must be recapitulated, and the faith which bears public testimony to it must draw upon the political dimension of his history. Christianity then poses the question, for resolution by open trial: Christ—or Caesar?

The theology of the cross is not 'pure theology' in a modern, non-political sense, or in the sense of private religion. Faith in the crucified Christ is in the political sense a public testimony to the freedom of Christ and the law of grace in the face of the political religions of nations, empires, races and classes. Between faith in Christ and the deified rulers of the world, the personal cults and the social and political fetishes of society, Jesus himself stands. The recollection of his crucifixion is something both dangerous and liberating. Let us break off here, to return to this political dimension later in the context of the resurrection of the crucified Jesus.

(c) Jesus and God: 'The godforsaken'

The theological conflict of Jesus with the understanding of the law on the part of the Pharisees, and his theological and political conflict with the Zealots and the Romans, provide an explanation of his condemnation as a 'blasphemer' and his crucifixion as a 'rebel'; but they do not explain the true inner pain of his suffering and death.

Let us begin by looking at this from the outside.

Socrates died as a wise man. Cheerfully and calmly he drank the cup of hemlock. This was a demonstration of magnanimity, and was also a testimony to the immortality of the soul, which Plato tells us he taught. For him, death was a breakthrough to a higher, purer life. Thus his farewell was not difficult. He had a cock sacrificed to Asclepius, which was only done on recovery from a severe illness. The death of Socrates was a festival of liberty.[63]

The Zealot martyrs who were crucified after the unsuccessful revolts against the Romans died conscious of their righteousness in the sight of God, and looked forward to their resurrection to eternal life just as they looked forward to the resurrection of their lawless enemies, and of the transgressors of the law who had betrayed them, to eternal shame. They died for their righteous cause, the cause of the righteousness of God, conscious that this would ultimately triumph over their enemies. Many of them succeeded in cursing their enemies even as they died. Rabbi

Akiba found in his death on the cross the freedom for which he had longed, to give himself utterly to the God who, according to Israel's Shema, can only be loved 'with the whole heart, the whole soul and the whole might'.

The wise men of the Stoics demonstrated to the tyrants in the arena, where they were torn to pieces by wild animals, their inner liberty and their superiority. 'Without fear and without hope,' as we are told, they endured in freedom and demonstrated to their fearful overlords and horrified crowds their complete lack of terror even at their own death.

The Christian martyrs too went calmly and in faith to their death. Conscious of being crucified with Christ and receiving the baptism of blood, and of thereby being united for ever with Christ, they went to their death in 'hope against hope'. The last words of Dietrich Bonhoeffer, with which he took leave of his fellow-prisoner Payne Best as he went to the place of execution in Flossenburg extermination camp were: 'This is the end—for me the beginning of life.'[64] As he had written in a letter, he was certain 'that our joy is hidden in suffering, and our life in death'.[65]

Jesus clearly died in a different way. His death was not a 'fine death'. The synoptic gospels agree that he was 'greatly distressed and troubled' (Mark 14.33 par.) and that his soul was sorrowful even to death. He died 'with loud cries and tears', according to the Epistle to the Hebrews (5.7). According to Mark 15.37 he died with a loud, incoherent cry. Because, as the Christian tradition developed, this terrible cry of the dying Jesus was gradually weakened in the passion narratives and replaced by words of comfort and triumph, we can probably rely upon it as a kernel of historical truth. Jesus clearly died with every expression of the most profound horror. How can this be explained? The comparison with Socrates, and with Stoic and Christian martyrs, shows that there is something special here about the death of Jesus. We can understand it only if we see his death not against his relationship to the Jews and the Romans, to the law and to the political power, but in relation to his God and Father, whose closeness and whose grace he himself had proclaimed. Here we come upon the theological dimension of his life and death. Mark 15.34 reproduces the cry of the dying Jesus in the words of Psalm 22.2: 'My God, why hast thou forsaken me?' This is certainly an interpretation of the church after Easter, and indeed Psalm 22 as a

whole had a formative influence on the Christian passion narratives.[66] But it seems to be as near as possible to the historical
reality of the death of Jesus.[67] The Western group of texts of
Mark 15.34 have watered down the words, and read: 'My God,
what hast thou to reproach me for?' Luke omits these words completely and replaces them by the confident utterance of the
Jewish evening prayer from Ps. 31.6: 'Father, into thy hands I
commit my spirit' (23.46). Therefore the disciples in Luke do not
flee from the cross, for in his view Jesus did not die 'forsaken by
God', but as an exemplary martyr. In John, for different theological reasons yet again, we read: 'It is finished' (19.30), since
for John Jesus' struggle ends with his victory and glorification on
the cross. The history of the tradition being as it is, it can be
accepted that the difficult reading of Mark is as close as may be to
historical reality. To complete the paradox, in Mark the Gentile
centurion responds to the cry with which Jesus breathes his last
by professing that Jesus is the Son of God: 'Truly this man was
the Son of God' (15.39). In the pages that follow, therefore, we
start from the assumption that Jesus died with the signs and
expressions of a profound abandonment by God.[68]

In order to understand the mystery of the death of Jesus, which
is so unlike comparable narratives of the death of great witnesses
of faith, let us begin once again with the context of his life and
ministry. Like no one before him in Israel, Jesus had proclaimed
the imminence of the kingdom of God and demonstrated amongst
the incurable, the rejected and the hated that it was a gracious
imminence, not to judge but to save. In his own relationship to
the God of this kingdom, he himself had gone beyond the framework of the tradition of God's covenant with Israel, in which the
closeness of God to his people was mediated through the covenant,
the law and Moses. Note in passing that Jesus often called God
exclusively 'My Father'.[69] This is the expression of a fellowship
with God which is not mediated through the covenant, the nation
and tradition, and must therefore be termed a direct fellowship.
The unparalleled claim of Jesus includes the forgiveness of sins
here on earth, through the exercise of the divine right of grace. By
identifying himself with God in this way, Jesus was clearly
assuming that God identified himself with him and his words. But
anyone who lived and preached so close to God, his kingdom and
his grace, and associated the decision of faith with his own person,

could not regard his being handed over to death on the cross as
one accursed as a mere mishap, a human misunderstanding or a final
trial, but was bound to experience it as rejection by the very God
whom he had dared to call 'My Father'. When we look at his
non-miraculous and helpless suffering and dying in the context
of his preaching and his life, we understand how his misery cried
out to heaven: it is the experience of abandonment by God in the
knowledge that God is not distant but close; does not judge, but
shows grace. And this, in full consciousness that God is close at
hand in his grace, to be abandoned and delivered up to death as
one rejected, is the torment of hell.[70] Thus in the context of his
life, his abandonment on the cross, which he expressed in his last
cry, should not be interpreted as the ultimate test of a deeply
religious man in temptation and suffering, on the pattern of the
martyr christology which ever since Luke has repeatedly presented
Jesus as the archetype or example of faith under temptation. Nor,
in the context of his preaching, can his end be represented as a
'failure'. Heroes such as Leonidas 'failed' and demonstrated their
heroism by a heroic death. For this reason they are admired by
posterity. Bultmann says:

We cannot tell whether or how Jesus found meaning in it (viz., his death).
We may not veil from ourselves the possibility that he suffered a
collapse.[71]

This is certainly correct from the historical point of view, but is
much too biographical and psychological in its approach, something which in this very passage Bultmann is trying to avoid. The
understanding of the death of Jesus in the context of his life must
be theological, and must take into account the God for whom he
lived and spoke. Jesus did not live as a private person, which the
historical account of the liberal nineteenth century was the first
to make him, but as far as we can tell from the sources as a public
person, on the basis of the closeness of his God and his Father,
and for the sake of God's coming kingdom. The splendour of his
life and the horror of his death can be understood only on the basis
of that by which and for which he lived. The two Zealots who were
crucified with him may have 'broken down' and 'failed', but the
cause for which they had lived and fought was to them inviolable
and could not be destroyed by any death. They could die in the
consciousness that the coming world judgment would vindicate

them. But as we have shown, for Jesus, according to his whole preaching, the cause for which he lived and worked was so closely linked with his own person and life that his death was bound to mean the death of his cause. It is this which makes his death on the cross so unique. Other men, too, have been misunderstood and brought to disaster by the failure of men to understand them. Prophets, too, have been cursed as blasphemers by their own people. Many brave men have been executed by crucifixion and worse tortures. None of this distinguishes the death of Jesus from other crosses in the history of human suffering. Not until we understand his abandonment by the God and Father whose imminence and closeness he had proclaimed in a unique, gracious and festive way, can we understand what was distinctive about his death. Just as there was a unique fellowship with God in his life and preaching, so in his death there was a unique abandonment by God. This is something more than and something different from 'collapse' and 'failure'.

Why did Jesus die? He died not only because of the understanding of the law by his contemporaries or because of Roman power politics, but ultimately because of his God and Father. The torment in his torments was this abandonment by God. It leads us to understand, in the context of his life itself, what happened on the cross as something which took place between Jesus and his God, and between his Father and Jesus. The origin of christology, the purpose of which is to say who Jesus is in reality, consequently lies not in Jesus' understanding of himself or in his messianic consciousness, nor in the evaluation of him by his disciples, nor solely in his call to decision, which might imply a christology. It lies in what took place between Jesus and his God, between that 'Father' and Jesus, in what was given expression in his preaching and his actions and was literally 'put to death' in his abandonment as he died.

Let us attempt to test what took place between Jesus and his God in his death, by an interpretation of the words of Ps. 22.2 as Jesus spoke them. We shall take into account the fact that the church attempted to interpret Jesus' dying cry in these words, but shall regard this interpretation as the most accurate. Interpreters have usually understood the cry of Jesus in the sense of the prayer of Ps. 22. But even when the two use the same words, they do not necessarily mean the same thing, and a consideration purely from

the point of view of the history of tradition can easily overlook
this. Thus it is not right to interpret the cry of Jesus in the sense of
Ps. 22, but more proper to interpret the words of the psalm here
in the sense of the situation of Jesus. In the original Ps. 22 'My
God' means the covenant God of Israel, and the 'I' who has been
forsaken is the other partner of the covenant, the righteous
sufferer. But in Jesus' case the cry 'My God' implies the same
content as his own message of God who comes close in grace,
the message he had often expressed in the exclusive words 'My
Father'. And the community which may have placed these words
from the psalm on the lips of the dying Jesus must have regarded
them in this way and related the psalm to Jesus' situation. He is
no longer crying for Israel's covenant God. Were that the case, the
Zealots who were crucified with him could have echoed him. He is
crying for 'his' God and Father. Jesus is speaking not of any other
god, but of a special relationship to God by comparison with the
traditions of Israel. Similarly, the 'I' of the forsaken speaker is no
longer simply identical with the 'I' of a righteous man, faithful to
the covenant, from the Old Testament, but must be understood
in a special way as the 'I' of the Son. What is Ps. 22 lamenting,
and what in his turn is the dying Jesus lamenting? The prayer of
the Old Testament itself is not lamenting the speaker's own fate
in a mood of self-pity, but in the words of the psalm is calling
upon the faithfulness of God, which as a righteous man he is
defending. Psalm 22 is a legal plea. Jesus is not calling for the
compassion of God upon his own person, but for the revelation of
the righteousness of the God who promised 'not to forsake the
work of his hands'. Abandoned by God, the righteous man sees
God's deity itself at stake, for he himself is the faithfulness and
honour of God in the world. And therefore the prayer of Ps. 22
calls upon the faithfulness of God for God's sake. Likewise, the
cry of Jesus, as interpreted by Ps. 22, is not one of self-pity and
an expression of personal distress, but is once again a call upon
God for God's sake, a legal plea. However, unlike the speaker in
Ps. 22, Jesus is not just making a claim upon the faithfulness of the
God of Israel to his covenant, as he had promised to the whole
people; in a special way he is laying claim upon the faithfulness
of his Father to himself, the Son who has taken his part. In the
words 'My God, why hast thou forsaken me?' Jesus is putting at
stake not only his personal existence, but his theological existence,

his whole proclamation of God. Thus ultimately, in his rejection, the deity of his God and the fatherhood of his Father, which Jesus had brought close to men, are at stake. From this point of view, on the cross not only is Jesus himself in agony, but also the one for whom he lived and spoke, his Father. In the words of Ps. 22 Jesus is making a claim upon his own being in the particular relationship of his life and preaching to the Father. If we take this as our starting point, then in the death of Jesus more is at stake than Yahweh's covenant fellowship with the righteous of his people Israel. In the death of Jesus the deity of his God and Father is at stake.[72] Jesus is then calling upon the deity and faithfulness of his Father against his rejection and the non-deity of his Father. This can be put in an exaggerated form: the cry of Jesus in the words of Ps. 22 means not only 'My God, why hast thou forsaken *me*?' but at the same time, 'My God, why hast thou forsaken *thyself*?' In the theological context of what he preached and lived, the unity of Jesus and God must be emphasized as strongly as this.

If this were not so, then Ps. 22 on the lips of Jesus would merely show that after all his conflicts with the Pharisees and Zealots and their understanding of the law, Jesus had returned at his death to the God of the fathers. But this would mean the end of his novel message and the liquidation of his special mission. There is therefore nothing to be gained by emphasizing, in the words of the psalm which Jesus spoke as he died, first the rejection and secondly the confidence which is expressed in the term 'My God', in order to go on to the affirmation that in extreme despair, Jesus cast himself into the arms of God.[73] This, of course, is also the case with the Old Testament figure who utters the prayer of Ps. 22; and to imitate him and to die in 'comforted despair' there is no need for the passion narrative of Jesus. In the theological context of his life and preaching, the issue in his death is not the general paradox of confidence in God in abandonment by God, but above all that of the deity of *his* God and *his* Father. The rejection expressed in his dying cry, and accurately interpreted by the words of Ps. 22, must therefore be understood strictly as something which took place between Jesus and his Father, and in the other direction between his Father and Jesus, the Son—that is, as something which took place between God and God. The abandonment on the cross which separates the Son from the Father is something which takes place within God himself; it is *stasis* within God—'God against God'—particularly if we are to maintain that Jesus bore witness to and lived out the truth of God. We must not allow ourselves to overlook this 'enmity' between God and God by failing to take seriously either the rejection of Jesus by God, the gospel of God which he lived out, or his last cry to God upon the cross.

As a 'blasphemer', Jesus was rejected by the guardians of his people's law. As a 'rebel' he was crucified by the Romans. But finally, and most profoundly, he died as one rejected by his God and his Father. In the theological context of his life this is the most important dimension. It is this alone which distinguishes his cross from the many crosses of forgotten and nameless persons in world history. In his conflict with the law it was possible to speak of a 'misunderstanding' on the part of the Jews. In the political conflict of his crucifixion as a rebel it is customary to speak of a 'misunderstanding' on the part of the Romans. But is it possible to speak of a 'misunderstanding' in the theological context of his abandonment by God? If so, either Jesus must have misunderstood God in his preaching, or God must have misunderstood Jesus at the end of his life. But in view of his message concerning God, his abandonment on the cross cannot be interpreted as a misunderstanding unless Jesus is to be explained as a liar, or God as non-God.

The theology of the cross must take up and think through to a conclusion this third dimension of the dying of Jesus in abandonment by God. If, abandoned by his God and Father, he was raised through the 'glory of the Father', then eschatological faith in the cross of Jesus Christ must acknowledge the theological trial between God and God. The cross of the Son divides God from God to the utmost degree of enmity and distinction. The resurrection of the Son abandoned by God unites God with God in the most intimate fellowship. How is this Easter day fellowship of God with God to be conceived in the Good Friday cross? To comprehend God in the crucified Jesus, abandoned by God, requires a 'revolution in the concept of God': *Nemo contra Deum nisi Deus ipse.*[74] Here the Christian concept of God itself becomes a revolt in a quite different sense from the revolt which scandalized the Pharisees and priests over Jesus and which the Romans suppressed by executing him.[75]

There are two traditions in Christian theology which have taken account of this 'revolt' in the Christian concept of God: the development of the doctrine of the *Trinity* and the elaboration of the *theology of the cross*. But apart from these tentative steps, which we hope to take up again and continue in Chapter 6, every theology which claims to be Christian must come to terms with Jesus' cry on the cross. Basically, every Christian theology is consciously or unconsciously answering the question, 'Why has thou forsaken me?', when their doctrines of salvation say 'for this reason' or 'for that reason'. In the face of Jesus' death-cry to God, theology either becomes impossible or becomes possible only as specifically Christian theology. Christian theology cannot come to terms with the cry of its own age and at the same time always be on the side of the rulers of this world. But it must come to terms with the cry of the wretched for God and for freedom out of the depths of the sufferings of this age. Sharing in the sufferings of this time, Christian theology is truly contemporary theology. Whether or not it can be so depends less upon the openness of theologians and their theories to the world and more upon whether they have honestly and without reserve come to terms with the death-cry of Jesus for God. By the standards of the cry of the dying Jesus for God, theological systems collapse at once in their inadequacy. How can Christian theology speak of God at all in the face of Jesus' abandonment by God? How can Christian theology not speak of God in the face of the cry of Jesus for God on the cross?

In the context of the gospel of God which he lived out, the life of Jesus ends with an open question concerning God. In the context of the resurrection and of eschatological faith there must be a return to this abandonment of Jesus by God, and the trial that takes place between God and God must be recapitulated.

NOTES

1. Cf. E. Jüngel, *Tod*, 1971, 132.
2. The church dispute in Japan mentioned in ch. 1 significantly leads to a polarization of 'Iesuron' (Jesuology) and 'Kirisutoron' (Christology). The picture of the human, revolutionary Jesus, oriented on force, was set against the picture of the transcendent reactionary Christ of the establishment. Toshikazu Takao set the revolutionary Jesus in the context of the Jewish Zealots and found his true followers in the rebelling students. Kazoh Kitamori, who wrote the first Japanese theology of the cross, was attacked as a representative of the Christ of the establishment

of the church and society. For the protesting students of theology, the revolutionary Jesus became the model for radical self-denial in an inhuman and alienated society.

3. See the attractive *bon mot* by H. Conzelmann, 'The Method of the Life-of-Jesus Research', in Carl E. Braaten and Roy A. Harrisville (eds.), *The Historical Jesus and the Kerygmatic Christ*, New York and Nashville 1964, 56, 'the attempt is made to grow a systematic Christ-rose from the soil of historical scepticism'.

4. M. Kähler, *The So-Called Historical Jesus and the Historic, Biblical Christ*, Philadelphia 1964.

5. R. Bultmann, *Jesus and the Word*, Fontana Books 1958; *Primitive Christianity in its Contemporary Setting*, Fontana Books 1960; 'The Primitive Christian Kerygma and the Historical Jesus', in C. E. Braaten and R. A. Harrisville, op. cit., 15–42.

6. Cf. J. Moltmann, 'Exegese und Eschatologie der Geschichte', in *Perspektiven der Theologie*, 1968, 57ff.

7. M. Kähler, 'Das Kreuz', 302.

8. Thus W. Trillhaas critically on E. Käsemann, *EvKomm* 3, 1970, 682.

9. On this see W. Pannenberg, 'Hermeneutic and Universal History', in *Basic Questions in Theology* 1, SCM Press 1970, 96–136.

10. This is the question posed by G. Ebeling, *Word and Faith*, SCM Press 1963, 201ff., 305ff.; *The Nature of Faith*, Collins 1961, 44ff., 58ff.; 'Towards a Christology', in *Theology and Proclamation*, Collins 1966, 82ff.

11. So too W. Pannenberg, *Jesus—God and Man*, SCM Press 1968, 19.

12. E. Käsemann, *Essays on New Testament Themes*, SCM Press 1964, 25.

13. See H. Diem, *Was ist schriftgemäss?*, 1958.

14. A. Schweitzer, *The Quest of the Historical Jesus*, A. & C. Black ³1950, 1ff.; P. Tillich, *Systematic Theology* II, Nisbet 1957, 112ff.

15. E. Käsemann has used the contrast 'continuity-discontinuity' in his article 'The Problem of the Historical Jesus', op. cit., 15. G. Ebeling has criticized it as being inappropriate to the historical context: 'This terminology is unsatisfactory because in it either continuity or discontinuity are not seen as real alternatives, but stand in a dialectical relationship to one another, in such a way that they can be predicated of every sequence of events, and as such already give expression to a material relationship; or else they are conceived so formally' (*Theology and Proclamation*, 59). In 'Blind Alleys in the "Jesus of History" Controversy', *New Testament Questions of Today*, SCM Press 1969, 36ff., E. Käsemann has gone on to distinguish between historical and material continuity, but has not given up the terminology. We shall replace the terminology used by Käsemann and Ebeling with the terms analogy and 'the new', 'novelty', because this enables us to give a more concrete description of the historical relationship between tradition and innovation.

16. Thus E. Bloch, 'Die Formel *incipit vita nova*', in *Tübinger Einleitung in die Philosophie* 2, 1964, 151.

17. Against E. Troeltsch, 'Über historische und systematische Methoden in der Theologie', *Gesammelte Schriften* II, 1913, 729–53.

18. W. Dilthey, *Gesammelte Schriften* VIII, 225.

19. J. M. Robinson, *A New Quest of the Historical Jesus*, SCM Press 1959, 75.

20. This sums up the provisional result of the dispute over Bultmann's answer in 'The Primitive Christian Kerygma', though individual questions still remain to be considered.

21. For this see once again E. Jüngel, *Paulus und Jesus*, 82.

22. Thus W. Wrede, *Paulus*, 1907, 94.

23. J. Weiss, *Paulus und Jesus*, 1909, 3. For the context see E. Jüngel, *Paulus und Jesus*, 5ff.

24. R. Bultmann, *Faith and Understanding*, SCM Press 1969, 223.

25. R. Bultmann, op. cit., 286ff.

26. Cf. R. Bultmann, *Theology of the New Testament* I, SCM Press 1952, 'The Message of Jesus', 3–32.

27. This has been emphatically demonstrated both systematically and exegetically by E. Fuchs, *Studies of the Historical Jesus*, SCM Press 1964.

28. R. Bultmann, *Faith and Understanding*, 292.

29. J. Schniewind, 'Messiasgeheimnis und Eschatologie', in *Nachgelassene Reden und Aufsätze*, ed. E. Kähler, 1952, 1ff.

30. Thus W. Marxsen, 'The Resurrection of Jesus as a Historical and Theological Problem', in C. F. D. Moule (ed.), *The Significance of the Message of the Resurrection for Faith in Jesus Christ*, SCM Press 1968, 15–50; id., *The Resurrection of Jesus of Nazareth*, SCM Press 1970. In that case one cannot follow R. Bultmann in saying that 'nothing needs to be taught about Jesus except "that" (sc. the eschatological "that" of his preaching), nothing except *that* in his historical life the event had its beginning and the event continues in the preaching of the community' (*Faith and Understanding*, 311).

31. R. Bultmann, *Faith and Understanding*, 283.

32. Here I am transferring D. F. Strauss's saying to christology: 'The true criticism of dogma is its history' (*Die christliche Glaubenslehre* I, 1840, 71) and making it more radical.

33. P. Vielhauer, *Aufsätze zum Neuen Testament*, 90. Similarly already H. Cremer, *Die paulinische Rechtfertigungslehre*, ²1900, 345: 'Jesus himself, who deliberately did not mention Christ in his proclamation until he had to swear that he was the Christ, therefore had to talk of the kingdom of God and leave it to his hearers whether they recognized the presence of this kingdom in his person or not. But now, where it was important to bear witness to Jesus as the one in whom all the promises of God are Yes and Amen (II Cor. 1.20), now it was no longer possible to preach that the kingdom of God was at hand, but rather that Jesus was the Christ—this is the apostolic form of Jesus' preaching of the kingdom.'

34. J. Moltmann, *Theology of Hope*, SCM Press 1967, 172ff.

35. H. Conzelmann, 'Historie und Theologie in den synoptischen Passionsberichten', in *Zur Theologie des Todes Jesu*, 1967, 37.

36. E. Käsemann, *Essays on New Testament Themes*, 23: 'The historical Jesus meets us in the New Testament, our only real and original

documentation of him, not as he was in himself, not as an isolated individual, but as *the* Lord of the community which believes in him. Only in so far as, from the very outset, he was potentially and actually this Lord, does the story of his earthly life play any part in our Gospels.' Nevertheless, the community had a genuine interest in the recollection of his earthly life and death because of their present experiences of the exalted Lord. If their 'historical' recollection is determined by their eschatological faith, 'the problem of history is a special form of the problem of eschatology' (29). Can history, as history writing, ever neglect the significance of history for the hopes of the present?

37. Thus H. Kessler, *Die theologische Bedeutung des Todes Jesu. Eine traditionsgeschichtliche Untersuchung*, 1970, 229ff.

38. Thus O. Betz, *What do we know about Jesus?*, SCM Press 1968, 86ff.

39. For what follows see G. Bornkamm, *Jesus of Nazareth*, Hodder and Stoughton 1960; E. Schweizer, *Jesus*, SCM Press 1971; H.-W. Bartsch, *Jesus—Prophet und Messias aus Galiläa*, 1970; O. Betz, *What do we know about Jesus?*, SCM Press 1968; W. Schrage, 'Das Verständnis des Todes Jesu im Neuen Testament', in: *Das Kreuz Jesu Christi als Grund des Heils*, 1967, 51–89; H. Kessler, *Die theologische Bedeutung des Todes Jesu*, 1970; E. Käsemann, *Essays on New Testament Themes*, SCM Press 1964; id., *New Testament Questions of Today*, SCM Press 1969.

40. E. Käsemann, *Essays on New Testament Themes*, 37f.

41. For blasphemy as the curse of God see the regulations in Lev. 24.16: 'He who blasphemes the name of the Lord shall be put to death; all the congregation shall stone him,' also Ex. 22.28; I Kings 21.10,13. In Num. 15.30 blasphemy is understood in wider terms: any deliberate sin with a high hand is regarded as cursing the name of the most Holy. In this wider form, mockery of the people of God (II Kings 19.4,6,22) or oppression of it (Isa. 52.5) by Assyrian kings, any shaming of those who fought for God (II Macc. 8.4; 12.4), mocking the holy land (Ez. 35.12 by Edom) and threats against the temple (I Macc. 7.38,41f.) are designated blasphemy. At the time of Jesus the understanding of blasphemy seems to have been so wide that impudent talk against the *Torah* and even the one 'who stretches out his hand against God', fall under it. Post-Christian *halachah*, on the other hand, took a narrower view: the blasphemer must have expressed the name of God clearly in the form of a curse (Mishnah Sanh. 7.5). In the case of Jesus it cannot have been a renunciation of God by a curse, but can only have been the blasphemy of a false Messiah made by a 'hand stretched out against God', someone intervening in a matter where rights are reserved for God alone.

42. E. Sjöberg, *Der verborgene Menschensohn in den Evangelien*, 1955, 244.

43. The distinction between Jesus and John the Baptist is particularly emphasized by E. Käsemann in order to underline the new element in his preaching (*New Testament Questions of Today*, 121ff.). That does not mean, as W. Pannenberg understands the matter (*Jesus—God and Man*, 62), that Jesus is thus 'detached from the apocalyptic atmosphere that preceded

him and followed him', whereas a connection with the apocalyptic message of the Baptist is more probable. In his structural comparisons of the proleptic sayings of John, Jesus and the primitive Christian kerygma, Pannenberg overlooks the new understanding of the content of the righteousness of God in Jesus and the Christ kerygma in comparison with the message of John. But Käsemann speaks of it in the earlier context.

44. The concept of prolepsis has been common material of New Testament theology since the time of J. Weiss, and is no new invention.

45. W. Schrage, op. cit., 57.

46. See W. Schrage, op. cit., 57f.

47. See in more detail J. Moltmann, *Theology of Hope*, SCM Press 1967, 139–54. Criticism of my use of the concept of the 'realization' of the promise through the gospel is quite superfluous, and does not note my remarks about the deconditionalizing and universalizing of the promise through Jesus and his history. The promise, freed from the limits and conditions of the law understood in nomistic terms, and taken up in the gospel of Christ, is something different from an unbroken continuation of the history of promise with other means. H. G. Geyer, H. Fries, W. Kreck and B. Klappert have been too light with their criticism at this point. Similarly B. Klappert, *Die Auferweckung des Gekreuzigten. Der Ansatz der Christologie K. Barths im Zusammenhang der Christologie der Gegenwart*, 1971, 323ff.

48. Cf. the German version in O. Weber, *Lebendiges Bekenntnis*, 1959, 67f.

49. See T. Mommsen, *Römische Geschichte* III, ⁷1882, 84ff.

50. C. Schmitt, *Politische Theologie II, Die Legende von der Erledigung jeder Politischen Theologie*, 1970, 117 n.3, writes as follows on my grounding of Christian 'political theology' in the remembrance of the 'Christ crucified for political reasons': 'The crucifixion was a political measure against slaves and those placed outside the law; it was the *supplicium sumptum de eo in servilem modum* ... Otherwise Moltmann is right in stressing the intensively political significance which is indestructibly contained within the worship of a God crucified in this fashion and which does not allow itself to be sublimated into something "purely theological".'

51. O. Cullmann, *Jesus und die Revolutionären seiner Zeit*, 1970, 47.

52. Thus M. Hengel, *Was Jesus a Revolutionist?*, Philadelphia 1971, against H. Braun, *Jesus*, 1969, 50, who asserts: 'The inscription on the cross, which is not put in Jewish terms, seems to be an unhistorical Christian interpretation which derives from the confession of Jesus as the Messiah.' Nevertheless, Braun concedes: 'Jesus may have seemed to the Romans to be a political disturber of the peace; his Jewish opponents, who were brought up against the uncomfortable admonisher, may have stressed to the Romans that some themes of the preaching of Jesus ... were politically suspicious.'

53. R. Bultmann, 'The Primitive Christian Kerygma', op. cit., 24. E. Käsemann, *New Testament Questions of Today*, 50f., already objected: 'I should, further, not myself wish to characterize the Cross simply as the result of a political misunderstanding on the part of the Romans, and I

should raise the question as to whether it must not rather be understood as arising out of the internal logic of Jesus' own activity.'

54. Here I follow M. Hengel, *Die Zeloten. Untersuchungen zur jüdischen Freiheitsbewegung in der Zeit von Herodes I bis 70 n. Chr.*, 1961; S. G. F. Brandon, *Jesus and the Zealots*, Manchester University Press, 1967; M. Hengel, *Victory over Violence*, Philadelphia 1973; ' "Politische Theologie" und neutestamentliche Zeitgeschichte', *KuD* 18, 1972, 18–25, and also the works already mentioned.

55. Thus O. Cullmann, op. cit., 23.

56. O. Cullmann, ibid.

57. M. Hengel, *Was Jesus a Revolutionist?*.

58. P. Lapide, cited in M. Hengel, ibid., 12.

59. M. Hengel, *Was Jesus a Revolutionist?*, 27; *Victory*, 54, 41. I believe that Hengel is right historically, but believe the ethical consequences in which he limits the revolution to the heart and discipleship to private morality to be unconsidered.

60. Cullmann, op. cit., 57.

61. R. Seeberg, *Lehrbuch der Dogmengeschichte* I, 333f.

62. H. Berkhof, *Kirche und Kaiser*, 1947, 31f.

63. R. Guardini, *The Death of Socrates*, Sheed and Ward 1948.

64. E. Bethge, *Dietrich Bonhoeffer*, Collins 1970, 830.

65. D. Bonhoeffer, *Letters and Papers from Prison*, The Enlarged Edition, SCM Press 1971, 391.

66. Cf. H. Gese, 'Psalm 22 und das Neue Testament', *ZThK* 65, 1968, 1ff. For Psalm 22 and the passion narrative in Jewish interpretation see E. Fromm, *Die Herausforderung Gottes und des Menschen*, 1970, 227–32.

67. W. Schrage, op. cit., 67.

68. Thus essentially also R. Bultmann, H. Braun and W. Schrage, when they speak of collapse, failure, etc.

69. Cf. J. Jeremias, *The Prayers of Jesus*, SCM Press 1967.

70. In fact Luther rightly referred Christ's descent into hell to his dying forsaken by God and not to his preaching in the kingdom of the dead.

71. R. Bultmann, 'The Primitive Christian Kerygma', op. cit., 24.

72. R. Weth, 'Heil im gekreuzigten Gott', *EvTh* 31, 1971, 227ff.

73. So too W. Schrage, op. cit., 67 n.48: 'The word is certainly not simply the expression of naked despair or pure meaninglessness, because Jesus did not abandon himself to despair but, *in* despair, to the arms of God.'

74. C. Schmitt, *Politische Theologie* II, 116, has made an important reference to a theological doctrine of *stasis*. He uses the saying of Gregory of Nazianzus (*Or. Theol.* III 2) quoted by E. Peterson: 'The one—*to hen* —is always in uproar—*stasiatsōn*—against itself—*pros heauton*' and remarks: 'Here we find a true political theological stasiology at the heart of the doctrine of the Trinity' (118). The dictum '*Nemo contra Deum nisi Deus ipse*', which describes the same situation, comes from Goethe, stands as a motto over the fourth book of *Dichtung und Wahrheit*, and is of christological derivation: 'These men cannot be overcome by anything

but the universe itself, with which they began their struggle . . . and from
such observations that remarkable but tremendous saying may have
arisen.' According to C. Schmitt it comes from J. M. Lenz, *Catharina von
Siena*, where Catharina laments at the flight of her father:

'Like a loving, injured God
my father looked threateningly at me.
Yet had he stretched out both hands—
God against God
   (she takes a small crucifix from her breast and kisses it).
Rescue me, save me,
My Jesus, whom I follow, from his arm . . .
Rescue me, save me from my father,
and his love, his tyranny.'

C. Schmitt rightly remarks: 'If a unity is a duality and consequently the
possibility of an uproar, a *stasis*, is immanent, then theology seems to
become "stasiology" ' (123). In that case it is no longer a matter of
'theological politics' in earthly friend-enemy relationships, but of 'political
theology', namely the talk of the enmity manifest and overcome in God
himself, from which theological politics can only draw the conclusion of
reconciliation through dissolution of the friend-enemy pattern. If the
conflict in God is overcome by God himself, the external conclusion is:
'All feuds now have an end'.

   75. Cf. H. Gollwitzer, *Krummes Holz—aufrechter Gang. Zur Frage
nach dem Sinn des Lebens*, 1970, 258: 'The rift goes not only through
Jesus but through God himself. God himself is abandoned by God and
God casts himself out.'

5

THE ESCHATOLOGICAL TRIAL OF
JESUS CHRIST

1. *Eschatology and History*

In Chapter 4 we have tried to understand the death of Jesus on
the cross in the context of his theological life and work. In the
three dimensions which we described, Jesus' way to the cross
ended with open questions: with the question of the righteousness
of God, between Jesus and the understanding of law in his time;
with the question of the authority of freedom, between Jesus and
the religio-political power of Rome; and with the question of the
divinity of God, between Jesus and his Father. Now we face the
task of understanding his death and his life and thus his whole
historical appearance in the context of his resurrection from
the dead and of eschatological faith. Both perspectives must be
reciprocally related to one another, if his truth is to be both
perceived and understood. Here one cannot separate historical
consideration from eschatological understanding, nor put the two
things together afterwards. The historical Jesus is not 'half Christ',
nor is the risen Christ the other half of Jesus.[1] It is a question of
one and the same person and his unique history. The risen Christ
is the historical and crucified Jesus, and *vice versa*. The reason
for the 'differentiated connection'[2] of the historical and eschatological perspectives is the uniqueness of the person of Jesus and
his history; because of his death on the cross, the only way in
which they can adequately be described is by the double formulae
'Jesus Christ' and 'crucified and risen'. But what makes possible
the eschatological recognition of his person, his life and death in
the light of his resurrection from the dead? What justifies it?

The decisive element for primitive Christianity was not just the history of the life and death, the proclamation and the work of Jesus; it attached equal weight to the unexpected and un-derivable new factors of his resurrection by God, of the gift of the spirit and of faith among Jews and Gentiles. The union of Jesus with God and of God with Jesus was constituted for it by that event which it originally and—as we shall see—rightly called 'the resurrection of Jesus'. The first creeds that we know speak of 'Jesus the Lord', and of 'God who has raised him from the dead' (Rom. 10.6; I Cor. 15.1), in the same breath. They combine a formula about a person with a formula about a work. The confession of the crucified Jesus as *kyrios* was grounded on faith in the God who had raised him. Conversely, this faith in God was completely and utterly a resurrection faith and concerned the person of the crucified Christ, in whom God had acted and in whom the God who raises from the dead had manifested himself. As a process and as an event, the resurrection was so to speak a light into which it was impossible to look directly. It was necessary to look at the one whom it illuminated and manifested, and that was none other than Jesus, the crucified. If the person and history of Jesus, and God's act in raising him, are both constitutive of Christian faith, then it is not a question of establishing the life and death of Jesus as a historical fact, and regarding the resurrec-tion, the appearances of Jesus and the Easter faith as inter-changeable interpretations of that fact. That would not do justice to the rise of the Christian faith at all. Rather, the legitimate critical question is: does the primitive Christian belief in the resurrection do justice to the life and death of Jesus, or has it put something else in Jesus' place? The true criticism of dogma is its history, remarked D. F. Strauss. We have changed that and said: the true criticism of faith in the resurrection is the history of the crucified Christ. So we must subject belief in the resurrection to the history of the crucified Christ as its true criticism.

'If Christ is not risen, then our preaching is vain and your faith is vain,' says Paul in I Cor. 15.14. If one calls the cross of Jesus the 'nuclear fact' of Christian faith, one must call his resurrection the primal datum of that faith.[3] An analysis of the process of primitive Christian tradition confirms the fact. There was hardly any dispute over Jesus' resurrection, but there was over the inter-pretation of his death on the cross in the light of the resurrection. Primitive Christian recollections of Jesus were determined from the start by the experience of his resurrection through God. That was the only reason why his words and his story were remembered and why people were concerned with him. Even today, it is doubtful whether there is any other adequate reason for being concerned with the person and history of Jesus Christ which lie so far back in the past. As a merely historical person he would long have been forgotten, because his message had already been contradicted by his death on the cross. As a person at the heart of an eschatological faith and proclamation, on the other hand, he becomes a mystery and a question for every new age.

If we are to understand the truth about Jesus according to the witness of the New Testament, we must take two courses at the same time: we must read his history both forwards and backwards, and relate both readings, the ontic-historical and the noetic-eschatological, to each other and identify the results we achieve.

Just as, historically speaking, the crucifixion precedes the Easter appearances, so for the faith of the primitive church all knowledge of Jesus (in the sense of certainty of salvation) was only possible after Easter. This applies to the one who was incarnate and crucified as well as to the one who was pre-existent and exalted. Nor must we confine this observation to the experience of the primitive church. It is a basic truth and applies at all periods. If this were not so, a theology of the Word would be quite unjustifiable.[4]

First of all, this applies only to Christian faith. As the New Testament shows, not only in the epistles but also in the gospels, Christian faith essentially reads the history of Jesus back to front: his cross is understood in the light of his resurrection, his way to the cross in the light of the saving meaning of his cross, his words and miracles in the light of his Easter exaltation to be Lord. Even his insignificant birth is recalled and narrated in the light of his crucifixion. Ernst Bloch is right about this reading of the history of Jesus Christ in the light of his resurrection: 'Indeed, even the end of Christ was nonetheless his beginning.' Jesus' resurrection from the dead by God was never regarded as a private and isolated miracle for his authentication, but as the beginning of the general resurrection of the dead, i.e. as the beginning of the end of history in the midst of history. His resurrection was not regarded as a fortuitous miracle in an unchangeable world, but as the beginning of the eschatological transformation of the world by its creator. Thus the resurrection of Jesus stood in the framework of a universal hope of eschatological belief, which was kindled in it. The first titles of Christ to be formulated under the impact of the appearances of the crucified Jesus in the light of the coming glory of God are titles of promise and hope: 'The first fruits of them that are asleep', 'the first fruits of the resurrection of the dead', the 'pioneer of life'.[6] That means that the crucified Christ was understood in the light of his resurrection and that his resurrection was understood in the light of his future in the coming God and his glory. Therefore his historical crucifixion was understood as the eschatological event of judgment and his resurrection as a hidden anticipation of the eschatological kingdom of glory in which the dead will be raised. The 'future' of which the first real anticipation was seen in his resurrection was not understood as future history and thus as part of transitoriness, but eschatologically as the future of history and thus as the pledge of the new creation. 'Easter' was a prelude to, and a real anticipation of, God's qualitatively new future and the new creation in the midst of the history of the world's suffering. So in the light of this prelude to the coming God and the coming end of this abandoned world it was also necessary to recall, understand and proclaim in eschatological terms the one who presented this prelude, Jesus of Nazareth. For the Easter hope shines not only forwards into the unknown newness of the history which it opens up, but also backwards over the graveyards of history, and in their midst first on the grave of a crucified man who appeared in that prelude. The symbol of the 'resurrection *of the* dead' which is used by eschatological belief combines God's future with the past of the dead and expresses not only hope for those to come, but also hope for those who have passed on in God. Correspondingly, the creed of early Christian faith that 'Jesus was raised *from* the dead' expresses a certainty about the future of the Jesus who was killed and by his death was condemned to the past. The Christian resurrection hope is kindled by the appearances of Jesus; as a result it first casts its light backwards on to the Jesus who died on the cross. Only from him and through him does the resurrection hope then extend to the living and the dead. 'For to this end has Christ died and come alive again, that he might be Lord of both dead and living' (Rom. 14.9).

In the modern historical sense we talk of *Jesus of Nazareth*, because in historical terms and temporality his origin should explain his future and his beginning his end. But eschatological faith speaks of Jesus whom God has raised from the dead, and of Jesus as the Christ of God, the one who 'reserves a place for the God who is to come' (which is how one can interpret the title 'Christ'), because his future determines and explains his origin and his end his beginning. The historical title 'Jesus of Nazareth' binds Jesus to his past. The eschatological title 'Christ' binds him to his future.

Are there starting points for this eschatological reading of Jesus' history in historical thought generally? Rudolf Bultmann once remarked:

> Events or historical figures are not historical phenomena in themselves, not even as members of a sequence of cause and effect. They are 'historical phenomena' only in the way in which they are related to their future, for which they have significance and for which the present bears the responsibility.[7]

Unfortunately, he himself then abandoned this fruitful notion for fear of Hegelianism and replaced the 'eschatological interpretation' of history which is suggested here by an existentialist interpretation of the eschatological historicity of existence. But if his remark quoted above is correct, in the present case it follows that as a 'historical phenomenon' Jesus will be understood 'historically' only in the way in which he is related to his future, for which he has significance, and that the responsibility of present faith is for such a historical understanding of Jesus, together with his future. Faith's own historicity arises only from the eschatological connection between Jesus and his future, which it perceives.

F. Rosenzweig has spoken even more aptly of history as an 'unfinished world':

> This state of becoming and unfinishedness can only be grasped by a reversal of the objective relationships of time. Whereas the past, that which is already finished, lies there from its beginning to its end and can be narrated . . . the future can only be grasped as what it is, namely the future, by means of anticipation.[8]

If history were finished and we were standing at its end, one would be able to narrate world history from the beginning to the end, and one would be able to estimate the significance of each part for the whole. But as we are not at the end, but in the midst of history, we always associate, consciously or unconsciously, recollections of the past with hopes and fears for the future, and interpret the past in respect of the future of our own present. With historical recollections we connect an outline of the whole of history, i.e. of the end of history.

W. Benjamin has expressed the dialectical identity of eschatology and history in a still more subtle manner:

Only the Messiah himself brings to consummation all historical events, in the sense that he himself resolves, completes, creates their relationship to the messianic. Therefore nothing historical can of itself want to be related to the messianic. Therefore the kingdom of God is not the *telos* of historical *dynamis*. From a historical point of view it is not the goal, but the end . . . Thus the profane is not a category of the kingdom, but a category, perhaps the most appropriate category, for its slightest approach.[9]

Only the historian has the gift of kindling the sparks of hope in the past which is permeated by it; *even the dead* will not be safe from the enemy when he conquers. And this enemy has not ceased to conquer.[10]

Benjamin has expressed things similarly in his picture of the *angelus novus*.[11] Since for him history is fundamentally a history of suffering, it cannot itself become pregnant with a messianic future. The messianic history of life runs counter to the history of the suffering of the world which leads to death, and approaches it from the future. But in this counter-course it has a redemptive relationship to the whole history of death and the dead. This view comes very near to being an eschatological theology of the crucified Christ, if it is in a position to unfold hope and liberation in the history of the suffering of the world from the history of the suffering of the risen Christ. Thus the reversed 'eschatological reading of history' is not so alien among the general problems of universal history-writing as positivists might think. Rather, historical positivism is eschatological in its solemn concern to 'end' history by dissolving its facts and laws in positivistic epistemology.[12] The general structural connections of recollection and hope, profanity and messianic nature, when applied to historical knowledge and historical writing in the midst of an 'open' history of suffering and death, do not 'prove' the justification of the primitive Christian eschatology of the life and death of Jesus, but they do make it more comprehensible.

2. *Jesus' Resurrection from the Dead*

We must first ask what Easter faith says and what it does not say, and begin with the situation of the eye-witnesses. Jesus was crucified in public. But at first only his disciples learned of his resurrection by God through the 'appearances of Jesus'. After that they spoke again of Jesus as the Christ in public. What had happened to them, according to their own account? Easter faith arose among those who knew Jesus, who had gone about with him and who had experienced his crucifixion in human helplessness and abandonment by God. It arose first among those who without exception had fled from the place where he was crucified and whose faith in Jesus had been refuted by this harsh fact. The situation of the Easter witnesses was therefore determined: 1. by the preaching of Jesus and their discipleship; 2. by the crucifixion of Jesus and their faith which was shattered by it; 3. by the themes and symbols of the general apocalyptic expectation held by the Judaism of their time, under Roman domination. This sequence must be noted, so that Easter faith is not derived directly from the general apocalyptic mood of the Judaism of the time. The Easter faith was given its Christian determination primarily by Jesus' proclamation of the righteousness of the kingdom of God which was approaching in grace, and which already represented a change from the apocalyptic pattern of righteousness. This faith was also determined by the death of Jesus as a 'lawless man', a 'rebel' and 'one abandoned by God'. Between the eschatological Easter faith and the various forms of late-Jewish apocalyptic stood Jesus himself and his cross.[13] If the first enthusiastic forms of Christian belief in the resurrection do not always betray a clear consciousness of this fact, the more time goes on the less it can be missed.

How did the eye-witnesses see the risen Christ? In the Easter kerygma the Easter faith is constantly grounded in a 'seeing'. What was the structure of this seeing? The expression ὤφθη, which already occurs in pre-Pauline tradition, is presumably the earliest. It can mean that *Christ was seen*; it can also mean that Christ *appeared* and *showed himself*. Finally, following the passive periphrasis of the divine name which is to be found in Judaism, it can also mean that *God showed him*.[14] In that case, it is a revelation formula such as also appears in theophanies in the Old

Testament. The activity lies with the one who appears or with the one who makes someone else appear. The man affected by the appearance is passive. He experiences the appearance of God in his knowledge of God. It is the seeing of something which is given to someone to see. It is therefore not the seeing of something which is always there. Nor is it a seeing that can be repeated and can be verified because it can be repeated. In Gal. 1.15 Paul associates this 'appearing' and 'seeing' with the expression ἀποκάλυψις. If the group of words relating to appearing and seeing is associated with this group of words connected with revelation, then we have a very definite meaning: God is disclosing something which is concealed from the knowledge of the present age of the world. He is revealing something which cannot be known by the mode of knowledge of the present time. Now it is 'the mysteries of the end-time', i.e. God's future and the righteousness of his kingdom, which are concealed and cannot be known under the conditions of the present age.[15] The present age of unrighteousness cannot tolerate the righteousness of God, and so the righteousness of God brings about a new age. This is manifest only at the end of the unrighteous world as a ground for the new world. So too God himself will reveal himself in his glory only at the end of the old age and at the beginning of the new. But in the history of the unrighteous world there are already anticipatory revelations of his future. That is an old prophetic and apocalyptic tradition: 'Surely the Lord God does nothing without revealing his secret to his servants the prophets' (Amos 3.7).[16] 'For just as with respect to all that has happened in the world the beginning is obscure but the end manifest, so also are the times of the Most High: the beginnings are visible in portents and secret signs, and the end in effects and marvels' (IV Ezra 9.5).[17] Anticipatory revelations of God's future in the Old Testament are constantly associated with prophetic calls and the sending of prophets into this world. Even Paul understood the appearance of the risen Christ which he experienced as his call to the apostolate, following the pattern of the prophetic calls. But that means that in the view of those concerned, the appearances of the risen Christ had the structure of anticipatory vision, and were bound up with a call to special service of the one who was to come, in the transitory world. They were therefore not mystical transportations into another world beyond, nor were they inner illuminations, but a sight and a foretaste in the countenance of the crucified Christ of the God who was to come, a matter of being seized by the coming change in the world through God's glory. The Easter visions had two sides: the eye-witnesses 1. had a foretaste of the coming glory of the kingdom of God in the form of Jesus and 2. recognized Jesus again by the marks of crucifixion. So we can say that the visions were a reunion in anticipation and an anticipation in reunion. The disciples saw Jesus in the glory of the coming God and the glory of the coming God in Jesus. It was a reciprocal process of identification.

This form of the Easter visons explains the return of the disciples from Galilee to Jerusalem, 'although any other place clearly offered better protection to the adherents of the crucified Nazarene'.[18] They had to wait for the kingdom of the crucified Christ, an anticipation of which they had seen, in Jerusalem, for in the first place he had been crucified there; and in the second place, according to apocalyptic tradition Jerusalem was the place where the expected Messiah or Son of Man would appear. When they reached Jerusalem they will have found there stories about the empty tomb and will have accepted these as confirmation of the new eschatological belief in Jesus that they had brought with them. According to this analysis of the Easter appearances and visions, the original significance of the Easter faith is that the eye-witnesses perceived the earthly, crucified Jesus of the past in the glory of God's coming and drew conclusions from that in their experience of a call and mission. In that case it must be said that Jesus was raised into God's future and was seen and believed as the present representative of this future, of the free, new mankind and the new creation. In that case he was not raised into heaven and in that sense eternalized or divinized. Nor was he raised into the kerygma or into faith, for both kerygma and faith are understood eschatologically as the promise and hope of what is to come. Jesus 'rose into the final judgment of God'[19] to which both kerygma and faith bear witness.

Now when it is seen in terms of the hope that sheds its light backwards, that means that the glory of the coming God has been manifested in the helplessness and shame of the crucified Jesus. The final judgment has already been made in his execution. Jesus' deliverance to men and their attitude to him are decisive for the final judgment. His forgiveness of sins is God's law of grace.

The coming God has been made flesh in Jesus of Nazareth. The future of the qualitatively new creation has already begun through the history of Jesus' suffering in the history of the suffering of the abandoned world. The judgment has been anticipated and by his death has already been decided in favour of the accused. If, as the Easter vision implies, God has identified himself, his judgment and his kingdom with the crucified Jesus, his cross and his helplessness, then conversely the resurrection of the crucified Jesus into the coming glory of God contains within itself the process of the incarnation of the coming God and his glory in the crucified Jesus. When John stresses that Jesus was glorified on the cross, the converse implication is that the glory of God was crucified in him and thus made manifest in this unjust world. The Christian belief in resurrection is the foundation not only of the transcendence but also of the immanence of this faith, because it sees the transcendent God immanent in Jesus, and conversely the immanent Jesus transcended in God.

Here we come to matters about which the Easter faith says nothing. No witness claims to have seen what happened between Good Friday and Easter. There are no eye-witnesses to the process of the resurrection of Jesus from the tomb. But in that case why did they talk of his 'resurrection' and not, say, of his elevation or his eternalization? If 'seeing' Jesus after his death had the structure of anticipation on the ground of the anticipatory vision of his future in the coming God, it then becomes comprehensible why those concerned spoke of his 'resurrection from the dead' and adopted this apocalyptic symbol for the new creative action of God. It is a symbol for the 'end of the history', of unrighteousness, evil, death and abandonment by God, and for the beginning of the new world of the righteousness of God. Is this symbol appropriate to the matter with which it is concerned?

'Resurrection of the dead' first of all excludes any idea of a revivification of the dead Jesus which might have reversed the process of his death. Easter faith can never mean that the dead Jesus returned to this life, which leads to death. Were that the case, then he would have to be expected to die once more like, Lazarus, who according to John 11 was raised by Christ, although his corpse was already stinking, and who then later died again. The symbol of 'resurrection from the dead' means a qualitatively new life which no longer knows death and therefore cannot be a continuation of this mortal life. 'Christ being raised from the dead will never die again,' says Paul (Rom. 6.9). Resurrection means 'life from the dead' (Rom. 9.15), and is itself connected with the annihilation of the power of death. On the other hand, 'resurrection of the dead' excludes any idea of 'a life after death', of which many religions speak, whether in the idea of the immortality of the soul or in the idea of the transmigration of souls. Resurrection life is not a further life after death, whether in the soul or the spirit, in children or in reputation; it means the annihilation of death in the victory of the new, eternal life (I Cor. 15.55). The notion of 'life after death' can coexist peacefully with the experience that this life is a 'life towards death'. But the 'resurrection of the dead', understood as a present hope in the midst of the 'body of death', contradicts the harshest facts of life which point in the opposite direction, and cannot leave either death or the dead in peace, because it symbolizes the future of the dead. Thus the expression 'resurrection of the dead', which seemed to follow from the Easter visions, does not deny the fatality of death, whether this death is the death of Jesus on the cross or death in general, with the help of ideas of a life after death in some shape or form. Nor does it reduce the new element which the disciples perceived in Jesus to a dimension of the earthly Jesus, like the continuing influence of his cause or his spirit, or to a dimension of the faith of the disciples, like their longing for their own justification despite the disappointment of the cross or their desire for hope for their crucified past. It is therefore appropriate to the two experiences—the experience of his death on the cross and the experience of his appearances in the light of the coming glory of God. But can it be used further in Christianity, once the thought-world of Jewish apocalyptic has faded far into the past and become incomprehensible? The symbol of the resurrection of the dead comes from Jewish apocalyptic and was a firm ingredient of Jewish expectations among many groups at the time of Jesus. What does this symbol convey in that context, and what does it say in the Christian context?

At the end of days God will raise the dead, and in so doing will demonstrate his power over the power of death. The end-time of the world and the beginning of the new creation dawns with the general resurrection of the dead. Now the proclamation of the Easter witnesses that God has 'raised' this dead Jesus 'from

the dead' amounts to nothing less than the claim that this future of
the new world of the righteousness and presence of God has already
dawned in this one person in the midst of our history of death. All
who hear and believe this, move from a distant expectation of an
uncertain future to a sure hope in a near future of God which has
already dawned in that one person. Whereas Jewish apocalyptic
says that men should wait for 'the resurrection *of the dead*', Easter
faith says that men should believe in 'the resurrection of Jesus
from the dead'. This is already an important alteration in the
symbol of the resurrection of the dead itself. The alteration
asserts that this one man has been raised before all others and that
with him the process of the raising of the dead has been set in
motion, to the degree that this world of death and the coming
world of life are no longer set over against each other like two
different periods of the world. Believers no longer live in this
unredeemed world of death. In that one man the future of the
new world of life has already gained power over this unredeemed
world of death and has condemned it to become a world that
passes away. Therefore, in faith in the risen Jesus, men already
live in the midst of the transitory world of death from the powers
of the new world of life that have dawned in him. There is already
true life in the midst of false life, though only in communion with
the one who had been crucified by that false life.[20] 'The future has
already begun.' Jesus' resurrection already makes possible the
impossible, namely reconciliation in the midst of strife, the law
of grace in the midst of judgment, and creative love in the midst
of legalism. Just as Jesus proclaimed, 'The kingdom of God is
near at hand', so, on the basis of his resurrection from the dead,
with a similar structure the early church proclaimed, 'The day
(viz. of God) has come near' (Rom. 13.12) and 'the end of all
things is at hand' (I Peter 4.7). Thus the 'night' of false life and
unrighteousness and the 'unredeemed world' is 'far spent'. Over
against Jewish apocalyptic we find expressed here a new eschatological understanding of time, and it is this, for all the change in
cosmological ideas, that is constitutive for the eschatological faith
of Christianity. Without this eschatological consciousness of time,
all the things that the Christian church claims and proclaims as
being present: the forgiveness of sins, reconciliation and discipleship in love, are fundamentally impossible. The attested resurrection of Jesus before all other men is in fact meant proleptically.[21]

Now according to the apocalyptic order of hope, such an anticipation of the future which was to affect all men was not expected
at all. The redemption of the unredeemed world is public and
universal, or it has not yet come about. Nevertheless, in the
apocalyptic tradition there were also legends of a premature
ascension of particular righteous men, like Elijah and Enoch. There
was also the notion that great spirits of the past so to speak
'rise again' in their great followers. So, for example, it was asked
whether John the Baptist or Elijah had 'risen again' in Jesus.
Wolfhart Pannenberg thinks that the special feature in Christian
faith, as opposed to apocalyptic, is this prolepsis. Just as Jesus
proleptically claimed the distant kingdom of God and referred
his claim to God for future confirmation, so Easter faith proclaimed the 'end of history', in which God will fully reveal
himself, as 'anticipated' by his resurrection. 'In the fate of Jesus
the end of history has taken place beforehand as an anticipation.'[22]
As far as the formal structure of the Easter visions and the
Christian symbol of the 'resurrection of Jesus from the dead',
together with the Easter kerygma, are concerned, that is hard
to dispute. But it still does not provide any historical proof for
Jesus' claim, since in the case of the claim of the earthly Jesus
and his resurrection from the dead the verification pattern of claim
and confirmation has again been referred to the confirmation of his
resurrection *from the dead* by the general resurrection *of the dead*.
What has taken place in Jesus is for its part again referred for its
confirmation to the end of history, which is here said to be
anticipated. It is true that the proclamation of the 'resurrection of
Jesus *from the dead*' only makes sense in the eschatological horizon
of the 'resurrection *of the dead*'. But an anticipation can confirm
that it is an anticipation and confirm that which is to be anticipated
only in the context of what has been itself anticipated. And to
recognize what has been anticipated eschatologically in the
sequence of historical anticipations which refer to each other and
confirm each other requires faith, namely faith in what has been
anticipated, which can only be recognized in anticipation. Whereas
Jesus anticipated the coming kingdom by his word and was
publicly crucified for it, the Easter anticipation of the resurrection
was manifested in a different way. Knowledge of it led directly to
faith in Jesus, to certain hope in his coming and to the actions of
the apostolate. This was therefore no unpartisan knowledge

established on a neutral basis, but a knowledge that engaged men, claimed their allegiance and called them to the apostolate. Thus it is removed from what in modern times is understood as a factual historical proof. The resurrection of Jesus from the dead by God does not speak the 'language of facts', but only the language of faith and hope, that is, the 'language of promise'. I have therefore denoted the proleptic structure of the proclamation of Jesus and the Christian resurrection faith by the word 'promise'.[23] In the sphere of speech this expresses the very anticipation which for Pannenberg lies in the fact itself. There is no need here to be involved in a dispute between the expressions 'verbal prolepsis' (promise) and 'real prolepsis' (anticipatory event). Both expressions say the same things on different levels. My own view is that the expression 'promise event' corresponds more really to the continuing difference between the demonstrably 'unredeemed world' and faith in the coming of reconciliation in the midst of strife than the verbally pacifying talk of the actual anticipation of the end.

The point of difference lies elsewhere. Only the new creation in Christ and through Christ will demonstrate the new element in the proclamation of Jesus and the new element in his anticipated resurrection from the dead. This points to 'eschatological verification'. Conversely, this means that the old, unredeemed and unchanged world of suffering, guilt and death is not capable of demonstrating the new creation, in which there will be no more sorrow, no more crying and no more tears. This 'scandal of the qualitative difference'[24] between the unfree world and the free world, between false and true life, between the unredeemed world and redeemed existence, may not be brought down to a single level. In so far as and so long as the cross of Jesus is a scandal and foolishness in the world, his resurrection cannot be demonstrated to this world, except through the freedom of a faith which runs contrary to this world and is therefore constantly on trial. It lies with reality in the dispute over the future of true being. For Christians, the 'scandal of qualitative difference' cannot be an abstract one, which attests the dream of the other life through a 'great refusal'.[25] The Christian scandal of the qualitative difference lies in the cross of the Christ whom God has raised.

Let us therefore ask once again: was the proleptic feature of anticipation really the special element in the Christian Easter faith?

As Daniel 12 shows, in apocalyptic expectation the expectation of a general resurrection of the dead was an integral part of the expectation of God. God will raise the dead in the last days. But why? In the apocalyptic expectation this was no longing for eternal life. 'Resurrection of the dead' was not an anthropological or a soteriological symbol, but a way towards expressing belief in the righteousness of God. God is righteous. His righteousness will conquer. As the righteousness of God, it cannot be limited even by death. So God will summon both dead and living before his judgment seat. But that is only possible if he has raised the dead beforehand, so that they can identify themselves with the deeds and omissions of their earthly life at his judgment. In the judgment God returns to the past life of the dead. Hence the notion of a general resurrection of the dead arose logically from thinking through to the end the irresistible and victorious righteousness of God. The starting point was the question, 'Why must the righteous suffer and why do the godless fare well here?' 'Why is Israel to the heathen given over for reproach, thy beloved people to godless tribes given up?' (IV Ezra 4.23). The apocalyptist's answer is: 'Why has thou not considered what is to come, rather than what is now present?'[26] Now if the future is taken to heart in the question of righteousness, then God's righteousness is put in question by the death of the innocent and also by the death of the unrighteous. Does death then set a limit to the righteousness of God? In view of the belief in the divinity of God this is inconceivable. Daniel 12.2 is therefore the first to answer this question with the symbol of the expectation of a general resurrection of the dead for the final judgment, so that the righteousness of God can assign some 'to eternal life' and others to eternal shame and damnation. Those here who are righteous according to the law of the divine covenant gain eternal life. The lawless and the lawbreakers come to eternal damnation. Is this symbol of the general resurrection of the dead a symbol of hope? For the unrighteous it is rather a symbol of fear. It would be better for them to stay dead. But for the righteous it is an uncertain hope, for no one can say with certainty that he is righteous. Ernst Bloch has understood better than some theologians that the hope for resurrection is not a human hope for good fortune, but is an expression of the expectation of divine righteousness;[27] thus it represents a hope for God, for the sake of God and his right.

In the framework of the question of righteousness, which is fundamental for apocalyptic, one cannot say that the question of righteousness has become obsolete along with the ideas through which it is expressed here, and cannot now be understood by modern men. Any look at world history raises the question why inhuman men fare so well and their victims fare so badly. Only on a superficial level is 'world history' a problem of universal history, by the solution of which a meaningful horizon can be found for the whole of existence. At the deepest level the question of world history is the question of righteousness. And this question extends out into transcendence. The question whether there is a God or not is a speculative question in the face of the cries for righteousness of those who are murdered and gassed, who are hungry and oppressed. If the question of theodicy can be understood as a question of the righteousness of God in the history of the suffering of the world, then all understanding and presentation of world history must be seen within the horizon of the question of theodicy. Or do the executioners ultimately triumph over their innocent victims? Even the Christian Easter faith in the last resort stands in the context of the question of the divine righteousness in history: does inhuman legalism triumph over the crucified Christ, or does God's law of grace triumph over the works of the law and of power? With this question we go beyond the formal statements about the proleptic structures of eschatological faith to the matter of Christian faith itself. We must not only ask whether it is possible and conceivable that one man has been raised from the dead before all others, and not only seek for analogies in the historical structure of reality and in the anticipatory structure of reason, but also ask *who* this one man was. If we do, we shall find that he was condemned according to his people's understanding of the law as a 'blasphemer' and was crucified by the Romans, according to the divine ordinance of their *Pax Romana*, as a 'rebel'. He met a hellish death with every sign of being abandoned by his God and Father. The new and scandalous element in the Christian message of Easter was not that some man or other was raised before anyone else, but that the one who was raised was this condemned, executed and forsaken man. This was the unexpected element in the kerygma of the resurrection which created the new righteousness of faith. Then, and probably even now, the problematical question was and is not just whether the resurrection of Jesus is physically, biologically or historically possible and conceivable, but also whether the resurrection of the crucified Christ corresponds to the righteousness of God. If God raised this dishonoured man in his coming righteousness, it follows that in this crucified figure he manifests his true righteousness, the right of the unconditional grace which makes righteous the unrighteous and those without rights.

In the context of the apocalyptic expectation of the final triumph of the law, the 'resurrection of the dead' is a two-edged expectation. But the resurrection of the crucified Christ reveals the righteousness of God in a different way, namely as grace which makes righteous and as the creator's love of the godless. Therefore the resurrection hope of Christian faith is no longer ambivalent, threatened by an uncertain final judgment and its verdict; it is unequivocally a 'joyful hope'. It shows the cross of Christ as the unique and once-for-all anticipation of the great world judgment in the favour of those who otherwise could not survive at it. Thus resurrection is no longer the ontic presupposition of the accomplishment of the final judgment on the dead and the living, but is already itself the new creation. So the Pauline resurrection kerygma contains within itself the proclamation of the new creation. In that case righteousness no longer means the rewarding of the righteous with eternal life and the punishing of the unrighteous with eternal condemnation, but the law of grace for unrighteous and self-righteous alike.

Wolfhart Pannenberg has stressed the formal structure of prolepsis in the claim of Jesus and its confirmation in the resurrection event so one-sidedly that it has become easy to overlook the significance of the harsh antithesis between the claim of Jesus and its confirmation in his cross.[28] He has interpreted apocalyptic and christology too much in terms of their significance for universal history, so that the fundamental question of righteousness can be neglected. Finally, as a result, in his hermeneutics he has been able to contemporize the apocalyptic context in which the symbol of the 'resurrection of Jesus from the dead' is expressed, only by means of an anthropology of the openness of modern man to the world.[29] It is not wrong to establish such structural analogies, since the modern anthropology of man's openness to the world is itself derived from the influence of the history of apocalyptic and christology. But Jesus' claim and his resurrection can easily become a mere example of a universal-historical or anthropological notion here, the truth of which is in the end independent of the history of Jesus.[30] Only when one goes beyond the formal categories of anticipation to the material content of the proclamation of Jesus and the Christian kerygma of the resurrection of the crucified Christ does the irreplacably Christian element emerge. And only in the question of righteousness in suffering the evil and misery of the world of man does one, in my view, come up against the abiding question of apocalyptic which cannot be settled, and the answer of Jesus and his history, the scandal of which cannot be laid aside.

To sum up:

1. Apocalyptic is a syncretistic formation with more than one idea. But at its centre we do not find anthropology or universal history, but the expectation of the future victory of the righteousness of God over dead and living. The 'resurrection of the dead' has no significance of its own, but is thought of as *a conditio sine qua non* for the universal achievement of righteousness in the judgment upon righteous and unrighteous.

2. Jesus' proclamation was apocalyptic in form, as far as, like John the Baptist, he proclaimed the imminence of the distant kingdom. In fact, however, Jesus broke through legalistic apocalyptic, because he proclaimed *justitia justificans* rather than *justitia distributiva* as the righteousness of the kingdom of God, and anticipated it in the law of grace among the unrighteous and those outside the law.

3. In form, the resurrection message of the early community was an apocalyptic anticipation of what was to come, but in content it was the proclamation of the crucified Christ as the Lord of righteousness. The scandal was not the message that one man had been raised before all others in the final judgment and the kingdom of God, but the certainty that this one man was the crucified Jesus. In form, Christian faith in the resurrection is eschatological faith. In content, this eschatological faith is Christian, because it proclaims the resurrection of the crucified Christ. The Christian belief in the resurrection does not proclaim world-historical tendencies or anthropological hopes, but the nucleus of a new righteousness in a world where dead and living cry out for righteousness.

4. The hermeneutic point for the understanding of Christian faith in the resurrection must therefore be sought in the question of righteousness in the history of the suffering of the world. This is an open question, which cannot either be answered or given up. The horizon of universal history and the depths of historical existence provide a framework to help in answering this question. The horizon of universal history makes clear the breadth of the question of righteousness in the form of the question of theodicy, whereas the existential dimension makes clear the depth of this question of righteousness in the question of justification.

5. The dispute over the resurrection of Jesus is concerned with the question of righteousness in history. Does it belong to the *nomos* which finally gives each man his deserts, or does it belong to the law of grace as it was manifest by Jesus and in the resurrection of the crucified Christ? The message of the new righteousness which eschatological faith brings into the world says that in fact the executioners will not finally triumph over their victims. It also says that in the end the victims will not triumph over their executioners. The one will triumph who first died for the victims and then also for the executioners, and in so doing revealed a new righteousness which breaks through the vicious circles of hate and vengeance and which from the lost victims and executioners creates a new mankind with a new humanity. Only where righteousness becomes creative and creates right both for the lawless and for those outside the law, only where creative love changes what is hateful and deserving of hate, only where the new man is born who is neither oppressed nor oppresses others, can one speak of the true revolution of righteousness and of the righteousness of God.

3. *The Significance of the Cross of the Risen Christ*

In the light of the Easter events the community first looked forwards into the future. The one who appeared to them in the splendour of divine glory was their guarantee that the glory of God and his new creation were not distant, but near. In recognizing his 'resurrection from the dead', they also traced in themselves the 'spirit of resurrection', the 'spirit which brings life' (Rom. 8.11), and waited in the 'power of the resurrection' (Phil. 3.10) for the coming appearance of Christ in glory. They understood his resurrection as a preparatory and preliminary action of God in Jesus for the good of themselves and the world. God had answered the evil deed of men in crucifying Jesus in a glorious way by raising him from the dead (Acts 2.24). As the primitive Christian hymns show, his humiliation on the cross faded into the background behind the present experience of his exaltation to be Kyrios, to be the Lord who ushers in the end-time. The eschatological enthusiasm expressed in the early hymns was filled full of the present of the one who came in the spirit. There was no longer any need to think of the earthly way of this Lord to the cross. The spirit shone beyond the experience of the still unredeemed world. The Lord's future weighed more heavily than his past. Nevertheless, the situation inevitably prompted the question: if Jesus is now Lord in the Spirit—who was he in his earthly life and in his suffering and death on the cross? This question is once again not only a historical question but also a systematic question for any christology.

The earliest titles which say who Jesus is come from the experience of the appearances of Jesus and have their foundation in the resurrection event.[31] By his resurrection Jesus was made Christ, Son of God, Kyrios, by God.[32] *Formulas of adoption* were used for this act: by his resurrection Jesus was adopted as the Son of God (Rom. 1.4). *Enthronement formulas* were also used: by the resurrection Jesus was exalted and appointed to be Lord. The purpose behind these titles was to say that by his resurrection it was not just that one man was raised from the dead before all others. At the same time, the other men were provided with a divine commission and a calling. This is the first thing that the Christ titles express. They do not so much express his exaltation, rank and status as his function, his call, his divine task and his mission. They can therefore be understood as *titles of representation.* The Christ of God represents God himself in a still unredeemed world. The Son of God represents the Father in a godless and forsaken world. The Kyrios is the mediator between man who is passing away and the God who is coming, that is, between the transitoriness of man the sinner, which puts him in this situation, and the holy God who comes in judgment. The adoption and enthronement of Jesus through his resurrection from the dead defines his actual and temporal role as mediator between God and man. So it is said again and again that we only have 'access through Christ to God, the Father'. That is why in primitive Christian liturgy Jesus the Lord is invoked in time of need and God the Father is addressed in praise.[33] According to I Cor. 15.20–28, God the Father has handed over the rule to his Kyrios with the resurrection of Jesus, so that after the end of his rule Jesus may hand over the kingdom to the Father, that 'God may be all in all'. With the early christological titles, then, Jesus is designated God's lieutenant on earth, 'God's representative', who stands for God before men and for men before God. The rule of God's Christ is limited and provisional. 'The only goal it serves is to give way to the sole lordship of God. Christ is God's representative over against a world which is not yet fully subject to God, although its eschatological subordination is in train since Easter and its end is in sight.'[34] For Paul 'the reign of Christ' is characterized by the fact that he—though not we ourselves—is delivered from death. 'It is therefore defined by the two poles, his resurrection and ours, and must be described materially as the realm of the power of the resurrection in a world which has fallen a prey to death, and thus to the other cosmic powers.'[35] The titles coined at the appearances of the risen Jesus thus display throughout an 'eschatological subordinationism'.[36] Christology is at the service of the eschatology of the God who is coming and his righteousness that makes all things new.

Now we also established that the resurrection hope sheds its light not only forwards, into God's future, by giving a foretaste of that future in the anticipations of the spirit, but also *backwards*, into the mystery of the suffering and death of the exalted Lord. If his future in God and his being sent into the world for the future of God are manifested in the appearances of the risen Christ, then at the same time the significance of his cross and his way to the cross must also be manifested backwards; otherwise the identity of his person would not be maintained, and resurrection faith would be a way of separating oneself from the crucified Christ and the recollection of his career. If the future of God 'has already begun' with his resurrection, what is the significance of his suffering and death? As the suffering and death of a righteous man it would not be a riddle, for to be unrecognized and misunderstood was the fate of many righteous men in Israel and many wise men outside Israel. Nor would it be a riddle as the end of a prophet born out of his time. There were plenty of precedents in the history of Israel. But if for Easter faith resurrec-

180

tion by God qualifies the person of Jesus of Nazareth as the Christ of God, the question inevitably arises: 'Why did the Christ have to suffer these things?' (Luke 24.26). Easter does not solve the riddle of the cross, but makes Christ's cross a mystery. The qualification of his person to be the Christ of God and his enthronement as Kyrios could not be dated from his resurrection on, as though it had not happened before, or as though the earthly Jesus was merely the forerunner of the heavenly Christ. That would not do justice to the identity of his person, but would tear it apart into two persons, one earthly and one eschatological. In fact the unity of his person requires it to be said that the crucified Jesus of Nazareth is exalted to be the Kyrios of God. Pannenberg has given a basis for this connection with the 'retroactive force' of the Easter confirmation of the claim of Jesus by God and has used for it the analogy of laws and regulations which are put in force retrospectively. By this he means to say that the resurrection of Jesus gives a basis to his nature retroactively, from the end of his career, and that this is not only retroactive for our knowledge, but also for his being.[37] This is a helpful idea for understanding the resurrection faith which leads to Christian belief in Jesus. But in my view the *person* of Jesus who was identified through the resurrection is not expressed sufficiently clearly in the accord between Jesus' claim and God's confirmation of it.

One of the earliest, pre-Pauline confessions says:

Christ died for our sins in accordance with the scriptures and was buried, and he was raised on the third day in accordance with the scriptures (I Cor. 15.3b–4).

In his own words, Paul says: 'Christ died for us' (Rom. 5.8). We can follow W. Kramer in taking the Pauline formula as being more original, because the first, traditional formula already interprets the 'for us' in the special sense of 'for our sins'.[38] The first important thing is that at a very early stage the community understood the death of Jesus Christ as an event 'for us', that is in our favour, though the Pauline formula leaves it open whether the 'for us' implies personal representation or is understood in the cultic sense of expiation 'for our sins'. The interpretation 'for us' seems to be a fundamental phrase which occurs over and over again. The more detailed and very different interpretations in terms of a theory of expiatory sacrifice or a doctrine of justification seem to be meant as a secondary interpretation of that fundamental 'for us'. The significance of Christ's death can affect the realm 'for all' and 'for us' horizontally. It can have the material significance of expiation for sins or the reconciliation of the world. It can be a personal expression of 'Christ for us' and 'God for us'. Apart from occasional sayings which also relate the 'for us' to Christ's resurrection (Rom. 4.25), the interpretation is throughout applied to the death of Christ. The formula in I Cor. 15.3b–4 speaks in the second line only for the fact of his resurrection and his appearance among the disciples, whereas the first line mentions the saving significance of his death. 'Precisely in this way the material unity of the two statements is preserved. For whereas the resurrection constitutes or confirms the eschatological status of Jesus, the ὑπὲρ ἡμῶν is the interpretation of the dying of Jesus as the dying of this eschatological person.'[39] By his resurrection Jesus is qualified in his person to be the Christ of God. So his suffering and death must be understood to be the suffering and death of the Christ of God. Only in the light of his resurrection from the dead does his death gain that special, unique saving significance which it cannot achieve otherwise, even in the light of the life that he lived. 'The resurrection of Jesus does not relativize the cross so that it becomes a past datum of history or a transitory stage on the way to heavenly glory, but qualifies it so that it becomes an eschatological saving event',[40] because only it says *who* really suffered and died here. So the crucified Christ has not changed into a risen and glorified figure. Rather, his resurrection qualifies the one who has been crucified as the Christ, and his suffering and death as a saving event for us and for many. The resurrection 'does not evacuate the cross' (I Cor. 1.17), but fills it with eschatology and saving significance. From this it follows systematically that all further interpretations of the saving significance of Christ's death on the cross 'for us' must start from his resurrection. Furthermore, when it is said at length that only his death has a saving significance for us, that means that his death on the cross expresses the significance of his resurrection for us and not, vice versa, that his resurrection expresses the significance of his cross. The resurrection from the dead qualifies the person of the crucified Christ and with it the saving significance of his death on the cross for us, 'the dead'. Thus the saving significance of his cross manifests his resurrection. It is not his resurrection that shows that his death on the cross took place for us, but on the contrary, his death on the cross 'for us' that makes relevant his resurrection 'before us'.[41] This must be stressed, because the early Jewish-Christian idea of the dying Christ as an expiatory offering for our sins, which has constantly been repeated throughout the tradition in varied forms, cannot display any intrinsic theological connection with the kerygma of the resurrection. One can hardly talk of the resurrection of an expiatory offering, any more than one can talk of the resurrection of the Son of God who sacrificed himself to satisfy the injured honour of God. Within the framework of the idea of expiatory offerings, both individuals and the people as a whole need expiation for their sins, so that the righteousness of the law of the covenant may be restored. This expiation was offered in the sacrificial cult of the Jerusalem temple. The exemplary martyrs' death of the righteous had atoning force for the whole community. The idea of the special expiatory power of the 'blood of Jesus' (Rom. 3.25; I Cor. 10.16, etc.) has its roots here. The phrase 'died for our sins' means that the cause of his suffering was our sins, the purpose of his suffering is expiation for us, the ground of his suffering is the love of God for us. It is very difficult to harmonize the resurrection of Jesus with these interpretations of his death and very difficult to harmonize these interpretations of his death with his resurrection from the dead. For the ideas of expiatory offerings move consistently within the framework of the law: sins trangress the law, expiation restores the law. By sin man falls short of the righteousness of the law and comes under the accusation of the law; by expiation he is restored to the righteousness of the law. Expiation for sins always has a retrospective character. Its future concern is the *restitutio in integrum*, not the beginning of a new life. Nevertheless, these ideas of expiation are important in that they show: 1. how little unrighteous man can achieve his own righteousness, how there can be no new future for him without the acceptance of guilt and liberation from it, at least through good intentions by which he only denies himself; 2. that as the Christ of God, Jesus took the place of helpless man as his representative and in so doing made it possible for man to enter into communion before God in which he otherwise could not stand and survive; 3. that in the death of Christ God himself has acted in favour of this man.

But if we want to understand the cross strictly as the cross of Christ, that is of the risen Christ, we must go beyond the ideas of expiatory sacrifice which we find here. Instead, we must try once again to read history eschatologically with a 'reversed sense of time' and return from the future of Christ to his past. In terms of history and its sense of time, Jesus first died and was then raised. In eschatological terms the last becomes the first: he died as the risen Christ and was made flesh as the one who was to come. In historical terms Christ can be called the *anticipation* of the coming God on the basis of his resurrection from the dead. In eschatological terms, however, he must be called the *incarnation* of the coming God in our flesh and in his death on the cross. It is one-sided and a mistaken interpretation of his death on the cross if on the basis of the proleptic resurrection of Jesus one looks only into the future of God and to the end of history.[42] With the reversal of the noetic and the ontic order, it is also necessary to recognize in this anticipation the incarnation of the future of that redeeming kingdom in the past of the crucified Christ. In that case, what is the significance of his death on the cross? Why did the rebel, God's lieutenant, man's representative before God, die on the cross?

For Paul and Mark, the theological accent is placed entirely on the reversal of the noetic and ontic orders and on the transformation of the historical sense of time into an eschatological sense of time. The risen Christ is the crucified Christ.[43] The proleptic-eschatological christology described at the beginning hangs in the air, because everyone has to ask himself, Why was only this one man raised? Why were not all men raised at the same time? This is in essence the nucleus of the Christian question of theodicy, which is usually described as the phenomenon of the 'delay of the parousia';[44] why only Jesus at first, and not the whole salvation of the world at a stroke? The answer lies in the cross of Christ, just as only the knowledge of the cross is adequate to explain the so-called experience of disappointment at the delay of the parousia. Through his suffering and death, the Christ who was raised from the dead *before us* becomes the Christ *for us*, just as the 'God before us' becomes the 'God for us'.[45] The anticipation of the resurrection of the dead in him gains its saving significance for us only through his offering for us on the cross. His prolepsis forms the basis of his pro-existence and in it becomes significant for us. Only when the one who was raised proleptically takes our place and dies does his prolepsis have saving significance for us. The basic New Testament idea of Christ as the representative for us, 'for all', must therefore be developed systematically from the concept of prolepsis used for the resurrection. The theology of Easter hope must be changed into the theology of the cross, if it is to set our feet on the ground of the reality of the death of Christ and our own death. The reversal just mentioned makes that possible. God has anticipated the future of his liberating righteousness in this one man and sent him before in order that this one man may communicate it to others. If the resurrection has already been anticipated in him, then 'resurrection, life and righteousness' come through the death of this one man in favour of those who have been delivered over to death through their unrighteousness. Through his suffering and death, the risen Christ brings righteousness and life to the unrighteous and the dying. Thus the cross of Christ modifies the resurrection of Christ under the conditions of the suffering of the world so that it changes from being a purely future event to being an event of liberating love. Through his death the risen Christ introduces the coming reign of God into the godless present by means of representative suffering. He anticipates the coming righteousness of God under the conditions of human injustice in the law of grace and in the justification of the godless by his death. The countenance of the Christ raised before all the dying is, for these dying, the countenance of the one who was crucified for them. By sharing in the fellowship of Christ's suffering they gain a share in the resurrection (Phil. 3.10–12). The coming kingdom, the certainty of which the disciples found in the Easter appearances of Christ, has then, as a result of this Christ, taken the form of a cross in the alienated world. The cross is the form of the coming, redeeming kingdom, and the crucified Jesus is the incarnation of the risen Christ. In the crucified Jesus the 'end of history' is present in the midst of the relationships of history. Therefore in him can be found reconciliation in the midst of strife and hope for the overcoming of strife.

Without the representative saving significance of his death on the cross, the Christ raised from the dead would be a miracle or at best a model or a forerunner of the future. But that does not help those who suffer under their own unrighteousness and that of the world, and live in the shadow of death. It is only his death on the cross that makes the meaning of his resurrection manifest for these men, for it is only through his action as their representative that the glory anticipated in him enters into their misery. Only through his death 'for them' does that new life begin for them which he lives by virtue of being raised by God.

The anticipation of the resurrection of the dead in the resurrection of Jesus from the dead may have a stimulating effect on men who are open to the world and to the future. But for men who are closed to the future, and without hope, for the *homo incurvatus in se* and for the Narcissus who is sadly in love with himself, it means nothing, for it does not reach them. Only Christ's representative suffering and sacrifice 'for them' in his death on the cross brings hope to the hopeless, future to those who are passing away and new right to the unrighteous.

Therefore we must say that Christ's death on the cross is 'the significance' of his resurrection for us. Conversely, any interpretation of the meaning of his death which does not have as a presupposition his resurrection from the dead is a hopeless matter, because it cannot communicate the new element of life and salvation which came to light in his resurrection. Christ did not die only as that expiatory offering in which the law was restored or the original creation was reconstituted after the fall of man. He died 'for us', to give us, 'the dead', a share in his new life of resurrection and in his future of eternal life. His resurrection is the content of the significance of his death on the cross 'for us', because the risen Christ is himself the crucified Christ. His resurrection from the dead can be known in his death 'for many'. It is not that his 'resurrection' is a dimension of his death on the cross; on the contrary, his sacrifice on the cross for the reconciliation of the world is the immanent dimension of his eschatological resurrection in the glory of the coming kingdom. By understanding Christ's death as having taken place 'for many', one can understand his resurrection from the dead as having taken place in favour of those who are still dead. If that is the case, then his death on the cross 'for us' can be understood as a *proof* of his resurrection. To understand the representative significance of his death is to understand his resurrection. In his dying for us the risen Christ looks on us and draws us into his life. In the one who became poor for our sake, God's riches are opened up for us. In the one who became a servant for our sake, we are grasped by God's freedom. In the one who became sin for us, sinners become the righteousness of God in the world.

The one whom the Easter kerygma proclaims as the Lord became a servant for us (Phil. 2) in order to transform us from being servants to being free lords of all things. Thus his death on the cross 'for us' makes us sinners and godless and at the same time righteous and sons of God. 'The cross is his method, and lasts until his future.'[46]

It is precisely when we understand the representative significance of his death in terms of the anticipatory form of his resurrection before us that the provisional and eschatological manner of his representativeness becomes clear. If the kingdom of Christ is limited in content and time by his resurrection from the dead, which has happened for him, but still awaits us, then his representativeness is grounded and limited in the same way. The reconciling power of his suffering and death is the power of the resurrection. However, its purpose is not to make itself superfluous, but to become the basis for new, redeemed existence, which it owes to the crucified Christ.

4. *The Future of God in the Sign of the Crucified Christ*

We conclude this chapter with the question of the concept of God which follows on the one hand from the *resurrection* of the crucified Christ and on the other hand from the *cross* of the risen Christ. In this question we can speak of two stages of knowledge in the primitive Christian tradition of the kerygma of Christ.

The first stratum in the primitive Christian theology of Easter says: 'You killed him, but God raised him up' (Acts 2.23; 3.15; 4.10, etc.). The mission speeches of Acts are determined by the theme of this contrast.[47] They are speeches about Christ to Jews, and set out to say that God has raised Jesus from the dead and thus has vindicated him. This has been accomplished by the God of the covenant and the law, the righteous God. The Jews have condemned Jesus and delivered him to crucifixion because of ignorance and lawlessness, against the will of God and therefore against the law. If they now recognize the true will of God in his action in raising Jesus from the dead, they will understand

God's will in the law rightly, as it is interpreted by Jesus, and follow it, observing the twofold commandment of love. The Jewish-Christian community which spoke in this way understood itself in the form of the 'twelve apostles' as the people of the twelve tribes renewed in accordance with God's will, as a Christian messianic revival movement within Israel. As can be seen in the dispute between Peter and Paul, they were therefore not concerned to go beyond the bounds of Israel and the synagogue and address themselves to the Gentiles. In the Israelite order of hope it was a question of the Jews first and then the Gentiles. Once Zion has been restored by the Messiah or Son of Man, the Gentiles will make a pilgrimage there of their own accord, in order to receive justice and righteousness. But if Gentiles already come to the Christian faith in the Diaspora, they must observe the law and be circumcised. This Jewish-Christian community spoke of the 'raising of Jesus'. The subject of the action was God, the object of the suffering was the executed Jesus, and the event was regarded as an eschatological event. According to this belief, God had revealed himself 'at last', and therefore finally, in the resurrection of Jesus. For Paul, too, 'raise' was therefore a term used with reference to the God of Jesus Christ. According to Rom. 8.11 God is the one 'who has raised Christ Jesus from the dead'. Galatians 1.1 characterizes God as the one 'who has raised him from the dead'. That means that God has finally, in the end-time, defined himself through the resurrection of Jesus as *the God who raises the dead*.[48] All earlier divine statements from the history of Israel, from the law of the covenant or from the state of the world in general fade into insignificance, become no more than historical statements, in comparison with this new eschatological definition given by God of himself as the one who raises the dead. Paul took up this Easter kerygma and in Rom. 4.17 mentioned the 'God who gives life to the dead and calls into existence the things that do not exist'. Here he has drawn a conclusion from the eschatological designation of God as the one who raises the dead to the one who creates all things from nothing. And he found, as the context shows, the presence of this creative God who raises the dead in the word of the promise which creates faith.

The eschatological resurrection of the dead does not mean a restoration of the creation which has been made obsolete by human sin, but the 'creation of the end-time' that is now dawning.[49]

188

For Paul, the resurrection of the dead is no longer the ontic pre-supposition for the righteousness of God in the final judgment over dead and living, but is itself already the new righteousness of God and the new creation from this righteousness. This new creation goes further in the 'spirit of the resurrection' and in the justification of the godless, until it is completed in the appearance of Christ and his handing over the kingdom to the Father. The mass of predicates current in Judaism like 'before the world, sole ruler, incorruptible, unstained, unbegotten' retreat into the background in favour of the new name of God which identifies God with the new element of the resurrection of Christ: this new name is ὁ ἐγείρας Ἰησοῦν Thus at its heart the Easter message bears a new divine message. It not only contains a new divine predicate, but speaks of God as the subject of his eschatological action in Jesus; it must therefore be understood as a divine name. But this divine name has been formulated as an exact parallel to the first commandment of the covenant of Israel. There we read: 'I am the Lord your God who brought you up out of the land of Egypt, out of the house of slavery.' Here there is mention of the God who has raised Jesus from death on the cross into his glory. In each case the name of God is connected with a historical action which manifests God. In each case the historical action of God brings freedom to those concerned: in the one case it brings the people freedom from a historical tyrant, in the other it brings Jesus freedom from the tyranny of death. So in the one case there is talk of a historical event which happened in the past but which has continuing force for Israel, whereas in the other there is talk of an eschatological event which has anticipatory force for all who are seized by it.

According to this first stratum in the Easter kerygma, the eschatological action of God in the resurrection of Jesus blotted out and replaced the historical action of man in his crucifixion. This understanding of God in the light of the resurrection of Jesus matches certain strata in the Israelite understanding of God in terms of his actions in history. The only difference is that the resurrection of a dead man falls outside the framework of history, which is dominated by death and men's dying.

Therefore the eschatological understanding of God in terms of the resurrection of Jesus emerges with a final claim. In this sense one can say that the 'notion of an indirect self-revelation of God in the mirror of his historical action'[50] is finally valid here because the resurrection of Christ is an eschatological event.

But let us return again from the perspective of a history which looks from the past into the future, to eschatology, which looks from the future into the past. If we do, the question arises: What was the 'God who raised Jesus' doing in and during the crucifixion of Jesus? If there was here only the action of evil, ignorant men, Jews and Romans, then that God evidently did not act, but restrained himself and allowed things to happen. But why did he keep silent over the cross of Jesus and his dying cry? Had he forgotten him? Was he absent? If, like the first theology of Easter, one sees the eschatological action of God in Jesus' resurrection only in his power over death, the cross of Jesus will be incomprehensible in respect of God and God will be incomprehensible in respect of the cross.

But in their theology of the cross and passion, Paul and Mark understood the risen Christ *as the crucified Christ*. This meant that they had to understand the God who raised him as the God who crucified him and was crucified. If they saw God in action in the resurrection of Jesus, they had to seek to understand God in passion, in the crucifixion of Jesus. But how can the death of Jesus on the cross be understood as God's action, even as God's suffering? Paul goes even one stage further in II Cor. 5.19ff., when he says 'God *was* in Christ'. In other words, God not only acted in the crucifixion of Jesus or sorrowfully allowed it to happen, but was himself active with his own being in the dying Jesus and suffered with him. 'If God has reconciled the world to himself through the cross, then this means that he has made himself visible in the cross of Christ and, as it were, says to man, "Here I am!".'[51] Here we are confronted with a paradox. How can the almighty God be in a helpless man? How can the righteous God be in a man who has been condemned in accordance with the law? How can God himself be in one who has been forsaken by God? Must one not abandon all that has been imagined, desired or feared in respect of 'God' if one is to understand God thus in the crucified Christ? Can one still understand the crucified Christ on the presupposition of a concept of God imported 'from elsewhere'? On the contrary, must one not understand this 'God and Father of Jesus Christ' completely in the light of what happened on the cross?

The primitive Christian theology of the resurrection saw the event of the resurrection as constituting Jesus to be Son of God. The pre-Pauline formula in Rom. 1.3b speaks of the earthly and the heavenly modes of being of Jesus: κᾱτὰ σάρκα he is son of David, κατὰ πνεῦμα ἁγιωσύνης ἐξ ἀναστάσεως νεκρῶν he is Son of God. Correspondingly, his appointment as Son of God became the interpretation of his resurrection.[52] But Paul himself constantly associated this Easter formula of the Son of God with the sending of the Son and his sacrifice by the Father in his eschatological retrospect on the life and death of Jesus.

The *sending* is intended to bring the whole career and the whole of the appearance of Jesus under the heading: 'When the time had fully come, God sent forth his Son, born of woman, born under the law, to redeem those who were under the law, so that we might receive adoption as sons' (Gal. 4.4f.). The foundation of the coming of Jesus is his being sent by God. The purpose of the sending of the Son of God is liberation from slavery under the law for the freedom of the children of God.

On the other hand, the *giving up* of the Son (Rom. 8.32; Gal. 2.20; John 3.16; Eph. 5.25, etc.) is meant to be an interpretation of the particular suffering and death of Jesus.[53] 'God did not spare his own Son, but gave him up for us all; will he not also give us all things with him?' (Rom. 8.32). The formula παραδιδόναι used here is passion terminology, but whereas there it means 'deliver over', 'betray', 'abandon', here it is used by Paul as an expression of the love and the election of God. 'The Son of God loved me and gave himself for me', Paul confesses in Gal. 2.20. If according to Rom. 8.32 it is God who acts in giving up Jesus, according to Gal. 2.20 it is Jesus himself who is active here. In both passages, and also especially in John 3.16, what is meant is self-surrendering, self-emptying love. In Rom. 4.25 ('who was delivered up for our sins . . .') it becomes clear that the reference is to the death of Jesus.

That God delivers up his Son is one of the most unheard-of statements in the New Testament. We must understand 'deliver up' in its full sense and not water it down to mean 'send' or 'give'. What happened here is what Abraham did not need to do to Isaac; Christ was quite deliberately abandoned by the Father to the fate of death; God subjected him to the power of corruption, whether this be called man or death . . . God made Christ sin (II Cor. 5.21), Christ is the accursed of God. A theology of the cross cannot be expressed more radically than it is here.[54]

191

Paul certainly takes over from the tradition the conception that Jesus was constituted Son of God by his resurrection from the dead, but he sees it at work in the sending of Jesus by God and in his being given up by the Father, which is at the same time his own self-surrender. That means that Jesus as Son of God is not painted with the colours of his resurrection glory, but with the colours of his passion and his death on the cross. The Son of God is not first at work in his exaltation and glory, but in his humiliation and lowliness. The 'Son of God' is here the representative and revealer of God in a godless and godforsaken world. That means that God represents and reveals himself in the surrender of Jesus and in his passion and death on the cross. But where God represents and reveals himself, he also identifies and defines himself. Therefore Paul can say: 'God (himself) was in Christ' (II Cor. 5.19). Logically this means that God (himself) suffered in Jesus, God himself died in Jesus for us. God is on the cross of Jesus 'for us', and through that becomes God and Father of the godless and the godforsaken. He took upon himself the unforgivable sin and the guilt for which there is no atonement, together with the rejection and anger that cannot be turned away, so that in Christ we might become his righteousness in the world. Taken to its final consequence, that means that God died that we might live. God became the crucified God so that we might become free sons of God. So what did God do in the crucifixion of Jesus? Whereas the resurrection of Jesus was understood as a revelation of the power (*dynamis*) and glory (*doxa*) of God and as an action that makes things new, God was not silent and uninvolved in the cross of Jesus. Nor was he absent in the godforsakenness of Jesus. He acted in Jesus, the Son of God: in that men betrayed him, handed him over and delivered him up to death, God himself delivered him up. In the passion of the Son, the Father himself suffers the pains of abandonment. In the death of the Son, death comes upon God himself, and the Father suffers the death of his Son in his love for forsaken man. Consequently, what happened on the cross must be understood as an event between God and the Son of God. In the action of the Father in delivering up his Son to suffering and to a godless death, God is acting in himself. He is acting in himself in this manner of suffering and dying in order to open up in himself life and freedom for sinners. Creation, new creation and resurrection are external works of God against chaos, nothingness and death. The suffering and dying of Jesus, understood as the suffering and dying of the Son of God, on the other hand, are works of God towards himself and therefore at the same time passions of God. God overcomes himself, God passes judgment on himself, God takes the judgment on the sin of man upon himself. He assigns to himself the fate that men should by rights endure. The cross of Jesus, understood as the cross of the Son of God, therefore reveals a change in God, a *stasis* within the Godhead: 'God is other.' And this event in God is the event on the cross. It takes on Christian form in the simple formula which contradicts all possible metaphysical and historical ideas of God: 'God *is* love.'

Like Paul, Mark too depicted the divine Sonship of the risen Christ in the way of Jesus to the cross. Right at the beginning of his gospel he calls Jesus 'the Son of God' (1.1) and declares that Jesus became Son of God with the baptism, through the spirit of God (1.11). Consequently the sayings and miracles of Jesus are presented as sayings and miracles of the Son of God. Still more, however, the suffering and the death of Jesus on the cross are reported in his proclamation as the passion and death of the Son of God. And for Mark Jesus dies on the cross with the cry, 'My God, why hast thou forsaken me?' (15.34): the Son of God dies forsaken by God. When Jesus 'gives up the ghost with a loud cry' (15.39), the Gentile centurion answers with the confession, 'Truly, this man was the Son of God' (15.39). This seems to be paradoxical in a number of respects.

1. The eschatological cry of godforsakenness by the Son of God, directed towards the God who has left him, is followed by the human answer of faith and the confession that Jesus is the Son of God. According to Mark, this faith does not first follow in the divine act of power at the resurrection, which would have easily been conceivable against the background of contemporary apocalyptic, but at the cross of the one who has been forsaken by God. The Jesus who dies with crying and tears provoked, according to Mark, a confession that he was the Son of God and awoke the faith which changes men from slaves of the law to free sons of God.

2. The confession of faith does not come from a pious disciple of Jesus, nor even from a Jew, who might have some

understanding, but from the Gentile, Roman centurion who was presumably in charge of the execution squad. Whereas only the disciples who had fled had a part in the Easter appearances, and they shared with the Jews a certain common context in which to set Jesus' 'resurrection from the dead' when they began to preach, according to Mark the passion and the cross of Jesus is directed immediately towards the Gentiles. If the Easter appearances were only perceived in the utmost privacy by the disciples, and if the message of the resurrection was at first understandable only in the realm of Israelite apocalyptic traditions, this happened publicly through the crucifixion of Jesus. Indeed, it even happened outside the gate of the city of Jerusalem with its temple, and therefore outside the boundary of Israel, on Golgotha, and outside the 'hedge of Israel', i.e., its legal tradition. It happened, in fact, on the boundary of human society, where it does not matter whether a person is Jew or Gentile, Greek or barbarian, master or servant, man or woman, because death is unaware of all these distinctions. So the crucified one does not recognize these distinctions either. If his death is proclaimed and acknowledged as the death of the Son of God 'for many', as by that centurion, then in this death God's Son has died for all, and the proclamation of his death is for all the world. It must undermine, remove and destroy the things which mark men out as elect and non-elect, educated and uneducated, those with possessions and those without, the free and the enslaved. The Gentile-Christian proclamation concerns all men, because confronted with the cross all men, whatever the differences between them and whatever they may assert about each other, 'are sinners and fall short of the glory of God' (Rom. 3.23). 'Here there is no distinction' (Rom. 3.23a). Gentile-Christian proclamation must therefore essentially be the proclamation of the crucified Christ, i.e. the word of the cross (I Cor. 1.18). The proclamation of the cross is 'Christianity for all the world' (Blumhardt), and may not erect any new distinctions between men, say between Christians and non-Christians, the pious and the godless. Its first recognition leads to self-knowledge: to the knowledge that one is a sinner in solidarity with all men under the power of corruption. Therefore the theology of the cross is the true Christian universalism. There is no distinction here, and there cannot be any more distinctions. All are sinners without distinction, and all will be made righteous without any merit on their part by his grace which has come to pass in Christ Jesus (Rom. 3.24).

As the crucified one, the risen Christ is there 'for all'. In the cross of the Son of God, in his abandonment by God, the 'crucified' God is the human God of all godless men and those who have been abandoned by God.

What are the implications of this move from the resurrection to the cross of Christ for the concept of God?

1. 'Without Jesus I would be an atheist,' remarked the Ritschlian J. Gottschick.[55] If God's being is manifest in the passion and the death of Jesus, through Jesus' suffering and death 'for us' and for our salvation, he is known by that faith which is called freedom. The God of freedom, the true God, is therefore not recognized by his power and glory in the world and in the history of the world, but through his helplessness and his death on the scandal of the cross of Jesus. The gods of the power and riches of the world and world history then belong on the other side of the cross, for it was in their name that Jesus was crucified. The God of freedom, the human God, no longer has godlike rulers as his political representatives. If the crucified one is the 'Son of God', then Pharaoh and Caesar are no longer 'God's son', though this may be what they have called themselves. If the crucified one is Kyrios, then the Caesars must renounce the title. These divinized rulers belong more on the other side of the cross of Jesus, for he was crucified in the name of those like them. 'Without Jesus I would be an atheist,' remarked Gottschick. But 'atheist' is a relative term and a polemical expression. We must therefore use a more pointed expression and say, 'For Christ's sake I am an atheist,' an atheist in respect of the gods of the world and world history, the Caesars and the political demigods who follow them. 'Only a Christian can be a good atheist,' I once remarked to Ernst Bloch, turning round his remark 'Only an atheist can be a good Christian'. He accepted this offering.[56] But a 'good Christian' is like the Gentile centurion who said of the crucified Jesus, 'Truly this is the Son of God,' and for whom as a result the world, the history of the world and the rulers of the world have been de-divinized.

2. 'If I did not find God in Jesus, I would have to take God for the devil,' Zinzendorf remarked to his Community of Brethren,

taking up Luther's: 'You might just as well pray to the devil if you have to have any God but Jesus.'[57] For the Christian there is no gradation between the crucified Jesus and the gods, as though God were less evident in the world, world history and world politics, and more evident in Christ. This notion of a gradation between a natural theology and a Christian theology can easily be unmasked as the ideology of a state church which seeks to set itself up on the existing political religion of a society as its higher consummation and thus seeks to be its supernatural justification, or holds itself to be the 'crown of society'. Between 'God in Christ' and the gods outside and in other representations there stands the cross of that God, and with it the alternative '*aut Christus—aut Caesar*', just as Elijah once posed the alternatives 'either Yahweh or the Baals'. Hence Luther and Zinzendorf did not speak of other gods or other revelations of the same God, but of 'God and non-God', of 'God and the devil'. The cross of Jesus marks a divide between the human God who is freedom and love and the 'counter-God' who keeps men under his sway and dominated by fear, like demons, and sucks them up into nothingness. However, the 'crucified God' here cannot be interchanged with the 'God of Christians', for by the terms of a psychological or sociological analysis the God of the Christians is not always the 'crucified God'. Only rarely is this the case. Even for historical Christianity the cross, if it is understood radically and down to its final consequences, is a scandal and foolishness. The freedom of faith in the crucified God is not 'everyone's business' just because the human God is there for everyone. For who wants to be 'everyone' and 'all sinners together?'

NOTES

1. E. Grässer has made this remarkable assertion in 'Politisch gekreuzigter Christus', *ZNW* 62, 1971, 279: 'But the historical Jesus is only half the Christ. The whole Christ is the one who lived, died and rose again.' His critical discussion of my lecture to the doctors' conference in Regensburg, 'Politische Theologie', 1969, is also less exegetical than ideological. He thinks that the New Testament supports the ideology of our society in that 1. it concerns the individual; 2. politics is a matter for the professionals; 3. an unpolitical church is a political element because it is 'incomparably free to do what this society can expect of us' (278). It is easy to see whom such an ideology benefits.

2. B. Klappert, *Die Auferweckung des Gekreuzigten*, 1971.

3. H. Conzelmann, 'Historie und Theologie in den synoptischen Passionsberichten', in *Zur Bedeutung des Todes Jesu*, 1967, 35ff.
4. E. Käsemann, *Perspectives on Paul*, SCM Press 1971, 54.
5. E. Bloch, *Verfremdungen* I, 1962, 218.
6. Cf. J. Moltmann, *Theology of Hope*, SCM Press 1967, 18f., 197ff.; W. Pannenberg, *Jesus—God and Man*, SCM Press 1968, 66ff.
7. R. Bultmann, *Glauben und Verstehen* III, 113; on this see J. Moltmann, *Perspektiven der Theologie*, 128ff.
8. F. Rosenzweig, *Der Stern der Erlösung*, 170.
9. W. Benjamin, *Illuminationen*, 1961, 280.
10. Ibid., 270f.
11. W. Benjamin, *Angelus Novus*, 1969.
12. For the messianic pathos of positivism in Saint-Simon and Auguste Comte cf. J. L. Talmon, *Politischer Messianismus*, 1963, 21ff.
13. It seems that W. Pannenberg has paid too little attention to this in his chapter 'The Significance of Jesus' Resurrection', *Jesus—God and Man*, SCM Press 1968, 66ff. Nor is it adequate to speak here of a 'borrowing of apocalyptic ideas' because the Easter message proclaimed that the 'eschaton had already arrived' and thus burst through the 'nature of apocalyptic,. Cf. G. Ebeling, *Theology and Proclamation*, Collins 1966, 92. But Ebeling's observation that the crucified Christ sets us in the situation of faith is correct (ibid.).
14. For the Easter 'seeing' see most recently U. Wilckens, *Auferstehung*, 1970, 69ff., and the literature reviewed in Pannenberg, op. cit., 88f.
15. Cf. Wilckens, op. cit., 90ff.
16. On this see H. W. Wolff, *Gesammelte Studien zum Alten Testament*, ThB 22, 1964, 289ff.
17. P. Stuhlmacher, *Gerechtigkeit Gottes bei Paulus*, 1965, 79 n.1.
18. E. Käsemann, *New Testament Questions of Today*, SCM Press 1969, 114.
19. U. Wilckens, op. cit., 145ff. On the other hand see E. Fuchs, *Marburger Hermeneutik*, 1968, 200: Jesus is 'risen in the word of love'.
20. T. W. Adorno, *Negative Dialektik*, 1966, 354.
21. I agree with W. Pannenberg in understanding the 'resurrection of Jesus' in eschatological terms and seeing it as an anticipation of the resurrection of the dead. The difference certainly does not lie in my 'resource to divine promise', the justification for which is grounded in 'an authoritarian principle like the "Word of God" in dialectical theology' and 'seems to live on in Moltmann's conception of promise' (W. Pannenberg, preface to *Grundfragen systematischer Theologie*, 1967, 5 n.2). 1. 'Dialectical theology' had no 'authoritarian concept of the Word of God'. Anyone who still asserts that, misunderstands both its understanding of the Word and the concept of authority. There is much to be learned here from H.-G. Gadamer, 'Rhetorik, Hermeneutik und Ideologiekritik', in *Hermeneutik und Ideologiekritik*, 1971, 73ff. 2. I have grounded the concept of the promise in the particular historical differences which lie in the event of liberation: in Israel in the Exodus event, in Christianity in the event of the resurrection of the crucified

The Crucified God

Christ. A standpoint by the crucified Christ is 'extra-historical' in its own way.

22. Thus W. Pannenberg, *Offenbarung als Geschichte*, 1961, 98.

23. Thus against W. Pannenberg, *Offenbarung als Geschichte*, 112, 114; J. Moltmann, *Theology of Hope*, 204ff.

24. H. Marcuse, *Das Ende der Utopie*, 1967, 20, used this relevant expression.

25. H. Marcuse, *One Dimensional Man*, Abacus 1972, 200; 'The critical theory of society possesses no concepts which could bridge the gap between the present and its future; holding no promise and showing no success, it remains negative. Thus it wants to remain loyal to those who, without hope, have given and give their life to the Great Refusal.' For criticism of this see E. Fromm, *The Revolution of Hope*, New York 1968, 8 n.3, and W. F. Haug, 'Das Ganz und das ganz Andere. Zur Kritik der revolutionären Transzendenz', in *Antworten auf Herbert Marcuse*, ed. J. Habermas, 1968, 50ff., 63: 'Instead of challenging the lords of this world over this world, Marcuse works out a second world.'

26. On this see L. Mattern, *Das Verständnis des Gerichtes bei Paulus*, 1966, 15ff.

27. E. Bloch, *Das Prinzip Hoffnung*, 1959, 1324: 'The breakthrough of immortality first came about in Judaism through the *prophet Daniel* . . . and the drive towards it did not come from the old wish for a long life, for wellbeing on earth, now extended into the transcendent. It came, rather, from Job and the prophets, from the thirst after righteousness.'

28. W. Pannenberg, *Jesus—God and Man*, 66: 'Measured by the imminent nearness of these events of the end, it must have been of secondary significance for Jesus whether he himself would have to endure death before the end came.' Cf. however, his remarks in §7 on Jesus' death on the cross.

29. Ibid., 83ff.

30. The following remarks by Pannenberg, *Jesus—God and Man*, 83, can easily be directed against his own anthropological continuation of apocalyptic: 'The knowledge of Jesus obtained within this apocalyptic horizon of expectation certainly can subsequently be translated into different patterns of thought, for example, into Gnostic thought; but it cannot be established from the perspective of these other patterns of thought. Where such a new basis has been sought, Jesus again and again has become merely the example of a Gnostic or a philosophical idea whose truth is ultimately independent of the history of Jesus . . .' Thus e.g. H.-G. Geyer, 'The Resurrection of Jesus Christ: A Survey of the Debate in Present-Day Theology', in C. F. D. Moule (ed.), *The Significance of the Message of the Resurrection for Faith in Jesus Christ*, SCM Press 1968, 131, who thinks that in Pannenberg, 'the resurrection of Jesus, as the declared basis of Christian faith, [is] subject to the historical confirmation of an inherent structural principle in human life, existing independently.' This is hardly apt as a bald statement, but it points to a weakness in the dialectic between Pannenberg's historical heremeneutics of origin and his historical hermeneutics of effect.

31. Here I agree with Pannenberg. Cf. also R. Schnackenburg, 'Die Auferweckung Jesu als theologischer Ansatzpunkt der urchristlichen Theologie', *Mysterium Salutis* III, 1, 1970, 237–47.

32. W. Kramer, *Christ, Lord, Son of God*, SCM Press 1966.

33. H. Conzelmann, 'Christus im Gottesdienst der neutestamentlichen Zeit', *MPTh* 55, 1960, 361.

34. E. Käsemann, *New Testament Questions of Today*, 133. Similarly D. Sölle, *Christ the Representative*, SCM Press 1967, 130ff., for whom provisionality is part of the structure of personal representation.

35. E. Käsemann, op. cit., 134.

36. E. Brunner, *Das Ewige als Zukunft und Gegenwart*, 1964, 226f.; P. Stuhlmacher, op. cit., 208.

37. Pannenberg, *Jesus—God and Man*, 135ff.

38. W. Kramer, op. cit., 26.

39. W. Kramer, ibid.

40. W. Schrage, op. cit., 61.

41. This reversal must be stressed over against Bultmann's view of the resurrection: 'Can talk of the resurrection of Christ be anything but an expression of the significance of the cross?', *Kerygma und Mythos* I, 1948, 478.

42. Cf. also my criticism in *Diskussion über die 'Theologie der Hoffnung'*, 1967, 215ff.

43. W. Schrage, op. cit., 65.

44. On this see J. Moltmann, 'Problem der neueren evangelischen Theologie', *VuF* 1966, 120ff.

45. This does not remove the idea of 'God with us', but makes it more profound. See J. B. Metz, 'Gott vor uns', in *Ernst Bloch zu ehren*, 1965, 227ff.

46. Zinzendorf, quoted in S. Eberhard, *Kreuzestheologie. Das reformatorische Anliegen in Zinzendorfs Verkündigung*, 1937, 89.

47. Cf. U. Wilckens, *Die Missionsreden der Apostelgeschichte*, ²1963.

48. On this see J. Schniewind, *Nachgelassene Reden und Aufsätze*, 1951, 120, 130.

49. H. Schwantes, *Schöpfung der Endzeit*, 1962, esp. 88ff.

50. W. Pannenberg, *Offenbarung als Geschichte*, 16.

51. R. Bultmann, 'Jesus and Paul', in *Existence and Faith: The Shorter Writings of Rudolf Bultmann*, ed. Schubert M. Ogden, Fontana Books 1962, 197.

52. W. Kramer, op. cit., 108–11.

53. Thus against W. Kramer, op. cit., 115–18, with W. Schrage, op. cit., 72 n.66.

54. W. Popkes, *Christus traditus, Eine Untersuchung zum Begriff der Dahingabe im Neuen Testament*, 1967, 286f.

55. See H. Benckert, 'Ohne Christus wäre ich Atheist', *EvTh* 18, 1958, 445ff.

56. This has been taken into the sub-title of E. Bloch, *Atheismus in Christentum*, 1969.

57. Cf. S. Eberhard, *Kreuzestheologie*, 1937, 89.

6

THE 'CRUCIFIED GOD'

The three christological chapters above are now to be followed by three systematic chapters which will develop the consequences of this theology of the crucified Christ for the concept of God (Chapter 6), for anthropology (Chapter 7) and for a critical theory of church and society (Chapter 8). From this point we shall proceed in reverse order, beginning with the concept of God which seeks to understand 'the godforsakenness of Jesus' on the cross. After that we shall attempt to arrive at an understanding of man which does justice to the crucified 'blasphemer', and finally we shall look for a 'political theology' in which the significance of the political dimension of his crucifixion for church and society is explored.

1. The 'Death of God' as the Origin of Christian Theology?

Over recent years, many Christians and theologians have been made uneasy by the controversy over the existence of God and belief in God. Long-familiar religious notions have been shattered, and many people feel disoriented when faced with the slogans 'God is dead' and 'God cannot die'.[1] Nevertheless, within these public controversies, new converging trends in theological thinking have begun to emerge, which may lead us to expect a consistent *Christian* doctrine of God. As this new development is happening in both Catholic and Protestant theology, we may speak of an ecumenical task and hope. It is true that in the struggle for a new church and a humane society there are those who have excluded the question of God from current discussion. It is true that others have turned only to Jesus, his example and his human features in a neo-Protestant fashion, following the poetical 'death of God' in modern times. But such superficialities do not resolve

200

the crisis. Behind the political and social crisis of the church, behind the growing crisis over the credibility of its public declarations and its institutional form, there lurks the christological question: Who really is Christ for us today? With this christological crisis we have already entered into the political crisis of the church. And rooted in the christological question about Jesus is ultimately the question about God. Which God motivates Christian faith: the crucified God or the gods of religion, race and class?

Without new certainty and new insight in Christian faith itself, Christianity will not achieve any public credibility in the human and social problems of the divided world.

The new converging trends in theological thought today concentrate the question and the knowledge of God on the death of Christ on the cross and attempt to understand God's being from the death of Jesus. The rather solemn-sounding 'death of God theology' has at least been successful in compelling theologians to begin with christology and thus to speak of God for Jesus' sake, in other words to develop a particular theology within earshot of the dying cry of Jesus.[2] The theological traditions have always considered the cross and the resurrection of Jesus within the horizon of soteriology. Even the studies produced by the Protestant Church Union, to which we have referred in previous chapters, only examine the cross of Jesus in the context of a search for the 'ground of salvation'.[3]

This is by no means false, but it is not radical enough. We must go on to ask: '*What does the cross of Jesus mean for God himself?*' 'Jesus died for God before he died for us', said Althaus in an ambiguous way, meaning that a serious fault of earlier Protestant theology was that it did not look at the cross in the context of the relationship of the Son to the Father, but related it directly to mankind as an expiatory death for sin. Later Protestant Jesuology was even worse, as it saw his death only as exemplary obedience in suffering and the proof of his faithfulness to his calling.[4] But how can the 'death of Jesus' be a *statement about God*? Does that not amount to a revolution in the concept of God?

In Catholic theology, since 1960 Karl Rahner has understood the death of Jesus as the death of God in the sense that through his death 'our death [becomes] the death of the immortal God himself'. This statement appears in his 'On the Theology of the

Incarnation',[5] and is meaningful only in a trinitarian context. Here Rahner issues an invitation to consider the death of Jesus not only in its saving efficacy but also in its very nature. As we may not assume that this death 'does not affect' God, 'this death itself expresses God'. 'The death of Jesus is a statement of God about himself.'[6] But to what degree is God himself 'concerned in' or 'affected by' the fate of Jesus on the cross? Did he suffer there in himself or only in someone else? Does the involvement go so far that the death of Jesus can be identified *as* the death of God? And in that case, who is God: the one who lets Jesus die or at the same time the Jesus who dies? What dichotomy does this presuppose in God? Hans Urs von Balthasar has similarly taken up the ominous formula 'the death of God' and developed the 'paschal mystery' under the title 'The Death of God as the Source of Salvation, Revelation and Theology'.[7] He too derives knowledge of God and receiving salvation from the crucified Christ, understands the church as the church 'under the cross' and 'from the cross', and develops the doctrine of God as a trinitarian theology of the cross. This leads him repeatedly, for all his precautions, to Luther's *theologia crucis*, to Hegel and Kierkegaard, to the German, English and Russian kenotic theologians of the nineteenth century, and to Karl Barth. With a more profound theology than that of Rahner, he traces the self-surrender, the grief and the death of the crucified Christ back to the inner mystery in God himself and conversely finds in this death of Jesus the fullness of the trinitarian relationships of God himself. The fundamental questions of the mutability of God, his passibility and his 'death' are not, however, made the subject of thematic discussion in this book.

This attempt has been made by H. Mühlen in a short work on 'The Mutability of God as the Horizon of a Future Christology'[8] and by Hans Küng in excursuses to his book on Hegel entitled 'Incarnation of God. An Introduction to Hegel's Theological Thought as Prolegomena to a Future Christology', dealing with the questions 'Can God Suffer?' and 'Does God Change?'[9]

On the Protestant side, after Adolf Schlatter[10] and Paul Althaus, Karl Barth has developed a *theologia crucis* in the sections of his *Church Dogmatics* on predestination and reconciliation.[11] The 'crucified Jesus is the "image of the invisible God"'.[12] His well-known christological concentration of theology, which never became 'Christomonism', led him in his doctrine of reconciliation to combine the traditional doctrines of the two natures of Christ, the divine and the human, and the two states of Christ, those of humiliation and exaltation. Accordingly, the divinity of Jesus is revealed precisely in his humiliation and his manhood in his exaltation. In this way Barth has consistently drawn the harshness of the cross into his concept of God.[13] His criticism of a one-sided Lutheran *theologia crucis* itself leads him to take up the theology of the cross and make it more profound, for only in connection with the resurrection of Jesus can the theology of the cross be theology and at the same time a radical recognition of the for-sakenness of the crucified Christ. Because Barth thought consistently of 'God in Christ', he could think historically of God's being, speak almost in theopaschite terms of God's suffering and being involved in the cross of the Son, and finally talk of the 'death of God', *de facto*, if not in those very words. 'In God's eternal purpose it is God Himself who is rejected in His Son', for 'God wills to lose that man may win'.[14] Remarkably, I see the critical limitation of Barth in the fact that he still thinks too *theo*logically, and that his approach is not sufficiently trinitarian.[15] In stressing constantly and rightly that '*God* was in Christ', *God* humbled himself, *God* himself was on the cross, he uses a simple concept of God which is not sufficiently developed in a trinitarian direction. For this reason, like Karl Rahner he has to make a distinction in the 'God was in Christ' between the God who proceeds from himself in his primal decision and the God who is previously in himself, beyond contact with evil.[16] For all his polemic against Luther's distinction between the *deus revelatus* and the *deus absconditus*, Barth himself comes very close to the same sort of thing. It can, however, be avoided at this point if one makes a trinitarian differentiation over the event on the cross. The Son suffers and dies on the cross. The Father suffers with him, but not in the same way. There is a trinitarian solution to the paradox that God is 'dead' on the cross and yet is not dead, once one abandons the simple concept of God. Theopaschite talk of the 'death of God' can be a general metaphor, but on closer inspection it will not hold.

Eberhard Jüngel has followed Barth in developing the fundamental notion of 'the death of the living God', largely as a result of the 'death of God theology'.[17] He has been followed by H.-G. Geyer, who takes issue with both theism and atheism.[18] Further trinitarian criticism of Barth's way of talking about God in connection with the cross of Jesus would also affect them. When one considers the significance of the death of Jesus for God himself, one must enter into the inner-trinitarian tensions and relationships of God and speak of the Father, the Son and the Spirit. But if that is the case, it is inappropriate to talk simply of 'God' in connection with the Christ event. When one uses the phrase 'God in Christ', does it refer only to the Father, who abandons him and gives him up, or does it also refer to the Son who is abandoned and forsaken? The more one understands the whole event of the cross as an event of God, the more any simple concept of God falls apart. In epistemological terms it takes so to speak trinitarian form. One moves from the exterior of the mystery which is called 'God' to the interior, which is trinitarian. This is the 'revolution in the concept of God' which is manifested by the crucified Christ. But in that case, who or what is meant by 'God'?

The death of Jesus on the cross is the *centre* of all Christian theology. It is not the only theme of theology, but it is in effect the entry to its problems and answers on earth. All Christian statements about God, about creation, about sin and death have their focal point in the crucified Christ. All Christian statements about history, about the church, about faith and sanctification, about the future and about hope stem from the crucified Christ. The multiplicity of the New Testament comes together in the event of the crucifixion and resurrection of Jesus and flows out again from it. It is one event and one person. The addition of 'cross and resurrection' represents only the inevitable temporality which is a part of language; it is not a sequence of facts. For cross and resurrection are not facts on the same level; the first expression denotes a historical happening to Jesus, the second an eschatological event. Thus the centre is occupied not by 'cross and resurrection', but by *the resurrection of the crucified Christ*, which qualifies his death as something that has happened for us, and *the cross of the risen Christ*, which reveals and makes accessible to those who are dying his resurrection from the dead.

In coming to terms with this Christ event, the christological tradition closely followed the Christ hymn in Phil. 2. It therefore understood the incarnation of the Son of God as his course towards the humiliation on the cross. The incarnation of the Logos is completed on the cross. Jesus is born to face his passion. His mission is fulfilled once he has been abandoned on the cross. So it is impossible to speak of an incarnation of God without keeping this conclusion in view. There can be no theology of the incarnation which does not become a theology of the cross. 'As soon as you say incarnation, you say cross.'[19] God did not become man according to the measure of our conceptions of being a man. He became the kind of man we do not want to be: an outcast, accursed, crucified. *Ecce homo*! Behold the man! is not a statement which arises from the confirmation of our humanity and is made on the basis of 'like is known by like'; it is a confession of faith which recognizes God's humanity in the dehumanized Christ on the cross. At the same time the confession says *Ecce deus*! Behold God on the cross! Thus God's incarnation 'even unto the death on the cross' is not in the last resort a matter of concealment; this is his utter humiliation, in which he is completely with himself and completely with the other, the man who is dehumanized. Humiliation to the point of death on the cross corresponds to God's nature in the contradiction of abandonment. When the crucified Jesus is called the 'image of the invisible God', the meaning is that *this* is God, and God is like *this*. God is not greater than he is in this humiliation. God is not more glorious than he is in this self-surrender. God is not more powerful than he is in this helplessness. God is not more divine than he is in this humanity.[20] The nucleus of everything that Christian theology says about 'God' is to be found in this Christ event. The Christ event on the cross is a God event. And conversely, the God event takes place on the cross of the risen Christ. Here God has not just acted externally, in his unattainable glory and eternity. Here he has acted in himself and has gone on to suffer in himself. Here he himself is love with all his being. So the new christology which tries to think of the 'death of Jesus as the death of God', must take up the elements of truth which are to be found in *kenoticism* (the doctrine of God's emptying of himself).[21] It cannot seek to maintain only a dialectical relationship between the divine being and human being, leaving each of these unaffected; in its own way the divine being must encompass the human being and vice versa. That means that it must understand the event of the cross in God's being in both trinitarian and personal terms. In contrast to the traditional doctrine of the two natures in the person of

Christ, it must begin from the totality of the person of Christ and understand the relationship of the death of the Son to the Father and the Spirit. The doctrine of kenosis, the self-emptying of God, was still conceived within the framework of the distinction of the two natures of God and man. It attempted, however, to understand God's being in process. It has found few followers, because the framework of thought which it has preserved leads to difficult and impossible statements. But Paul Althaus is right in saying:

Christology must be done in the light of the cross: the full and undiminished deity of God is to be found in the complete helplessness, in the final agony of the crucified Jesus, at the point where no 'divine nature' is to be seen. In faith in Jesus Christ, we recognize as a law of the life of God himself a saying of the Lord which Paul applied to his own life ('My strength is made perfect in weakness', II Cor. 12.9). Of course the old idea of the immutability of God shatters on this recognition. Christology must take seriously the fact that God himself really enters into the suffering of the Son and in so doing is and remains completely God. This divine miracle cannot be rationalized by a theory which makes God present and active in Jesus Christ only so long as the limits of being human as we understand it are not crossed. Yet on the other hand the Godhead may not be located ontologically in the humanity of Jesus. The Godhead is there hidden under the manhood, only open to faith and not to sight. It is therefore beyond any possibility of a theory. That this is the case, that God enters into the hiddenness of his Godhead beneath the human nature, is kenosis.[22]

With this attitude to the old doctrine of kenosis, Althaus comes very near to a personal understanding of the suffering and death of Jesus as that of the Son in relationship to the Father. He has put in question the theory of the immutability of God and with it the axiom of the impassibility of the divine nature. But at that point he has returned to the old dialectic of Godhead and manhood and has therefore barred the way towards a trinitarian understanding of kenosis. The 'mystical theology of the Eastern church', unrestricted by the doctrine of the two natures by which God and man are distinguished, could go further here and say: 'The kenosis . . . (and) the work of the incarnate Son (is) the work of the entire most holy Trinity, from which Christ cannot be separated.'[23] But if the kenosis of the Son to the point of death upon the cross is the 'revelation of the entire Trinity', this event too can only be presented as a God-event in trinitarian terms. What happens on the cross manifests the relationships of Jesus, the Son, to the Father, and vice versa. The cross and its liberating effect makes possible the movement of the Spirit from the Father to us. The cross stands at the heart of the trinitarian being of God; it divides and conjoins the persons in their relationships to each other and portrays them in a specific way. For as we said, the theological dimension of the death of Jesus on the cross is what happens between Jesus and his Father in the spirit of abandonment and surrender. In these relationships the person of Jesus comes to the fore in its totality as the Son, and the relationship of the Godhead and the manhood in his person fall into the background. Anyone who really talks of the Trinity talks of the cross of Jesus, and does not speculate in heavenly riddles.

Consequently, we must make more of a differentiation than is suggested by the phrase 'the death of God' which appeared at the beginning of this section. Jesus' death cannot be understood 'as the death of God', but only as death *in* God. The 'death of God' cannot be designated the origin of Christian theology, even if the phrase has an element of truth in it; the origin of Christian theology is only the death on the cross in God and God in Jesus' death. If one uses the phrase, it is advisable to abandon the concept of God and to speak of the relationships of the Son and the Father and the Spirit at the point at which 'God' might be expected to be mentioned. From the life of these three, which has within it the death of Jesus, there then emerges who God is and what his Godhead means. Most previous statements about the specifically Christian understanding of talk about 'the death of God' have lacked a dimension, the trinitarian dimension. 'On the cross, God stretched out his hands to embrace the ends of the earth,' said Cyril of Jerusalem. This is a symbolic expression. He invites the whole earth to understand his suffering and his hopes in the outstretched arms of the crucified Jesus and therefore in God. 'O blessed tree on which God was outstretched.'[24] This symbol is an invitation to understand the Christ hanging on the cross as the 'outstretched' God of the Trinity.

2. *Theism and the Theology of the Cross*

Whereas in the late Middle Ages the theology of the cross was an expression of the mysticism of suffering, Luther uses it strictly as a new principle of theological epistemology. For him the cross is not a symbol for the path of suffering that leads to fellowship with God, a reversal of the way of works that are well-pleasing to God; rather, as the cross of the outcast and forsaken Christ it is the visible revelation of God's being for man in the reality of his world. The Heidelberg disputation on 26 April 1518 was a regular theological conference of the chapter of the Augustinian monks.[25] Luther presented his new principle of theological epistemology by means of an exegesis of Psalm 22. Then he had to go to Worms. Thus the *theologia crucis* stands at the climax of his 'decision for reformation' and represents its theoretical basis. For Luther understands the cross of Christ in a quite unmystical way as God's protest against the misuse of his name for the purpose of a religious consummation of human wisdom, human works and the Christian imperialism of medieval ecclesiastical society. It is a protest for the freedom of faith. With the *theologia crucis* there begins the Reformation struggle over the true or the false church, over the liberation of man enslaved under the compulsion of works and achievements. With it, indeed, begins a new relationship to reality itself.[26]

Thesis 19: 'He is not rightly called a theologian who perceives and understands God's invisible being through his works. That is clear from those who were such 'theologians' and yet were called fools by the apostle in Romans 1.22. The invisible being of God is his power, Godhead, wisdom, righteousness, goodness, and so on. Knowledge of all these things does not make a man wise and worthy.'

Here Luther is not talking of theology as knowledge of God in itself, but of the theologian, i.e. the man who seeks to know God. For him, every Christian is a 'theologian', i.e. one who knows God. What does knowledge of God make him? Luther does not consider theological theory in itself, its subject-matter and its method, but theory in connection with its use by men. In Chapter 2 we called this a transition from a pure theory to a critical theory,[27] because here Luther is already reflecting on knowledge and interest in their conscious and unconscious connections. He is looking into the element of heuristic interest in the knowledge of God and the use of knowledge by man. So he does not speak of a *theologia gloriae* but of a *theologus gloriae*.

The epistemological course which he criticizes is the course of natural theology following the *Sentences* of Peter Lombard, not a theology in the realm of glory. According to Luther's Thesis 19, this method begins from the works of God—*ea quae facta sunt*—and draws conclusions from the effects to the cause, from the works to the one who performs them, and thus by means of a process of induction arrives back at the indirect knowledge of the invisible nature of God: his power, Godhead, wisdom and righteousness. This is what Paul said of the Gentiles in Rom. 1.19–20: 'For what can be known about God is plain to them, because God has shown it to them, that God's invisible being, that is his power and his Godhead, can be seen, so that it is perceived in his works, namely in the creation of the world.' Peter Lombard expressed this natural knowledge of God in the following way: 'Man perceives him (the Creator) in what is created in the world by virtue of the excellence through which he towers above all other creatures and by virtue of his accord with all creation.'[28] Here, first of all, is old Stoic tradition: (*a*) the cosmos is permeated by the divine Logos and its rationality corresponds to that of the divine being itself; (*b*) the seed of wisdom is innate in all men. Man comes to know the rationality of the cosmos with the aid of his innate ideas, his reason (like is known only by like), and in this way he achieves a life in accordance with his nature. But if nature (*physis*) corresponds to God and is itself divine, then by a life in accord with nature and reason, man achieves a life in accord with God. The Christian theological formulation used by Lombard breaks away from Stoic pantheism and pan-rationalism by introducing the difference between the Creator and the creature, but it bridges this difference between the creation and the Creator by means of the *analogia entis*. Furthermore, it maintains the *excellentia* of man as compared with everything else and his *convenientia* with all other creatures. As a being with intelligence, man is not only a part of creation but also stands over against it. This gives him his 'ex-centric position',[30] which is also called his self-transcendence. By his intelligence he transcends creation, and by his insight, his ability to see through things, he gains a share in the wisdom of God. His capacity is heightened by his power to reason for the visible to the invisible, from the many to the one, from realities to the one who brings about reality. The heuristic interest lies in man's *excellentia*. The consequence is the exaltation of man above all creatures and his departure from *convenientia* with all creatures. This course of knowledge is the basis of all cosmological arguments for the existence of God. Hegel said: 'The starting point of these arguments is finitude, but this has several determinations, and so there are a number of different arguments.'[31] According to Thomas Aquinas, the starting point of the five ways of this knowledge of God is the perception of motion, of effect, of contingent being, of finite being, of ordered being.[32] The method is that of logical inference. The ontological presupposition for this inference is the ontic connection between motion and mover, between effect and cause, between the contingent and the necessary, the finite and the infinite, between ordered being and the one who gives it rational order. There must be a community of being between effect and cause, etc., as otherwise logical inference would be impossible. There must be a reality accessible in experience and perception, which is at the same time related to God and corresponds to him, otherwise there would be no knowledge of God immediately accessible to every man.

The cosmological arguments for the existence of God presuppose a God who is indirectly evident and manifest through his works. Therefore they draw conclusions from *ea quae facta sunt* to the invisible being of God. This process of argument is not questionable in itself, but stringent; however, its presupposition, that everything that is corresponds to God and is connected with his being through an *analogia entis*, probably is. Logical inference really only advances these correspondences of being to correspondences in knowledge. Therefore two things are recognized in the intelligible knowledge which it produces:

1. God's invisible being is known from his works and realities in the world; conversely, the reality of the world is recognized as God's world, that is, as the visible body of the Godhead (the Stoa), i.e. in Christian terms, as his good creation. The reality of the world that can be experienced and known is like a mirror in which God's divinity, God's power, God's wisdom and God's righteousness can indirectly be known, for it is a created, accomplished world, set in motion, ordered and regulated. It is cosmos, or creation.

When in his five ways Thomas reaches the last point beyond which no further questions may be asked, the *causa prima*, the *primum movens*, the *ens per se necessarium* and the *maxima ens*, he says, '*et hoc omnes intelligunt Deum*'. The last element in this course of knowledge is the first element in being. He calls 'God' that which must be conceived of as the first, the all-embracing, the origin and the principle, if the finite world is to be conceived of as a unity. That is, he conceives of a last, first, absolute, unconditioned and final principle for the sake of the concept of the world as a whole. God is then not thought of for his own sake but for the sake of something else, for the sake of finite being. The heuristic interest is that of 'securing' God in and for finite being.

Thesis 20: But he is rightly called a theologian who understands that part of God's being which is visible and directed towards the world to be presented in suffering and in the cross. That part of God's being which is visible and directed towards the world is opposed to what is invisible, his humanity, his weakness, his foolishness ... For as men misused the knowledge of God on the basis of his works, God again willed that he should be known from suffering, and therefore willed to reject such wisdom of the invisible by a wisdom of the visible, so that those who did not worship God as he is manifested in his works might worship him as the one who is hidden in suffering (I Cor. 1.21). So it is not enough and no use for anyone to know God in his glory and his majesty if at the same time he does not know him in the lowliness and shame of his cross ... Thus true theology and true knowledge of God lie in Christ the crucified one.

Here Luther follows the train of thought in Rom. 1.18ff., but he connects it with I Cor. 1 and therefore opposes the knowledge of God in the cross to the natural knowledge of God from his works. He does not dispute the possibility of natural knowledge of God, but he does dispute its reality. He disputes it on the basis of I Cor. 1.21: 'Because men did not know God from creation'— but perverted this truth into the lie of idolatry—'it pleased God through the folly of what we preach (the crucified Christ) to save those who believe'. Natural knowledge of God is potentially open to men, but in fact they misuse it in the interest of their self-exaltation and their self-divinization. Just as man misuses his works to justify himself, to conceal his anxiety from God and from himself, so too he misuses the knowledge of God to serve his hybris. In this situation, this knowledge of God is useless; it merely does him damage, because it 'puffs him up' and gives him illusions about his true situation. On the other hand, the knowledge of God in the suffering and death of Christ takes this perverse situation of man seriously. It is not an ascending, exalting knowledge, but a descending, convincing knowledge. God is not in

heaven here, but wants something on earth. In revealing himself
in the crucified Christ he contradicts the God-man who exalts
himself, shatters his hybris, kills his gods and brings back to him
his despised and abandoned humanness. The theology of the
cross therefore takes quite seriously God's interest in his knowledge
through man. God reveals himself in the contradiction and the
protest of Christ's passion to be against all that is exalted and
beautiful and good, all that the dehumanized man seeks for
himself and therefore perverts. So God here is not known through
his works in reality, but through his suffering in the passiveness
of faith, which allows God to work on it: killing in order to make
alive, judging in order to set free. So his knowledge is achieved
not by the guiding thread of analogies from earth to heaven, but
on the contrary, through contradiction, sorrow and suffering. To
know God means to endure God. To know God in the cross of
Christ is a crucifying form of knowledge, because it shatters
everything to which a man can hold and on which he can build,
both his works and his knowledge of reality, and precisely in so
doing sets him free. The 'ascent of knowledge of God' takes
place in the 'descent of self-knowledge', and the two come together
in the knowledge of Christ.[33]

According to Luther, the theology of the cross does not begin
from the visible works of God in order to disclose God's invisible
being, but takes the opposite starting point, 'that part of God's
being which is visible and directed towards the world'. For him
this visible being of God is the passion and cross of Christ. It is
set over against the 'invisible being' of God in the ascending
knowledge of the *theologus gloriae* and contradicts it. Christ the
crucified alone is 'man's true theology and knowledge of God'.
This presupposes that while indirect knowledge of God is possible
through his works, God's being can be seen and known directly
only in the cross of Christ and knowledge of God is therefore real
and saving. In the one place one looks so to speak only at his
hands; in the other one looks into his heart. This again is possible
only if God has descended of his own accord as the crucified
Christ and has become man and makes himself visible for man in
Christ. In fact Luther's *theologia crucis* here is a radical development
of the doctrine of the incarnation with a soteriological intent.

Through the regime of his humanity and his flesh, in which we live by
faith, he makes us of the same form as himself and crucifies us by making

212

us true men instead of unhappy and proud gods: men, that is, in their misery and their sin. Because in Adam we mounted up towards equality with God, he descended to be like us, to bring us back to knowledge of himself. That is the significance of the incarnation. That is the kingdom of faith in which the cross of Christ holds sway, which sets at naught the divinity for which we perversely strive and restores the despised weakness of the flesh which we have perversely abandoned.[34]

The one who knows God in the lowliness, weakness and dying of Christ does not know him in the dreamed-of exaltation and divinity of the man who seeks God, but in the humanity which he has abandoned, rejected and despised. And that brings to nothing his dreamed-of equality with God, which has dehumanized him, and restores to him his humanity, which the true God made his own.

Whereas medieval mysticism understood the way of suffering and the *meditatio crucis* as a way to the divinization of man by means of the *via negationis*, Luther reverses this approach and sees in the cross God's descent to the level of our sinful nature and our death, not so that man is divinized, but so that he is de-divinized and given new humanity in the community of the crucified Christ. Hence Thesis 21 reads: 'The theologian of glory calls the bad good and the good bad; the theologian of the cross calls things by their right names (*dicit quod res est*).' The theologian of glory, and that is the 'natural man', who is incurably religious (Berdyaev), hates the cross and passion. He seeks works and success and therefore regards the knowledge of an almighty God who is always at work as being glorious and uplifting. But the theologian of the cross, and that is the believer, comes to knowledge of himself where he knows God in his despised humanity, and calls human things by their real names and not by images of their attractive appearance. He does not name them as they would wish out of fear of nothingness, but as they are accepted by the boundless suffering love of God. The 'theologian of glory' of the invisible being of God secretly creates for himself free room for activity in his own interest which will allow him 'to love what is like'. For his theology needs equations and confirmations. But the 'theologian of the cross' is led by the visible nature of God in the cross. He is freed to love that which is different and other. This has far-reaching consequences: religious desire for praise and might and self-affirmation are blind to suffering—their own and that of others—because they are in love with success. Their love is eros for the beautiful, which is to make the one who loves beautiful himself. But in the cross and passion of Christ faith experiences a quite different love of God, which loves what is quite different. It loves 'what is sinful, bad, foolish, weak and hateful, in order to make it beautiful and good and wise and righteous. For sinners are beautiful because they are loved; they are not loved because they are beautiful.'[35]

With this we come to the confrontation between the theology of the cross and the philosophical theism of indirect knowledge of God from the world.[36]

Is the theistic concept of God applicable to Christian belief in the crucified God?

For metaphysics, the nature of divine being is determined by its unity and indivisibility, its lack of beginning and end, its immovability and immutability. As the nature of divine being is conceived of for the sake of finite being, it must embrace all the determinations of finite being and exclude those determinations which are directed against being. Otherwise finite being could not find a support and stay against the threatening nothingness of death, suffering and chaos in the divine being. Death, suffering and mortality must therefore be excluded from the divine being. Christian theology has adopted this concept of God from philosophical theology down to the present day,[37] because in practice down to the present day Christian faith has taken into itself the religious need of finite, threatened and mortal man for security in a higher omnipotence and authority. Even Schleiermacher conceived of God as pure causality for the feeling of absolute dependence,[38] and therefore had to exclude God, as pure activity, from all suffering which would make God the object of human activity. In the metaphysical concept of God from ancient cosmology and the modern psychological concept of God, the being of the Godhead, of the origin of all things or the unconditioned mover, as the zone of the impossibility of death, stands in juxtaposition to human being as the zone of the necessity of death.[39] If this concept of God is applied to Christ's death on the cross, the cross *must* be 'evacuated' of deity, for by definition God cannot suffer and die. He is pure causality. But Christian theology must think of God's being in suffering and dying and finally in the death of Jesus, if it is not to surrender itself and lose its identity. Suffering, dying and similar negations simply cannot be predicated of that which is conceived of as pure causality and the unconditioned mover.[40] The God who was the subject of suffering could not be truly God.[41]

At this point, the controversy between Christian theology and the philosophical concept of God must now be taken further. After the very long period during which the theologian has been confronted in the picture of Christ with the 'unmoving, unemotional countenance of the God of Plato, bedecked with some features of Stoic ethics',[42] the time has finally come for differentiating the Father of Jesus Christ from the God of the pagans and the philosophers (Pascal) in the interest of Chistian faith. On the theoretical level this corresponds to the critical disestablishment of Christianity from the bourgeois religions of the particular societies in which that theism has predominated. The theology of the early church advanced furthest in this direction in developing the trinitarian doctrine of God, for the doctrine of the Trinity speaks of God in respect of the incarnation and the death of Jesus and in so doing breaks the spell of the old philosophical concept of God, at the same time destroying the idols of national political religions.[43]

The modern surrender of the doctrine of the Trinity or its reduction to an empty, orthodox formula is a sign of the assimilation of Christianity to the religions felt to be needed in modern society.

With the Christian message of the cross of Christ, something new and strange has entered the metaphysical world. For this faith must understand the deity of God from the event of the suffering and death of the Son of God and thus bring about a fundamental change in the orders of being of metaphysical thought and the value tables of religious feeling. It must think of the suffering of Christ as the power of God and the death of Christ as God's potentiality. Conversely, it must think of freedom from suffering and death as a possibility for man. So Christian theology cannot seek to understand the death of Jesus on the presupposition of that metaphysical or moral concept of God. If this presupposition holds, the death of Jesus cannot be understood at all in theological terms. Rather, faith must take an opposite course and 'understand God's Godness from the event of this death'.[44] Christianity cannot therefore any longer be represented as a 'monotheistic form of belief' (Schleiermacher).[45] Christian faith is not 'radical monotheism'.[46] As a theology of the cross, Christian theology is the

criticism of and liberation from philosophical and political monotheism. God cannot suffer, God cannot die, says theism, in order
to bring suffering, mortal being under his protection. God suffered
in the suffering of Jesus, God died on the cross of Christ, says
Christian faith, so that we might live and rise again in his future.
Thus at the level of the psychology of religion, Christian faith
effects liberation from the childish projections of human needs for
the riches of God; liberation from human impotence for the
omnipotence of God; from human helplessness for the omnipotence of God; from human helplessness for the responsibility of
God. It brings liberation from the divinized father-figures by
which men seek to sustain their childhood. It brings liberation
from fear in the ideas of political omnipotence with which the
powers on earth legitimate their rule and give inferiority complexes
to the impotent, and with which the impotent compensate their
impotence in dreams. It brings liberation from the determination
and direction from outside which anxious souls love and at the
same time hate. This God of the cross is not the 'great huntsman'
(Cardonnel),[47] who sits over man's conscience like a fist on the
neck. Anyone who understands God in this way misuses his
name and is far from the cross.

Is Christian faith applicable to the theistic concept of God?

We have seen that Christian faith stands over against the
theistic concept of God in its philosophical, political and moral
variations. But does this already solve the problems which have
led to that concept of God? For Christian faith, is the world no
longer finite, transitory and threatened by chaos? Is man no longer
a being who is aware of his finitude in death and of the absurdity
of his existence in experiencing his nothingness? It is nonsense to
drive out metaphysics from Christian theology with the aid of the
'end of metaphysics' proclaimed by Nietzsche, if one can put
nothing in its place in the experience of the world and man's
experience of himself. In that case, why did the church's tradition
take up philosophical theology as a task of Christian theology?
The mere separation of Christian theology from philosophical
theology and the interpretation of the world, time and man's self
leads only to the self-isolation of theology and helps no one. It
leads to a *theologia gloriae* from below. The important thing,
therefore, is to think of the God of the cross quite consistently
not only in the sphere of theology but also in the sphere of social

life and the personality of man, in the realm of society, politics
and finally even that of cosmology.

At this point the analogous attempts of H.-G. Geyer and E.
Jüngel break off remarkably abruptly. Both try to think of the
death of Christ as a possibility of God's being, i.e. to understand
the death of Christ as the 'death of God', and end by saying that
in that case man becomes free to comprehend the 'transformation
of destiny, of dying into the freedom of being able to die'.[48]
'The death which has become a phenomenon *of God* still awaits
the believer as a phenomenon of the world. But as such it is
demythologized so that it becomes dying ... Dying no longer
alienates man and *God*, but from the beginning belongs to
Christian existence.'[49] If the curse of death which separates man
from God is abolished in the death of God, natural death remains,
which existentialist interpretation makes it possible to accept: the
resurrection hope means 'God is my beyond'.

Now a tranquil ability to die has always been part of the Stoic
and Christian *ars moriendi*. But the phenomenon which has been
described in modern times with the symbol of the 'death of God'
does not concern the death of the individual at all, but the 'darkness of God' (Buber), the inescapability of the process of the world
and the absurdity of existence. Is the world too to learn to die
tranquilly, or are there hopes for the world which must be
answered in personal and socio-political terms? Men must go
beyond the significance of the Christian 'death of God' for their
own ability to die and seek the significance of the death of God on
Christ's cross for the universal death of God today—Hegel's
'speculative Good Friday'. The death of Christ cannot only come
to fruition in an existentialist interpretation, in the ability of the
believer to die in peace, important though that may be. The
crucified Christ must be thought of as the origin of creation and
the embodiment of the eschatology of being. In the cross of his
Son, God took upon himself not only death, so that man might
be able to die comforted with the certainty that even death could
not separate him from God, but still more, in order to make the
crucified Christ the ground of his new creation, in which death
itself is swallowed up in the victory of life and there will be
'no sorrow, no crying, and no more tears'. Revelation 5.12 and
7.17 therefore say that 'the lamb that was slain is worthy to
receive power and riches, wisdom and strength and honour and

thanksgiving and praise' and the 'conqueror will lead them to living streams of water' and 'death will be no more, because the former things have passed away' (21.4). This includes being able to die tranquilly in faith, because it includes faith in the universal hope for the new creation in Christ. *Like* the metaphysics of finite being, the theology of the cross sees all creatures subject to transitoriness and nothingness. But because it does not arise in this context, but sees nothingness itself done away with in the being of God, who in the death of Jesus has revealed himself and constituted himself in nothingness, it changes the general impression of the transitoriness of all things into the prospect of the hope and liberation of all things. 'For the creation was subjected to nothingness, not of its own will but by the will of him who subjected it in hope' (Rom. 8.20). Thus the metaphysical longing of all that is transitory for intransitoriness and of all that is finite for infinity undergoes an eschatological transformation and is taken up into the hope of the freedom of the sons of God and the freedom of the new creation that does not pass away. Anyone who says 'resurrection of the dead' says 'God' (Barth).[50] On the other hand, anyone who says 'God' and does not hope for the resurrection of the dead and a new creation from the righteousness of God, has not said 'God'. What other belief in God can be held by those who are 'dead' unless it is 'resurrection faith'?[51]

Christian theology is not the 'end of metaphysics'. Precisely because metaphysical theism is not applicable to it, it is for its part free to take up metaphysics as a task of theology and to think through the consequences of faith in the sphere of the experiences and hopes of the world. A 'philosophy of the cross' can easily lead to Gnostic speculations. Nevertheless, the theology of the cross also has cosmological dimensions, because it sees the cosmos in the eschatological history of God. For the 'history of God', whose nucleus is the event of the cross, cannot be thought of as history in the world, but on the contrary makes it necessary to understand the world in this history. The event of the resurrection of the crucified Christ makes it necessary to think of the annihilation of the world and the creation of every being from nothing. The 'history of God' is no 'inner-worldly' possibility, but on the contrary the world is a possibility and a reality in this history. No Christian eschatology is possible without the knowledge of the God who creates from nothing and raises the crucified

Christ. But if one looks at the world and all that happens in this history, the metaphysical decisions are made in the light of a hope which is both this-worldly and transcendent. The new possibilities in the world spring from the world as a possibility of the creator God.[52] The history of God is then to be thought of as the horizon of the world; the world is not to be thought of as the horizon of his history. The cross is 'set up in the cosmos to establish the unstable', we read in the apocryphal Acts of Andrew.[53] There is a truth here: it is set up in the cosmos in order to give future to that which is passing away, firmness to that which is unsteady, openness to that which is fixed, hope to the hopeless, and in this way to gather all that is and all that is no more into the new creation.

3. *The Theology of the Cross and Atheism*

We have identified the *theologia gloriae* attacked by Luther in the philosophical theology of the cosmological arguments for the existence of God. This metaphysical theology makes use of logical inference from *ea quae facta sunt* to the invisible properties of God, his absolute causality, his power and his wisdom, and in this way arrives at the intelligible preception of infinite being which it calls 'God'. It conceives of divine being in its qualitative superiority over finite and threatened being for the very sake of this finite being. This logical inference proves both the divine being and the finite and mortal being caused, moved and sustained by him. It proves both God and the world as God's world. Now it is not the logical inference as such that may be questionable, but its presupposition. Atheism does not address itself to this logical inference but to its ontic presupposition of the community of being between the finite being which can be experienced and the invisible divine being. In so doing atheism itself makes use of logical inference. It does not doubt the existence of God in itself, as this does not concern any being that is not God; it does doubt whether the world of experience is grounded in a divine being and is guided by this divine being. Metaphysical atheism, too, takes the world as a mirror of the deity. But in the broken mirror of an unjust and absurd world of triumphant evil and suffering without reason and without end it does not see the countenance of a God, but only the grimace of absurdity and nothingness. Atheism, too, draws a conclusion from the existence of the finite world as it is

to its cause and its destiny. But there it finds no good and righteous
God, but a capricious demon, a blind destiny, a damning law or an
annihilating nothingness. As long as this world is not 'God-
coloured', it does not allow any conclusions to God's existence,
righteousness, wisdom and goodness.[54] Thus, as the world has
really been made, belief in the devil is much more plausible than
belief in God. The hells of world wars, the hells of Auschwitz,
Hiroshima and Vietnam, and also the everyday experiences
which make one man say to another 'You make my life hell',
often suggest that the world as a whole should be thought of as a
'house of the dead', a house of discipline, a madhouse or a *univers
concentrationnaire*, and not the good earth under the gracious
heaven of a righteous God. Strindberg declared: 'Jesus Christ
descended to hell, but his descent was his wandering here on
earth, his way of suffering through the madhouse, the house of
discipline, the mortuary of this earth.'[55] In Schiller's 'Ode to Joy'
we find:

> Be patient, O millions!
> Be patient for the better world!
> There above the starry sky
> A great God will give a reward.

Against this theodicy of German idealism, in Dostoevsky's novel
Ivan Karamazov tells a story of a poor serf child who hit his
master's hunting dog with a stone while he was playing. The
master had him seized and the next morning he was hunted and
torn to pieces by the master's hounds before his mother's eyes.
Ivan says:

And what sort of harmony is it, if there is a hell? I want to forgive. I want
to embrace. I don't want any more suffering. And if the sufferings of
children go to make up the sum of sufferings which is necessary for the
purchase of truth, then I say beforehand that the entire truth is not worth
such a price. I do not want a mother to embrace the torturer who had her
child torn to pieces by his dogs. She has no right to forgive him. And if
that is so, if she has no right to forgive him, what becomes of the harmony?
I don't want harmony. I don't want it out of the love I bear to mankind.
I want to remain with my suffering unavenged. Besides, too high a price
has been placed on harmony. We cannot afford to pay so much for admission. And therefore I hasten to return my ticket of admission. And
indeed, if I am an honest man, I'm bound to hand it back as soon as
possible. This I am doing. It is not God that I do not accept, Alyosha. I
merely most respectfully return him the ticket. I accept God, understand
that, but I cannot accept the world that he has made.[56]

This is the classical form of *protest atheism*. The question of the existence of God is, in itself, a minor issue in the face of the question of his righteousness in the world. And this question of suffering and revolt is not answered by any cosmological argument for the existence of God or any theism, but is rather provoked by both of these. If one argues back from the state of the world and the fact of its existence to cause, ground and principle, one can just as well speak of 'God' as of the devil, of being as of nothingness, of the meaning of the world as of absurdity. Thus the history of Western atheism becomes at the same time the history of nihilism. In this atheistic, de-divinized world, literature is full of the 'monotheism of Satan' and the mythologoumena of evil. It varies the images: God as deceiver, executioner, sadist, despot, player, director of a marionette theatre—or it introduces the images of the sleeping, erring, bored, helpless and clownish God. 'I would not want to be God at the present moment.'[57] These blasphemies are fundamentally provocations of God, for there is something that the atheist fears over and above all torments. That is the indifference of God and his final retreat from the world of men.

Here atheism demonstrates itself to be the brother of theism. It too makes use of logical inference. It too sees the world as the mirror of another, higher being. With just as much justification as that with which theism speaks of God, the highest, best, righteous being, it speaks of the nothingness which manifests itself in all the annihilating experiences of suffering and evil. It is the inescapable antithesis of theism. But if metaphysical theism disappears, can protest atheism still remain alive? For its protest against injustice and death, does not it need an authority to accuse, because it makes this authority responsible for the state of affairs? And can it make this authority responsible if it has not previously declared it to be behind the way in which the world is and exists? Following Dostoevsky, Camus called this atheism a 'metaphysical rebellion'.[58] It is 'the means by which a man protests against his condition and against the whole of creation. It is metaphysical because it disputes the ends of man and of creation.' According to Camus, the metaphysical rebellion does not derive from Greek tragedy but from the Bible, with its concept of the personal God. 'The history of the rebellion that we experience today is far more that of the descendants of Cain than the pupils of Prometheus. In this sense, it is above all others the God of the Old Testament who sets in motion the energies of the rebellion.'[59] Where does this metaphysical rebellion of atheism lead? 'I rebel— therefore we exist,' says Camus. As those who suffer and are revolted at injustice, 'we are', and we are even more than the gods or the God of theism. For these gods 'walk above in the light' as 'blessed spirits' (Hölderlin). They are immortal and omnipotent. What kind of a poor being is a God who cannot suffer and cannot even die? He is certainly superior to mortal man so long as this man allows suffering and death to come together as a doom over his head. But he is inferior to man if man grasps this suffering and death as his own possibilities and chooses them himself. Where a man accepts and chooses his own death, he raises himself to a freedom which no animal and no god can have. This was already said by Greek tragedy. For to accept death and to choose it for oneself is a human possibility and only a human possibility. 'The experience of death is the extra and the advantage that he has over all divine wisdom.'[60] The peak of metaphysical rebellion against the God who cannot die is therefore freely-chosen death, which is called suicide. It is the extreme possibility of protest atheism, because it is only this that makes man his own god, so that the gods become dispensable. But even apart from this extreme position, which Dostoevsky worked through again and again in *The Demons*, a God who cannot suffer is poorer than any man. For a God who is incapable of suffering is a being who cannot be involved. Suffering and injustice do not affect him. And because he is so completely insensitive, he cannot be affected or shaken by anything. He cannot weep, for he has no tears. But the one who cannot suffer cannot love either. So he is also a loveless being. Aristotle's God cannot love; he can only be loved by all non-divine beings by virtue of his perfection and beauty, and in this way draw them to him. The 'unmoved Mover' is a 'loveless Beloved'. If he is the ground of the love (eros) of all things for him (*causa prima*), and at the same time his own cause (*causa sui*), he is the beloved who is in love with himself; a Narcissus in a metaphysical degree: *Deus incurvatus in se*. But a man can suffer because he can love, even as a Narcissus, and he always suffers only to the degree that he loves. If he kills all love in himself, he no longer suffers. He becomes apathic. But in that case is he a God? Is he not rather a stone?

Finally, a God who is only omnipotent is in himself an incomplete being, for he cannot experience helplessness and powerlessness. Omnipotence can indeed be longed for and worshipped by helpless men, but omnipotence is never loved; it is only feared.[61] What sort of being, then, would be a God who was only 'almighty'? He would be a being without experience, a being without destiny and a being who is loved by no one. A man who experiences helplessness, a man who suffers because he loves, a man who can die, is therefore a richer being than an omnipotent God who cannot suffer, cannot love and cannot die. Therefore for a man who is aware of the riches of his own nature in his love, his suffering, his protest and his freedom, such a God is not a necessary and supreme being, but a highly dispensable and superfluous being.

However, protest atheism is in error if it divinizes man in place of God, in order to declare him to be the supreme being for man: almighty, righteous, infinite and good. Protest atheism is in error if it supplies a human genre or human society or its vanguard, a humanistic party, with inherited theistic divine predicates, saying that it is immortal, that it is always right, that it grants security and authority, etc. It will only arrive at its own truth if it recognizes man, erring, loving and suffering, unrighteous and protesting against injustice, helpless man, in his humanity, and sees that in his human experiences he is greater than all gods and all divinities and idols.

But what keeps Ivan Karamazov's protest alive? What keeps alive the protester himself, when he wants to hand back his ticket to 'such a world'?

Suicide removes the protester himself from the game and resolves the contradiction by putting the contradicter to one side. Theistic confidence resolves the contradiction by a prohibitive and useless answer. Max Horkheimer once expressed the quintessence of his critical theory in the remark: 'The longing that the murderer should not triumph over his innocent victim.' Horkheimer has thought through this longing and righteousness in his critical theory of capitalist society, and has also drawn attention to the injustice of the societies which call themselves Marxist under Stalin and his admirers.[62] He has criticized the religious idols of religion, and also the idols and the totalization which have appeared in capitalism, in nationalism and in established Marxism as true images of earlier religious idols. His critical theory of society takes over 'the productive criticism of the present state of affairs which was expressed in earlier times in faith in a heavenly judge'.[63] His 'longing for the wholly other' is the longing for the righteousness of God in the world. Were this longing not there, suffering for unrighteousness and evil would not be an unquenchable sorrow.

Without the notion of truth and what guarantees it, there can be no knowledge of its opposite, the abandonment of men, because of which true philosophy is critical and pessimistic; indeed, there cannot even be the sorrow without which joy is impossible.[64]

Horkheimer has never given the name 'God' to 'the wholly other', a formula from early dialectic theology. Rather, his critical theory is based on the presupposition that we do not know what God is. This is an old theological principle: *Deus definiri nequit*. His critical theory is therefore in essence *a negative theology which prohibits images*: it is critical, to the degree that it cannot be satisfied with any immanent idols and righteousnesses, but seeks a universal beyond contradiction into which the subjects of society could enter without compulsion; it is negative, in so far as it cannot allow the validity of any positive definitions of God, whether these are dogmatic or secularized. His negative talk of the unspeakable God, the wholly other, is demonstrated in the way in which the world can only be assigned relative validity.[65] He does not assert that there is an omnipotent, righteous and gracious God, but he questions radically whether any immanent substitute could take his place. In his critical theory he challenges both traditional theism and its brother, traditional atheism. There is no theistic answer to the question of suffering and injustice, but far less is there any atheistic possibility of avoiding this question and being content with the world. It is impossible to be content with one's own possibilities, which are always limited. So Horkheimer uses the formula of 'longing for the wholly other', which hovers between theism and atheism.

This longing for perfect righteousness can never be realized in secular history; for even if a better society were to resolve the present social disorder, it could not make good past misery nor take up past distress into all-embracing nature.[66]

In Horkheimer we find a protesting faith which takes us beyond the crude opposition of theism and atheism. 'In view of the suffering in this world, in view of the injustice, it is impossible to believe the dogma of the existence of an omnipotent and all-gracious God,' he says against optimistic theism.[67] In view of the suffering in this world, in view of the injustice, however, it is also impossible not to hope for truth and righteousness and that which provides them. That must be said on the other side. For radical criticism of the here and now is impossible without a desire for the wholly other. Without the idea of truth and that which provides it, there is no knowledge of its opposite, the forsakenness of men.[68]

However, Horkheimer has gone one step nearer to the mystery of God and suffering which underlies the dispute between theists and atheists, by going past that dispute. If innocent suffering puts the idea of a righteous God in question, so conversely longing for the righteousness of the wholly other puts suffering in question and makes it conscious sorrow. It makes consciousness of sorrow a protest against suffering. Sorrow is a special feeling in general suffering. It takes upon itself the freedom to see suffering as something special and to protest against it. If we call the sting in the question *unde malum? God,* then conversely the sting in the question *an Deus sit?* is *suffering.* Cosmological theism answers this double question with a justification of this world as God's world. In so doing it passes over the history of suffering of this world. Either it must be tolerated, or it will be compensated for by the second world in heaven.

This answer is idolatry.

Traditional atheism seeks to take the ground from under the question of God prompted by suffering. 'The simplest answer: there is no God,' said Voltaire. Stendhal's *bon mot,* for which Nietzsche envied him, is more refined: 'The only excuse for God would be for him not to exist.' Here the non-existence of God is made into an excuse for him in view of an unsuccessful creation. That is atheism as a theodicy.

But Horkheimer's critical theory is not content with any answer and keeps the question alive. Its negative theology therefore comes close to the critical theology which has its basis in the open question to the crucified Jesus: 'My God, why hast thou forsaken me?'

A radical theology of the cross cannot give any theistic answer to the question of the dying Christ. Were it to do so it would evacuate the cross. Nor can it give an atheistic answer. Were it to do so it would no longer be taking Jesus' dying cry to God seriously. The God of theism cannot have abandoned him, and in his forsakenness he cannot have cried out to a non-existent God.

Critical theology and critical theory meet in the framework of open questions, the question of suffering which cannot be answered and the question of righteousness which cannot be surrendered. 'All these wishes for eternity and above all for the dawn of universal righteousness and goodness are common to both the materialist thinker and the religious thinker, in contrast to the bluntness of the positivistic attitude.'[69] Camus comes nearer to the mystery when he writes:

Christ came to solve two main problems: evil and death, both of which are the problems of rebellion. His solution first consisted in taking them upon himself. The God-man also suffers, and does so with patience. Evil cannot be as fully ascribed to him as death, as he too is shattered and dies. The night of Golgotha only has so much significance for man because in its darkness the Godhead, visibly renouncing all inherited privileges, endures to the end the anguish of death, including the depths of despair. This is the explanation of the *Lama sabachthani* and Christ's gruesome doubt in agony. The agony would have been easy if it could have been supported by eternal hope. But for God to be a man, he had to despair.[70]

But did Christ really solve the 'problems of rebellion', evil and death, on Golgotha, in the way in which Camus portrays him, as a divine sufferer?

That was not Camus' view. He saw Christ too much in terms of the traditional passion mysticism and too little as the protesting God involved in human sorrow and suffering. He understood well that Christ's cross must mean that God himself renounced his long-standing privileges and himself experienced the agony of death, as the kenotic theology of the cross indicates, but he could not see on the other hand the cross and the deathly anguish of the godforsakenness in God. He saw God vanish on the cross, but he did not see Christ's death on the cross taken up into God. Yet only this change of perspective indicates why the night of Golgotha gained so much significance for mankind.

Crude atheism for which this world is everything is as superficial as the theism which claims to prove the existence of God from the reality of this world. Protest atheism points beyond both God and suffering, suffering and God, sets them one against the other and becomes an atheistic protest against injustice 'for God's sake'. In the context of the question which sets God and suffering over against each other, a God who sits enthroned in heaven in a glory that no one can share is unacceptable even for theology. Equally so, a grief which only affects man externally and does not seize him and change him in his very person does not do it justice. But in that case must not Christian theology take up once again the old theopaschite question 'Did God himself suffer?', in order to be able to think of God not in absolute terms, in the usual way, but in particular terms as in Christ? Before it can talk of the significance of the history of Christ's suffering for the history of the world's suffering, Christian theology must have faced the intrinsic problem of the history of Christ's suffering and have understood God's being in the godforsakenness of Christ. Only when it has recognized what took place between Jesus and his Father on the cross can it speak of the significance of this God for those who suffer and protest at the history of the world.

The only way past protest atheism is through a theology of the cross which understands God as the suffering God in the suffering of Christ and which cries out with the godforsaken God, 'My God, why have you forsaken me?' For this theology, God and suffering are no longer contradictions, as in theism and atheism, but God's being is in suffering and the suffering is in God's being itself, because God is love. It takes the 'metaphysical rebellion' up into itself because it recognizes in the cross of Christ a rebellion in metaphysics, or better, a rebellion in God himself: God himself loves and suffers the death of Christ in his love. He is no 'cold heavenly power', nor does he 'tread his way over corpses', but is known as the human God in the crucified Son of Man.

4. *The Doctrine of Two Natures and the Suffering of Christ*

More recent Protestant and Catholic accounts of the history of the dogmas of the early church are agreed that a central difficulty for early christology was the undisguised recognition of the forsakenness of Jesus.[71] Ignatius could say without reflecting that he was a disciple of the 'passion of my God' (Rom. 6.3), and even the worship of the crucified Christ in the Good Friday liturgies demonstrates something like a 'religion of the cross'. But theological reflection was not in a position to identify God himself with the suffering and the death of Jesus. As a result of this, traditional christology came very near to docetism, according to which Jesus only appeared to suffer and only appeared to die abandoned by God: this did not happen in reality. The intellectual bar to this came from the philosophical concept of God, according to which God's being is incorruptible, unchangeable, indivisible, incapable of suffering and immortal; human nature, on the other hand, is transitory, changeable, divisible, capable of suffering and mortal. The doctrine of the two natures in Christ began from this fundamental distinction, in order to be able to conceive of the personal union of the two natures in Christ in the light of this difference. But the intellectual barrier in the other direction came from the longing for salvation. For where can transitory and mortal man find salvation if not in intransitoriness and immortality, that is, in participation in the divine being in that communion with God which was called *theiosis*? It is wrong merely to criticize the metaphysical framework of the christology of the early church, to replace it with a moral framework, which was the course of historians of dogma and dogmatic theologians at the end of the nineteenth century.[72] If the onto-theological presupposition no longer holds, then the eschatological hope for likeness to God also lacks weight, and there remains the modest comfort that the morally sinless Jesus will allow his followers to live better or more easily. The doctrine of the two natures became the framework for christology not just because of the world-picture of the time, but even more because of the transcendent hope of salvation: God became man that we men might participate in God (Athanasius). The theistic concept of God according to which God cannot die, and the hope for salvation, according to which man is to be immortal, made it impossible to regard Jesus as really being God and at the same time as being forsaken by God.

If one considers the event on the cross between Jesus and his God in the framework of the doctrine of the two natures, then the Platonic axiom of the essential *apatheia* of God sets up an intellectual barrier against the recognition of the suffering of Christ, for a God who is subject to suffering like all other creatures cannot be 'God'. Therefore the God-man Christ can only have suffered 'according to the flesh' and 'in the flesh', that is in his human nature. Granted, the much-disputed theopaschite formula asserted that 'One of the holy Trinity suffered in the flesh',[73] but the christological attack on the predominance of the axiom of *apatheia* in christology did not go further. This theopaschite formula was rejected. Even Cyril of Alexandria, who more than any one else stressed the personal unity of Christ against those who pressed for the differentiation of the two natures, was not able to remedy the 'error'[74] which the whole of early Christian theology demonstrates at this point. As a consequence of his christology of unity he really had to refer the cry of the forsaken Christ on the cross to the complete, divine and human person of the Son. 'But Cyril cannot manage that. Certainly, it is Christ who says that, but it is not his own personal and human need that leads him to it. Anyone who claims that Christ is overcome with fear and weakness here, says Cyril, refuses to confess him God. Christ does not say this in his own name, but in the name of his total nature, because only this and not he himself fell prey to corruption. He is calling to the Father for us, and not for himself.'[75] This understanding of Christ's cry for desolation in Cyril is a last retreat before the axiom of *apatheia*. According to Thomas Aquinas, too, the suffering is only a *suppositum* of the divine nature in respect of the human nature which it assumed and which was capable of suffering; it did not relate to the divine nature itself, for this was incapable of suffering.[76]

First let us adopt the presuppositions of the christology of the early church and of traditional christology and ask: Was it really impossible to ascribe Christ's suffering to God himself? Was it really necessary to dissolve the personal union of the two natures in Christ in his cry of desolation?

1. Nicaea rightly said against Arius: God is not changeable. But that statement is not absolute; it is only a simile. God is not changeable as creatures are changeable. However, the conclusion should not be drawn from this that God is unchangeable in every respect, for this negative definition merely says that God is under no constraint from that which is not of God.[77] The negation of changeableness by which a general distinction is drawn between God and man must not lead to the conclusion that he is intrinsically unchangeable. If God is not passively changeable by other things like other creatures, this does not mean that he is not free to change himself, or even free to allow himself to be changed by others of his own free will. True, God cannot be divided like his creation, but he can still communicate himself. Thus the relative definition of his unchangeableness does not lead to the assertion of his absolute and intrinsic unchangeableness.

2. The mainstream church maintained against the Syrian monophysites that it was impossible for God to suffer.[78] God cannot

suffer like creatures who are exposed to illness, pain and death. But must God therefore be thought of as being incapable of suffering in any respect? This conclusion is not convincing either. Granted, the theology of the early church knew of only one alternative to suffering and that was being incapable of suffering (*apatheia*), not-suffering. But there are other forms of suffering between unwilling suffering as a result of an alien cause and being essentially unable to suffer, namely active suffering, the suffering of love, in which one voluntarily opens himself to the possibility of being affected by another. There is unwilling suffering, there is accepted suffering and there is the suffering of love. Were God incapable of suffering in any respect, and therefore in an absolute sense, then he would also be incapable of love. If love is the acceptance of the other without regard to one's own well-being, then it contains within itself the possibility of sharing in suffering and freedom to suffer as a result of the otherness of the other. Incapability of suffering in this sense would contradict the fundamental Christian assertion that God is love, which in principle broke the spell of the Aristotelian doctrine of God. The one who is capable of love is also capable of suffering, for he also opens himself to the suffering which is involved in love, and yet remains superior to it by virtue of his love. The justifiable denial that God is capable of suffering because of a deficiency in his being may not lead to a denial that he is incapable of suffering out of the fullness of his being, i.e. his love.⁷⁹

3. Finally, can the salvation for which faith hopes be expressed significantly by means of the general predicates of God from the *via negativa*, like unchangeableness, immortality and incorruptibility? If change, mortality and corruption are experienced as disaster and misery, salvation can primarily be described here only in phrases which negate the negative.⁸⁰ But these are no more than paraphrases, for the positive position does not arise magically or miraculously from the negation of the negative. If no information can be given about the content of faith, and the negative paraphrases are taken as the content itself, then in the end incorruptibility and immortality do not appear to be especially desirable, but rather seem to be terrifying and boring. They also negate the relative goodness of creation and the transitory and mortal happiness of this life with the experience of the misery of 'failing'—in the twofold sense of being guilty and dying. If

salvation is described only as being wholly other it cannot even be salvation, for final corruption is also wholly other. So if we are to speak seriously of salvation in fellowship with God, we must go beyond the general distinctions between God and the world, or God and man, and penetrate the special relationships between God and the world and God and man in the history of Christ. In that case, however, Athanasius' formula changes its shape and becomes like that of Luther: God became man that dehumanized men might become true men. We become true men in the community of the incarnate, the suffering and loving, the human God. This salvation, too, is outwardly permanent and immortal in the humanity of God, but in itself it is a new life full of inner movement, with suffering and joy, love and pain, taking and giving; it is changeableness in the sense of life to its highest possible degree.

The doctrine of two natures in christology attempted not only to make a neat separation between the natures of Godhead and manhood, but also to assert their unity in the person of Christ and to reflect upon it. It put the two natures in a reciprocal relationship in the personal union, in conditions which were not to apply in abstract terms to the relationship between Godhead and manhood, creator and creature, but only and exclusively in concrete terms to the God-man Christ. Here the divine nature is originally identical with the person of Christ, in so far as the person of Christ is the second person of the Trinity, the eternal Son of God. That is, the divine nature is at work in Christ not as a nature, but as a person. The second person of the Trinity is the centre in the God-man Christ which forms his person. The human nature of Christ, on the other hand, is not originally identical with the person of Christ, but is assumed by the divine person of the Son of God through his incarnation (*assumptio humanae naturae*), and in the person of Christ becomes the concrete existence of Jesus Christ.[81] The divine nature displays itself hypostatically in Christ as a person, but the human nature displays itself anhypostatically as the particular existence of the divine person. But if the centre in Christ which forms his person has a divine nature, how can it be said of the whole of the divine and human person of Christ that he suffered and died forsaken by God? Scholastic theology asked with stringent logic whether the

predicates of the divine nature could be transferred to the human
nature and the predicates of the human nature could be transferred
to the divine nature on the grounds of the unity of the two natures.
These questions were dealt with in the doctrine of the *communicatio
idiomatum*. It was maintained that there could be no *communicatio
idiomatum in abstracto*, that is, apart from the person of Christ.
So there could only be a *communicatio idiomatum* in the particular
instance.[82] That is, one can say: Christ, the Son of God suffered
and died. With the help of the notion of the *communicatio idiomatum*
one can attribute the human characteristics of suffering and death
to the whole person of Christ. One cannot say: Therefore the
divine nature can suffer and die; it is only possible to say: Therefore the person of Christ is mortal. One cannot say: Therefore
the body of the risen Christ is omnipresent, but only: Therefore
the person of Christ is omnipresent. Reformation theology took
this theology further in its disputes over the eucharist.

Zwingli still had a good rhetorical conception of the pattern of
the *communicatio idiomatum* along scholastic, humanistic lines:
'then *communicatio idiomatum*, that is, community of the properties,
is called *alloiosis* among us'. *Alloiosis* here is a figure of speech for
the preaching of the God-man Christ. In Christ's being itself the
two natures remain what they had been before. Thus in the personal union in Christ Zwingli sees only two natures common in
one person and stresses the difference between the natures, for
God is Creator and man is creature.[83] Melanchthon and his
disciples followed the early church and scholasticism in saying:
'*Communicatio idiomatum est praedicatio, qua proprietas unius
naturae tribuitur personae in concreto.*' It is a *praedicatio*, not a
communicatio, though the proclamation of Christ belongs to the
Christ event itself.[84] Luther, on the other hand, took seriously the
fact that it is not a matter of thinking of two natures of equal
worth in one person, but rather that a divine person assumed an
anhypostatic human nature. For him, the unity of the God-man
Christ took place and is determined by the action of the divine
person himself. Consequently the divine-human unity in Christ
stems not only verbally, but in reality, from the action of the Son
of God. Lutherans like Brenz therefore spoke of a *communicatio
idiomatum realis* and uttered polemic against Melanchthon and
Reformed teaching, which they termed a mere *communicatio
idiomatum verbalis*. 'For Luther the *unitio naturarum* is already

an "event in the being of the person" which goes beyond a mere combination of the two natures or a union of them in thought.'[85]

No, friend, where you set aside God you must set aside the manhood with him. They cannot be divided and separated from one another. One person has come into being, and the manhood is not set aside as master Hans takes off his coat and puts that aside when he goes to sleep.[86]

For Luther, therefore, Christ and God form a unity not only in revelation, but already in their very being, as his formula indicates: 'Christ alone and no other God.' Jesus Christ is 'the Lord Sabaoth'. 'The one whom the whole circle of the world never encompassed, lies in Mary's womb,' we find in his hymns. 'For God is not solely present and substantial in him as in all other (creatures), but also dwells in him corporeally in such a way that one person is man and God. And while I can say of all creatures, "There is God" or "God is in that", I cannot say of them "that is God himself". But faith says of Christ not only that God is in him but also that Christ is God himself.'[87] The talk of God which has recently become usual, namely that 'God is in Christ', is thus taken further: God is Christ and Christ is God.

For Zwingli, God remains untouched in his sovereignty by taking the human nature of Christ. Christ suffers and dies according to his manhood, his veil of flesh, on our behalf. But for Luther the person of Christ is determined by the divine person. Therefore the divine person also suffers and dies in the suffering and death of Christ. So he can say: '*Vere dicitur: Iste homo creavit mundum et Deus iste est passus, mortuus, sepultus, etc.*'[88] Although he again divides the person of Christ with this phrase '*iste Deus*' and '*iste homo*', it is in fact possible to talk of the 'death of God', while saying at the same time that Jesus created the world and that the man from Nazareth is present everywhere. The critical counter-question of the Reformed tradition is whether a third being, a monster with fleshly Godhead and divinized flesh, has not taken the place of God and man and their personal unity in Christ.

In the Good Friday hymn of Johann Rist we read:

O great distress, God himself lies dead,
He died upon the cross,
In this he won the kingdom of heaven
For love of us.[89]

In the German Protestant Church Hymn Book of 1915 and in

the Protestant Hymn Book, no. 73, this verse appears with the dogmatic correction:

O greatest need, God's son lies dead. . . .

Luther himself had said: 'In his nature God cannot die. But now that God and man are united in one person, when the man dies, that is rightly called the death of God, for he is one thing or one person with God.'[90] This corresponds to his distinction between the (external) nature of God in relation to the world and the (internal) person of the Son of God in the relations of the Trinity. But where he does not distinguish the two, but uses 'God' to refer both to the nature of the Trinity and to one person in the Trinity, and where these distinctions in 'God' are not made, paradoxes arise, as for example that 'God strives with God' on the cross of Christ, that in the godforsakenness of Jesus God himself is forsaken and dies, and vice versa that the dead Jesus is himself God and creator.

If one begins only from 'God' *in genere* and then goes on to speak of God in Christ and then of the death of God on the cross, this death itself becomes a 'phenomenon of God'.[91] This must be said of the death of Jesus on the cross on Golgotha, but cannot be transferred to death generally. If this death of Jesus is the revelation of God, then love is all the more a 'phenomenon of God'.

In making a critical summary of the tradition, we might say:

1. By means of the doctrine of the *communicatio idiomatum* Luther made special efforts to overcome the intellectual barrier against perceiving God in the death of Christ, a barrier which arose out of the doctrine of the two natures. This doctrine made external distinctions between God and man and in so doing destroyed all attempts by man at self-divinization. On this presupposition the *communicatio idiomatum* penetrated into the inner relationships between God and Jesus and thought through the inner life of the God-man Christ, which communicates fellowship with God to men.

2. It made it possible to conceive of God himself in the godforsakenness of Christ and to ascribe suffering and death on the cross to the divine-human person of Christ. If this divine nature in the person of the eternal Son of God is the centre which creates a person in Christ, then it too suffered and died.

3. It is important to distinguish between the divine nature *in genere* and the second person of the Trinity *in concreto*. Luther continually kept this in mind, though he did not always maintain it. He used this distinction to recognize God in person in the suffering and death of Christ. However, he left out of account the relationships in which this suffering and dying person of the Son is involved with the persons of the Father and the Spirit. In other words, his christology was formed in terms of incarnation and the theology of the cross, but not always in trinitarian terms. He used the name 'God' generically and promiscuously for (*a*) the nature of God, (*b*) the person of the Son of God, and (*c*) the persons of the Father and the Spirit. Because he spoke emphatically of God and man, of the incarnate God and the man Jesus who became divine, he arrived at paradoxical distinctions between God and God: between the God who crucifies and the crucified God; the God who is dead and yet is not dead; between the manifest God in Christ and the hidden God above and beyond Christ.

4. Luther's christology of the crucified God remains within the framework of the early church's doctrine of two natures, represents an important further development of the doctrine of the *communicatio idiomatum* and radicalizes the doctrine of the incarnation on the cross. By presupposing the concept of God gained from his general distinction between God and the world, God and man in his christology, in the theology of the cross he came later to change his concept of God, but he never arrived at a developed christological doctrine of the Trinity.

5. *Trinitarian Theology of the Cross*

In all the Christian churches, the cross has become the sign which distinguishes the churches from other religions and modes of belief. At the same time, it must be noted that in the ancient world of religion, the doctrine of the Trinity in the concept of God was the doctrine which marked off Christianity from polytheism, pantheism and monotheism. When Islam conquered Asia Minor, Christian churches in many places were turned into mosques, and were given an inscription directed against Christians who still might be present: 'God did not beget and is not begotten.' The element in Christianity which was above all the object of passionate polemic from Islam monotheism was belief in the Trinity. Is this an indispensable part of Christian belief in God? Is there an inner logical connection between the two special features of Christianity, faith in the crucified Jesus and in the triune God? We are not concerned here to mediate in ecumenical fashion between two Christian traditions of which one has been fostered particularly in Protestantism and the other above all in Greek orthodoxy. Our question, rather, is: if we are to understand the 'human', the 'crucified' God, must we think of God in trinitarian terms? And conversely, can we think of God in trinitarian terms if we do not have the event of the cross in mind?

The doctrine of the Trinity enjoys no special significance in the history of Western theology. It seems to have been hard enough to speak of 'God' at all in the life of the churches and in the understanding of believers with any degree of honesty. True, liturgies begin with the traditional formula 'In the name of the Father, the Son and the Holy Spirit', and the Apostles' Creed and its more modern versions have three articles and, in the view of many, claim to speak of God the Creator, the Reconciler and the Redeemer.

In practice, however, the religious conceptions of many Christians prove to be no more than a weakly Christianized monotheism. However, it is precisely this general monotheism in theology and the belief of Christians which is involved in a crisis of identity. For this general religious monotheism is a permanent occasion for protest atheism, and rightly so. Karl Rahner is also right about Protestant theology when he observes that in theological and religious contexts people only say that 'God' has been made man and not that 'the Word has been made flesh' (John 3.16). 'One could suspect that as regards the catechism of the head and the heart, in contrast to the catechism in books, the Christian idea of the Incarnation would not have to change at all, if there were no Trinity.'[92] Even the doctrine of grace is monotheistic, and not trinitarian, in practice. Man shares in the grace of God or the divine nature. It is still said that we acquire this grace through Christ, but no trinitarian differentiation in God seems to be necessary. The same thing is true of the doctrine of creation. Faith in the one creator God seems to be sufficient—as among Mohammedans. In eschatology, too, at best there is talk of the coming God and his kingdom or of God as the absolute future. Understandably,

Christ then fades away to become the prophet of this future, who fills his function as the representative of the now absent God and can go when God himself comes to occupy his place. Finally, Christian ethics establishes the obedience of man under the rule of God and Christ, and rarely goes beyond a moral monarchy.

From the time of Melanchthon, and particularly since Schleiermacher and the moral theology of the nineteenth century, the doctrine of the Trinity seems to have been regarded in Protestantism as no more than a theological speculation with no relevance for life, a kind of higher theological mystery for initiates. Although Melanchthon later thought completely in trinitarian terms, the only quotation to be made from his writings by liberal Protestantism in the nineteenth century was that passage from the *Loci communes* of 1521 which was so much in accord with the modern spirit:

We do better to adore the mysteries of Deity than to investigate them. The Lord God Almighty clothed his Son with flesh that he might draw us from contemplating his own majesty to a consideration of the flesh, and especially of our weakness . . . Therefore there is no reason why we should labour so much on those exalted topics such as 'God', 'The Unity and Trinity of God', 'The Mystery of Creation', and 'The Manner of the Incarnation' . . . To know Christ means to know his benefits, and not as *they* teach, to reflect upon his natures and the modes of his incarnation . . . In his letter to the Romans when he was writing a compendium of Christian doctrine, did Paul philosophize about the mysteries of the Trinity, the mode of incarnation, or active and passive creation? . . . He takes up the law, sin, grace, fundamentals on which the knowledge of Christ exclusively rests.[93]

The transition among the Reformers from pure theological considerations to a critical theory of theological practice for faith in fact led to a surrender of the doctrine of the Trinity, because in the tradition of the early church the doctrine of the Trinity had its place in the praise and vision of God, and not in the economy of salvation.[94] But does the doctrine of the Trinity in fact belong in the 'consideration of the divine majesty', quite separately from the revelation of God through Christ for us, in our history and our flesh? Once this distinction is made, it is correct to turn from the doctrine of the Trinity as pure speculation and apply ourselves to the history of law, sin and grace with which we are concerned. But such a distinction is itself fundamentally false. One does not 'philosophize' speculatively about the mysteries of the Trinity, as

Melanchthon put it, but stands before the question how God is to be understood in the event of the cross of Christ. This is a quite different set of problems.

The move from pure theory to the theory of practice is further demonstrated in the whole of modern thought. This is no longer contemplative thought but operational thought. Reason is no longer perceptive, but productive. It no longer seeks to recognize permanent being in reality, but seeks to recognize in order to change. Modern thought is thought concerned with work and production. It is pragmatic: reality is efficiency. Theories are not verified by eternal ideas but through practice and its results. As has been shown, this also dominated the hermeneutics of nineteenth-century theology. According to Kant, the canon of the interpretation of the biblical and theological traditions is 'what is practical'. He explains this in lapidary fashion:

'Virtually no practical consequence can be drawn from the doctrine of the Trinity taken literally, if one seeks to understand it, and still less, once it is realized that it transcends all our concepts.' For 'by principles of belief is not to be understood that which should be believed (. . .) but that which is possible and purposeful to accept in a practical (moral) intent, though this cannot be demonstrated, but only believed.' 'Thus such a belief, because it neither makes a better man nor proves one to be such, is no part of religion.'[95]

According to Schleiermacher, theological statements must be possible as statements of Christian self-awareness. He therefore put the doctrine of the Trinity at the end of *The Christian Faith* and indeed in an appendix, and remarked: 'But this doctrine itself, as ecclesiastically framed, is not an immediate utterance concerning the Christian self-consciousness, but only a combination of several such utterances.'[96] Nevertheless, Schleiermacher was open to a complete reshaping of the doctrine of the Trinity. 'We have the less reason to regard this doctrine as finally settled since it did not receive any fresh treatment when the Evangelical (Protestant) Church was set up; and so there must still be in store for it a transformation which will go back to its very beginnings.'[97] Precisely this must be attempted today. We cannot achieve it in the form of the pure theory of antiquity; that appears to us to be pure speculation. *Quod supra nos nihil ad nos!*[98] We cannot say of God who he is of himself and in himself; we can only say who he is for us in the history of Christ which reaches us in our history. Nor can we achieve it in the forms of modern thought which are so related to experience and practice. Or can we make something practical and relevant to Christian self-understanding out of the way in which God acts towards God? In that case we would have to give up the distinction made in the early church and in tradition between the 'God in himself' and the 'God for us', or between 'God in his majesty' and 'God veiled in the flesh of Christ', as Luther and Melanchthon put it. We would have to find the relationship of God to God in the reality of the event of the cross and therefore in our reality, and consider it there. In practice that would amount to a 'complete reshaping of the doctrine of the Trinity', because in that case the nature of God would have to be the human history of Christ and not a divine 'nature' separate from man.

Why did the doctrine of the Trinity become isolated speculation and a mere decoration for dogmatics after the Middle Ages? Karl Rahner has pointed out that after the supplanting of the *Sentences* of Peter Lombard by the *Summa* of Thomas Aquinas, a momentous distinction was introduced into the doctrine of God. This was the distinction between the tractates *De Deo uno* and *De Deo triuno* and the order in which they are put, which is still felt to be a matter of course even today. The purpose behind this separation and arrangement was apologetic. Following Thomas, one began with the question 'Is there a God?', and demonstrated with the help of the natural light of human reason and the cosmological arguments for the existence of God that there was a God and that God was one. Then, with the same method, conclusions were drawn as to the metaphysical, non-human properties of the divine nature. This knowledge was assigned to natural theology. Only then was a move made to describe the inner being of God with the aid of the supernatural light of grace, a move towards *theologica christiana, theologia salvifica*, the saving knowledge of God.

In the first tractate there was a discussion of the metaphysical properties of God in himself, and in the second of his salvation-historical relationships to us. Even in Protestant orthodoxy, first a general doctrine of God '*De deo*' was outlined, after which there followed teaching on the '*mysterium de sancta trinitate*'. The great Greek theology of the Cappadocians certainly understood all theology as the doctrine of the Trinity. But it made a distinction between the 'immanent Trinity' and the 'Trinity in the economy of salvation', and thus distinguished in its own way between the inner being of God and salvation history, as between original and copy, idea and manifestation. Karl Barth, who differed from the Protestant tradition of the nineteenth century by making his *Church Dogmatics* begin not with apologetic prolegomena or with basic rules for hermeneutics but with the doctrine of the Trinity, which for him was the hermeneutic canon for understanding the Christian principle 'Jesus Christ the Lord', followed the Cappadocians in distinguishing between the immanent Trinity and the economy of the Trinity. God is 'beforehand in himself' everything that he reveals in Christ. God corresponds to himself.

Karl Rahner[99] has advanced the thesis that both distinctions are inappropriate and that we must say:

1. The Trinity *is* the nature of God and the nature of God *is* the Trinity.

2. The economic Trinity *is* the immanent Trinity, and the immanent Trinity *is* the economic Trinity.

God's relationship to us is three-fold. And this three-fold (free and unmerited) relationship to us is not merely an image or analogy of the immanent Trinity; it *is* this Trinity itself, even though communicated as free grace.[100]

Thus the unity and the Trinity of God belong together in one tractate. One cannot first describe the unity of the nature of God and then distinguish between the three divine persons or hypostases, as in that case one is essentially dealing with four beings. The being of God then becomes the hypostasis of God, so that the three persons can be renounced and one can think in monotheistic terms.

Before we consider this question further, we must also look at the particular context in which trinitarian thought is necessary at all. Otherwise these considerations could easily become a new version of traditional teaching under the changed conditions of modern times, just for the sake of a tradition which once existed. As Schleiermacher rightly said, any new version of the doctrine of the Trinity must be 'a transformation which goes right back to its first beginnings'. The place of the doctrine of the Trinity is not the 'thinking of thought', but the cross of Jesus. 'Concepts without perception are empty' (Kant). The perception of the trinitarian concept of God is the cross of Jesus. 'Perceptions without concepts are blind' (Kant). The theological concept for the perception of

the crucified Christ is the doctrine of the Trinity. The material
principle of the doctrine of the Trinity is the cross of Christ.
The formal principle of knowledge of the cross is the doctrine of
the Trinity. Where do the first beginnings lie? As is well known, the
New Testament does not contain any developed doctrine of the
Trinity. That only arose in the controversies of the early church
over the unity of Christ with God himself. I believe that B.
Steffen, in his long-forgotten book *Das Dogma vom Kreuz. Beitrag
zu einer staurozentrischen Theologie* (1920: 'The Dogma of the
Cross. A Contribution to a Staurocentric Theology'), saw something quite astonishing:

> The scriptural basis for Christian belief in the triune God is not the scanty
> trinitarian formulas of the New Testament, but the thoroughgoing,
> unitary testimony of the cross; and the shortest expression of the Trinity
> is the divine act of the cross, in which the Father allows the Son to
> sacrifice himself through the Spirit.[101]

We must test this argument, according to which the theology of
the cross must be the doctrine of the Trinity and the doctrine of
the Trinity must be the theology of the cross, because otherwise the human, crucified God cannot be fully perceived.[102]

What happened on the cross of Christ between Christ and the
God whom he called his Father and proclaimed as 'having come
near' to abandoned men? According to Paul and Mark, Jesus himself was abandoned by this very God, his Father, and died with a
cry of godforsakenness.

> That God delivers up his Son is one of the most unheard-of statements in
> the New Testament. We must understand 'deliver up' in its full sense and
> not water it down to mean 'send' or 'give'. What happened here is what
> Abraham did not need to do to Isaac (cf. Rom. 8.32): Christ was quite
> deliberately abandoned by the Father to the fate of death: God subjected
> him to the power of corruption, whether this be called man or death. To
> express the idea in its most acute form, one might say in the words of the
> dogma of the early church: the first person of the Trinity casts out and
> annihilates the second . . . A theology of the cross cannot be expressed
> more radically than it is here.[103]

Consequently we shall begin with a theological interpretation of
those sayings which express the abandonment of Christ by God.

In the passion narratives, which present Jesus' death in the
light of the life that he lived, the word for deliver up, $\pi\alpha\rho\alpha\delta\iota\delta\acute{o}\nu\alpha\iota$,
has a clearly negative connotation. It means: hand over, give up,
deliver, betray, cast out, kill. The word 'deliver up' (Rom. 1.18ff.)

also appears in Pauline theology as an expression of the wrath and judgment of God and thus of the lostness of man. God's wrath over the godlessness of man is manifest in that he 'delivers them up' to their godlessness and inhumanity. According to Israelite understanding, guilt and punishment lie in one and the same event. So too here: men who abandon God are abandoned by God. Godlessness and godforsakenness are two sides of the same event. The heathen turn the glory of the invisible God into a picture like corruptible being—'and God surrenders them to the lusts of their heart' (Rom. 1.24; par. 1.26 and 1.28). Judgment lies in the fact that God delivers men up to the corruption which they themselves have chosen and abandons them in their forsakenness. It is not the case that Paul threatens sinners, whether Jews or Gentiles, with a distant judgment; rather, he sees the wrath of God as now being manifest in the inhuman idolatry of the Gentiles and the inhuman righteousness by works of the Jews. Guilt and punishment are not separated temporally and juristically. In the godforsakenness of the godless idolaters Paul now already sees the revelation of the wrath of God, the judgment that is being accomplished.[104] In this situation (Rom. 1.18) he proclaims the saving righteousness of God in the crucified Christ. But how can deliverance and liberation for godforsaken man lie in the figure of the godforsaken, crucified Christ?

Paul introduces a radical change in the sense of 'deliver up' when he recognizes and proclaims the godforsakenness of Jesus in the eschatological context of his resurrection rather than in the historical context of his life. In Rom. 8.31f., we read: 'If God is for us, who is against us? He who did not spare his own Son but gave him up for us all, will he not also give us all things with him?' According to this God gave up his own Son, abandoned him, cast him out and delivered him up to an accursed death. Paul says in even stronger terms: 'He made him sin for us' (II Cor. 5.21) and 'He became a curse for us' (Gal. 3.13). Thus in the total, inextricable abandonment of Jesus by his God and Father, Paul sees the delivering up of the Son by the Father for godless and godforsaken man. Because God 'does not spare' his Son, all the godless are spared. Though they are godless, they are not godforsaken, precisely because God has abandoned his own Son and has delivered him up for them. Thus the delivering up of the Son to godforsakenness is the ground for the justification of the godless and the acceptance of enmity by God. It may therefore be said that the Father delivers up his Son on the cross in order to be the Father of those who are delivered up. The Son is delivered up to this death in order to become the Lord of both dead and living. And if Paul speaks emphatically of God's 'own Son', the not-sparing and abandoning also involves the Father himself. In the forsakenness of the Son the Father also forsakes himself. In the surrender of the Son the Father also surrenders himself, though not in the same way. For Jesus suffers dying in forsakenness, but not death itself; for men can no longer 'suffer' death, because suffering presupposes life. But the Father who abandons him and delivers him up suffers the death of the Son in the infinite grief of love. We cannot therefore say here in patripassian terms that the Father also suffered and died. The suffering and dying of the Son, forsaken by the Father, is a different kind of suffering from the suffering of the Father in the death of the Son. Nor can the death of Jesus be understood in theopaschite terms as the 'death of God'. To understand what happened between Jesus and his God and Father on the cross, it is necessary to talk in trinitarian terms. The Son suffers dying, the Father suffers the death of the Son. The grief of the Father here is just as important as the death of the Son. The Fatherlessness of the Son is matched by the Sonlessness of the Father, and if God has constituted himself as the Father of Jesus Christ, then he also suffers the death of his Fatherhood in the death of the Son. Unless this were so, the doctrine of the Trinity would still have a monotheistic background.

In Gal. 2.20 the 'delivering up' formula also occurs with Christ as its subject: '... the Son of God, who loved me and gave himself for me'. According to this it is not just the Father who delivers Jesus up to die godforsaken on the cross, but the Son who gives himself up. This corresponds to the synoptic account of the passion story according to which Jesus consciously and willingly walked the way of the cross and was not overtaken by death as by an evil, unfortunate fate. It is theologically important to note that the formula in Paul occurs with both Father and Son as subject, since it expresses a deep conformity between the will of the Father and the will of the Son in the event of the cross, as the Gethsemane narrative also records. This deep community of will between Jesus and his God and Father is now expressed precisely at the point of their deepest separation, in the godforsaken and accursed death of Jesus on the cross. If both historical godforsakenness and eschatological surrender can be seen in Christ's death on the cross, then this event contains community between Jesus and his Father in separation, and separation in community.

As Rom. 8.32 and Gal. 2.20 show, Paul already described the godforsakenness of Jesus as a surrender and his surrender as love. Johannine theology sums this up in the sentence: 'God so loved the world that he gave his only-begotten Son that all who believe in him should not perish but have everlasting life' (3.16). And I John sees the very existence of God himself in this event of love on the cross of Christ: 'God is love' (4.16). In other words, God does not just love as he is angry, chooses or rejects. He *is* love, that is, he exists in love. He constitutes his existence in the event of his love. He exists as love in the event of the cross. Thus in the concepts of earlier systematic theology it is possible to talk of a *homoousion*, in respect of an identity of substance, the community of will of the Father and the Son on the cross. However, the unity contains not only identity of substance but also the wholly and utterly different character and inequality of the event on the cross. In the cross, Father and Son are most deeply separated in forsakenness and at the same time are most inwardly one in their surrender.[105] What proceeds from this event between Father and Son is the Spirit which justifies the godless, fills the forsaken with love and even brings the dead alive, since even the fact that they are dead cannot exclude them from this event of the cross; the death in God also includes them.

In this way we have already used trinitarian phrases to understand what happened on the cross between Jesus and his God and Father. If one wanted to present the event within the framework of the doctrine of two natures, one could only use the simple concept of God (*esse simplex*). In that case one would have to say: what happened on the cross was an event between God and God. It was a deep division in God himself, in so far as God abandoned God and contradicted himself, and at the same time a unity in God, in so far as God was at one with God and corresponded to himself. In that case one would have to put the formula in a paradoxical way: God died the death of the godless on the cross and yet did not die. God is dead and yet is not dead. If one can only use the simple concept of God from the doctrine of two natures, as tradition shows, one will always be inclined to restrict it to the person of the Father who abandons and accepts Jesus, delivers him and raises him up, and in so doing will 'evacuate' the cross of deity. But if one begins by leaving on one side any concept of God which is already presupposed and taken from metaphysics, one must speak of the one whom Jesus called 'Father' and in respect of whom he understood himself as 'the Son'. In that case one will understand the deadly aspect of the event between the Father who forsakes and the Son who is forsaken, and conversely the living aspect of the event between the Father who loves and the Son who loves. The Son suffers in his love being forsaken by the Father as he dies. The Father suffers in his love the grief of the death of the Son. In that case, whatever proceeds from the event between the Father and the Son must be understood as the spirit of the surrender of the Father and the Son, as the spirit which creates love for forsaken men, as the spirit which brings the dead alive. It is the unconditioned and therefore boundless love which proceeds from the grief of the Father and the dying of the Son and reaches forsaken men in order to create in them the possibility and the force of new life. The doctrine of two natures must understand the event of the cross statically as a reciprocal relationship between two qualitatively different natures, the divine nature which is incapable of suffering and the human nature which is capable of suffering. Here we have interpreted the event of the cross in trinitarian terms, as an event concerned with a relationship between persons in which these persons constitute themselves in their relationship with each other. In so doing we have not just seen one person of the Trinity suffer in the event of the cross, as though the Trinity were already present in itself, in the divine nature. And we have not interpreted the death of Jesus as a divine-human event, but as a trinitarian event between the Son and the Father. What is in question in the relationship of Christ to his Father is not his divinity and humanity and their relationship to each other but the total, personal aspect of the Sonship of Jesus. This starting point is not the same as that to be found in the tradition. It overcomes the dichotomy between immanent and economic Trinity, and that between the nature of God and his inner tri-unity. It makes trinitarian thought necessary for the complete perception of the cross of Christ.

Faith understands the historical event between the Father who forsakes and the Son who is forsaken on the cross in eschatological terms as an event between the Father who loves and the Son who is loved in the present spirit of the love that creates life.

If the cross of Jesus is understood as a divine event, i.e. as an event between Jesus and his God and Father, it is necessary to speak in trinitarian terms of the Son and the Father and the Spirit. In that case the doctrine of the Trinity is no longer an exorbitant and impractical speculation about God, but is nothing other than a shorter version of the passion narrative of Christ in its significance for the eschatological freedom of faith and the life of oppressed nature. It protects faith from both monotheism and atheism because it keeps believers at the cross. The content of the doctrine of the Trinity is the real cross of Christ himself. The form of the crucified Christ is the Trinity. In that case, what is salvation? Only if all disaster, forsakenness by God, absolute death, the infinite curse of damnation and sinking into nothingness is in God himself, is community with this God eternal salvation, infinite joy, indestructible election and divine life. The 'bifurcation' in God must contain the whole uproar of history within itself. Men must be able to recognize rejection, the curse and final nothingness in it. The cross stands between the Father and the Son in all the harshness of its forsakenness. If one describes the life of God within the Trinity as the 'history of God' (Hegel), this history of God contains within itself the whole abyss of godforsakenness, absolute death and the non-God. '*Nemo contra Deum nisi Deus ipse.*' Because this death took place in the history between Father and Son on the cross on Golgotha, there proceeds from it the spirit of life, love and election to salvation. The concrete 'history of God' in the death of Jesus on the cross on Golgotha therefore contains within itself all the depths and abysses of human history and therefore can be understood as the history of history. All human history, however much it may be determined by guilt and death, is taken up into this 'history of God', i.e. into the Trinity, and integrated into the future of the 'history of God'. There is no suffering which in this history of God is not God's suffering; no death which has not been God's death in the history on Golgotha. Therefore there is no life, no fortune and no joy which have not been integrated by his history into eternal life, the eternal joy of God. To think of 'God in history' always leads to theism and to atheism. To think of 'history in God' leads beyond that, into new creation and *theopoiesis*. To 'think of history in God' however, first means to understand humanity in the suffering and dying of Christ, and that means all humanity, with its dilemmas and its despairs.

In that case, what sense does it make to talk of 'God'? I think that the unity of the dialectical history of Father and Son and Spirit in the cross on Golgotha, full of tension as it is, can be described so to speak retrospectively as 'God'. In that case, a trinitarian theology of the cross no longer interprets the event of the cross in the framework or in the name of a metaphysical or moral concept of God which has already been presupposed—we have shown that this does not do justice to the cross, but evacuates it of meaning—but develops from this history what is to be understood by 'God'. Anyone who speaks of God in Christian terms must tell of the history of Jesus as a history between the Son and the Father. In that case, 'God' is not another nature or a heavenly person or a moral authority, but in fact an 'event'.[106] However, it is not the event of co-humanity, but the event of Golgotha, the event of the love of the Son and the grief of the Father from which the Spirit who opens up the future and creates life in fact derives.

In that case, is there no 'personal God'? If 'God' is an event, can one pray to him? One cannot pray to an 'event'. In that case there is in fact no 'personal God' as a person projected in heaven. But there are persons in God: the Son, the Father and the Spirit. In that case one does not simply pray to God as a heavenly Thou, but prays *in* God. One does not pray to an event but *in* this event. One prays through the Son to the Father in the Spirit. In the brotherhood of Jesus, the person who prays has access to the Fatherhood of the Father and to the Spirit of hope. Only in this way does the character of Christian prayer become clear. The New Testament made a very neat distinction in Christian prayer between the Son and the Father. We ought to take that up, and ought not to speak of 'God' in such an undifferentiated way, thus opening up the way to atheism.

'God *is* love,' says I John 4.16. Thus in view of all that has been said, the doctrine of the Trinity can be understood as an interpretation of the ground, the event and the experience of that love in which the one who has been condemned to love finds new possibility for life because he has found in it the grace of the impossibility of the death of rejection. It is not the interpretation of love as an ideal, a heavenly power or as a commandment, but of love as an event in a loveless, legalistic world: the event of an unconditioned and boundless love which comes to meet man, which takes hold of those who are unloved and forsaken, unrighteous or outside the law, and gives them a new identity, liberates them from the norms of social identifications and from the guardians of social norms and idolatrous images. What Jesus commanded in the Sermon on the Mount as love of one's enemy has taken place on the cross through Jesus' dying and the grief of the Father in the power of the spirit, for the godless and the loveless. Just as the unconditional love of Jesus for the rejected made the Pharisees his enemies and brought him to the cross, so unconditional love also means enmity and persecution in a world in which the life of man is made dependent on particular social norms, conditions and achievements. A love which takes precedence and robs these conditions of their force is folly and scandal in this world. But if the believer experiences his freedom and the new possibility of his life in the fact that the love of God reaches him, the loveless and the unloved, in the cross of Christ, what must be the thoughts of a theology which corresponds to this love? In that case it is a love which creates its own conditions, since it cannot accept the conditions of lovelessness and the law. Further, it cannot command love and counterlove. As its purpose is freedom, it is directed towards freedom. So it cannot prohibit slavery and enmity, but must suffer this contradiction, and can only take upon itself grief at this contradiction and the grief of protest against it, and manifest this grief in protest. That is what happened on the cross of Christ. God is unconditional love, because he takes on himself grief at the contradiction in men and does not angrily suppress this contradiction. God allows himself to be forced out. God suffers, God allows himself to be crucified and is crucified, and in this consummates his unconditional love that is so full of hope. But that means that in the cross he becomes himself the condition of this love. The loving Father has a parallel in the loving Son and in the Spirit creates similar patterns of love in man in revolt. The fact of this love can be contradicted. It can be crucified, but in crucifixion it finds its fulfilment and becomes love of the enemy. Thus its suffering proves to be stronger than hate. Its might is powerful in weakness and gains power over its enemies in grief, because it gives life even to its enemies and opens up the future to change. If in the freedom given through experience of it the believer understands the crucifixion as an event of the love of the Son and the grief of the Father, that is, as an event between God and God, as an event within the Trinity, he perceives the liberating word of love which creates new life. By the death of the Son he is taken up into the grief of the Father and experiences a liberation which is a new element in this de-divinized and legalistic world, which is itself even a new element over against the original creation of the word. He is in fact taken up into the inner life of God, if in the cross of Christ he experiences the love of God for the godless, the enemies, in so far as the history of Christ is the inner life of God himself. In that case, if he lives in this love, he lives in God and God in him. If he lives in this freedom, he lives in God and God in him. If one conceives of the Trinity as an event of love in the suffering and the death of Jesus— and that is something which faith must do—then the Trinity is no self-contained group in heaven, but an eschatological process open for men on earth, which stems from the cross of Christ. By the secular cross on Golgotha, understood as open vulnerability and as the love of God for loveless and unloved, dehumanized men, God's being and God's life is open to true man. There is no 'outside the gate' with God (W. Borchert), if God himself is the one who died outside the gate on Golgotha for those who are outside.

To conclude this chapter we must relate the Christian concept of the trinitarian event of God on the cross of Jesus which we have developed to the problems of theism and atheism.

6. *Beyond Theism and Atheism*

In their struggle against each other, theism and atheism begin from the presupposition that God and man are fundamentally one being. Therefore what is ascribed to God must be taken from man and what is ascribed to man must have been taken from God.[107] Theism thinks of God at man's expense as an all-powerful, perfect and infinite being.[108] Consequently man appears here as a helpless, imperfect and finite being. There are good historical grounds for arguing that while the Christian church gained the ancient world with its proclamation of God, from Justinian at the latest the Caesars conquered in the church. We can see this in the concept of God in the fact that God was now understood in terms of the image of the Egyptian pharaohs, the Persian kings and the Roman emperors.[109] The church bestowed on God those attributes which formerly belonged exclusively to the Caesar. In so doing it certainly brought the Caesars under the authority of God, in a critical sense, but at the same time it formulated the authority of God in terms of the image of the Caesars, in an affirmative sense. In the great period of the origin of theistic philosophy and theology, which essentially led to Islam, thought took three main lines: 1. God in the image of the imperial ruler; 2. God in the image of the personification of moral energy; 3. God in the image of the final principle of philosophy.[110] But measured by the origin of Christian faith in the crucified Christ, these three images are idols. This theism is tantamount to idolatry. For as Whitehead points out,

There is in the Galilean origin of Christianity yet another suggestion which does not fit well with any of the three main strands of thought. It does not emphasize the ruling Caesar, or the ruthless moralist, or the unmoved mover. It dwells upon the tender elements of the world, which slowly and in quietness operate by love; and it finds purpose in the present immediacy of a kingdom not of this world. Love neither rules, nor is it unmoved; also it is a little oblivious as to morals. It does not look to the future; for it finds its own reward in the immediate present.[111]

If we can follow Whitehead in describing theism in moral, political and philosophical respects as idolatry, it follows, conversely, that theism removes man from his humanity and alienates him from his freedom, his joy and his true being. 'If man is free, then there is no such God; if there is such a God, then man is not free.' These are the alternatives in the face of such a hypostatized idol.

A God who is conceived of in his omnipotence, perfection and infinity at man's expense cannot be the God who is love in the cross of Jesus, who makes a human encounter in order to restore their lost humanity to unhappy and proud divinities, who 'became poor to make many rich'. God conceived of at man's expense cannot be the Father of Jesus Christ. Zinzendorf saw this rightly when he complained of the 'legalistic and servile situation of the human race in face of God'. 'So-called Christianity has preserved the princely idea of God and blotted out the idea of the lamb, his merit and his death.'[112] It is indispensable for the liberated believer to dispense with the inhuman God, a God without Jesus, for the sake of the cross. Here 'Christian atheism' is in the right.

But atheism in rebellion against this kind of political, moral and philosophical theism has long been nothing more than a reversed form of theism, especially in modern times. It has not been able to break free from its opponent. It thinks of man at God's expense as a powerful, perfect, infinite and creative being. It makes 'man the supreme being for man' (Marx) and applies all the old theistic divine predicates to man for the purpose of man's incarnation. It is not God who created man in his image but man who creates God in his. Man is the ground and creator of himself (*causa sui*).[113] Humanity is perfect and infinite in its totality. The more humanistic atheism dethrones the theistic God politically, morally and philosophically, the more it sets man on the throne that was his, adorned with the attributes of which it has robbed him, 'The attributes are taken away from God, who is now ineffable, and are given back to the Creation, to Love and Death ... Everything here that is deep and inward, that the church has embezzled for the beyond, returns, and all the angels sing together on earth.' This is Rilke's message in the Duinser Elegies and the Sonnets to Orpheus.[114] The 'gospel of the death of God' is said to lead to 'liberated humanity' even in the American 'God is dead' movement, because it liberates from the alien, hostile, other God.[115]

According to Feuerbach, atheism is the surrender of a God separated from the world and from man, crouching outside the world.[116] But if this theistic God is given up, where is he? Is not the position of power connected with the God of theism preserved? In that case, God is man come to himself, and man himself is God. In that case God and man are no longer separated and alienated from each other in religious terms, but are one being. This antitheistic atheism leads unavoidably to anthropotheism, to the divinization of man, of humanity and those parties who claim to be a cadre representing non-alienated, divine humanity in the realm of alienation. If for this atheism 'man is finally man's God', this may be morally fine as an ideal in face of the situation where man is man's wolf. But a century's experience with such anthropotheism has shown that even these human deities can become man's wolf. If the consequence of Feuerbach's dethroning of God is that 'the state is unlimited, infinite, true, perfect divine man', and politics becomes religion,[117] then the history of atheism against theism returns to its beginning, and the old theism would have to be called relatively human, in so far as it ascribes to God the properties and functions which it is better for men not to exercise against other men. If God is other than man, then a man can at least not play god over other men.

In the enthusiasm of their religious inheritance, the anthorpotheists of modern times from Feuerbach to Rilke, from Marx to Bloch, have overlooked the dark side of evil in man and the problem of suffering in the world.

With a trinitarian theology of the cross faith escapes the dispute between and the alternative of theism and atheism: God is not only other-worldly but also this-worldly; he is not only God, but also man; he is not only rule, authority and law but the event of suffering, liberating love. Conversely, the death of the Son is not the 'death of God', but the beginning of that God event in which the life-giving spirit of love emerges from the death of the Son and the grief of the Father.

7. *Beyond Obedience and Rebellion*

With this we return to the only serious atheism, the atheism of Camus and Horkheimer, the atheism of 'metaphysical rebellion' and the longing for righteousness, the atheism which one can follow Bloch in calling 'atheism for God's sake'. Does the Christian concept of the trinitarian event of God say anything about these deeper problems of inextricable suffering and the inescapable longing for eschatological righteousness? What can the knowledge of the 'crucified God' mean for helpless and suffering men?

Anyone who suffers without cause first thinks that he has been forsaken by God. God seems to him to be the mysterious, incomprehensible God who destroys the good fortune that he gave. But anyone who cries out to God in this suffering echoes the death-cry of the dying Christ, the Son of God. In that case God is not just a hidden someone set over against him, to whom he cries, but in a profound sense the human God, who cries with him and intercedes for him with his cross where man in his torment is dumb. The one who suffers is not just angry and furious and full of protest against his fate. He suffers because he lives, and he is alive because he loves. The person who can no longer love, even himself, no longer suffers, for he is without grief, without feeling and indifferent. This apathy is the sickness of our time, a sickness of person and systems, a sickness to death, to personal and universal death. But the more one loves, the more one is open and becomes receptive to happiness and sorrow. Therefore the one who loves becomes vulnerable, can be hurt and disappointed. This may be called the dialectic of human life: we live because and in so far as we love—and we suffer and die because and in so far as we love. In this way we experience life and death in love.

The God of theism is poor. He cannot love nor can he suffer. The protesting atheist loves in a desperate way. He does not want suffering because he loves. But at the same time he protests against love which makes him so vulnerable and wants to 'hand back his ticket', as Ivan Karamazov said. Love makes life so lively and death so deadly. Conversely, it also makes life deadly and death lively. The problem of its existence is sustaining this dialectic: how can one continue to love despite grief, disappointment and death?

The pure longing that the murderer shall not triumph over his victim is a protest of the impotence of love. It is a true and worthy human attitude, but it is hard to sustain without becoming bitter or superficial. The faith which springs from the God event on the cross does not give a theistic answer to the question of suffering, why it must be as it is, nor is it ossified into a mere gesture of protest, but leads sorely tried, despairing love back to its origin. 'Whoever abides in love abides in God and God in him' (I John 4.17). Where we suffer because we love, God suffers in us. Where he has suffered the death of Jesus and in so doing has shown the force of his love, men also find the power to continue to love, to sustain that which annihilates them and to 'endure what is dead' (Hegel).

Hegel termed this the life of mind:

But the life of mind is not one that shuns death, and keeps clear of destruction; it endures death and in death maintains its being. It only wins to its truth when it finds itself utterly torn asunder. It is this mighty power, not by being a positive which turns away from the negative, as when we say of anything it is nothing or it is false, and, being then done with it, pass on to something else: on the contrary, mind is this power only by looking the negative in the face, and dwelling with it. This dwelling beside it is the magic power that converts the negative into being.[118]

What Hegel here calls the dialectical power of mind, he had earlier called love or simply life (*Theologische Jugendschriften*), and he depicted this life of mind in accordance with the event of Good Friday, because in this 'death of God' love had killed death. He hoped for the life of mind after a Good Friday of the unfathomable and individual features of nature-religions and philosophies. In manifest religion the True is shown, in absolute knowledge it is brought to awareness and in logic—in theory—it is vindicated. As the God-man, in his passion, Jesus sustained the contradiction between life and death, identity and difference, and thus achieved reconciliation. 'The death of Christ is the death of this death itself, the negation of negation' (*Philosophy of Religion*). God has made this death part of his life, which is called love and reconciliation.

'God himself is dead', as it is said in a Lutheran hymn; the consciousness of this fact expresses the truth that the human, the finite, frailty, weakness, the negative, is itself a divine moment, is in God Himself.[119]

Therefore anyone who enters into love, and through love experiences inextricable suffering and the fatality of death, enters into the history of the human God, for his forsakenness is lifted away from him in the forsakenness of Christ, and in this way he can continue to love, need not look away from the negative and from death, but can sustain death.

It remains for us to note that at the end of this section of the *Philosophy of Religion* Hegel expressly acknowledges the doctrine of the Trinity, because only this makes it possible to understand the cross as the 'history of God'.

This is the form which the history of God's manifestation takes for the Church; this history is a divine history, whereby it reaches a consciousness of the truth. It is that which elates the consciousness, the knowledge, that God is a Trinity.

The reconciliation believed in as being in Christ has no meaning if God is not known as Trinity, if it is not recognized that He *is* but is at the same time the Other, the self-differentiating, the Other in the sense that this Other is God Himself and has potentially the divine nature in it, and that the abolishing of this difference, of this otherness, this return, this love, is Spirit.[120]

For eschatological faith, the trinitarian God-event on the cross becomes the history of God which is open to the future and which opens up the future. Its present is called reconciliation with grief in love and its eschaton the filling of all mortal flesh with spirit and all that is dead with this love. It is a transformation into the fullest degree of life. As we always use images in our thought, whether consciously or unconsciously, it seems clear that the divine Trinity should not be conceived of as a closed circle of perfect being in heaven. This was in fact the way in which the immanent Trinity was conceived of in the early church. Barth also uses this figure of the 'closed circle' for God. In contrast to this, though, one should think of the Trinity as a dialectical event, indeed as the event of the cross and then as eschatologically open history. The Spirit, love, is open to the future for the whole of forsaken humanity; in positive terms, for the new creation. The one who believes and loves first experiences an *arrabon*, an anticipation of this Spirit. Thus even the relationship of the Son to the Father is still incomplete in respect of the function of the Son in the world as Kyrios; this is clear from I Cor. 15, according to which, after the Son has completed his liberating functions, he will hand over the kingdom to the Father, that 'God may be all in all' (I Cor. 15.28). Thus the Trinity means the Christ event in the eschatological interpretation of faith. The Trinity therefore also means the history of God, which in human terms is the history of love and liberation. The Trinity, understood as an event for history, therefore presses towards eschatological consummation, so that the 'Trinity may be all in all', or put more simply, so that 'love may be all in all', so that life may triumph over death and righteousness over the hells of the negative and of all force. If Christian belief thinks in trinitarian terms, it says that forsaken men are already taken up by Christ's forsakenness into the divine history and that we 'live in God', because we participate in the eschatological life of God by virtue of the death of Christ. God is, God is in us, God suffers in us, where love suffers. We participate in the trinitarian process of God's history. Just as we participate actively and passively in the suffering of God, so too we will participate in the joy of God wherever we love and pray and hope. 'In this sense God is the great companion—the fellow-sufferer, who understands.'[121] Understood in trinitarian terms, God both transcends the world and is immanent in history, as process theology says in the bipolar concept of God without trinitarian thought.[122] He is, if one is prepared to put it in inadequate imagery, transcendent as Father, immanent as Son and opens up the future of history as the Spirit. If we understand God in this way, we can understand our own history, the history of suffering and the history of hope, in the history of God. Beyond theistic submissiveness and atheistic protest this is the history of life, because it is the history of love.

8. *Trinity and Eschatology*

Eschatology has come closer for modern theology than for many earlier theological periods. A particular eschatology has grown out of an abstract 'doctrine of the last things'; a confused appendix to dogmatics, *'de novissimis'*, has become the 'theology of hope'. 'From first to last, and not merely in the epilogue, Christianity is eschatology, is hope, forward looking and forward moving, and therefore also revolutionizing and transforming the present.'[123] God is no longer understood as the 'God above us' or 'in the depths of being', but as the 'God before us', going before us in history as the 'God of hope'.[124] The Bible is read as testimony to the history of promise, and faith is seized as a living hope and as a contradiction to a present which establishes itself in inner apathy and external systems. 'Hope is suffering and the passion which arises over the Messiah.' Therefore Jesus is given a new title as *the anticipator of the future* of God, his righteousness and the freedom of man.[125] This anticipation of the future, which can be recognized in his whole manifestation, in his person, his functions and his history of crucifixion and resurrection, has led to his being seen as the unconditional and universal *realization of the promise.* He has been named the unique *anticipation of the end* in the midst of history, or *God's lieutenant* in a godless world, as the *provisional representative* of the still absent God.[126] This general trend of theology and practice towards eschatological hope— whatever the differences between individual theologians may seem to be—is not something that can be taken back. But it must be made more profound if it is not to become the superficial sanctioning by religion of an officially optimistic society, sworn to economic growth and political and cultural expansion. Therefore eschatological theology must also think its own problems through to the end in theory. To think eschatologically means to think a matter through to the end. But where is the end, and what is it? We shall consider this by means of a dispute in the christological tradition.

Does Christ make himself superfluous when the kingdom of God comes? The question may sound speculative, but fundamental decisions of supreme importance depend on it. Any eschatologically oriented and functionally developed christology comes 'at the end' to the question whether its mediator has not made himself superfluous. Its conceptions of the mediation and representative function of Christ are determined by what is decided in this 'last question'. Three examples will make this clear.

Jean Calvin arrived at this question in his exegesis of I Cor. 15.28, which says that in the end Christ will hand over the kingdom to the Father, that God may be all in all.[127] His christology is conceived in functional terms: who Jesus is follows from his functions for man as prophet, priest and king. Jesus received his power as the one who had appeared in the flesh (*deus manifestus in carne*). The Father handed over the divine rule to the Christ when he sent him in the flesh. The Father indeed rules, but he has handed on his government to the incarnate Christ.[128] For this reason Calvin was fond of calling Christ the *lieutenant de Dieu*. Christ is the governor and representative of God in his exercise of God's rule in this godless world. However, as God's representative he exercises this rule in communion with the Father. But we recognize God only in the incarnate Christ. 'So we believe in God as the supreme Lord, but we see him only in the countenance of the man Jesus.' God descended into the manhood of Jesus not for his own sake but for the sake of our dullness and weakness.[129] This accommodation of God coming to meet us is also to be found in the governorship of Christ. For Calvin, the rule of the incarnate Christ is limited in time and scope. It begins with the incarnation and ends with the eschatological surrender of the kingdom to the Father. It is grounded in the free mercy of God, but conditioned in its Christ form by the sin of man. As Calvin does not make a distinction in principle between a political rule and one that is merely religious, but sets the confession of 'Christ the Lord' in the manifest and real struggle for world rule, his exegesis of I Cor. 15.24–28 becomes the nucleus of his doctrine of the 'divine monarchy'. Eschatological hope says: 'But Christ must reign until he puts all enemies under his feet' (v. 25). For Calvin, that is the triumph of Christ over the devil and his powers, and finally over death. Furthermore, 'Christ will destroy every rule and every authority and power' (v. 24) when he delivers up the kingdom to the Father. For Calvin, even worldly powers and authorities exercise 'a certain governship for God'. But they have only a transitory, provisional function. 'But all this is superfluous if the kingdom of God as it has now been created in us, quenches our present life.'[130] Therefore the day of Christ, when he hands over the kingdom to the Father, will see the annihilation of these mediating intermediary authorities. 'Then all supremacy must be laid low, so that God's glory alone may shine forth.'[131] For any intermediary introduces an element of prevention.[132] Further, the consummation of the rule of Christ is also the end of all earthly ordinances and communications of the church, in which Christ rules through the service of man in the medium of word and sacrament.[133] Finally, for Calvin, even the mediation of Christ himself and thus the humanity of Christ, assumed for the sake of this mediation, ceases when the kingdom is handed over to the Father. In the consummation the mediator is removed from the middle, so that the redeemed may depend immediately upon God himself. Even the humanity of Christ, which acts as intermediary between the holy God and sinful man, contains an element of hindrance, since for Calvin it is a veil with which the Godhead clothes itself in order to draw near to us. 'Then the veil will fall and we shall see the glory of God without hindrance, as he reigns in his kingdom. Christ's humanity will no longer stand in the middle, keeping us from the final view of God.'[134] Here Calvin is not thinking of an annihilation of Christ in person, but of a transference of the divine rule from the humanity of Christ to the divinity of Christ. If the incarnation in humanity was conditioned by sin and directed towards redemption, it will become superfluous in the redemption. The personal union took place for the sake of the redemption of sinners and will therefore be given up in redeemed existence. In that case the rule of God falls back on the Trinity—this is what is meant by the Godhead of Christ—and the whole Trinity will dwell immediately in the new creation, so that the whole creation will contain its glory directly. The eternal Son of God so to speak retreats into the

Trinity, and the man Jesus enters the host of the redeemed, or conversely, the whole of redeemed existence enters into the divine relationship of the *unio personalis*, i.e. into immediacy with God. The manhood of Christ which was crucified for the redemption of sinners no longer has a place in existence which has been redeemed and placed in immediacy to God.

Calvin's generally acknowledged spiritualist eschatology, which here leads to a rather docetic christology, can excite some criticism.[135] However, in principle a christology which is understood merely in functional terms must logically lead to the crucified Christ becoming superfluous in the realm of redeemed existence which is immediate to God. Because Calvin thinks of the doctrine of two natures only in the light of Christ's function as representative, which has become necessary because of the sin of man, for him the unity of Christ's person dissolves when the kingdom is handed over to the Father. Without the sin of man, the Son of God would not have become man. As a consequence, when he completes his lordship and hands over the kingdom, his incarnation is transcended. It follows from this that in the eschaton the creation will confront God immediately with the same purity and goodness that it had at the beginning, and will participate in his glory.

Following Calvin, but not without his one-sidedness, *A. A. van Ruler* has put forward his doctrine of theocracy again in modern times.[136] With Christ and his church, God is concerned only for creation and the kingdom. Sin is a problem which has intervened. So, as the reconciler, Christ is 'God's emergency measure'. God's special presence in Christ is only one element in his total action towards the world. It is his will in and through Christ that the whole of reality shall become his image, that his name shall be hallowed, his kingdom shall come and his will shall be done. The cross, the overcoming of sin by vicarious expiation, is the centre of the gospel. But its horizon is the kingdom, the purified heart, the sanctified life, the exorcized state, the society made at peace.[137] Israel and the Christian state are historical forerunners of the kingdom. But these forerunners of the kingdom in history are also emergency measures. It is not a matter of a Christian stamp on culture, but of humanity itself, of the kingdom of glory. Therefore all Christianizations of state, society and culture are necessary, but are at the same time torsos and failures. As we are not men to become Christians, but on the contrary are Christians in order to be able to be truly men, there must always be such anticipations in history by Christian states and Christian cultures. Here the state is particularly important for van Ruler, as it is 'the last collection of all thing-elements in human existence'.[138] Thus the church must intercede for theocracy. Theocracy is not clericalism and the church state, but an ordering and shaping of state life in the light of Christ, the gospel, the word of God. 'In theocracy the Bible is the spiritual foundation of the state'[139]—and this is not meant in a biblicist way. With this, van Ruler too puts the confession of Christ as Lord in the real struggle for world rule. The question of theocracy in the New Testament is the question 'who will inherit the earth'. In the New Testament everything is directed towards the new earth on which righteousness dwells.

In his christology van Ruler follows Calvin in beginning from 'the idea of representation, understood radically in Anselm's terms'.[140] God is only in Christ in his particular form in order to bear the guilt of sin and to take it away from the life of created reality so that this may stand before the face of God. Because Christ is only present in his form as God-man as an emergency measure on the part of God, because of the distress that mankind has brought upon itself by sin, in this form he becomes superfluous once the distress has been removed.

Over against Barth, one must keep the creation neat and not mix in anything of Christ, the Son of God in the flesh. One should also keep the kingdom of glory neat and not mix in anything of Christ. The *assumptio carnis* is necessary only because of sin. In the last judgment, the crisis will affect this too and it will be made subject: at that time, the veil of the flesh, the special form of God in Christ, will be laid aside.

Protologically and eschatologically, all things will then be directed towards the naked existence of things as such before God, without the veil of sin and without the veil of Christ . . . But the whole of Christianization is also directed towards that: it has its origin in the midst, in the special form of God in Christ. And it has its final purpose in the protological and eschatological purpose of God: not in the Immanuel, in the God with us, but in the humanity, in the man before God.[141]

The ultimate goal is the endless play of redeemed and liberated creation in the immediately present glory of God himself.

Here van Ruler makes Calvin more radical. What Calvin expressed in eschatological suggestions, with van Ruler becomes a firm thesis. If the Christ event contains only representation for the guilt of sin, the divine and human person of the representative is determined only by his function in forgiving transgressions and overcoming the consequences of sin. Only the functional titles like Kyrios, Christ and sacrifice denote the person of the God-man. In that case the title of Son can only denote the Godhead of Christ and not the relationship of the whole person of Jesus to the Father. In the Christ event there is a negation (expiation) of the negative (sin). The positive element is reality itself, which is understood as creation and as kingdom. The aim of the mission of Christ is the restoration of the original creation and humanity. Like Calvin, van Ruler dissolves the humanity of Christ in the eschaton. But unlike Calvin, for him the state, as the 'collection of all thing-elements', belongs to human existence both in creation and in the kingdom of God. It is in no way done away with, but emerges purified from transgression and sin. Whereas in Calvin it was still possible to think that the eschaton might also be the completion of the first creation in Christ, for van Ruler the eschaton is none other than the *restitutio in integrum*. If Christ is not the negation of the negative, then nothing new has come into the world with him over against the original creation. But can the consummation be understood as being quite untouched by this history out of which it emerges? Does not an unhistorical conception of God and human reality emerge from the identification of kingdom and creation? Can it really be said of the first creation that in it God was 'all in all'? Against such a conception of grace which only makes sin good, the theological tradition has raised the speculative question when the next fall would take place. For if the guilt of sin is removed by grace, this by no means signifies that the possibility of sin is also removed. If it too is to be removed, grace must contain some boundless 'more' over and above sin (Rom. 5.20), and consequently redeemed existence must be more than created existence, and finally the new freedom of the children of God must be greater than the first freedom of men. But if grace, by overcoming even the possibility of sin, adds something more to existence, that is, a new being in the world, then Christ must be regarded as more than the representative understood radically in Anselm's terms. In that case the assumption of the flesh contains not only the possibility of representation but also an anticipation of existence in the new creation and with it the fulfilment of the first promise of creation. In that case, Christ belongs as a foundation in the new creation and the kingdom of glory, whereas the state is done away with in its mediating authority.

Finally, the thesis that the mediator himself becomes superfluous also emerges in *Dorothee Sölle*. She sets out to make clear what 'the represented hope for and the genuine representative aims at, namely, the self-elimination of representation'.[142] Starting from the question of the identity of man in his alienated world and ending with the question of the identity of God in a godless world, she rightly seeks a personal understanding of the traditional christological notion of the representative and his act of representation on the cross. Wherever there are pointers towards advocacy, and these are to be found in every society, there is also representation. This reality of man comes to awareness of itself in Christian faith. But if representation is to preserve the longing for identity and is not to destroy it, it must not become replacement. The representative must keep open the place of the one whom he represents and retreat when the latter himself occupies the place. Only in this way does he preserve the latter's identity and responsibility for himself. To represent anyone therefore means to intercede for him for a time. Otherwise representation is inconceivable in the personal age of modern times. In this way all magical and materialistic conceptions of the expiatory sacrifice and the substitute in God's judgment come to nothing when applied to Christ. 'Representation cannot possibly be conceived in personal terms without provisionality and temporariness.' 'Only when representation is eschatologized, when it is therefore provisional, does it preserve the dignity of those entrusted to it.' 'By its provisionality, representation makes hope possible', namely, 'hope that it will eliminate itself'.[143] It follows from this that the representation effected by Christ before God, for men who are not identical with him, in connection with his resurrection from the dead, can only be an eschatologically provisional representation. Christ keeps open man's future before God, and as forerunner of God he keeps open his future in the world. In this sense there is a double identification in Christ with man and with God. It will only be superseded in the new heaven and the new earth in which non-identical man achieves his full identity before God and the absent God comes to his complete identity in the world.

With Dorothee Sölle the general theology of hope has been

subsumed under a Christian concept. On the basis of her stress on the non-identity of man as he is, the absence of God and the cross as a two-sided transitory representation, one can speak of a negative theology of hope. But for all its elements of truth, this eschatological christology is ultimately questionable at the following points, in an analogous way to that of Calvin and van Ruler:

1. A representative can only make himself superfluous when the place is objectively there and cannot be occupied for a while by the real occupant for reasons of subjective weakness and incapacity. But if the place is not there or is not yet there in its full and free form, but first must be made ready, then the representative does not make himself superfluous like an employment agency, but so to speak founds a new firm. In that case he has an effect not only on the subjective incapacity of the occupant of the place, but also on the making of the place. He not only represents but creates.

2. If we apply this picture to Christianity, this suggests a representation of Christ for us which is not only intervention as a mediator but is also creative action (John 14.3: 'I go to prepare a place for you'). In that case his representation is not just mediation for a while but also the basis for the new being and the new identity which goes beyond the self-identity that men always desire (I John 3.2).[144]

3. Not only is Christ the representative of the kingdom of the identity of God and man, but this kingdom is already present in him and has been given a fundamental definition in his history. As an eschatological forerunner he paves a way for men through judgment and godforsakenness, which is only passable for men in his company. It is not that through the representative work of Christ men are relieved of something of their needs, but that Christ experiences a hell of rejection and loneliness on the cross which need no longer be suffered by believers in this way. As a forerunner he paves the way. The way is laid open for his successors. Christ experiences death and hell in solitude. His followers experience it in his company. That is no substitution, but a liberation. Understood as a substitution, representation alienates men. But personal representation has within itself an element of liberation. It offers not only a chance to shift responsibility for oneself, but also liberation from impossible burdens and from solitude.

4. If the representative is to make himself superfluous, then it is necessary to presuppose identity, even if this is lost and therefore sought for. It is kept open by representation and restored in fulfilment. But is that not an idealistic concept of identity, which at all events ultimately becomes asocial in respect of the sociality of Christ the representative? If Christ is superseded by 'the new heaven and the new earth', in which their *lost* identity smiles again for God and for man, then there cannot be a really new heaven and a really new earth, a *new* identity for God and man, but only the restoration of old conditions. The category of the novel, which is involved in the primitive Christian experience of Christ, is concealed by the thesis of the supersession of the representative in a merely functional christology. The place of the vision of what is new is taken by romantic dreams of the original creation or the original identity of man in respect of which christology is then made functional. Here the notion of representation is not 'eschatologized', as Dorothee Sölle thinks, but protologized. What comes out at the end is only what was presupposed at the beginning. The interplay between non-identity and representation becomes a shadow play before the light that always was, is and will be.

The passage in I Cor. 15 in *Paul*, to which Calvin and van Ruler refer, gives no proof that the mediator will one day become superfluous.[145] In a striking way, Paul changes from the title Christ in v. 24 to the title Son in v. 28. The rule of Christ ends when he hands over the kingdom to the Father. At that time his representation, lieutenancy and governorship also end. In fact the rule of Christ only serves 'to give way to the sole lordship of God. Christ is God's representative over against a world which is not yet fully subject to God'.[146] But Paul does not speak here of a dissolution of the mediating rule of Christ through the immediate rule of God; rather, he speaks of the 'rule of God' which is handed over by Christ to the Father. This is no historical-eschatological event in which the provisional is replaced by the final, but a process within the Trinity. The 'kingdom of God' passes from the incarnate Son to the Father. As a result Jesus becomes superfluous as 'Christ' and 'Kyrios'. His mediating functions between the Father and abandoned mankind come to an end. But he remains as 'Son', indeed his Sonship only becomes complete as he hands over the kingdom to the Father. For Paul, the title Son not only expresses a function of Jesus for men, but also denotes his whole being in relationship to the Father. The obedience of Jesus is accomplished in the subordination of the Son to the Father (v. 28). The word used for subordination does not mean making superfluous, but obedience. The relationship of Jesus to his God and Father is described by Paul as Sonship in the formulae which denote surrender. The title 'Son' does not therefore concern a Godhead separated from the manhood of Christ, but the whole person of the Christ who is delivered up, raised and given power to rule, in his relationship to the Father. The relationships in the Trinity between Father and Son are not fixed in static terms once and for all, but are a living history. This history of God or this history in God begins with the sending and delivering up of the Son, continues with his resurrection and the transference of the rule of God to him, and only ends when the Son hands over this rule to the Father. The delivering up on the cross is the central point of this history in God, not its conclusion. Only with the handing over of rule to the Father is the obedience of the Son, and thus his Sonship, consummated.

In the light of this future it becomes clear that the rule of the crucified Christ, too, is not just that of a forerunner of the coming sole Lordship of Christ, but in its eschatological provisionality already itself represents the lordship of the Son. However, the rule of Christ involves not only representation for the coming rule of God but also the incarnation and the realization of this rule of God. The Christ does not just intervene for the future consummation, but this consummation already acquires its permanent form in his suffering love. The eternal God has by no means merely 'veiled' his majesty in the manhood of Jesus, in order to draw near to men in grace. Such a modalistic christology must ultimately end in un-Christian monotheism or pantheism. A merely functional christology must end in a non-Christian eschatology of being, obtained from somewhere else. Here the purpose for which Christ has come cannot be defined in terms of Christ, but must be defined in some other terms. Only when, as in Paul, eschatological-functional christology is taken up from beginning to end into a trinitarian christology, is it and does it remain Christian. But conversely, for trinitarian christology that means an alteration in the concept of God. The cross does not bring an end to the trinitarian history in God between the Father and the Son in the Spirit as eschatological history, but rather opens it up.

The goal of the subordination of the Son to the Father and the significance of the transference of the kingdom to the Father is not simply the sole rule of God, but the consummation of the Fatherhood of the Father. If according to I Cor. 15.49 man will bear the image (*eikon*) of the heavenly, this will be accomplished in men being made like the image of the Son, so that, as Rom. 8.29 says, he may be the firstborn among many brothers. The goal of the consummation does not lie in the dissolution by Christ of his rule so that it is taken up into the rule of God, but in the consummation of the obedience of the Son and thus in the consummation of the brotherhood of believers. In respect of the world, the godless powers and death one can see the consummation of salvation in the transition from the rule of Christ to the sole rule of God. But in respect of the inner relationship of the Son to the Father, the consummation of the salvation of the world lies in the consummation of the history of God within the Trinity. In the first respect it is possible to speak of the provisional functions of God's Christ as representative and mediator becoming superfluous. In the second respect, however, one must speak of the abiding significance of the Son who is delivered up and then raised. It follows from this that the crucified Christ does not disappear when the fulfilment comes, but rather becomes the ground for redeemed existence in God and the indwelling of God in all. In that event the crucified Christ in fact no longer has representative functions. But new existence is indebted to him for ever. The functional and soteriological representative-christology then becomes a doxological Son-christology. And as the end brings about this reversal, so too it is present in the confession of the Christian believer from the beginning. Historical christology, too, must do more than provide a functional representation of the significance and use of Christ for salvation, righteousness and identity; it must itself be an expression of the brotherhood of the believer with the Son and express that doxologically in thanksgiving and praise. Thus the necessity of representation 'for us' becomes the freedom of thankfulness 'from us'. Christ is more than necessary; he is free and sets free. He belongs both to the realm of necessity and the realm of freedom, because he is himself the transition.[147]

9. The Experience of Human Life in the Pathos of God

Man develops his manhood always in relationship to the God-head of his God. He experiences his existence in relationship to that which illuminates him as the supreme being. He orients his life on the ultimate value. His fundamental decisions are made in accordance with what unconditionally concerns him. Thus the divine is the situation in which man experiences, develops and shapes himself. Theology and anthropology are involved in a reciprocal relationship. Therefore the theology of the 'crucified God' also leads to a corresponding anthropology. Hitherto our dominant concern has been with the question of the history and the quality of the suffering of God; now we must enquire into the development of the humanity of man in this situation with God. A comparison of Christian theology with the *apathetic theology* of Greek antiquity and the *pathetic theology* of later Jewish philosophy of religion may help to define the context more clearly. We started by asserting that the adoption of the Greek philosophical concept of the 'God incapable of suffering' by the early church led to difficulties in christology which only more recent theology has set out to overcome. But before the 'suffering of God' had become a theme of Christian theology in the present, Jewish theology had already been discussing the theme. Christian theology cannot but learn from this new Jewish exegesis of the history of God in the Old Testament and in the present suffering of the Jewish people.

(a) The apatheia of God and the freedom of man

In the ancient world, early Christianity encountered *apatheia* as a metaphysical axiom and an ethical ideal with irresistible force.[148] On this concept were concentrated the worship of the divinity of God and the struggle for man's freedom. Like *pathos*, the word *apatheia* has many connotations. It means incapable of being affected by outside influences, incapable of feeling, as is the case with dead things, and the freedom of the spirit from inner needs and external damage. In the physical sense *apatheia* means unchangeableness; in the psychological sense, insensitivity; and in the ethical sense, freedom. In contrast to this, *pathos* denotes need, compulsion, drives, dependence, lower passions and un-willed suffering. Since Plato and Aristotle the metaphysical and ethical perfection of God has been described as *apatheia*. According to Plato, God is good and therefore cannot be the cause of anything evil, of punishment and sorrow. The poetic conceptions of the gods as capricious, envious, vengeful and punitive, which were meant to arouse emotions, *pathe*, among the audience of the tragedy, which would lead to *katharsis*, are rejected as 'inappropriate to God'. They do not fit the moral and political 'guidelines for the doctrine of the gods'.[149] It is inappropriate to present God as the *auctor malorum*. As that which is perfect, the Godhead needs nothing.[150] If it has no needs, it is therefore also unchangeable, for any change shows a deficiency in being. God does not need the services or the emotions of men for his own life. Because he is perfect, he needs no friends nor will he have any. 'Friendship occurs where love is offered in return. But in friendship with God there is no room for love to be offered in return, indeed there is not even room for love. For it would be absurd if anyone were to assert that he loved Zeus.'[151] As like is only known and loved by like, the Godhead is self-sufficient. From the time of Aristotle onwards, the metaphysical principle which has been derived from this has been θεὸς ἀπαθής.[152] As *actus purus* and pure causality, nothing can happen to God for him to suffer. As the perfect being, he is without emotions. Anger, hate and envy are alien to him. Equally alien to him are love, compassion and mercy. 'The blessed and incorruptible being does not itself endure tribulation, nor does it burden others with it. Therefore it knows neither wrath nor favour. This sort of thing is to be found only in a weak being.'[153] God thinks himself eternally and in this is the thought of thought. God is ever-willing. Therefore both will and thought are part of his apathic being.

If it is the moral ideal of the wise man to become similar to the divinity and participate in its sphere, he must overcome needs and drives and lead a life free of trouble and fear, anger and love, in *apatheia*. He will find rest in God in the thinking of thought. He will find the eternal presence of God in the eternal will. The school of the Sceptics demanded the withholding of judgment (ἐποχή). The man of understanding must stand firm in *ataraxia*, and the wise man will possess *apatheia*. His knowledge is not disturbed by any emotions of the soul or any interests of the body. He lives in the higher sphere of the Logos. He does not even feel what other men regard as good or evil. He uses all things as though they had a value, although he ascribes no value to them. Imperturbability, dispassionateness, mildness follow the *epoche* of the Sceptics like a shadow.[154] The middle situation (μετριοπάθεια) in the life of feeling and the senses which was originally praised, even by Aristotle, was then superseded by the Stoic ethic of the *apatheia* for which the wise man strives. In the struggle for virtue, the wise man acquires that which the Godhead possesses by nature.

Ancient Judaism, above all in the person of Philo, and ancient Christianity, took up this ideal of *apatheia* in theology and ethics and sought to fulfil it and go beyond it. Philo presents Abraham as the model of *apatheia*, but also praises his *metriopatheia*. He too regards *apatheia* as the goal of perfection. But man does not strive to be free for himself and content with himself. Rather, he strives to become free and without needs in the service of God who alone gives the power to achieve *apatheia*. Because Philo is in the area influenced by the Old Testament understanding of God, his doctrine of *apatheia* differs from that of the Stoics, although he has taken over their form of it. For him the *apatheia* strived for is indeed meant to lead to similarity with God, but in essence it leads to a different 'situation of God'.[155]

An examination of the discussion of *apatheia* in ancient Greece, Judaism and Christianity shows that *apatheia* does not mean the petrification of men, nor does it denote those symptoms of illness which are today described as apathy, indifference and alienation. Rather, it denotes the freedom of man and his superiority to the world in corresponding to the perfect, all-sufficient freedom of the Godhead. *Apatheia* is entering into the higher divine sphere of the Logos. On the other hand, only the lower drives and compulsions were understood as *pathos*. What today is described as the *pathos of life*, the meaning which fills a life, brings it alive and enhances it, was not included among the *pathe*. What Christianity proclaimed as the *agape* of God and the believer was rarely translated as *pathos*. Because true *agape* derives from liberation from the inward and outward fetters of the flesh (*sarx*), and loves without self-seeking and anxiety, without *ira et studio*, *apatheia* could be taken up as an enabling ground for this love and be filled with it. Love arises from the spirit and from freedom, not from desire or anxiety. The apathic God could therefore be understood as the free God who freed others for himself. The negation of need, desire and compulsion expressed by *apatheia* was taken up and filled with a new positive content.[156] The *apathetic theology* of antiquity was accepted as a preparation for the trinitarian theology of the love of God and of men. Only a long history of use in Judaism and Christianity changed the word and provided it with another context of meanings. It associated passion with love out of freedom for others and those who were different, and taught an understanding of the meaning of the suffering of love from the history of the passion of Israel and of Christ. These changes must be noted if justice is to be done to the apathetic theology of antiquity and its acceptance in Judaism and Christianity. Nevertheless, the question remains open whether the positive side of the new relationship with God did not inevitably have to break out of the framework of the presupposed negation of the negative, and still must do so.

(b) The pathos *of God and the* sympatheia *of men*

It was Abraham Heschel who, in controversy with Hellenism and the Jewish philosophy of religion of Jehuda Halevi, Maimonides and Spinoza which was influenced by it, first described the prophets' proclamation of God as *pathetic theology*.[157] The prophets had no 'idea' of God, but understood themselves and the people in the *situation of God*. Heschel called this situation of God the *pathos of God*. It has nothing to do with the irrational human emotions like desire, anger, anxiety, envy or sympathy, but describes the way in which God is affected by events and human actions and suffering in history. He is affected by them because he is interested in his creation, his people and his right. The *pathos* of God is intentional and transitive, not related to itself but to the history of the covenant people. God already emerged from himself at the creation of the world 'in the beginning'. In the covenant he enters into the world and the people of his choice. The 'history' of God cannot therefore be separated from the history of his people. The history of the divine *pathos* is embedded in this history of men. Because creation, covenant and history of God spring from his freedom, his effective *pathos* is quite different from that of the capricious, envious and heroic divinities of the mythical sagas, who are indeed subject to fate (*ananke*). It is the *pathos* of his free relationship to creation, to the people and to history. The prophets never identified God's *pathos* with his being, since for them it was not something absolute, but the form of his relationship to others. The divine *pathos* is expressed in the relationship of God to his people. The concept of an apathic God was inevitably alien to them. Prophecy, therefore, is in essence not a looking forward into the future to see what is appointed in unalterable destiny or a predestined divine plan of salvation, but insight into the present *pathos* of God, his suffering caused by Israel's disobedience and his passion for his right and his honour in the world. If the divine *pathos* is grounded in his freedom, it is not pure will, as in the Islamic concept of God. Rather, it is his interest in his creation and his people, by which God transfers his being into the history of his relationship and his covenant with man. God takes man so seriously that he suffers under the actions of man and can be injured by them. At the heart of the prophetic proclamation there stands the certainty that God is interested in the world to the point of suffering.

As Abraham Heschel shows in a comparison with Greek philosophy, with Confucianism, Buddhism and Islam, the Israelite understanding of the *pathos* of God is unique.[158] But in a way parallel to that taken by Christian theology, Jewish scholasticism in the Middle Ages also sought to adapt itself to the idea of the *theos apathes*. 'Any passion is evil.' Therefore Jehuda Halevi thought that compassion and sympathy could only be signs of weakness in the soul and were not appropriate to God. 'He is a just judge; he ordains the poverty of one individual and the wealth of another without any change in his nature, without feelings of sympathy with one or anger against another'.[159] According to Maimonides, no predicate which involves corporeality and the capacity for suffering may be applied to God. 'God is free from passions; he is moved neither by feelings of joy nor feelings of grief.' So too Spinoza asserted that strictly speaking 'God neither loves nor hates'.[160] So for a long time the apathic God became a fundamental principle for Jewish theology too.

Now if one starts from the *pathos* of God, one does not think of God in his absoluteness and freedom, but understands his passion and his interest in terms of the history of the covenant. The more the covenant is taken seriously as the revelation of God, the more profoundly one can understand the historicity of God and history in God.[161] If God has opened his heart in the covenant with his people, he is injured by disobedience and suffers in the people. What the Old Testament terms *the wrath of God* does not belong in the category of the anthropomorphic transference of lower human emotions to God, but in the category of the divine *pathos*. His wrath is injured love and therefore a mode of his reaction to men. Love is the source and the basis of the possibility of the wrath of God. The opposite of love is not wrath, but indifference. Indifference towards justice and injustice would be a retreat on the part of God from the covenant. But his wrath is an expression of his abiding interest in man. Anger and love do not therefore keep a balance. 'His wrath lasts for the twinkling of an eye,' and, as the Jonah story shows, God takes back his anger for the sake of his love in reaction to human repentance. As injured love, the wrath of God is not something that is inflicted, but a divine suffering of evil. It is a sorrow which goes through his opened heart. He suffers in his passion for his people.[162]

In the sphere of the apathic God man becomes a *homo apatheticus*. In the situation of the *pathos* of God he becomes a *homo sympatheticus*.[163] The divine *pathos* is reflected in man's participation, his hopes and his prayers. Sympathy is the openness of a person to the present of another. It has the structure of dialogue. In the *pathos* of God, man is filled with the spirit of God. He becomes the friend of God, feels sympathy with God and for God.[164] He does not enter into a mystical union but into a sympathetic union with God. He is angry with God's wrath. He suffers with God's suffering. He loves with God's love. He hopes with God's hope. Abraham Heschel has developed his theology of the divine *pathos* as a *dipolar theology*. God is free in himself and at the same time interested in his covenant relationship and affected by human history. In this covenant relationship he has spoken of the *pathos* of God and the *sympatheia* of man, and in so doing has introduced a second bipolarity. For the *sympatheia* of man answers the *pathos* of God in the spirit. The prophet is an *ish haruach*, a man driven and emboldened by the spirit of God. There is probably a hint here of the idea of a dual personality in God. Both notions can be followed further in the theology of the rabbis and are further deepened by them.

As P. Kuhn has demonstrated,[165] the rabbis at the turn of the ages spoke of a number of stages in the self-humiliation of God: in the creation, in the call of Abraham, Isaac and Jacob and the history of Israel, in the exodus and in the exile. Psalm 18.36:

'When you humble me you make me great' was understood to mean: 'You show me that you are great by your humiliation of yourself.' God dwells in heaven and among those who are of a humble and contrite spirit. He is the God of gods and brings justice to widows and orphans. He is lofty and yet looks upon the lowly. So he is present in two opposite ways. God already renounces his honour in the beginning at creation. Like a servant, he carries the torch before Israel into the wilderness. Like a servant he bears Israel and its sins on his back. He descends into the thornbush, the ark of the covenant and the temple. He meets men in those who are in straits, in the lowly and the small. These *accommodations* of God to the limitations of human history at the same time contain *anticipations* of his future indwelling in his whole creation, when in the end all lands will be full of his glory. He enters not only into the situation of the limited creature, but even into the situation of the guilty and suffering creature. His lamentation and sorrow over Israel in the exile show that God's whole existence with Israel is in suffering. Israel is 'the apple of his eye'. He cannot forget Israel's suffering, for were he to do that he would have to forget 'his own rights'. So God goes with Israel into the Babylonian exile. In his 'indwelling' in the people he suffers with the people, goes with them into prison, feels sorrow with the martyrs. So conversely the liberation of Israel also means the liberation of that 'indwelling of God' from its suffering. In his *Shekinah* the Holy One of Israel shares Israel's suffering and Israel's redemption, so that in this respect it is true that 'God has redeemed himself from Egypt together with his people: "The redemption is for me and for you." God himself "was led out (with Israel from Egypt)" '. [165] Because his name has been bound up with Israel, Israel is redeemed when God has redeemed himself, that is, has glorified his name; and the suffering of God is the means by which Israel is redeemed. God himself is 'the ransom' for Israel. [167]

A shattering expression of the *theologia crucis* which is suggested in the rabbinic theology of God's humiliation of himself is to be found in *Night*, a book written by E. Wiesel, a survivor of Auschwitz:

The SS hanged two Jewish men and a youth in front of the whole camp. The men died quickly, but the death throes of the youth lasted for half an hour. 'Where is God? Where is he?' someone asked behind me. As the youth still hung in torment in the noose after a long time, I heard the man call again, 'Where is God now?' And I heard a voice in myself answer: 'Where is he? He is here. He is hanging there on the gallows . . .'[168]

Any other answer would be blasphemy. There cannot be any other Christian answer to the question of this torment. To speak here of a God who could not suffer would make God a demon. To speak here of an absolute God would make God an annihilating nothingness. To speak here of an indifferent God would condemn men to indifference.

But theological reflection must draw the consequence from such experiences of the suffering of God in suffering which cannot be accounted for in human terms. Rabbinic talk of God's humiliation of himself presses towards a distinction in God between God himself and his 'indwelling' (Shekinah), between God and the indwelling spirit of God. Judaism of the rabbinic period developed the notion of such a dual personality in God in order to be able to express the experience of the suffering of God with Israel and in suffering to protect that 'religion of sympathy', the openness for God against the curse of God (Job 2.9), hardening of the heart and the surrender of hope. But the intrinsic theological problem arises when one asks what is the cause of the suffering of the God who suffers with imprisoned, persecuted and murdered Israel. Does he merely suffer for human injustice and human wickedness? Does the Shekinah, which wanders with Israel through the dust of the streets and hangs on the gallows in Auschwitz, suffer in the God who holds the ends of the earth in his hand? In that case not only would suffering affect God's *pathos* externally, so that it might be said that God himself suffers at the human history of injustice and force, but suffering would be the history in the midst of God himself. We are not concerned here to set up paradoxes, but to ask whether the experiences of the passion and the suffering of God lead into the inner mystery of God himself in which God himself confronts us.

(c) *The fullness of life in the trinitarian history of God*

Christian faith does not believe in a new 'idea' of God. In the fellowship of the crucified Christ it finds itself in a new 'situation of God' and participates in that with all its existence.

Christian theology can only adopt the insight and the longing of Hellenistic *apathetic theology* as a presupposition for the knowledge of the freedom of God and the liberation of fettered man. For its own concerns it completely reverses the direction of that theology: it is not the ascent of man to God but the revelation of God in his self-emptying in the crucified Christ which opens up God's sphere of life to the development of man in him. This situation is related to the situation of the Jews, for the *pathos* of God perceived and proclaimed by the prophets is the presupposition for the Christian understanding of the living God from the passion of Christ. But the *pathetic theology* of Judaism must begin from the covenant of God with the people and from membership of this people of God. Therefore there is for it a direct correspondence between the *pathos* of God and the *sympatheia* of men. On the basis of the presupposition of election to the covenant and the people it is necessary only to develop a dipolar theology which speaks of God's passion and the drive of the spirit in the suffering and hopes of man. This presupposition does not exist for the Christian, especially for the Gentile Christian. Where for Israel immediacy with God is grounded on the presupposition of the covenant, for Christians it is Christ himself who communicates the Fatherhood of God and the power of the Spirit. Therefore Christian theology cannot develop any dipolar theology of the reciprocal relationship between the God who calls and the man who answers; it must develop a trinitarian theology, for only in and through Christ is that dialogical relationship with God opened up. Through Christ, God himself creates the conditions of entering into that relationship of *pathos* and *sympatheia*. Through him he creates it for those who cannot satisfy these conditions: the sinners, the godless and those forsaken by God. In Christian terms, therefore, no relationship of immediacy between God and man is conceivable which is separated from this person and his history. But in that God himself creates the conditions for communion with God through his self-humiliation in the death of the crucified Christ and through his exaltation of man in the resurrection of Christ, this community becomes a gracious, presuppositionless and universal community of God with all men in their common misery. For the sake of the unconditionality and universality of God's community of grace, Christian theology must therefore think simultaneously in both christocentric and trinitarian terms. Only the covenant founded one-sidedly by God and opened to all in the cross of Christ makes possible the covenant relationships of dialogue in the spirit, in *sympatheia* and in prayer. 'God was in Christ'—that is the presupposition for the fellowship of sinners and godless with God, since it opens up God's sphere for the whole of man and for all men. 'We live in Christ'—that is the consequence for the faith which experiences the full communion with God in communion with Christ.

But how can this sphere of God opened up in Christ be described? Is it comparable to the field of action of God's apathic freedom or to the field of force of God's *pathos*?

Following Philippians 2, Christian theology speaks of the final and complete self-humiliation of God in man and in the person of Jesus. Here God in the person of the Son enters into the limited, finite situation of man. Not only does he enter into it, descend into it, but he also accepts it and embraces the whole of human existence with his being. He does not become spirit so that man must first soar to the realm of the spirit in order to participate in God. He does not merely become the covenant partner of an elect people so that men must belong to this people through circumcision and obedience to the covenant in order to enter into his fellowship. He lowers himself and accepts the whole of mankind without limits and conditions, so that each man may participate in him with the whole of his life.

When God becomes man in Jesus of Nazareth, he not only enters into the finitude of man, but in his death on the cross also enters into the situation of man's godforsakenness. In Jesus he does not die the natural death of a finite being, but the violent death of the criminal on the cross, the death of complete abandonment by God. The suffering in the passion of Jesus is abandonment, rejection by God, his Father. God does not become a religion, so that man participates in him by corresponding religious thoughts and feelings. God does not become a law, so that man participates in him through obedience to a law. God does not become an ideal, so that man achieves community with him through constant striving. He humbles himself and takes upon himself the eternal death of the godless and the godforsaken, so that all the godless and the godforsaken can experience communion with him.

The incarnate God is present, and can be experienced, in the humanity of every man, and in full human corporeality. No one need dissemble and appear other than he is to perceive the fellowship of the human God with him. Rather, he can lay aside all dissembling and sham and become what he truly is in this human God. Furthermore, the crucified God is near to him in the forsakenness of every man. There is no loneliness and no rejection which he has not taken to himself and assumed in the cross of Jesus. There is no need for any attempts at justification or for any self-destructive self-accusations to draw near to him. The godforsaken and rejected man can accept himself where he comes to know the crucified God who is with him and has already accepted him. If God has taken upon himself death on the cross, he has also taken upon himself all of life and real life, as it stands under death, law and guilt. In so doing he makes it possible to accept life whole and entire and death whole and entire. Man is taken up, without limitations and conditions, into the life and suffering, the death and resurrection of God, and in faith participates corporeally in the fullness of God. There is nothing that can exclude him from the situation of God between the grief of the Father, the love of the Son and the drive of the Spirit.[169]

Life in communion with Christ is full life in the trinitarian situation of God. Dead in Christ and raised to new life, as Paul says in Rom. 6.8, the believer really participates in the suffering of God in the world, because he partakes in the suffering of the love of God. Conversely, he takes part in the particular suffering of the word, because God has made it his suffering in the cross of his Son.[170] The human God who encounters man in the crucified Christ thus involves man in a realistic divinization (*theosis*). Therefore in communion with Christ it can truly be said that men live *in God* and *from God*, 'that they live, move and have their being in him' (Acts 17.28). Understood in pantheistic terms, that would be a dream which would have to ignore the negative element in the world. But a trinitarian theology of the cross perceives God in the negative element and therefore the negative element in God, and in this dialectical way is panentheistic. For in the hidden mode of humiliation to the point of the cross, all being and all that annihilates has already been taken up in God and God begins to become 'all in all'. To recognize God in the cross of Christ, conversely, means to recognize the cross, inextricable suffering, death and hopeless rejection in God.

A 'theology after Auschwitz' may seem an impossibility or

blasphemy to those who allowed themselves to be satisfied with theism or their childhood beliefs and then lost them. And there would be no 'theology after Auschwitz' in retrospective sorrow and the recognition of guilt, had there been no 'theology in Auschwitz'. Anyone who later comes up against insoluble problems and despair must remember that the *Shema* of Israel and the Lord's Prayer were prayed in Auschwitz.

It is necessary to remember the martyrs, so as not to become abstract. Of them and of the dumb sacrifices it is true in a real, transferred sense, that God himself hung on the gallows, as E. Wiesel was able to say. If that is taken seriously, it must also be said that, like the cross of Christ, even Auschwitz is in God himself. Even Auschwitz is taken up into the grief of the Father, the surrender of the Son and the power of the Spirit. That never means that Auschwitz and other grisly places can be justified, for it is the cross that is the beginning of the trinitarian history of God. As Paul says in I Cor. 15, only with the resurrection of the dead, the murdered and the gassed, only with the healing of those in despair who bear lifelong wounds, only with the abolition of all rule and authority, only with the annihilation of death will the Son hand over the kingdom to the Father. Then God will turn his sorrow into eternal joy. This will be the sign of the completion of the trinitarian history of God and the end of world history, the overcoming of the history of man's sorrow and the fulfilment of his history of hope. God in Auschwitz and Auschwitz in the crucified God—that is the basis for a real hope which both embraces and overcomes the world, and the ground for a love which is stronger than death and can sustain death. It is the ground for living with the terror of history and the end of history, and nevertheless remaining in love and meeting what comes in openness for God's future. It is the ground for living and bearing guilt and sorrow for the future of man in God.

NOTES

1. For an introduction to the American 'Death of God theology' see T. Altizer and W. Hamilton, *Radical Theology and the Death of God*, Indianapolis 1966; for an introduction to the American and German discussion, S. M. Daecke, *Der Mythos vom Tode Gottes*, 1970. There is a simplified journalistic introduction in H. Zahrnt, *What Kind of God?*, SCM Press 1971. I will refrain from discussing their theses in what

follows, and keep to works which are in every respect more fundamental, which will be presented on the following pages.

2. This view, from which I have begun in the previous chapters, has recently been put forward by E. Jüngel, *Unterwegs zur Sache, Theologische Bemerkungen*, 1972, 297: 'Any Christian confession must be compatible with the death cry of Jesus—or it does not confess faith in God.'

3. Cf. the collection of studies by F. Viering, *Der Kreuzestod Jesu. Interpretation eines theologischen Gutachtens*, 1969.

4. P. Althaus, *Theologische Aufsätze*, 1929, 23. His article in this volume on 'The Cross of Christ' deserves special notice.

5. Karl Rahner, *Theological Investigations* IV, Darton, Longman and Todd 1966, 113.

6. Karl Rahner, *Sacramentum Mundi* II, Burns and Oates 1969, 207f.: '*Jesus' death as the death of God:* Christology at the present day must reflect more closely on Jesus' death, not only in its redemptive effect, but also in itself. Not in order to countenance a superficial and fashionable death of God theology but because it is called for by the reality itself . . . If it is said that the incarnate Logos died only in his human reality, and if this is tacitly understood to mean that this death therefore did not affect God, only half the truth has been stated. The really Christian truth has been omitted. The immutable God in himself of course has no destiny and therefore no death. But he himself (and not just what is other than he) has a destiny, through the Incarnation, in what is other than himself . . . And so precisely this death (like Christ's humanity) expresses God as he is and as he willed to be in our regard by a free decision which remains eternally valid. In that case, however, this death of God in his being and becoming in what is other than himself, in the world, must clearly belong to the law of the history of the new and eternal covenant in which we have to live. We have to share God's lot in the world. Not by declaring with fashionable godlessness that God does not exist or that we have nothing to do with him. Our "possessing" God must repeatedly pass through the deathly abandonment by God (Matt. 27.46: Mark 15.34) in which alone God ultimately comes to us, because God has given himself in love and as love, and this is realized and manifested in his death. Jesus' death belongs to God's self-utterance.'

7. Hans Urs von Balthasar, 'Mysterium Paschale', in *Mysterium Salutis. Grundriss heilgeschichtlicher Dogmatik* III, 2, 1969, 133–326, esp. 159ff.

8. H. Mühlen, *Die Veränderlichkeit Gottes als Horizont einer zukunftigen Christologie. Auf dem Wege zu einer Kreuzestheologie in Auseinandersetzung mit der altkirchlichen Christologie*, 1969.

9. H. Küng, *Menschwerdung Gottes*, 1970. The excursuses mentioned can be found on pp. 622ff. and 637ff.

10. A. Schlatter, *Jesus Gottheit und das Kreuz*, ²1913, deserves to be recalled from oblivion in the context of today's christological questions as does B. Steffen, *Das Dogma vom Kreuz. Beitrag zu einer staurozentrische Theologie*, 1920.

11. Karl Barth, *Church Dogmatics* II 2, T. & T. Clark 1957, and IV 1–4, T. & T. Clark 1956–69.

12. Ibid., II 2, 123. On this see E. Jüngel, *Gottes Sein ist im Werden. Verantwortliche Rede vom Sein Gottes bei Karl Barth. Eine Paraphrase*, 1965.

13. This is rightly stressed by B. Klappert, *Die Auferweckung des Gekreuzigten*, 1971, 180f.: 'In Barth, the rejection of paradox in christology has the function and intention of thinking through the *theologia crucis* consistently to the point of taking the cross up into the concept of God. This shows theology as talk of God that its primarily place is on the cross, that is, on earth.'

14. *Church Dogmatics* II 2, 167, 162. So we read in *Church Dogmatics* IV 1, 557f.: 'A *theologia gloriae*, the magnifying of what Jesus Christ has received for us in His resurrection, of what He is for us as the risen One, can have no meaning unless it includes within itself a *theologia crucis*, the magnifying of what He has done for us in His death, of what He is for us as the Crucified. But an abstract *theologia crucis* cannot have any meaning either. We cannot properly magnify the passion and death of Jesus Christ unless this magnifying includes within itself the *theologia gloriae*—the magnifying of the one who in His resurrection is the recipient of our right and life, the One who has risen again from the dead for us.'

15. Thus according to G. C. Berkouwer's criticism (*The Triumph of Grace in the Theology of Karl Barth*, Paternoster Press 1956, 387), see also B. Klappert, op. cit., 182 n.58.

16. Cf. *Church Dogmatics* II 2, 166 (in addition to 150, 162):

'God could have remained satisfied with Himself and with the impassible glory and blessedness of His own inner life. But He did not do so.' 169: 'In ordaining the overflowing of His glory God also and necessarily ordains that this glory, which in Himself, in His inner life as Father, Son and Holy Spirit, cannot be subjected to attack or disturbance, which in Himself cannot be opposed, should enter into the sphere of contradiction. . . .'

The 'rest of God in himself' and his 'being in decision' certainly do not exclude each other in his life, which is why I have spoken of a 'distinction' here. God chooses the malefactor's cross for his throne, says Barth (167). But if God exists in this way in the cross of Jesus, what does it mean for the cross to exist in God? Or does it not reach God's being in itself? In that case Barth's christological concept of God would still have a trans-christological proviso. W. Krötke, *Sünde und Nichtiges bei Karl Barth*, 1970, does not go into this problem.

17. E. Jüngel, 'Vom Tod des lebendigen Gottes. Ein Plakat', *ZThK* 65, 1968, 1-24, now in *Unterwegs zur Sache*, 80ff.

18. H.-G. Geyer, 'Atheismus und Christentum', *EvTh* 30, 1970, 255-274.

19. H. Urs von Balthasar, op. cit., 142.

20. On this cf. Gregory of Nyssa, *Or. cat.* 24 (quoted in H. Urs von Balthasar, op. cit., 152): 'In the first place, then, the fact that the omnipotent nature should have been capable of descending to the low estate of humanity provides a clearer proof of power than great and super-

natural miracles ... But the descent to our low estate is a surpassing display of this power which is in no way impeded even in conditions opposed to nature ... the lofty, coming to exist in lowliness, is seen in this lowliness, and yet descends not from its height' (ET by J. H. Srawley, SPCK 1917, 77).

21. P. Althaus, art. 'Kenosis', *RGG*[3] III, 1244–6; H. Urs von Balthasar, op. cit., 143: 'Kenosis and the new picture of God'.

22. P. Althaus, op. cit., 1243.

23. A. Lossky, cited in H. Urs von Balthasar, op. cit., 149.

24. Quotations in H. Urs von Balthasar, op. cit., 217.

25. Text follows *Luthers Werken in Auswahl* V, ed. E. Vogelsang, Berlin 1933, 375–92; German text in the Münchener Lutherausgabe I, 131–145. On this cf. W. von Loewenich, *Luthers Theologia Crucis*, [5]1967; H. J. Iwand, *Nachgelassene Werke* II, 1966, 281ff.: *Theologia Crucis*; K. Schwarzwäller, *Theologia crucis. Luthers Lehre von der Prädestination nach De servo arbitrio*, 1970.

26. H. J. Iwand, op. cit., 382.

27. On this see M. Horkheimer, *Kritische Theorie* II, 1968, 137ff., and J. Habermas, 'Erkenntnis und Interesse', in: *Technik und Wissenschaft als 'Ideologie'*, 1968, 160ff.

28. *Sent.* I, *dist.* 3.1, quoted following H. J. Iwand, op. cit., 385.

29. Diogenes Laertes VII, 88; on this E. Topitsch, 'Das Problem des Naturrechts', in *Naturrecht oder Rechtspositivismus*, ed. W. Maihofer, 1962, 159ff.; and E. Wolf, 'Menschwerdung des Menschen?', in *Peregrinatio* II, 1965, 119ff.

30. Thus H. Plessner, *Lachen und Weinen*, [3]1961, 42ff.

31. G. W. F. Hegel, *Vorlesungen über die Beweise vom Dasein Gottes*, PhB 64, 70.

32. Thomas Aquinas, *Summa Theologica* I, q 2 a 3.

33. Blaise Pascal, *Pensées* 526 and 527: 'The knowledge of God without that of man's misery causes pride. The knowledge of man's misery without that of God causes despair. The knowledge of Jesus Christ constitutes the middle cause, because in him we find both God and our misery', Dent 1908, 143.

34. M. Luther, WA V, 128, 36.

35. Explanation of thesis 28. As a commentary see the novels of Dostoevsky and on them M. Doerne, *Gott und Mensch in Dostojewskijs Werk*, 1957.

36. Theism here primarily refers to that natural knowledge of God which is taken up by the Catholic and Protestant tradition in the article '*De Deo uno*', and then more generally to monotheistic philosophy in its political, moral and cosmological significance. See A. N. Whitehead, *Process and Reality*, 1960, 520: 'In the great formative period of theistic philosophy, which ended with the rise of Mohametanism, after a continuance coeval with civilization, three strains of thought emerge which, amid many variations in detail, respectively fashion God in the image of an imperial ruler, God in the image of a personification of moral energy, God in the image of an ultimate philosophical principle.'

37. Cf. the article '*De Deo uno*' in early Protestant dogmatics.
38. F. D. E. Schleiermacher, *The Christian Faith*, §50–55.
39. H. G. Geyer, op. cit., 270.
40. E. Jüngel, 'Vom Tod des lebendigen Gottes', *ZThK* 65, 1968, 106.
41. H. Küng, *Menschwerdung Gottes*, 626.
42. W. Elert, *Der Ausgang der altkirchlichen Christologie*, 1957, 74.
43. E. Peterson, 'Monotheismus als politisches Problem', in *Theologische Traktate*, 1951, 104: 'But the doctrine of the divine monarchy inevitably had to fail when confronted with trinitarian dogma and the interpretation of the *pax Augusta* by Christian eschatology.'
44. E. Jüngel, op. cit., 188f.
45. F. D. E. Schleiermacher, *The Christian Faith*, §8, 11.
46. H. R. Niebuhr, *Radical Monotheism and Western Culture*, Faber 1961.
47. J. Cardonnel, *Gott in Zukunft. Aufforderung zu einer menschlichen Welt*, 1969, 24. Cf. also Nietzsche's Zarathustra poem:

> Bend myself, twist myself, tortured
> By every eternal torment,
> Smitten
> By you, cruel huntsman,
> You unknown—God

(F. Nietzsche, *Thus Spoke Zarathustra*, translated by R. J. Hollingdale, Penguin Books 1961, 265.)
48. H.-G. Geyer, op. cit., 272.
49. E. Jüngel, op. cit., 115. Cf. also E. Jüngel, *Tod*, 1971, ch. VI: 'The death of death—death as an eternalization of lived life.'
50. K. Barth, *The Resurrection of the Dead*, Hodder and Stoughton 1933, 202: 'Without any doubt at all the words "resurrection of the dead" are, for him [Paul], nothing else than a paraphrase of the word "God". What else could the Easter gospel be except the gospel become perfectly concrete that God is the Lord? But a *necessary* paraphrase and concretion.'
51. Cf. F. Dostoevsky, *The House of the Dead*. On this M. Doerne rightly notes (op. cit., 35): 'Real faith in God is faith in the resurrection, indeed it is itself already a beginning of eternal life.'
52. On this see E. Jüngel, 'Die Welt als Möglichkeit und Wirklichkeit. Zum ontologischen Ansatz der Rechtfertigungslehre', *EvTh* 29, 1969, 417–22, who despite his justified theological criticism of Aristotle and E. Bloch, leaves out of account the mediation between 'the world as possibility' and the possibilities of world history. His critical observations about *Theology of Hope* do not therefore affect the mediations attempted there.
53. Quoted following M. Hornschuh, 'Acts of Andrew', in E. Hennecke–W. Schneemelcher–R. McL. Wilson, *New Testament Apocrypha* II, Lutterworth Press 1965, 418.
54. Thus D. Sölle, *Christ the Representative*, SCM Press 1967, 147.
55. A. Strindberg, *Ghosts*, act 3.
56. See G. Steiner, *Tolstoy or Dostoevsky. An Essay in the Old Criticism*, New York 1971, 334ff.
57. K. S Guthke, *Die Mythologie der entgötterten Welt*, 1971, shows

the negative theodicy in the satanology of the literature of the nineteenth century in a generous way. 'Where there are no gods, spirits rule' (Novalis); H. Gollwitzer, 'Der Einspruch des neuzeitlichen Atheismus gegen den christlichen Glauben im Namen der leidenden Kreatur', in *Krummes Holz—aufrechter Gang*, 1970, 373ff.

58. A. Camus, *The Rebel* (abridged translation), Hamish Hamilton 1953, 29.

59. A. Camus, *L'homme révolté*, 1951, 39f. (this and other passages cited from the French are not in the English translation).

60. H.-G. Geyer, op. cit., 270.

61. Alain, quoted in H. Urs von Balthasar, op. cit., 169.

62. M. Horkheimer, *Kritische Theorie* I, 374ff.; *Die Sehnsucht nach dem ganz Anderen*, 1970, 11.

63. M. Horkheimer, *Die Sehnsucht*, 36; *Kritische Theorie* I, 274.

64. M. Horkheimer, *Die Sehnsucht*, 40.

65. M. Horkheimer, ibid., 57.

66. Ibid., 69. T. W. Adorno, whose *Negative Dialektik*, 1966, represents an attempt to carry through the theory sketched out by Horkheimer, takes the idea of righteousness to the point of transcendence. 'What would not be affected by demythologizing, without placing itself at the disposal of apologetics, would not be an argument—whose sphere is quite simply antinomian—but the experience that thought which does not behead itself ends in transcendence, to the point of the idea of a conception of the world in which not only existing sorrow is done away with, but even that would be recalled which is past beyond recall' (393). Expressed in positive symbols, and therefore inappropriately, that would mean that perfect righteousness is impossible without the resurrection of the dead and indeed without their physical resurrection. Horkheimer's 'critical theory' and Adorno's 'negative dialectic' have an important theme in the contemporization of the Old Testament prohibition against images in reason. Both are critical of any dogmatism in reason in order to free true needs and impulses from the images, dogmas and concepts which keep them occupied. 'By a negation of the ideas of the resurrection of the dead, the last judgment and eternal life as dogmatic propositions, man's need for eternal happiness becomes quite manifest and contrasts with the evil conditions on earth' (*Kritische Theorie* I, 371). 'Good will, solidarity with misery and the struggle for a better world have cast off their religious garb' (ibid., 375). 'Anyone who believes in God cannot believe in him for that reason. The possibility for which the divine name stands is maintained by the one who does not believe. The prohibition of images once extended to the naming of the name, but in this form it has itself fallen under suspicion of being a superstition. It has become more acute: hope even only to think outrages it and works against it' (*Negative Dialektik*, 392). According to Adorno, materialism must be 'imageless'. 'The enlightening intention of thought, demythologizing, blots out the imagery of consciousness. What is caught up with a picture remains trapped in mythology, idolatry' (ibid., 203). 'The materialistic desire to understand a matter seeks the opposite: it would only be possible to think of the entire object

without images. Such a lack of imagery converges with the theological prohibition against images. Materialism secularized it by not allowing utopia to be painted in positive terms; that is the content of its negativity. It goes beyond theology, however, where it is at its most materialist. Its desire would be a resurrection of the flesh; it is quite alien to idealism, the kingdom of the absolute spirit' (ibid., 205). But Horkheimer already noted a certain 'metaphysical mourning' in the writings of the great materialists (*Kritische Theorie* I, 372). Has Adorno escaped it in 'negative dialectic'? Is the carrying out of the prohibition against images in thought a dream as impossible as it is necessary? Horkheimer and Adorno have gone furthest down this road which began in European philosophy with Bacon. If they do not fall into idolatry, but want to arrive at God's concern, Jewish and Christian theology also fall under the judgment of the prohibition of images. Its final fulfilment is part of Jewish messianic hopes and prayers. For Christian theology, the reality of the cross of Jesus, his physical suffering and death is the point where the prohibition of images is fulfilled and its fulfilment is sought by permanent criticism. Therefore the physical pain and death of Christ is regarded as the negative side of its symbolism of God, resurrection, judgment and eternal life. Theology which does not take up the truth of negative theology by knowledge of the cross can hardly become a theology of the crucified God. Here it must become 'materialistic'.

67. M. Horkheimer, *Die Sehnsucht*, 56f.

68. Ibid., 56. Similarly A. Camus, *L'homme révolté*, 84: 'From the moment that man subjects God to a moral judgment, he kills him in himself. But what becomes of the basis of morality then? Man denies God in the name of righteousness, but can he understand the idea of righteousness without the idea of God?'

69. M. Horkheimer, *Kritische Theorie* I, 372.

70. A. Camus, op. cit., 50f.

71. W. Elert, 'Die Theopaschitische Formel', *ThLZ* 75, 1950, 195ff.; id., *Der Ausgang der altkirchlichen Christologie*, 1957; A. Grillmeier, *Christ in Christian Tradition*, Mowbray ²1974; H. Küng, *Menschwerdung Gottes*, Exkurs II ('Can God suffer?'), 622ff.; H. Mühlen, *Die Veränderlichkeit Gottes als Horizont einer zukünftigen Christologie*, 1969; W. Pannenberg, 'The Appropriation of the Philosophical Concept of God as a Dogmatic Problem of Early Christian Theology', *Basic Questions in Theology* 2, SCM Press 1971, 119–83.

72. This soteriological trend in the doctrine of the two natures in the early church was overlooked in the liberal sketch of metaphysics, a sketch which has constantly been repeated since A. Ritschl, 'Theology and Metaphysics' (1881), in *Three Essays*, Philadelphia 1972. The consequence is a reduction of soteriology to morality, which finds a place in a christology which, as desired, is free from metaphysics.

73. W. Elert, op. cit., 110ff.

74. W. Elert, op. cit., 95.

75. Ibid.

76. H. Küng, op. cit., 634; H. Mühlen, op. cit., 16ff.

77. M. Löhrer, *Mysterium Salutis* II, 1967, 311ff., who rightly points

to the difference between the philosophical *immutabilitas Dei* and the biblically attested faithfulness of God; similarly H. Mühlen, op. cit., 28ff. Cf. also O. Weber, *Die Treue Gottes und die Kontinuität der menschlichen Existenz*, 1967, 99ff., 105: 'For according to the Bible God's being is not his absoluteness in itself but the permanence of his free relationship with the creature, the permanence of his mercy and faithfulness in election.' For the problems of the doctrine of predestination which arose out of the axiom of the *immutabilitas Dei*, cf. J. Moltmann, *Prädestination und Perseveranz*, 1961.

78. Cf. H. Küng, op. cit., 647ff.

79. Ibid., 652.

80. E. Brunner, *Das Ewige als Zukunft und Gegenwart*, 219ff., 221, remarks on the form of style of the negation of the negative, 'The negative is clear, and indicates that "the form of this world is passing away", that death, that transitoriness will be no more. But apart from whatever concerns the new being of man and humanity, the positive element remains almost completely indeterminate. Evidently we need only know one thing about it, that there will also be a "world" in eternity.' J. Moltmann, *Umkehr zur Zukunft*, 1970, 120ff., differs: here the negation of the negative is formulated in the historical anticipation of the eschatological positive, because only here does the experience of the negativity of the negative emerge.

81. For what follows see E. Jüngel, 'Vom Tod des lebendigen Gottes', in *Unterwegs zur Sache*, 105ff.

82. See R. Schwarz, 'Gott ist Mensch. Zur Lehre von der Person Christi bei den Ockhamisten und bei Luther', *ZThK* 63, 1966, 289–351.

83. See G. Locher, *Die Theologie H. Zwinglis im Lichte seiner Christologie* I, 1952; E. Jüngel, op. cit., 112. O. Weber, *Grundlagen der Dogmatik* II, 1962, 687ff., gives a full account of Zwingli's christology in the framework of his doctrine of the eucharist and judges it fairly.

84. J. Moltmann, *Christoph Pezel und der Calvinismus in Bremen*, 1958, 66ff.; H. E. Weber, *Reformation, Orthodoxie und Rationalismus* I, 2, 1940, 123ff.; for Reformed christology, 131ff.; for the christology of the Lutherans, 150ff.

85. E. Jüngel, op. cit., 114, following R. Schwarz.

86. *Vom Abendmahl Christi, Bekenntnis*, BoA 3, 397.

87. WA 23, 141, 23. Cf. the generous article by E. Wolf, 'Die Christusverkündigung bei Luther', *Peregrinatio* I, 1954, 30–80, from which this reference is taken (56f.).

88. WA 39, II, 93ff.

89. First in J. Porst, *Geistliche und liebliche Lieder*, Berlin 1796, no. 114.

90. WA 50, 590, 19. Cf. also FC *Solid. decl.* VIII, 44.

91. E. Jüngel, op. cit., 125: 'In the event of the death of God, death is determined to become a phenomenon of God.'

92. K. Rahner, *Theological Investigations* IV, 79.

93. *Loci Communes* of 1521. English text in Wilhelm Pauck (ed.), *Melanchthon and Bucer*, Library of Christian Classics XIX, SCM Press 1969, 21f.

94. Cf. p. 66 above.

95. I. Kant, *Der Streit der Fakultäten*, A 50, 57.

96. F. D. E. Schleiermacher, *The Christian Faith*, §170, p. 738.

97. Ibid., §172, p. 747. He himself thought of a revival of Sabellianism. See M. Tetz, *F. Schleiermacher und die Trinitätslehre*, Texte zur Kirchen- und Theologiegeschichte, vol. II, 1969.

98. For the history of this formula cf. E. Jüngel, '*Quae supra nos, nihil ad nos*. Eine Kurzformel der Lehre vom verborgenen Gott — im Anschluss an Luther interpretiert', *EvTh* 32, 1972, 197–240.

99. K. Rahner, op. cit., 87ff.

100. Ibid., 96.

101. Op. cit., 152. On this see H. Mühlen, op. cit., 33, who also follows B. Steffen.

102. H. Urs von Balthasar, op. cit., 223: 'The scandal of the cross is tolerable for believers only as the action of the triune God, indeed it is the only thing in which the believer can boast.'

103. W. Popkes, Christus Traditus. *Eine Untersuchung zum Begriff der Dahingabe im Neuen Testament*, 1967, 286f.

104. Cf. on this G. Bornkamm, 'The Revelation of God's Wrath (Romans 1–3)', in *Early Christian Experience*, SCM Press 1969, 47–70.

105. H. Mühlen, op. cit., 32.

106. I have taken over this expression from H. Braun. According to his Greek understanding of God, God (more accurately, the divine) 'happens' where one man helps another. However, this can only be applied in a very loose way to the Christian understanding of the Holy Spirit and quickly succumbs to popular Ritschlianism.

107. Thus L. Feuerbach, *Das Wesen des Glaubens im Sinne Luthers*, ed. 1970, 2: 'Any lack in man is matched by a perfection in God: God is and has precisely those things which man is and has not. What is added to God is denied man, and conversely, what is allotted to man is removed from God . . . The less God is, the more is man; the less man is, the more is God.'

108. Thus rightly R. Weth, 'Heil im gekreuzigten Gott', *EvTh* 31, 1971, 227ff.

109. Cf. E. Peterson, *Monotheismus als politisches Problem*.

110. A. N. Whitehead, *Process and Reality*, New York 1960, 519f.

111. Ibid., 520.

112. Quoted after R. Weth, op. cit., 232. Cf. also E. Beyreuther, 'Christozentrismus und Trinitätsauffassung bei Zinzendorf', *EvTh* 21, 1961, 28–47.

113. M. Heidegger, 'Die Zeit des Weltbildes', in *Holzwege*, [3]1957, 69ff.

114. See R. Guardini, *Zu R. M. Rilkes Deutung des Daseins*, 1946, 21.

115. T. Altizer, *The Gospel of Christian Atheism*, Collins 1966.

116. See K. Löwith, *Die Hegelsche Linke*, 1962, 228: 'Atheism, that is, the surrender of a God who differs from man' (quotation from Feuerbach).

117. *Werke* II, 202, 419.

118. *Phenomenology of Mind*, 93.

119. *Philosophy of Religion*, III, 98.

120. Ibid., 99f.

121. A. N. Whitehead, op. cit., 532.

122. On this see S. M. Ogden, *The Reality of God*, SCM Press 1967, 59ff., 206ff.

123. J. Moltmann, *Theology of Hope*, SCM Press 1967, 16.

124. W. Pannenberg, 'Der Gott der Hoffnung', in *Ernst Bloch zu Ehren*, 1965, 209ff.; J. B. Metz, 'Gott vor Uns', ibid., 227ff.; J. Moltmann, 'Die Kategorie Novum in der christlichen Theologie', ibid., 243ff.; G. Sauter, *Zukunft und Verheissung*, 1965; U. Hedinger, *Hoffnung zwischen Kreuz und Reich*, 1968; E. Schillebeeckx, *God—The Future of Man*, New York 1969; K. Rahner, *Zur Theologie der Zukunft*, 1971; R. Alves, *A Theology of Human Hope*, Washington 1971; H. Cox, *On Not Leaving it to the Snake*, SCM Press 1967; G. O'Collins, *Man and his New Hopes*, New York 1969. For the theology of hope see C. Braaten, *The Future of God*, New York 1969; W. Capps, *Time invades the Cathedral. Tensions in the School of Hope*, New York 1972; B. Mondin, *I teologi della Speranza*, 1970.

125. Thus in the message of the Fourth Assembly of the World Council of Churches, Uppsala 1968. See Kenneth Slack, *Uppsala Report*, SCM Press 1968, vii: 'We ask you, trusting in God's renewing power, to join in these anticipations of God's Kingdom, showing now something of the newness which Christ will complete.'

126. J. Moltmann, op. cit., 129; W. Pannenberg, op. cit., 224; E. Käsemann, *New Testament Questions of Today*, 133; P. Stuhlmacher, *Gerechtigkeit Gottes bei Paulus*, 208; D. Sölle, *Christ the Representative*, SCM Press 1967, 107ff.

127. *Joannis Calvini in Novum Testamentum commentarii*, ed. A. Tholuck, vol. V, 1864, 226ff. See H. Quistorp, *Die letzten Dinge im Zeugnis Calvins*, 1941, 166ff.; T. F. Torrance, *Kingdom and Church. A Study in the Theology of the Reformation*, 1956, 90ff.: 'The Eschatology of Hope: John Calvin'; P. van Buren, *Christ in our Place. The Substitutionary Character of Calvin's Doctrine of Reconciliation*, Oliver and Boyd 1954.

128. This recalls the saying which about 1600 was directed, in Latin, against the king of Poland, Sigismund III: *rex regnat sed non gubernat*, and which then emerged again in France in the nineteenth century. C. Schmitt has used it for his political theology. Cf. *Politische Theologie*, [2]1934; *Politische Theologie* II, 1970, 52ff.: 'Le roi règne, mais il ne gouverne pas.'

129. Quotation in H. Quistorp, op. cit., 172.

130. CR 79, 339: 'When it is said that Jesus Christ has a sovereign name and is the image of God, his Father, this is because of our dumbness and weakness; the same is true when he is called God's lieutenant.'

131. Ibid.

132. On I Cor. 15.28, op. cit., 230: '*Impediunt enim quodammodo, ne Deus in se ipso nobis recta nunc appareat. Deus autem per se ipsum tunc et absque medio, coeli et terrae gubernacula tenens, omnia erit in hac parte: et tandem consequenter in omnibus non tantum personis, sed etiam creaturis.*'

133. On I. Cor. 15.24, op. cit., 227: '*Quin etiam tum in coelo principatus*

angelici, tum in Ecclesia cessabunt ministeria et praefecturae: ut solus Deus per se ipsum, non per hominum vel angelorum manus potestatem suam principatumque exerceat.'

134. On I Cor. 15.27, op. cit., 229f.: '*Tunc autem restituet Christus, quod accepit regnum, ut perfecte adhaereamus Deo. Neque hoc modo regnum a se abdicabit, sed ab humanitate sua ad gloriosam divinitatem quodammodo traducet: quia tunc patebit accessus, quo nunc infirmitas nostra arcet. Sic ergo Christus subiicietur Patri: quia tunc remoto velo palam cernemus Deum in sua majestate regnantem: neque amplius media erit Christi humanitas, quae nos ab ulteriore Dei conspectu cohibeat.*'

135. Thus H. Quistorp, op. cit., 175: 'But we should not take Calvin here to the point of absurdity. There remains in him a contradiction, the contradiction between his tendency to spiritualism—which here brings him near to docetic christology, and his biblical realism.'

136. I am restricting myself here to his German work *Gestaltwerdung Christi in der Welt. Über das Verhältnis von Kirche und Kultur*, 1956. His fundamental thought emerges very clearly here; those writings of his which have not been translated deal much more subtly with the specific question of christology.

137. Ibid., 18: 'The real subject of the Bible is the vision of human society which is instituted in accordance with the basis of righteousness and love. Jesus Christ came and offered himself as a sacrifice for the sake of this life of the community and of society. This is the only way of understanding the gospel in Israelite, rather than in gnostic terms.'

138. Ibid., 24.

139. Ibid., 24.

140. Ibid., 34. Ruler's thesis 'God in Christ is an emergency measure' (34) follows from his radical Anselmianism. He distinguishes the Anabaptist idea from this: 'In the special revelation we are not given a *recreatio*, a recreation, but a *nova creatio*, a new creation ... It is the fundamental notion of *diastasis* which prevails here' (33). He also rejects the Roman Catholic idea of synthesis: 'The creation itself is divided into nature and supernature. Supernature was lost at the fall. In the special revelation, in Jesus Christ, supernature is again added to nature ... Roman Catholic Christianization of culture has this supernatural intent' (34).

141. Ibid., 35. Thus for van Ruler, Paul, Irenaeus, Augustine, Barth and the traditions which follow them come near to what he calls 'baptist' solutions, for they all saw in the Christ event and in grace a superabundance of new being not only over against the deficiency of sin but also against the first creation and the initial freedom of men which contained the possibility of sin.

142. This is the main thesis of her book *Christ the Representative*, SCM Press 1967, 94. Against this see H. Gollwitzer, *Von der Stellvertretung Gottes. Christlicher Glaube in der Erfahrung der Verborgenheit Gottes*, 1967.

143. D. Sölle, *Christ the Representative*, 94, 96, 143.

144. See W. Schrage, *Göttinger Predigtmeditationen* 20, 1/1965, 35: 'Equality with God follows from being a child of God.'

145. For Zinzendorf, Paul's talk of handing of the kingdom to the Father was a heresy for which Paul was severely punished, according to II Cor. 12. For this conception threatens the whole idea of the Bible and is an 'accursed doctrine of the devil', because it says 'that the Father is more than the Son'. Against this, Zinzendorf asserted, 'Once the Saviour begins to reign he will never hand over the kingdom, but will rule and govern the whole creation for ever.' Cf. E. Beyreuther, 'Christozentrismus und Trinitätsauffassung bei Zinzendorf', *EvTh* 21, 1961, 28f.

146. E. Käsemann, *New Testament Questions of Today*, 133. For W. Pannenberg, 'The doctrine of the Trinity is the seal of the pure futurity of God, which does not harden into an impotent diastasis, a mere beyond contrasting with man's present, but which instead draws it into itself and through enduring the pain of the negative reconciles it with itself.' The basis of the *homoousion* of Jesus with God is that Jesus directed men away from himself entirely and towards the coming rule of the Father. In so doing he proved himself to be the Son of the Father. 'The difference between what is presently extant and the future of God and his lordship shows up in the personal relationship of Jesus to the Father' (*Basic Questions in Theology* 2, 249). But do these remarks go beyond an eschatologically orientated economic Trinity which then dissolves in the eschaton? The eschatological difference between what is present to hand and the future of God is in fact a difference in the 'history of God' itself, but only a trinitarian reflection which penetrates more profoundly can discover in it more than an eschatologically vanishing difference, in demonstrating that here God shows himself to be the Father of the Son.

147. Thus J. Moltmann, *Theology and Joy*, SCM Press 1973, 47ff., and E. Jüngel, *Unterwegs zur Sache*, 1972, 7. Cf. also the question which has been discussed time and again in the history of theology: would the Son of God have become man if the human race had remained without sin? J. Müller's work of the same name, written in 1870, now appears in *Christologische Texte aus der Vermittlungstheologie des 19. Jahrhunderts*, Texte zur Kirchen- und Theologiegeschichte, ed. J. Wirsching, 1968, 39–80.

148. On this see M. Pohlenz, *Vom Zorne Gottes. Eine Studie über den Einfluss der griechischen Philosophie auf das alte Christentum*, 1909; J. K. Mozley, *The Impassibility of God*, Cambridge University Press 1926; E. F. Micka, *The Problem of Divine Anger in Arnobius and Lactantius*, 1943; T. Rüther, *Die sittliche Forderung der Apatheia in den beiden ersten christlichen Jahrhunderten und bei Klemens Alexandrinus*, 1949; J. Woltmann, 'Απαθὴς ἔπαθεν *Apathie als metaphysisches Axiom und ethisches. Ideal und das Problem der Passion Christi in der Alten Kirche*, Erlangen Dissertation 1972.

149. J. Woltmann, 'Der geschichtliche Hintergrund der Lehre Markions vom "fremden Gott" ', in *Wegzeichen. Festgabe für H.M. Biedermann*, 1971, 23f.

150. *Philebus* 60c: 'That whatever living being possesses the good always, altogether, and in all ways, has no further need of anything, but is perfectly sufficient.'

151. Aristotle, *Magna Moralia* II, 1208b.
152. Aristotle, *Metaphysics* XII, 1073 a 11.
153. Quoted by Woltmann, op. cit., 26.
154. T. Rüther, op. cit., 11ff.
155. Ibid., 17ff.
156. Gregory Thaumaturgus occupies a special position in that for him God's inability to suffer becomes a suffering for suffering and is shown in its conquest. God's sharing in suffering is not a *pathos* in the Greek sense. Cf. V. Ryssel, *Gregor Thaumaturgos. Sein Leben und seine Schriften*, 1880, and U. W. Knorr, 'Gregor der Wundertäter als Missionar', *EMZ* 110, 1966, 70–84, esp. 76.
157. A. Heschel, *The Prophets*, New York 1962.
158. However, there are also beginnings in this direction in Islam, as has been shown by H. Corbin, 'Sympathie et Theopathie chez les Fidèles d'amour en Islam', *Eranos* XXIV, 1956, 199–301. There was agreement at one moment in the new dialogue between Christians and Muslims when Shi'iten declared that in their traditional belief in the sovereign God they did not find the God who suffers and therefore were not finished with the problem of suffering. Cf. H. J. Margull, *Dialog mit anderen Religionen*, 1972, 87.
159. Ibid., 252.
160. Spinoza, *Ethics* V, XVII.
161. Heschel, op. cit., 277.
162. Ibid., 209ff.
163. Ibid., 307ff.
164. Cf. E. Peterson, 'Der Gottesfreund', *ZKG* 42, 1923, 172ff.
165. P. Kuhn, *Gottes Selbsterniedrigung in der Theologie der Rabbinen*, 1968.
166. Ibid., 89.
167. Ibid., 90.
168. E. Wiesel, *Night*, 1969, 75f.
169. This is probably what D. Bonhoeffer meant when he said, 'God is beyond in the midst of our life ... but Christ takes hold of a man at the centre of his life' (*Letters and Papers from Prison*, The Enlarged Edition, SCM Press 1971, 282, 337).
170. D. Bonhoeffer, op. cit., 361: 'The Bible directs man to God's powerlessness and suffering; only the suffering God can help ... Man is summoned to share in God's sufferings at the hands of a godless world ... It is not the religious act that makes the Christian, but participation in the sufferings of God in the secular life. It is allowing oneself to be caught up into the messianic suffering of God in Jesus Christ.' Similarly, too, D. Sölle, *Christ the Representative*, 150ff.

7

WAYS TOWARDS THE PSYCHOLOGICAL
LIBERATION OF MAN

1. *Psychological Hermeneutics of Liberation*

As man develops his pattern of life in relation to the divinity of his God, we must now ask: who is man in the face of the rejected Son of Man who was raised up in the freedom of God? How does he develop his life in the field of force of the passion of the crucified God? 'Christ is the end of the law,' declares Paul (Rom. 10.4). What does that mean for the liberation of man?

If we attempt to draw out the consequences of the theology of the crucified God for anthropology, we cannot remain within the monologue of a theological anthropology, but have to enter into dialogue with other images of man. If we are attempting to track down the liberation of man and point to its traces, the first step is inevitably a dialogue with the anthropological science which is itself concerned with the therapy of sick men. Above all, this is a matter of the *psychoanalysis* of *Sigmund Freud*. Theological conversation with Freud has really got under way only in the last decades. A discussion of Freud's criticism of religion is therefore important for a critical theology. Of course this dialogue is only an extract from the many-layered pattern of Christian anthropology today, open to the world as it must necessarily be. It can therefore lay no claim to completeness. But it did seem more important to present the consequences of the theology of the cross at one point than to keep to abstract generalizations.[1]

Anyone who follows Paul in speaking of the freedom of the sons of God in faith in Christ must also seek out and present this freedom in specific psychological and political terms. He cannot restrict himself to making correct theological statements about what it must mean in the theological circle of true faith;

he must present his remarks in a specific controversy with general psychological phenomena of religion, particular pathological phenomena and therapeutic attempts at freeing men from psychological compulsions. Otherwise the freedom of faith would be discussed only in the freedom of theological reflection, and not as a new liveliness in the twilight of repressions and obsessions. What is needed here is therefore a *psychological hermeneutics* of the word of the cross, the spirit of freedom and the history of God. Psychological hermeneutics is an interpretation and not a reduction. Like *political hermeneutics*, it is a translation of the theological language of liberation for a particular sphere and into a particular dimension of life. As human life is complex and is lived at the same time in a number of spheres and dimensions, a number of hermeneutical processes are necessary. There is no one hermeneutical key and no one hermeneutical key experience. The process of translation involves various fields of experience and practice. It has to be adapted to a variety of different relationships, circumstances and patterns of practice and language. This does not mean that theology is dissolved into psychology; rather, Christian language should show its particular character in this area of experience and practice. Otherwise it would be of no interest to psychology. Theologians who go over to psychology and give up theology are no longer partners in conversation. Unfortunately they often corrupt psychology with their repressed and unconscious theological expectations of the substitute. None of the 'substance' of faith is lost in a psychological hermeneutics of faith. Rather, it gains a new dimension of its incarnation and enters into the utter this-worldliness of life as it is lived and obstructed.[2]

Christian theology thinks traditionally in terms of a dialectic of *law and freedom*. A psychological hermeneutics discovers points of correspondence between this theological dialectic and pathological phenomena and therapeutic processes. It therefore has to translate the theological dialectic on to the specific level of psychoanalysis and psychotherapy and reflect on it there. In so doing, it arrives at specific points, as at corrections and alterations, when it sees the man who is mentally ill in the situation of the crucified God and seeks his healing and his liberation in the free area opened up by this God. The theology of Paul and the Reformation speaks of the liberation of man by faith from the *obsession of works*. Psychological hermeneutics discovers a point of correspondence to this *obsession* in the *obsessive ideas* and *actions* of sick people and seeks how they may be freed for love and for unconstrained sympathy with life. In Rom. 7.7–11 Paul spoke of his imprisonment in the *vicious circle of sin, the law and death*: 'Apart from the law sin lies dead. But when the commandment came, sin revived and I died; the very commandment which promised life proved to be death to me. For sin, finding opportunity in the commandment, deceived me and by it killed me.' Sin and the law urge each other on and bring men to death. This is the diabolical strategy of evil: it takes the law, with which men fight against evil, into its regime and ensnares the man who obeys the law even more deeply in evil. He observes the law through fear of sin, but in so doing he only produces more and larger sins. He then takes up rigorous legalism, and this makes the evil even stronger. Even the best that he does serves evil. So this vicious circle of sin and the law results in man's death. It becomes a syndrome of decay (E. Fromm). Though hardly anyone today believes in a personal devil, many people speak, in a variety of spheres of life, of vicious circles, of the vicious circles of poverty, of violence, of alienation, of industrial pollution, of the vicious circles of the black, the immigrant worker, the prisoner, the mentally ill. What does it mean? There are clearly systems of a psychological, social and political nature which have become *fatal legalistic patterns*. They are vicious circles in which even the best leads to what is worse. They are therefore inescapable and without hope. They are processes of negative feedback in which orientation on life shifts over to become orientation on death. From a medical point of view, death is such a vicious circle, which has a negative effect on the basic relationships between the breathing, the brain, the heart and the circulation of the blood. 'This process leads to death only when the process of negative feedback can run its full course. But that means that any interruption of the vicious circle puts a check to dying.'[3]

It is easy to recognize the structural analogy between the vicious circle of sin, the law and death of which Paul and many theologians after him, including Augustine and Luther, spoke, and the processes of negative feedback among the dying, the imprisoned, the exploited and the oppressed. But how can liberation from the vicious circle of sin and the law by faith be introduced into these limited psychological, social and political situations, and what points of correspondence are there? How can it be experienced and practised in these situations? Here *the freedom of faith* must be developed into *freedom of experience and action*, and where this is possible, it is involved in competition and co-operation with other therapies and movements of liberation. In what follows we shall use the analytical and illuminative concepts of the law, compulsion and the vicious circle for the psychological and political hermeneutics of the Christian situation before God, in order to find corresponding processes and perspectives for liberation. Faith in the resurrection becomes faith that raises up, wherever it transforms psychological and social systems, so that instead of being oriented on death they are oriented on life. The prayer of Jesus, 'And deliver us from evil', is experienced and put into practice where men are liberated from these vicious circles, where the will to life is restored, and man comes out of the *rigor mortis* of apathy and regains his life once more.

2. *Patterns of the Dialogue between Theology and Psychoanalysis*

Sigmund Freud developed psychoanalysis in the therapy of sick individuals. But as time went on, he became more interested in the socio-psychological and cultural conditioning of illnesses. Although he was very careful in transferring the patterns of individual illnesses to society, he kept their determining conditions under constant investigation. This caution is less detectable in his followers like N. O. Brown, H. Marcuse and E. Fromm.[4] Their analysis of society with the help of the patterns of individual illnesses often float off into the clouds of speculation and no longer have any therapeutic effect. Here is a limit to psychotherapy which must be observed if a non-verifiable metapsychology is to be avoided: the analysis often demonstrates the sickness of society by the example of the sick man, but therapy can only begin with the individual. This does not make it superfluous, as sick people cannot be comforted with the promise of a future healing of the whole of society. But therapy must be aware of this limit to its potentiality, in which psychological vicious circles are bound up with vicious circles in society and in politics. The transference of patterns of individual illnesses to society as a whole is no more meaningful than the transference of a critique of society to an individual case. The dimensions are different. They condition each other reciprocally in a complex way. They can only be reduced to one another in rare cases. As in most historical contexts, monocausal derivations are nonsense.

Freud never entered into serious discussion with the theology of the theologians of his time.[5] His critique of religion is directed at 'the external forms of religion' and at 'what the common man understands by religion'. He was interested in religious rules, rites and symbols and their psychological functions; that is, in religious forms at the point of intersection of the individual and of society. The religious experiences of his patients were limited to the Victorian religion of the Vienna of his time and to the bourgeois world of the nineteenth century. But his own religious problems extended beyond this to the 'Mosaic religion', as it was called at that time, of his family and of Judaism. So he was fascinated by the figure of Moses from tradition, in the form of Michelangelo's statue in San Pietro in Vincoli, and at the level of his own inner feeling of guilt, which made him speak of the 'murdered prophet'.[6] He was increasingly more restrained towards the Christian religion, because he felt that he could not understand it. But Freud discovered pathological forms of private religion which occur among many men who have been influenced by Judaism and Christianity and indeed beyond that. His critique of religion was kindled by his interest in healing and liberation.

There are a number of different patterns in the conversation between psychotherapy and theology:

(*a*) Christian faith can identify itself with what Freud has criticized as 'religion' or 'the caricature of a religion'. In that case he is regarded as the 'worst enemy of religion' after Marx, a position which he occasionally accorded himself. But a Christianity which identifies itself with religion as it is attacked and criticized in this way has surrendered its own critique of religion. The best apologetic course for an equivalent religious theology would be not to reject Freud as irreligious but to demonstrate in its critique of religion the very religious implicates which he himself criticized. If his theory is itself conditioned by religion, it does not lead to the dissolution of religion at the hands of reason, but represents a dislocation of the religious element. This form of apologetic counter-criticism, which seeks to demonstrate the repressions of religious thought to irreligious thought, has today evidently been taken over by positivism. It occurs only rarely in theology. Just as H. Albert and E. Topitsch accused the Frankfurt school and their 'critical theory' of 'quasi-theological thought'[7]—not without a degree of truth—so D. Wyss has remarked about Marx and Freud:

It cannot be coincidence that Marx and Freud were familiar with the genesis of the Old Testament . . . In both, the suppression of religion and its statements about a violent, mythical beginning and a Utopian end . . . seems to emerge again in the characteristic religious elements of mythical conceptions and stereotyped thought-patterns which cannot, however, be verified in scientific terms. It is a 'return of what has been repressed'. Here the atheists Marx and Freud become the victims of their own repressions.[8]

The criticism of religion finds difficulty in escaping the categorical drive of its subject-matter. Theologians who feel that they have to defend the Christian religion against Freud, and positivists who want to get rid of both religion and the criticism of religion, should, however, recognize that Freud did not identify religion with neurosis. He simply saw neurosis as a 'caricature of religion', in the same way as he called hysteria a caricature of art and paranoia a caricature of philosophy.[9] It is therefore more appropriate to take up Freud's criticism in a positive way, in order to free faith from the caricatures of its pathological doubles which appear in superstition.

(*b*) If it is to be Christian, Christian faith must constantly make a distinction between its own forms of religion and its particular nature, and do so in a self-critical way. In that case faith is not the same thing as religion, but often has the same relationship to bourgeois religion and private religion as Yahweh to the Baalim, as the crucified Christ to the 'princes of this world', as the living God to the idols of anxiety. In the service of this distinction, Christian theology can adopt Marx's criticism of religion in order to detach the fellowship of Christ from the bourgeois-capitalist fetishism of gold and consumer goods, and can adopt Freud's criticism of religion in order to detach liberating faith from the religious superstition of the heart. In that case this criticism of religion is taken up as *aqua fortis* in order to bring out the gold of true faith from the dross of religion which has been through the fires of criticism. This is the way in which Karl Barth distinguished between faith and religion at the time of dialectical theology: 'Religion is unbelief, superstition and idolatry.'[10] P. Ricoeur, G. Crespy and R. de Pury follow him in this and use Freud as a bulldozer to clear the way for the gospel.[11] The gospel and the criticism of religion combine to kill the 'God' whom men bring into the world.[12] In fact this constellation of 'faith against religion' has a biblical predecessor in the prophetic criticism of religion, and above all in the Christian worship of the Christ who was crucified as a blasphemer. On the other side, Enlightenment criticism of idols from the time of Bacon has had its basis in the impact of the Old Testament prohibition against images.[13] The prohibition against making images and likenesses, bowing down to them and worshipping them, is meant to protect the freedom of God and the freedom of his image in every man. This freedom is lost where the prejudices of tradition or the fixed ideas of ideology hold man's understanding captive. It is lost where men worship their own works and bow themselves down to their own creatures, and where the objects that they have made gain power over them. The illumination of prejudices is therefore a liberation from the tutelage of tradition. The illumination of alienated conditions of work is liberation from the slavery that they impose. The illumination of psychological complexes, repressions and illusions corresponds to these movements towards freedom through iconoclasm.

(c) It is theologically legitimate to accept Freud's criticism of religion as a negation of the negative in order to present a true positive, but a mere distinction between faith and its caricatures in public and private religion often leads to no more than the non-observance and repression of these religious phenomena. In order to overcome them it is necessary to have understood them. It is not enough to ascribe such neurotic phenomena of religion to the devil, while combating them by keeping close to Jesus. It is also necessary to discover why man is evidently so 'incurably religious' (as Berdyaev supposed) that he cannot exist without certain obsessive actions and ideas, without 'something to which he can cling', and still remain sane. In fact, obsessions protect some patients from psychosis and the loss of reality. There are psychological pattern formations which stylize positive and negative experiences. The narcissistic pattern formation offers both protection and danger, by accommodating the unavoidable positive and negative idealizations, which derive from the early phase and are primarily concrete, in a 'world of symbols', that is, in ideas in which we believe.[14] This ambivalence of psychological formations should not be shattered in a senseless burst of iconoclasm.

That would bring no healing to the patient; it would make the iconoclasm a fatal obsession.

An attempt to mediate between the elements of truth in the two patterns would suggest that it would first be meaningful to 'accept Freud's criticism of religion as an attempt to extend the human conditions of understanding to the dimensions of the unconscious, to adopt it and to understand his psychoanalysis as a "method of finding meaning" '.[15] But in that case we must ask how the man who is possessed by drives and illusions and has therefore become apathetic can be made free in the situation of the crucified God and develop his humanity. Freud's criticism of religion should do more than help Christian faith to a better and more critical understanding of itself. His psychoanalysis must also show it the psychological barriers on which it can exercise its liberating power. The *homo sympatheticus* should be brought into the field of force of the *pathos* of God and the suffering of Christ, where pattern formations condemn man to a life of apathy.

3. *The Law of Repression*

About the year 1907, Freud became aware of the parallel between the obsessional actions of neurotics and the rituals of religious practice.[16] The neurotic patient is inclined to submit himself to a private ritual in order to unburden himself of sorrow, pressure or anxiety. For him there are particular times which call for special observance. There are places and objects which provoke either anxiety or obsessional observance. There are special actions which must be performed again and again if the patient is not to fall into a state of panic anxiety. Granted, he is not aware of the significance of such actions, but he needs them to survive. Freud described this obsessional neurosis as the 'caricature of a private religion' and investigated the hidden significance of the obsessional actions in unconscious motivations. It emerged that psychological pattern formations like obsessional washing, obsessional needs for assurance and attention, certain phobias and the like help the patient to soothe and damp down an intolerable feeling of guilt for emotional impulses of a libidinous nature. From this parallel, Freud drew the conclusion that the psychological rituals evidently help the neurotic individual in the same way as public religion has contributed at various times to the general government of society and its members by solving the problem of guilt or, better, offering the possibility of survival in face of the fatal pressures of guilt-ridden anxiety. He further remarked that the disappearance of a public religion of a generally binding character had contributed to an increase in the number of neurotics and their caricature of a private religion. Religion no longer makes its former contribution as a public ritual and symbol, namely compelling the renunciation of socially shameful impulses by a universal feeling of guilt and at the same time providing the possibility of shedding the burden of guilty anxiety. But feelings of guilt and the drives that are suppressed by these feelings are still there, and the man who is tortured by both produces neurotic private religions in order to survive. However, he no longer finds the compensation of shedding his burden in rituals of expiation.

These parallels observed by Freud can be interpreted in a number of ways.

(*a*) The neurotic regulations are without conscious significance for those who are subject to them. But public religious actions have a symbolic significance. Only when those who believe in public religion cease to ask after the significance of religious actions and symbols, and no longer understand them, do unburdenings become alienations. The symbols then become idols and the rituals become obsessional actions. Religion then assumes the features of a universal compulsive neurosis. It then becomes a caricature of itself and produces sick men. The critical statement 'religion is a universal obsessional neurosis' is true in this case.

(*b*) Conversely, however, Freud believed that the motives which compel religious observances are mostly fundamentally unknown to participants and are represented by pretended theological motives. True, he notes that in religion there have always been and still are 'occasional reforms' which restore the original context of meaning, but mostly the opposite is the case, that the unconscious motives are dominant. Religion which has become ossified in ritual and alienated from its real meaning can then be regarded in accordance with the standard of individual patterns of illness as a 'collective obsessional neurosis', as a 'neurosis of mankind', and often as 'mass hysteria'.

(*c*) Once public religion becomes a caricature of itself and can no longer contribute a meaningful restraint to impulses, it no longer brings man to maturity and no longer socializes him. It then acquires regressive functions. Freud long asked himself whether the universally widespread feeling of guilt and the anxiety of men were a basic datum of human existence or whether they had been evoked by religious education in childhood. In the second instance, religion would offer itself as a cure for the very illness which it had itself produced. He did not come to a final decision on this question. Nor can it be decided as long as the necessary verification cannot be produced by a religionless society which communicates psychological health on all sides. Both theses therefore remain primarily postulates, and can only be verified in terms of their therapeutic force. In negative terms, religion can eternalize the guilt of anxiety conditioned by history and society, but the thesis that religion has only a historical basis can also make men superficial and banal. However, that religion with its morality, its rituals and its symbols can find itself in the morass of regression is an important observation. In this function of religion Freud saw a 'regressive renewal of the infantile powers of protection' and came to the conclusion that in psychological terms the personal God is 'no more than an exalted father'. Anyone who is religious spares himself from developing an individual neurosis, and therefore from a psychological perspective, religion is nothing but a 'universal obsessional neurosis'.[17]

In this connection, J. Scharfenberg has pointed to the inconsistency of modern society which, while declaring adult religion to be a 'private matter', at the same time tenaciously holds on to the religious education of children.[18] The result is a schizophrenic consciousness: adult consciousness emancipates itself from children's religion, but the latter continues to have an unconscious affect on it. This leads to infantile religious conceptions among adults, and in many people to an intellectual marathon struggle against them. By baptizing infants, the churches produce the very problems and aggressions which they come up against in adults. Religious conceptions do not mature with men, and maturity is often achieved in the repression of these childish beliefs.

The real problem in neurotic pattern formations and in the alienated religion of idols and ossified rituals seems to me to lie not in the various attempts at explanation and derivation, but in the effect of this religion on man. Where the anxiety of guilt is suppressed, no matter what the cause of it may be, and where men flee to rituals and idols in order to be rid of the burden of ⋀grief, the result is apathy, insensitivity, the fixation of life in ⎣obsessional repetitions. The law of repressions reduces the liveliness of a man. He cannot accept the particular experiences of the anxiety of guilt, and so he builds up defence systems in which he encloses himself and which increasingly constrict his psyche. With images he builds a wall between himself and his intolerable experiences. He builds up a system with obsessional ritual actions in which he thinks he is unassailable. In this way he wants to survive. However, this costs him the liveliness of his life. The psychological and religious pattern formations are quite ambivalent: they guarantee protection and relief from pressure and to this extent work for him, but they also work for the anxiety of guilt and strengthen its pressure, making anxiety omnipresent. Thus they function simultaneously both for the survival of the patient and for his death. This can be seen above all in the way in which the repression of intolerable grief makes the patient increasingly apathetic. He becomes incapable of sorrow, incapable of loving others; his interest in his surroundings diminishes, because it is directed only towards repulsing the threat against him. The neurotic system may be called a vicious circle: it is meant to protect life and yet it destroys it. Everything that the neurotic man does in accordance with the law of repressions only leads him deeper into his neurosis. Here the apathy that sets in is often an anticipation in spiritual death of his real death.

There are similar manifestations in the *religion of anxiety*. Men who have not found their freedom in the humanity of God but, for whatever reason, feel anxiety at this God and the freedom that is expected of them, cling to the law of repressions. They then expect eternal support from things which offer no support. They hope for the absolute from relative values and eternal joy from transitory happiness. Instead of resolving conflicts, they construct aggressive images of enmity and make their enemies into demons in order to kill them spiritually. But because man knows at heart that in so doing he is making excessive demands of things, other men and himself, his anxiety remains. He has to suppress this anxiety by keeping his idols, images of his enemies and laws alive through constant repetitions of the same confessional formulae and rituals. At this point his life becomes ossified. He loses his openness for new experiences and becomes apathetic. The man who has not yet arrived at his humanity, the immature man who refuses maturity because of oppressive childhood experiences—and, because the process of maturing can never be regarded as complete, in the end this means every man—always makes himself idols and values which for him become identical with his own self, because he makes his existence dependent on them. He therefore regards attacks on his highest values as attacks on himself and reacts with fatal aggressiveness. He makes idols, to which he enslaves himself and without which he cannot live at a certain stage of his development without inner collapse. He needs them for his spiritual equilibrium. These were once the gods of power, fertility and man's own group: Moloch, Baal, Astarte, Amon and others. These today are the deities of fatherland, race, class, profit, consumption or anti-social attitudes.[19] But these are also objects, laws and rites of the Christian religion, which are used in this way by individuals and certain groups and are consequently misused. If objects from man's environment are divinized, they are made something which is said to exist independent of man, and are regarded as being more important and higher than he. These idolized realities are not there for his sake, but rather man is there to sustain these idols and laws. He sacrifices himself and others to them and is exploited and sacrificed by them.

There is no threat to man which arouses more hostility than to threaten his idols or those of his group. As long as a man identifies himself with such idols, he is not in a position to affirm himself as a free man while recognizing that the life of others may be different. He loves only what is like, and only acknowledges people who believe, think, love and do the things that he does. People like himself support him, and he needs this support to suppress his anxiety. People who differ from him disturb him, because they question his idols and laws and thus his world. So he loves only those who are like him, and hates other men. This is an important motive for xenophobia, antisemitism, racial hatred, the persecution of Communists and Christians and other manifestations of aggression. Love only for those who are like oneself is narcissistic. The religion of anxiety runs straight through all the public religions that we know. It also runs straight through the ideologies and institutions that we have. It is a widespread phenomenon.

The pattern formations of repression and the idols and laws of the religion of anxiety may not either suffer or die, since they have been erected against suffering and dying. They must be omnipotent and eternal, because they are meant to help impotent and mortal man and to relieve his anxiety. Anyone who damages the idols and laws, damages the holiest goods of those who worship them. But the crucified God renounces these privileges of an idol. He breaks the spell of the super-ego which men lay upon him because they need this self-protection. In humbling himself and becoming flesh, he does not accept the laws of this world, but takes up suffering, anxious man into his situation. In becoming weak, impotent, vulnerable and mortal, he frees man from the quest for powerful idols and protective compulsions and makes him ready to accept his humanity, his freedom and his mortality. In the situation of the human God the pattern formations of repressions become unnecessary. The limitations of apathy fall away. Man can open himself to suffering and to love. In *sympatheia* with the *pathos* of God he becomes open to what is other and new. The symbols which show him the situation of the human and crucified God give him protection as a result of which he can allow his own self-protection to fall. The hindrances of repression are not done away with through the ignorance of grief, anxiety and guilt. That would only be a further repression and would make man even more apathetic. They are done away with through sympathy and love, through the acceptance of what is otherwise unacceptable, through the ability to suffer, and through sensitiveness. When we speak positively here of suffering, we mean in general being affected by something else.[20]

4. *The Law of Parricide*

At a very early stage, Freud took up the historical-philosophical thesis of the Enlightenment that ontogenesis can be regarded as the repetition of phylogenesis.[21] The development of the child repeats in analogous fashion the development of humanity, so that it is possible to make inferences from one genesis to the other. The past Beyond of the mythical conception of the world recurs in the present Beyond of the unconscious activity of the soul. Metaphysics and the psychology of the unconscious correspond with each other. Freud used this thesis—leaving aside whether it is tenable or not—to clarify two observations: (*a*) the infantile religion of the exalted father which leads to neurosis is accompanied by rebellion against this super-ego; (*b*) during a holiday in the Tirol he saw the crucifixes which are called 'Lord Gods' there. This Christian fusion of the Father and the crucified Christ seemed to Freud to rest on the religious need for the depotentiation of the Father. 'Thus the Oedipus complex became the central problem of the "Lord Gods" of the Tirol for him.'

Freud applied the Oedipus complex as an interpretation of these events in the child's soul and in religion. True, it derives from ancient tragedy and therefore hardly allows modern, optimistic therapeutic conclusions to be drawn, but it is a good interpretation of the ambivalence of spiritual and religious systems. The feelings which tie a child to its father are both positive and negative at the same time. The longing for the protection given by the father is bound up with anxiety at his superiority. The positive feelings lead to identification with the father and internalize his authority in the super-ego. The negative feelings, however, give this super-ego despotic features. Freud further drew conclusions from neurotic animal phobias in children to totemistic religions. Here an animal is regarded as sacred and yet is sacrificed once a year and solemnly eaten. Freud found that this totem animal is a sub-stitionary offering for the father. It is worshipped and sacrificed so that the worshippers may acquire its power.

Following Darwin, Freud spoke of a powerful, prehistoric primal horde father. He prohibited his sons to possess their mother, that is, he castrated them and did not allow them to become potent. Even if the mother allowed it, the sons would become fathers only through the grace of the father. This is what makes the Oedipus situation so inextricable. Therefore the sons rise up against the father and kill him. But the recollection of this primal guilt remains, and so they attempt to incorporate the father into their expiatory cult. 'Totem religion emerged from the sons' awareness of guilt as an attempt to relieve this feeling and to reconcile the injured father through subsequent obedience . . . It makes it a duty to repeat the crime of parricide again and again in the sacrifice of the totem animal.'[22] Freud's mythology at this point is remarkable. He later told his critics that it was 'just a story'. Certainly he himself thought that it was impossible to derive 'something so complicated as religion from a single origin'.

Nevertheless, he allowed himself the generalization that all religions are fundamentally no more than attempts to solve the one problem which has arisen through feelings of guilt towards the primal Father. In Christianity he saw the sacrificial death of Christ as one such way of easing the primal feeling of guilt: 'He went and offered up his life, and by doing so delivered the host of his brothers from original sin.' Even the Christian eucharist is understood from a totemistic perspective as a 'renewed abolition of the Father, a repetition of the deed that has to be expiated'.

Every child of a patriarchal society goes ontogenetically through the same conflicts. It has to go through an intensive phase of ambivalent feelings towards the authority of the father, and then becomes a father itself. If phylogenesis begins with a revolution of brothers against the primal father, ontogenetically this revolution become the permanent drive of history, since it repeats itself in the conflicts between generations and authorities at any period. This permanent revolution of history gives rise to the constantly repeated experience of parricide in the dream by which men unburden themselves of real conflicts, in other words, in religion. If this revolution is again transposed to reality, there arises an eternal return of the same thing. According to this epigenetic principle, sons turn into fathers and continue the Oedipal circle from generation to generation. Thus many critics have supposed that Freud had a cyclical and ahistoric view of history: 'Running cyclically between rebellion, a feeling of guilt and renewed repression; ahistoric, as history is merely an environment for death.'[23] In fact, as his constant resort to the ancient symbols of tragedy shows, Freud did not have such confidence in progress as did the bourgeois nineteenth century. He stood under the impact of guilt which 'must continue to bring forth evil'. He persevered in depicting man's 'innate tendency to evil, to aggression, to destruction and thus to gruesomeness', even when he knew that the 'dear little children' were not pleased to hear what he said.

The model used by Freud for the father-son conflict and also for the ambivalent feelings in all theistic patriarchal religions derives from tragedy and has fatalistic features. Freud's principles in the early period are called 'Logos and Ananke'. He later said 'Eros and Ananke': 'healing through love', but through love on the ground of the reality of Ananke. One might ask why Freud did not use the biblical story of the Fall, which he knew, as a symbolic interpretation of primal guilt.[24] It speaks in essentially differentiated terms of guilt as self-divinization, of a reprieve in the punishment, and only after that of the fratricide of Cain and of his reprieve. This is no expression of tragic fatalism, for the dominant factor here is not Ananke, but the *pathos* of God, which maintains an abiding interest in the humanity of man. It is therefore simultaneously a history of guilt and hope.

The interpretation of the anxiety of guilt by means of the Oedipus story in essentials makes parricide the law according to which we have advanced. Iconoclasm against the authority of the father thus easily becomes an obsessional action. Just as Ananke is dumb and blind and cannot be influenced, so the man subjected to her, with an obsession about excluding his father from his life if he is to come to himself, is correspondingly unfeeling. He must do expiation and gain reconciliation in dreams and ritual repetitions. 'Healing through love' presupposes both liberation from the authority of the father and liberation from parricide, its repetitions and expiations. But can one add love and Ananke? Must one not seek a love which breaks even through Ananke?

Christian faith does not find itself in the situation of a despotic divine paternal authority which is both desired as a protective force and hated as a divine privilege. It finds itself in the situation of the *pathos* of God and brotherhood with the crucified Christ. But at the same time it in fact lives in particular religions based on authority and atonement, whose Oedipal structure Freud has aptly analysed. It follows from this that Christian faith must first cleanse its churches from the idols and taboos, the conceptions of authority and atonement which derive from Oedipal religion, if it is to extend its free situation in the *pathos* of God. In particular, it must cleanse the symbol of the cross from the Oedipal motives which have been painted over it. It must set the obsessional authoritarian and legalistic structures of church practice in the situation of the human God, and thus show them to be superfluous. For the problem of guilt in particular, that means that it is necessary to break through the eternal compulsion to repeat guilt and expiation by the recognition that guilt has been overcome 'once and for all' by God on the cross and that the obsessions of guilt have been shattered 'once and for all', so that men are no longer subject to them and that there is no need to repeat expiation. Finally, it means that Christian faith can separate itself from those father religions which depend on the images of Jupiter, Caesar and other fathers of the fatherland or the family.[25] In one respect Freud had a correct view of the crucified 'Lord Gods' of the Tirol when he interpreted them in his way. For the 'Lord God' was never the 'Father God'. Matthias Claudius once said that when he prayed the Lord's Prayer he always thought of his physical father. But the 'Lord Gods' in the Tirol compel one to think of the career of Jesus and what happened on the cross in connection with the Father of Jesus Christ. It is not the same father in the two places. The unknown Father of Jesus Christ has nothing to do with those idols of the father which lead to the Oedipus complex. The crucified Christ makes earthly fathers and earthly sons alike sons of God and brings them in community to the freedom which lies beyond the Oedipus complex. In origin Christianity is not a father-religion; if it is a religion at all it is a son-religion, namely a brotherly community in the situation of the human God, without privileges and without the rebellions that are necessary against them.[26] The parricide and blasphemer is out for annihilation and therefore falls into apathy. He rebels against the restrictions laid down by the authority of the father, but his rebellion does not free him from being a mirror image of his adversary. In the Oedipus conflict he remains clamped to his opponent.

For Christian faith the crucified Christ stands between the slaughtered God and his apathetic, witless slaughterers. The conflict between guilt and anxiety, between guilty liberation and necessary reconciliation, between authority and annihilation, is transferred to God himself. God allows himself to be humiliated and crucified in the Son, in order to free the oppressors and the oppressed from oppression and to open up to them the situation of free, sympathetic humanity. Knowledge and acceptance of the new situation extends God's freedom from the gods and antigods who produce the universal feeling of guilt and the need for compensation, right into the unconscious. Certainly the fathers and the parricides still dream in us. But if one can laugh at them, one need no longer repress them. They are still there, but they have lost their power. Freedom in faith can be described as a new spontaneity of the heart. But it only emerges when the emotions of anxiety and hate have been overcome and man emerges from his Oedipal situation.

5. *The Principle of Illusion*

In the course of his interpretation of dreams, Freud arrived at the view that the motive force of dreams was wish-fulfilment.[27] Dreams are attempts 'to overcome the world of the senses in which we are placed, by means of the world of our wishes'. Suppressed wishes and desires seek their fulfilment in dreams. He here arrived at a fundamental anthropological alternative: either men remain dependent on the *pleasure principle* and rooted in the prevalence of their wishes, or they mature into accepting the *reality principle* and come to terms with reality. The way to maturity is the way from the pleasure principle to the reality principle. It follows for an assessment of religion that religions cherish in their myths and utopias the 'oldest, strongest, most urgent wishes of mankind'. 'The secret of their strength is the strength of these wishes.' The analogy between infantile and religious wishes is evident. Religion has grown out of man's childish helplessness and need. Its content can be understood from the continuation of the wishes and needs of childhood into mature life. In the realm of religion all appears to be as we desire it. Anyone who adheres to this religious principle of illusion remains infantile, and through his refusal of reality tends towards neurosis. At this point Freud emphatically demands: 'Man cannot remain a child for ever.' Experience teaches us: 'The world is no kindergarten.' Therefore 'education for reality' is necessary. If a man is to live in this world, in the 'common world', he must inexorably give up the infantile dream world which has grown out of his desires. He must cease to interpret this world in terms of the world of his infantile wishes and desires.

Two conclusions follow from this for religion: religion must either renounce any interpretation of this world and transfer its kingdom to a quite other world or it must allow itself to come to terms with reality. In the second instance, the way from illusion to reality means withdrawing expectations from the Beyond of a dream world and concentrating all the powers that become free in this way on earthly life. This way would correspond to that of Feuerbach, and make men 'students of this world' instead of 'candidates of the Beyond', those who work instead of those who pray. Other-worldly religion would be transformed into this-worldly revolution. For Freud, however, no this-worldly utopia takes the place of the Beyond of wish-fulfilments. He knew well that on the way to the reality principle 'not all dreams blossom', and that almost all wither. To this degree there is still too much bad religion in revolutionary utopianism. For Freud, 'wise resignation' takes the place of religion and utopia. With this the mature man enters upon reality and accepts its conditions and limitations. 'The plan of creation does not provide for man's being happy.' Furthermore, the 'extraordinary progress of the natural sciences has not elevated the mass above the satisfaction of pleasure.' This is also true of human life in today's affluent society. Freud regarded even the progressive humanization of man and his relationships to be 'most probably a utopian hope'. He was too conscious of the deep-seated gruesomeness of man to agree with the optimists of his time. Certainly, he too hoped that 'all the energies which are now consumed in the production of neurotic symptoms in the service of a fantasy world isolated from reality . . . will help to strengthen the cry for those changes in our culture in which we can alone expect salvation for posterity.' But this hope was not very great. Freud persisted, rather, in an attitude which might be called resigned boldness or bold resignation. For him there was only one religious attitude of transcendence which can exist alongside the principle of reality, and that is the humour or the wisdom of Koheleth.

If it is true that faith can learn something from psycho-analysis about its own pathological double and thus also learn something about itself, it must illuminate its own wishes and hopes. Conversely, if psycho-analysis seeks to learn something from the power of faith, it must work for the overcoming of the unsatisfactory resignation which Freud put in the place of infantile illusions.

A hope which has been consolidated as illusion need not necessarily contradict reality. Its only characteristic is its basis in human wishes. Wherever it speaks of salvation, religion in fact has to do with elementary human wishes and hopes. It therefore also has to do with those wishes which derive from the child's primal trust and helplessness. But is it enough in attempting to achieve maturity for man, to move from the pleasure principle to the reality principle and to come to terms with unfulfilled hopes through wise resignation? Is not even wise resignation a renunciation of those hopes and therefore conditioned by their disappointment? Is man to show his maturity in being resigned and saturated,

albeit not without humour, being content with reality as it is?
Does not this resignation, for all its insight into reality and the
limits to human happiness, easily become the Stoic attitude of
apatheia? It no longer recalls any wishes and therefore no longer
has hopes for the future. How can it show sympathy and openness
for the wishes and the suffering of others?

'Do not despise the dreams of your youth,' says the Marquis
of Posa in Schiller's *Don Carlos*. Wishes and hopes can also mature
with men. They can lose their infantile form of drives and their
youthful enthusiasm without being given up. Freud interpreted
almost exclusively the dreams of ill people and the dreams that
made them ill. In them he found repressed childhood, unfulfilled
drives, incomplete experiences, forgotten wounds and disappoint-
ments. Therefore he saw in the work of dreams the regression by
means we return to the past that we have not mastered, in order
to work at it again. In this context, the work of psychology in
bringing to consciousness is the task of recalling the suppressed
past. The unconscious contains that of which one is no longer
aware. But in the adult culture at the end of the nineteenth century
in which Freud lived, such a return to phases of childhood
development was thought to be reprehensible, something that the
mature man should avoid. Today we regard such temporary periods
of regression as being not only useful but also enriching. They
enable us to relive various aspects of life with which otherwise we
would lose our relationship. They once again open up the present
to the past and make the past present. Then man does not run the
course of his life in a series of punctiliar presents which then
disappear, but collects himself for the full presence of his past
and present life. The surrender of the infantile phase and the
overcoming of the pleasure principle can easily lead the mature
man to apathy in respect of his youth. But that would not make
him richer, but poorer.

Ernst Bloch has criticized Freud's interpretation of dreams,
related as it is to the past, and countered the resigned reality
principle with a 'beyond the reality principle'.[28] Human wishes
are not only born from an inner helplessness; they are also
protentionally related to what is new. Their mode of time is the
future, and not just the return of what is lost. Human dreams are
concerned not only with regressive longing for the lost mother's
womb and for security, but at the same time with progressive

longing for freedom and curiosity over what is to come. Wishes and hopes represent a certain open sympathy on the part of man for the future, if they do not harden into caricatures and fixed ideas of the future. With a certain degree of simplification, one might say that in dreams by night man mostly returns to the past. But there are also day-dreams, and Aristotle called hope the 'dream of a waking man'. Dreams are ambivalent. What is articulated in them is not only that of which man is no longer aware but also that of which he is not yet aware, not only regressive but also utopian consciousness. Both affect each other reciprocally: recollection of early sorrow makes men dream beyond the present, and dreams of the future restore the memory of past happiness. If one were to analyse not only the dreams of neurotics at the nadirs of their illness but also the dreams of healthy people at the climactic experiences of their lives, one would probably come across this double presence of past and future.

Now Freud was concerned with overcoming the infantile pleasure principle with wise resignation over the constitution of the I, that is, with freedom. But it too is a utopia, though one which he thought was adequate to reality. Which reality? The basis of Freud's sense of reality will have lain not only in his strict morality but also in his estimation of death and the death-wish in men. He did not discover a future that overcomes death, and he did not trust the symbols of religion against the anxiety of death and the death-wish.

If we add Bloch's approach to Freud's interpretation of dreams, then religion itself is more ambivalent than Freud thought. It retains the infantile wishes of man and at the same time keeps his life open to the future. It contains both regressive and progressive elements. Along with man's memories, religion also preserves man's hopes. Here one must learn to make as neat a distinction as possible, so as not to put aside the caricatured healthy element along with the caricatures.

(*a*) Dream regressions into the world of infantile wishes can make men neurotic if they are bound up with a refusal of reality. But they can also enrich the sense of present reality in that they bring to consciousness not only the man of the moment but the whole man with all his life history. There is no present identity of a man without continuity with his past. Only then is a man present with all the strata of his life, for his childhood is a part of his present form. In that case, the free, unconstrained and un-repressed presence of the pleasure principle and the world of wishes is part of an existence which also includes childhood in itself. What is appropriate here is not wise resignation but open revision of infantile wishes. If a man develops himself in the *pathos* of God towards *sympatheia*, and *sympatheia* means openness, then in the situation of the crucified God man can develop openness backwards. There is no merely present or future authority before which he must separate himself from himself or deny his childhood. 'The infantile' is not a morally derogatory category.

(*b*) Utopian protensions into the utopia of the future can likewise lead to a denial of reality when the denial of reality fixes itself on utopian pictures of the future rather than on unacceptable suffering in the present of a man's own life or that of society. The incarnate hope of Christian belief must take care that its symbols are not used as idols and fetishes out of fear of suffering and refusal of the cross. Therefore it is necessary constantly to keep in mind the ground of human hope. It does not lie in disgust at and hate of the present, but in the situation of the crucified God, and is recognized by insight into the *pathos* of the loving and suffering God. The central symbol of Christian hope, the resurrection, is expressly related to the assumption of all human reality by God, including that reality which is spoilt by sin and condemned to death. It therefore represents a hope which is indissolubly coupled with the most intensive sense of reality. From this situation arises the freedom to abandon those apathetic pictures of the future with which past and present suffering is overplayed and compensated for, and in *sympatheia* to accept the suffering of God, in order to open oneself with the hopes of God to the future, and even to death. The fixated utopian is superstitious about the future. The apathic picture of the future makes him apathetic. In that case, day-dreaming in the field of force of God's passion corresponds to a free and human converse with the future. It follows from this that the dreams of the future which reckon with God's as yet unrealized possibilities do not contradict the reality principle and must not be destroyed by the transition to it. But the further the development of humanity goes in the situation of the *pathos* of God, and accepts the reality of suffering and death in love, the more even infantile wishes and dreams can mature with men. Enlightenment does not mean cynicism.

Maturity does not mean becoming an experienced, resigned or even cynical realist who merely smiles sympathetically at youth, his own at that of others. The enlightenment of wishes and hopes leads to enlightened and conscious wishes and hopes, not to a farewell from them. The word 'illusion' indeed has bad connotations, but literally it means becoming involved with the future, entertaining its possibilities in order to find what is worth realizing; and in Christian terms it also means playing with the possibilities in the history of God and developing into them. Prayers can be merely wish-projections born out of a refusal of reality. But they can also enter into the divine life in the situation of the passion of God and recall God, think with him. In that case, the openness of prayer is an openness in the history of God for the future of God. God's future is directed towards this openness in his history, for in theological terms it is the 'sighing of the spirit' which cries for fulfilment and consummation of the divine life in the world of the one who prays.

'Do not despise the dreams of your youth,' said Schiller. One would like to add: do not repress them and fix them in their infantile form, but work on them and with them and let them ripen with you! Openness to the future is conditioned by openness to the past. Constant faithfulness to hope is reciprocally bound up with faithfulness to the earth. Christian faith understands itself as faithfulness to hope as it is mindful of the resurrection of Christ, and as faithfulness to the earth as it is mindful of the cross of Christ. Because it leads man into this history of God, it frees him for an acceptance of human life which is capable of suffering and capable of love.

If man always develops his manhood in relationship to the Godhead of his God, this Godhead and consequently his manhood can take on very different appearances. Freud has shown how much the psychological pattern formations of repression, the Oedipus complex, narcissism and illusion correspond to religious systems and vice versa. These are two sides of the same coin. There are psychological and religious forms of straitened and hindered humanity, sick and on the way towards death. Their basic character seems to be apathy. There are situations of sick and oppressed humanity, and the element of sickness and oppression is expressed in these particular pattern formations which are meant to protect life from illness and oppression. If we understand

Christian faith as the development of a humanity that is capable of suffering and love in the situation of the passion of God, it will not be affected by the criticism of religion made by psycho-analysis. And if it is not affected by this criticism because it does not spread apathy in what is always the same, but on the contrary makes human apathy superfluous and destroys it by virtue of the passion of God, it is a partner in the attempt to liberate man from the gods and laws of repression, self-love, parricide and illusion. To free sick man from his psychological vicious circles it offers not only the critical rationality and ego-support which are often summoned up against the psychological strategies of evil, but also the new spontaneous liveliness which that critical rationality needs as the atmosphere in which it can develop freely. As is well known, the logic of the instincts differs from the logic of the understanding and is not always influenced by it. Therefore the logic of the understanding needs a corresponding level of instinct and feeling on which it can develop freely. It needs a barrier against anxiety and the threat of death on the level of the feelings also, that is, a love of life which brings intelligence to the understanding and orients it. These are fundamental decisions of the interest which make possible rationality and lead to the human use of rationality. On the level of the feelings and instincts man 'thinks' in notions and symbols. As is already shown by language, rational thought is directed for its freedom towards notions and symbols which do not constrict and fixate it, but open up free space for it. Rightly understood, the Christian symbolism which represents the situation of man in the passion of God, which wakens his remembrance and keeps alive his hope, cannot be a superstitious, dogmatistic and pathological pattern formation. It does not liberate an apathetic rationality of domination, but sympathetic reason. 'We know in so far as we love,' said Augustine, and in so doing made love the enabling ground for knowledge. The Christian symbolism of the situation of man in the *pathos* of God leads to the loving and suffering knowledge of man. It can therefore only take up the iconoclasm that is critical of religion and the psychotherapeutic liberation of man from his vicious circles and develop its own prophetic criticism of idolatry in parallel to that.

Any therapy is directed towards *health*. But health is a norm which changes with history and is conditioned by society. If in today's society health means 'the capability to work and the capability for enjoyment', as Freud could put it, and this concept of health even dominates psychotherapy, the Christian interpretation of the human situation must nevertheless also question the compulsive idolatry which the concepts of production and consumption introduce into this definition, and develop another form of humanity. Suffering in a superficial, activist, apathetic and therefore dehumanized society can be a sign of spiritual health. In this sense, we must agree with Freud's remark, 'As long as a man suffers, he can still achieve something.'[29]

NOTES

1. For other forms of Christian anthropology in present conflicts see J. Moltmann, *Mensch*, 1971.

2. For the psychological hermeneutics of faith see P. Ricoeur, *Freud and Philosophy: An Essay on Interpretation*, 1970. German text *Die Interpretation. Ein Versuch über Freud*, 1969, and J. Scharfenberg, *Religion zwischen Wahn und Wirklichkeit. Gesammelte Beiträge zur Korrelation von Psychoanalyse und Theologie*, 1972. For more recent psychology of religion see F. Meerwein, 'Neuere Überlegungen zur psychoanalytischen Religionspsychologie', *ZPMP* 17, 1971, 363–80.

3. H. Schaefer, 'Der natürliche Tod', in *Was ist der Tod?*, 1969, 20f., quoted following E. Jüngel, *Tod*, 1971, 31.

4. See N. O. Brown, *Life against Death*, Routledge and Kegan Paul 1959; H. Marcuse, *Eros and Civilization: Philosophical Inquiry into Freud*, Allen Lane: The Penguin Press 1969; E. Fromm, *The Heart of Man*, Routledge and Kegan Paul 1965.

5. J. Scharfenberg, *Sigmund Freud und seine Religionskritik als Herausforderung für den christlichen Glauben*, 1968, 137ff.

6. O. Mannoni, *Sigmund Freud*, 1971, 152ff.

7. H. Albert, *Traktat über kritische Vernunft*, 1968; E. Topitsch, *Die Sozialphilosophie Hegels als Heilslehre und Herrschaftideologie*, 1967.

8. D. Wyss, *Marx und Freud*, 1969, 58.

9. J. Scharfenberg, op. cit., 139.

10. K. Barth, *The Epistle to the Romans*, Oxford University Press 1933, deals with the limits, the meaning and the reality of religion in interpreting the vicious circles of sin, law and death in Rom. 7: 'Death is the meaning of religion' (253). 'Religion is the misfortune which every human being has to endure' (259). 'The reality of religion is man's dismay at what he is' (273).

11. P. Ricoeur, *Interpretation*, 555; R. de Pury, *Das Abenteuer der Freiheit. Sieben Meditationen über die Versuchung Jesu*, 1969.

12. Thus G. Crespy, quoted following R. de Pury, op. cit., 76f.: 'It is impossible for man to escape the urge to create religions. Clearly he can change his cultural perceptions, but religion lives on in and with the men who produce it. At least, that is the observation which Freud made in his

old age. So a concern to unveil this situation is like the efforts of Sisyphus. One would have to keep demonstrating with untiring wakefulness the attempts of religion at invasion through the Oedipus complex and then to annihilate its significance. In short, one would never have stopped killing God, and Nietzsche's cry: "God is dead and we have killed him!" would have to be taken up afresh in every generation ... Who can kill this God whom man brings into the world, and who can kill him so decisively that he never rises again?'

13. This has now been stressed again by C. Gremmels and W. Herrmann, *Vorurteil und Utopie. Zur Aufklärung der Theologie*, 1971.

14. I am grateful to Prof. Dr med. W. Loch of Tübingen, for this suggestion, and also for reading through the manuscript and offering friendly criticism.

15. Thus J. Scharfenberg in the books mentioned above, and W. Loch, 'Über die Zusammenhänge zwischen Partnerschaft, Struktur und Mythos', *Psyche* XXIII, 1969, 481–506.

16. Here I am following the account of Freud in J. Scharfenberg, *Sigmund Freud*, op. cit., 137ff. The Freud quotations come from his report.

17. J. Scharfenberg, op. cit., 140.

18. J. Scharfenberg, 'Zum Religionsbegriff S. Freuds', *EvTh* 30, 1970, 367ff.

19. E. Fromm has repeatedly pointed to the parallels between 'idolatry' and 'alienation'. Cf. *Die Revolution der Hoffnung. Für eine humanisierte Technik*, 1971, 146: 'The concept of alienation means the same thing as the biblical concept of idolatry.'

20. Cf. the unjustly forgotten study by F. J. J. Buytendijk, *Über den Schmerz*, 1948.

21. J. Scharfenberg, op. cit., 141.

22. Quoted by J. Scharfenberg, op. cit., 143.

23. D. Wyss, op. cit., 52. This remark is correct in so far as life progresses to death, but by maturity Freud meant the overcoming of the Oedipal return of the like.

24. Similarly one may ask why Freud applied the Narcissus myth to the diagnosis of sick self-love and not the Augustinian figure of *amor sui* or Luther's picture of the *homo incurvatus in se*. Both in fact mean the same thing, but do not stand in a tragic context.

25. See P. Ricoeur, *Interpretation*, 549ff., 562.

26. Thus J. Scharfenberg, following P. Ricoeur, op. cit., 161.

27. J. Scharfenberg, op. cit., 145ff.; P. Ricoeur, op. cit., 100ff.

28. E. Bloch, *Das Prinzip Hoffnung* I, 1959, 87ff.

29. S. Freud/Lou Andreas-Solome, *Briefwechsel*, 1966, 85.

8

WAYS TOWARDS THE POLITICAL
LIBERATION OF MANKIND

1. *Political Hermeneutics of Liberation*[1]

The psychological hermeneutics of life in the situation of the crucified God came up against a limit where psychological suffering becomes the suffering of society and suffering in society, and is determined by that. It therefore remains incomplete, if it is not supplemented by a corresponding political hermeneutics. What is meant by the contemporization of the crucified God in the political religions of society? In what dimensions must a human society develop in the free sphere of the history of this God? What are the economic, social and political consequences of the gospel of the Son of Man who was crucified as a 'rebel'? In the Reformation, the theology of cross was expounded as a criticism of the church; how can it now be realized as a criticism of society? If in the political trial of Jesus, the Caesar was the external reason for his end on the cross, how can the risen Christ become the internal reason for the end of Caesar?

If we attempt to draw the consequences of the theology of the cross for politics, the matter cannot be exhausted in general and abstract definitions of the relationship between church and state or dogmatic faith and political action. Concrete attention must be paid to religious problems of politics and to laws, compulsions and the vicious circles which for economic and social reasons constrict, oppress or make impossible the life of man and living humanity. The freedom of faith is lived out in political freedom. The freedom of faith therefore urges men on towards liberating actions, because it makes them painfully aware of suffering in situations of exploitation, oppression, alienation and captivity. The situation of the crucified God makes it clear that human situations where there is no freedom are vicious circles which must be broken through because they can be broken through in him. Those who take the way from freedom of faith to liberating action automatically find themselves co-operating with other freedom movements in God's history. Political hermeneutics calls especially for dialogue with socialist, democratic, humanistic and anti-racist movements. Political hermeneutics reflects the new situation of God in the inhuman situations of men, in order to break down the hierarchical relationships which deprive them of self-determination, and to help to develop their humanity. So there is need for critical solidarity with these movements; for solidarity with them in the struggle against the forms of in-humanity which threaten mankind; and for criticism and accept-ance of criticism of the aims and methods of liberation. Political hermeneutics of faith is not a reduction of the theology of the cross to a political ideology, but an interpretation of it in political discipleship. Political hermeneutics sets out to recognize the social and economic influences on theological institutions and languages, in order to bring their liberating content into the political dimension and to make them relevant towards really freeing men from their misery in certain vicious circles. Political hermeneutics asks not only what sense it makes to talk of God, but also what is the function of such talk and what effect it has. Even here, none of the so-called substance of faith is lost; rather, faith gains substance in its political incarnations and overcomes its un-Christian abstraction, which keeps it far from the present situation of the crucified God. Christian theology must be politi-cally clear whether it is disseminating faith or superstition.

Christian faith has hitherto made its political situation and function clear by means of two models: the model of unburdening and the model of correspondence. The *model of unburdening* says that church and faith must be freed from politics so that at the same time politics may be freed from religion.[2] The church relieves the state of the burden of religion and in so doing relieves religion of the burden of the state. The more unpolitical—in this critical sense—the church becomes, the more irreligious, secular and rationalist becomes the state. The more faith relieves reason of the enfleshed superstition of men, the more reasonable and realistic political reason becomes. This model is often misunderstood as a programme for the separation of church and state, faith and politics. Fundamentally, however, its concern is merely to make a proper distinction between what is always confused in political religion and religious politics. The distinction between the two realms which is constantly necessary in every new situation is thus not a-political, but to the highest degree a political-critical action. This distinction is directed against both the theological idea of a church state and against the political idea of a state church, against both theological politics and political theology in the old sense of the term. This model has an element of truth which must not be overlooked. But, as history shows, it is difficult to maintain the critical distinction of the two realms which has to be made in constantly new ways. There is a grave risk of the immediate separation of faith and reason as of church and state, followed by a *laissez-faire* addition of faith and the church to that form of political irrationality which declares itself to be rational, and to unjust and lawless forms of the state. The freedom experienced in faith and practised in the church can then coexist with any form of economic and social oppression. Furthermore, the freedom before God experienced in faith can be used as a substitute for the necessity of a real political liberation in the world. The latter is then often slandered as an apostasy from the righteousness of faith and as a righteousness achieved by works. Finally, if faith only has an indirect effect on the liberation of political reason for its supposed rationality, then no interests or criteria are offered for a use of reason which may be termed 'human' and 'rational'. What often happens is a theological blessing on positivist reason, a rationality of mere ways and means, and so-called 'real politics'. The model is fundamentally a transference of the old *potestas directa* of the church in politics into a *potestas indirecta*. The critical distinction of this model may be important, but it is of little help in the individual case when the decision is made. One can still be for or against the peasants in the German peasant war or for or against Nixon's policy in Vietnam, for in such cases what does 'reasonable' mean?

The *model of correspondence* presupposes the critical distinction between faith and politics mentioned above, but seeks to build a bridge from the realm of free faith and the liberated church into the realm of politics by means of correspondences, reflections and images.[3] The liberation of the believer from the prison of sin, law and death is brought about by God, not by politics, but this liberation calls for something to correspond to it in political life, so that liberations from the prisons of capitalism, racism and technocracy must be understood as parables of the freedom of faith. In this model a distinction is made between the 'great hope' of the gospel and the 'little hopes' which are necessary for the immediate future on earth.[4] A distinction is made between the 'last thing', which faith believes, and the 'next to the last thing', which faith does.[5] This distinction is not a quantitative but a qualitative one. God is God and man is man. So the gap can only be bridged by analogies from the side of God, the church and faith. This means that there can be no equations, but only parables; no unbroken continuity, but only continuity in discontinuity. But for that very reason, faith discovers these parables of the freedom of Christ and the kingdom of God not only in its own programmes and actions, but also in other movements in history. The kingdom of God can be socialism, but that does not mean that socialism is now the kingdom of God.[6] It can be regarded as a mirror and parable of the 'peace which is higher than all reason'. In the democratic movement the church can discover a parable of its own brotherly christocracy, and conversely offer itself in its order and ecumenical fellowship as a model for correspondences in social politics and international politics. This model, too, contains a grain of truth which is not to be forgotten. The critical distinction of what is qualitatively different remains without effect unless there are no correspondences. The model of parables and correspondences introduces faith in a liberating way into politically oppressed life, and at the same time preserves it from presumption and self-surrender. Nevertheless, the model of correspondence is often conceived in too hierarchical terms. In view of the qualitative difference between God and man, the correspondences go from above to below, and are often arbitrary. If the difference is transferred to the relationship between 'Christian community and civil community', the church is idealized so as to become the model of society. Its liberation is already presupposed, whereas in practice it only becomes free with the society in which it lives. If the difference is ultimately transferred to faith and action, faith easily comes to be understood as that powerful idea before which reality cannot hold out without adapting itself to it and corresponding to it. It would probably be more appropriate to history to regard these correspondences not as parables of what is perfect, but as anticipations and promises in the process of realization, in which the ultimate announces itself in the penultimate and the unconditional in the conditioned.[7] The identity and difference of God and man, of kingdom of God and the history of liberation, would then be associated dialectically. It is the history of the crucified Christ which binds together God and man and distinguishes one from the other. What God has really put together in Christ, no man should idealistically put asunder.

The models of unburdening and correspondence have been worked out to such a degree that they can only be introduced into the human history of God's liberation with difficulty. Both leave freedom in action in the realm of the possible and the arbitrary. They understand the Christian event of liberation in general terms first and only then look for 'concretions' of the abstract. To make a correct distinction between God and the world, the absolute and the relative, the last things and the things before the last is one thing. To look for what corresponds to God in the world, to the last things in the things before the last, to the great hope in the lesser hopes, is something else. But must we not go beyond that and from the start understand God *in* the world, the beyond *in* the this-worldly, the universal *in* the concrete and eschatology *in* the historical, in order to arrive at a political hermeneutics of the crucified Christ and a theology of real liberations?[8] That would lead beyond difference and parable in thought and language to a synecdochic understanding of the 'explosive', liberating presences of God in the extremities of inhuman misery. In that case we would have to understand the incarnations and anticipations of the presence of God in a history of 'transformations of God'. That would lead beyond difference and parable to a perception of God's identifications in history. The criterion of perception would be the identification of God with the crucified Christ. The horizon of perception would then be the kingdom of the perfected indwelling of God in the new creation, that is, the consummation of the trinitarian process of God in history. History is the 'sacrament' of Christian ethics, not just its material.

2. *Political Religion*

When Christian theology reflects on its political dimensions, it always finds this realm already occupied by political religions and political theologies, in which political interests dominate religion, theology and the churches.[9] Unless Christian theology frees itself from the needs and demands of the prevalent political religions, there can be no liberating theology. And on the other hand, without Christian criticism of religion, there can be no liberation of man in society.

From the beginning, Christian faith has had to struggle with the political religions of the societies in which it has been expanding. The Stoa distinguished three classes of divine figure: natural forces represented as divine persons, the gods of state religion and the gods of myth. Accordingly, they distinguished three forms of theology: the metaphysical theology of the philosophers, the political theology of the statesmen and the mythical theology of the poets.[10] Political theology teaches society which gods should be recognized because of the state and by which symbols and rites they should be reverenced. Because according to the doctrine of the state in antiquity it is the supreme purpose of the state to show due honour to the gods of the fatherland, so that they for their part bring the blessings of prosperity and peace to the country, the citizens were bound together with the aid of common religion. Religion became the supreme bond of society. The old and persistent trilogy of religion, authority and tradition comes from the political religion of Rome.[11] These are the symbols of the power which secures the existing state of affairs against chaos. Christians who no longer took part in the state cult in those societies of antiquity were regarded as 'atheists' and 'enemies of the human race'.[12] Their omission to observe the practices of the religious cult of the state made them guilty of the *crimen laesae religionis*. In martyrdom they followed their Lord, executed as a 'blasphemer' and 'enemy of the state'. However, when Christianity was elevated to the rank of a state religion by the legislation of the Christian emperors Theodosius and Justinian (*religio licita*), the charge of political atheism was shifted to Jews, pagans and heretics. This shows the political character of religion and also the inescapably political character of Christian belief.

From the time of Constantine and the Christianization of Europe Christianity has taken over the role of the political religion of society. It has indeed Christianized the existing state religions, but as a counter-move has been politicized in accordance with the standards of the reasons of state which have obtained at various times.

Remnants of this form of Christian state religion and popular
religion still survive. This is shown by the history of the blasphemy
paragraphs in penal legislation from the Carolina of 1532 down to
present penal law reform in Germany. It is further shown by the
theonomous justification for the death penalty, which has been
put forward again and again, and the religious roots of expiatory
penal law.[13] The political religion of society also keeps coming
into the foreground in the sphere of Christian religious education
which enjoys the protection of the state. Religion is to be integrated
into the needs of the prevailing society and is for its part to
contribute to social integration.[14]

The formation of new civic religions can also come about where
there is a democratic separation of church and state. These take
on different appearances depending on the history and structure
of a society. The nationalism of the nineteenth century evoked
patriotic religions which cultivated their own symbols, sacrifices
and altars. National acts of remembrance and festivals, school
books and presidential speeches were cultivated by these national
religions, as they contributed to the symbolic and ritual integration
of the different groups of peoples and classes and helped to rouse
them in case of conflict. There are also political religions of
imperialism, of the 'pre-eminence of white Christian civilization',
of capitalism, and unfortunately also of socialism. Imperialistic
religions are completely monotheistic, in order to lend religious
support to the central authority. Patriotic religions are for the
most part polytheistic, because each fatherland has its especial
gods. In socialism the political religions tend towards pantheistic
materialism. Capitalism in turn displays primitive forms of
fetishism, involving gold and possessions. As bearers of the
religions of society, the Christian churches are constantly subject
to one or other form of religion. When they regard themselves as
being either unpolitical or apolitical, this is only because of the
blindness which their social position inflicts on them.

Jean-Jacques Rousseau gave a classic analysis of the form of
réligion civile.[15] He distinguishes between the religion of man and
the religion of the citizen. He finds the former in Christianity,
which did not come into being as a national religion. It consists
in inward worship of the supreme God and the simple teachings
of the gospel of Jesus. For him, that is the true faith and the
divine law of nature. The second is limited to a country and gives

it its special gods and protectors. Every service performed for the fatherland is a sacrifice offered to the tutelary deity. There are also dogmas in the positive religion of the citizen. They are simple, few in number, expressed in definite terms and need no explanation. Like social life itself, they must be 'self-explanatory'. Rousseau names four: 1. the existence of the Almighty; 2. all-embracing providence; 3. a future life; 4. reward for the good and punishment for the godless. These are not really religious doctrines but general views; unless they are observed, a man can be neither a good citizen nor a true subject. Rousseau thought that it could be proved that there had never been a state which was not based on this kind of religion. He also recognized that little conflicted with the social spirit of this religion more than Christianity. Christianity did not come into being as a national religion and therefore cannot be one. It does not bind the hearts of citizens to the state, but lures them away from it. It separates the theological system from the political system and disquiets the people. This is why the pagans always regarded Christians as 'real rebels'. Rousseau therefore held the true religion of the gospel to be an ideal, but believed that it was politically impracticable and even dangerous. So he located the 'religion of the citizen' only in the social contract, and left the 'religion of man' free from the individual within the framework of whatever laws were valid.

More recent sociology of religion has taken up Rousseau's basic idea of a socially necessary civic religion.[16] It can point to equivalent state Shintos in capitalist and socialist societies. It shows how the established Christian churches are functionally adapted to the civil religion of a particular time. We will not therefore be far wrong in assuming that modern societies, too, need and produce political religions—if not with the help of the established churches, then without or against them. This produces a dilemma for political theology: the more the churches become departments of bourgeois religion, the more strongly they must suppress recollection of the political trial of Christ and lose their identity as Christian churches, for recollection of it endangers their religio-political relevance. However, if they retreat from the social theme of 'bourgeois religion', they become irrelevant sects on the boundary of society and abandon their place for others. The path of a theology of the cross that is critical of society goes between irrelevant Christian identity and social relevance without Christian identity. It must make the idols of bourgeois religion superfluous in their own place and destroy them. In place of the ritual integration of a people, a race or a class and its confirmation of itself as a symbol, it must develop openness for the recognition of others and a humanity that is free from anxiety and self-esteem. To make present one who was once crucified in the name of bourgeois religion means to replace bourgeois religion in a society with the churches as institutions which freely criticize society,[17] and which in this way are dysfunctional to themselves. This happens in theory through criticism of idols, taboos, hostile caricatures and self-justifications in political religion, and in practice in support for those 'others' who have become the victims of the political religions which are dominant at any particular time.

3. *Political Theology of the Cross*

Early Christianity was persecuted as godless and hostile to the state by both the Roman authorities and by pagan philosophers. Christian apologists were therefore all the more zealously concerned to rob these charges of their force and to present the Christian religion as the religion which truly sustained the state. Even before Constantine, and then explicitly in the imperial theology of Eusebius of Caesarea, a Christian-imperial political theology was developed. It was meant to secure the authority of the Christian emperor and the spiritual unity of the empire. It consisted of two basic ideas, one hierarchical and the other with a chiliastic philosophy of history. The authority of the emperor was secured by the idea of unity: one God—one Logos—one Nomos—one emperor—one church—one empire. His Christian empire was welcomed in chiliastic terms as the Christ's promised kingdom of peace. The *Pax Christi* and the *Pax Romana* were to be bound together by the *providentia Dei*. In this way Christianity became the unitive religion of the unitary Roman state. Recollection of the fate of the crucified Christ and his followers retreated into the background. As often happens in history, the persecuted became the rulers. E. Peterson and H. Berkhof have shown[18] how this first attempt at a Christian political theology shattered on the power of Christian faith itself, at two points in theology and at one in practice. Politico-religious monotheism was overcome by the development of the doctrine of the Trinity in the concept of

325

God. The mystery of the Trinity is to be found only in God, and not by reflection, in creation. In the doctrine of the Trinity Christian theology describes the essential unity of God the Father with the incarnate, crucified Son in the Holy Spirit. So this concept of God cannot be used to develop the religious background to a divine emperor. The identification of the *Pax Romana* with the *Pax Christi* shatters on eschatology. No emperor can guarantee that peace of God which is past all understanding; only Christ can do this. The political consequence is a struggle for the freedom and independence of the church from the Christian emperor. Trinitarian theologians like Athanasius and Lucifer of Cagliari thus incurred banishment and persecution.

According to E. Peterson, with the development of the doctrine of the Trinity, eschatology and the struggle for the freedom of the church in the Christian state, Christian theology made a fundamental break with all political religion and its ideology in political theology. Christian faith can no longer be misused to justify a political situation.[19] The theological and politico-religious systems are fundamentally separate.

The new 'political theology' and 'political hermeneutics' presuppose the early church's criticism of the political theology of political religions. But they become more radical when they seek to reclaim from the biblical tradition the awareness of a trial between the eschatological message of Jesus and social and political reality.

Salvation, the object of the Christian faith in hope, is not private salvation. Its proclamation forced Jesus into a mortal conflict with the public powers of his time ... This 'publicness' cannot be retracted nor dissolved, nor can it be attenuated ... *Every eschatological theology*, therefore, must become a political theology, that is, a (socio-) critical theology.[20]

Christian theology which wants to be aware of the present political restraints on and functions of its language, rites, institutions and practice will therefore do well to recall the political crucifixion and divine resurrection of the Christ who was executed as a 'rebel' and the consequence of discipleship. The memory of the passion and resurrection of Christ is at the same time both dangerous and liberating. It endangers a church which is adapted to the religious politics of its time and brings it into fellowship with the sufferers of its time. It frees the church from politico-religious church politics for a critical Christian political theology.

The new political theology is not concerned with the dissolution of the church into left-wing or right-wing politics, but with the Christianization of its political situation and function in terms of the freedom of Christ.

Christian theology has continually interpreted in soteriological terms the history of the Christ who was condemned in the name of the law, and in his exaltation by God brings to an end the law and the demands made on men by the law: man is not made righteous before God by works of the law, but by God's grace in faith. Faith brings liberation from the compulsion of works. But a theological interpretation of the political dimension of the crucifixion and resurrection of Jesus is absent. Because it has been assimilated to the state, the church has left this dimension unexplained. Now the death of Christ was the death of a political offender. According to the scale of social values of the time, crucifixion was dishonour and shame. If this crucified man has been raised from the dead and exalted to be the Christ of God, then what public opinion holds to be lowliest, what the state has determined to be disgraceful, is changed into what is supreme.[21] In that case, the glory of God does not shine on the crowns of the mighty, but on the face of the crucified Christ. The authority of God is then no longer represented directly by those in high positions, the powerful and the rich, but by the outcast Son of Man, who died between two wretches. The rule and the kingdom of God are no longer reflected in political rule and world kingdoms, but in the service of Christ, who humiliated himself to the point of death on the cross.

The consequence for Christian theology is that it must adopt a critical attitude towards political religions in society and in the churches. The political theology of the cross must liberate the state from the political service of idols and must liberate men from political alienation and loss of rights. It must seek to demythologize state and society. It must prepare for the revolution of all values which is involved in the exaltation of the crucified Christ, in the demolition of relationships of political domination. Now political representations and master-slave relationships continually arise when a people is capable of action in the medium of history. The citizen surrenders the right of self-determination to his representatives, so that they may act for him. This process of unburdening in political action is associated with the alienation of those who are relieved of their burdens. 'In representative institutions there is always subjection to a visible image, and that is idolatry.'[22] Political idolatry and political alienation arise when the representatives go over the heads of those whom they are meant to represent, and when the people bows to its own rulers. Alienation between government and people is then shown in an all-embracing apathy of the people towards those 'up there'. Because the representatives are out of their control, the citizens lapse into a passivity which allows further misuse of power to go unhindered. The democratic movement has clearly seen the connection between political idolatry, with the consequent apathy of its subjects, and the deprivation of political rights. 'Democracy has no monuments. It mints no medals. It does not bear a man's head on its coins. Its true nature is iconoclasm.'[23] If the nature of democracy is political iconoclasm, its reality lies in the demolition of master-slave relationships, in the limitation and control of the political exercise of power, and in activating the people from their apathy as subjects towards responsible participation in the processes of political decision.

If the Christ of God was executed in the name of the politico-religious authorities of his time, then for the believer the higher justification of these and similar authorities is removed. In that case political rule can only be justified 'from below'. Wherever Christianity extends, the idea of the state changes. Political rule is no longer accepted as God-given, but is understood as a task the fulfilment of which must be constantly justified. The theory of the state is no longer assertive thought, but justifying and critical thought.[24] The early church rejected the cult of the emperor and replaced it with prayer for the emperor which represented a limitation of his power. The Middle Ages and the Reformation relativized political ordinances so that they became necessary ordinances in the world, which served the well-being of people but not their salvation. Puritanism abolished the feudal system and replaced it by the covenant or the constitution of the free citizen.[25] A critical political theology today must take this course of desacralization, relativization and democratization. If the churches become 'institutions for the free criticism of society', they must necessarily overcome not only private idolatry but also political idolatry, and extend human freedom in the situation of the crucified God not only in the overcoming of systems of psycho-

logical apathy, but also in the overcoming of the mystique of
political and religious systems of rule which make men apathetic.
Christianity did not arise as a national or a class religion. As a
dominant religion of rulers it must deny its origin in the crucified
Christ and lose its identity. The crucified God is in fact a stateless
and classless God. But that does not mean that he is an unpolitical
God. He is the God of the poor, the oppressed and the humiliated.
The rule of the Christ who was crucified for political reasons can
only be extended through liberation from forms of rule which
make men servile and apathetic and the political religions which
give them stability. According to Paul, the perfection of his
kingdom of freedom is to bring about the annihilation of all rule,
authority and power, which are still unavoidable here, and at the
same time to achieve the overcoming of equivalent apathy and
alienation. Christians will seek to anticipate the future of Christ
according to the measure of the possibilities available to them, by
breaking down lordship and building up the political liveliness of
each individual.

4. *Vicious Circles of Death*

Political hermeneutics is not just a theoretical development of
tradition, nor is it accomplished only on an ideological and
religious level. It sets out to be a hermeneutics of life in the
situation of the passion of God, and therefore includes both
practice and the alteration of practice. Liberation of mankind
towards better mutual relationships is always practised in particular vicious circles which do not allow men to be men. Just as
there are psychological pattern formations which make men ill,
so too there are hopeless economic, social and political pattern
formations which drive life towards death. In such formations
there are always a number of vicious circles, each of which con-
tributes to another. So there is no sense in talking about a 'theology
of liberation'. It is necessary to speak of 'liberations' in the plural
and to advance the processes of liberation in several dimensions of
oppression at the same time. One cannot liberate a particular area
by setting up dictatorships elsewhere. So in what follows we are
in search of the traces of men's liberation in a series of realms
and dimensions. Only those will be introduced which cannot be
reduced to other dimensions. In each concrete instance these

dimensions work together. Distinguishing them will provide directives for action in particular instances. By this, one does not envisage any pyramid-like gradation in reality or any historical sequences with priorities. But in most cases a mutual influence of one dimension on another may be observed.

(*a*) In the economic dimension of life there is the *vicious circle of poverty*.[26] It consists of hunger, illness and early mortality, and is provoked by exploitation and class domination. There are vicious circles of poverty both in individual societies and between the developed industrial nations and the underdeveloped agrarian countries, the former colonial territories. The economic systems of labour and production keep producing unequal and unjust advances at different times. Granted, the overall *per capita* income increases, but this is not to everyone's advantage. For individual groups within a people and for entire peoples the result is a vicious circle of poverty, work, illness and exploitation. Millions of immigrant workers in Northern Europe have been caught up in this hopeless circle. Most negroes in the USA are caught in a similar trap; poverty, police, courts and prisons all being linked together. Within the larger circle, smaller vicious circles appear; poverty, drugs, crime, prison and further poverty all being linked together. From a global perspective, the economic systems of the world work in a spiral which makes the rich nations richer and the poor nations poorer. The prices of agrarian products decline and the prices of industrial products rise. Thus the underdeveloped countries fall increasingly into debt and cannot obtain freedom.

(*b*) In the political dimension, the vicious circle of force is inextricably bound up with the *vicious circle of poverty*.[27] It is produced in particular societies by the domination of dictatorships, upper classes or those with privileges. It is also produced through the relationships between powerful and weaker nations. The institutionalized rule of force produces counter-force. Human rights of self-determination and political co-determination are suppressed and then can only be asserted in revolutionary terms. Here, too, hopeless spirals develop: after the failure of reforms or revolutions the oppressors are better organized, and successful revolutions often organize new oppression. The growth of organized force and spontaneous counter-force is a threatening sign. No less threatening is the vicious circle of the international arms race.[28] Whereas previously military deterrent systems have secured peace, their escalation is now leading towards instability. The predictable course of the arms race is 'an open spiral upwards into nothingness'.[29] Mistrusts and interests in hegemony make the armament spiral a deadly threat to the whole world.

(c) Also involved with the vicious circles of poverty and force is the *vicious circle of racial and cultural alienation.* Men are adaptable and compliant once they have been robbed of their identity and characteristics and have been degraded to the point of becoming manipulable factors in the system. They are then shaped in the image of their rulers.[30] There can be no conquest of poverty and oppression without the liberation of men from their racial, cultural and technocratic alienation. The conquest of poverty and political oppression is often achieved only at the cost of alienations of this kind. Men then survive in relative freedom, but they no longer know who they really are. They become apathetic cogs in a technocratic mega-machine.[31]

(d) The vicious circles of poverty, force and alienation are now bound up in a greater circle, the *vicious circle of the industrial pollution of nature.*[32] Mindless faith in progress has irreparably destroyed the balance of nature by industrialization. It is possible to calculate the 'limits of growth'.[33] If no wise balance of progress and social equality is achieved, then ecological death is more than to be feared. The great undertaking of the industrial revolution comes to its end in the vicious circle of the ecological crisis. The destruction of the natural environment, the exploitation of nature, will also ruin the whole industrialized world and the rest of life on earth. Today a one-sided orientation on economic values and the hopes for self-liberation which earlier generations often rested with messianic fervour on work, the machine, profit and progress, are bringing about a reversal in the systems of men and nature from an orientation on life to an orientation on death.

(e) In the economic, political, cultural and industrial vicious circles one can see a deeper, more embracing drive: *the vicious circle of senselessness and godforsakenness.* Today we are making the world hell, say some, in view of our inextricable situation. The future has become obscure. So in the present people become perplexed, disheartened, and many men lose all sense of purpose. Just as the rabbit is transfixed by the snake's look, so today men are transfixed with future shock and become apathetic. Some seek escape in enjoyment of the present. Others look for peace in

331

dream-worlds. Others again anticipate the decline by terrorism. The general sense of disheartenment is experienced in different situations in different ways. But this makes men see the areas of misery outlined above as hopeless vicious circles. From the experience of senselessness arises apathy, and from apathy there often follows an unconscious death-wish.

5. *Ways towards Liberation*

Wherever the five vicious circles mentioned above work together, a general syndrome of decay develops. The vicious circles work together as a linked system and bring the human life involved in them to a state of dehumanization and death. Liberating action must therefore localize these vicious circles and recognize the way in which they work together. It must be active in all five dimensions at the same time, if it is to free the whole of life from oppression.

(a) In the *economic dimension of life*, liberation means the satisfaction of the material needs of men for health, nourishment, clothing and somewhere to live. A further part of this is a social justice which can give all members of society a satisfying and just share in the products they produce. In so far as the vicious circle of poverty is produced by exploitation and class domination, social justice can only be achieved by a redistribution of economic power. The privileges of capital over labour strengthen the vicious circle of poverty. The vicious circle of poverty can be broken only through economic co-determination and control of economic power by the producers. Social welfare for those who are economically weak and development aid for the so-called underdeveloped nations are necessary as transitional measures to keep men alive who would otherwise go to the wall. But they are only justified by a social policy which brings social justice to the poor, the exploited and the weak. If and in so far as socialism in this sense means the satisfaction of material need and social justice in a material democracy, *socialism is the symbol for the liberation of men from the vicious circle of poverty*.

(b) In the *political dimension of life*, liberation from the vicious circle of oppression also means democracy. By this we mean human dignity in the acceptance of political responsibility. This includes participation in and control of the exercise of economic and political power. The vicious circle of force can only be broken by giving each individual political responsibility and an active part in the processes of decision. Otherwise the exercise of power is not freed from the privileges and hegemonies of particular classes and groups. Only through equal and just distribution of political burdens can the alienation of the people from political power and its political apathy be overcome. The *Universal Declaration of Human Rights* may be taken as a standard for democratic justice. In the formulations which have been hitherto held to be valid it derives from the civic revolutions of the eighteenth and nineteenth centuries, and to that degree needs to be supplemented. Democracy means the recognition of human rights as the basic rights of the citizen in a state. The aim of the democratic movement, for we must speak of a movement and not of a condition or an ideal, is the making possible and the realization of human dignity through liberation from political oppression and control. If and to the degree that the democratic movement means the abolition of privilege and the establishment of political human rights, *democracy is the symbol for the liberation of men from the vicious circle of force*. This is true not only within a state but also between competing states, for the abolition of military deterrent systems and the construction of systems for political peace and control.

(c) In the *cultural dimension of life*, liberation from the vicious circle of alienation means identity in the recognition of others. By this we mean the 'human emancipation of man' (Marx), in which men gain self-respect and self-confidence in the recognition of others and fellowship with them. True, the struggle here is always one over integration or identity. But these are not contradictions. The recognition of racial and cultural and personal differences and the recognition of one's own identity belong together. Integration cannot lead to a grey mass of uniform men. Identity cannot mean ultimate separation. Identity and acknowledgment belong together and are not possible without each other. The human emancipation of men from self-alienation and alienating dealings with each other is only possible when different kinds of people encounter each other without anxiety, superiority or repressed feelings of guilt and regard their differences as fruitful, working together productively. If and in so far as emancipation means personalization in socialization and finding one's identity in the recognition of others, *emancipation is the symbol for liberation from the vicious circle of alienation.*

— (*d*) In the *relationship of society to nature*, liberation from the vicious circle of the industrial pollution of nature means peace with nature. No liberation of men from economic distress, political oppression and human alienation will succeed which does not free nature from inhuman exploitation and which does not satisfy nature. As far as we can see today, only a radical change of the relationship of man to nature will get us out of the ecological crisis. The models of self-liberation from nature and domination of it by exploitation lead to the ecological death of nature and humanity. They must therefore be replaced by new models of co-operation with nature. The relationship of working man to nature is not a master-servant relationship but a relationship of intercommunication which pays respect to the circumstances. Nature is not an object but man's environment, and in this has its own rights and equilibria. Therefore men must exchange their apathetic and often hostile domination over nature for a sympathetic relationship of partnership with the natural world. The hominization of nature in the sphere of human control only leads to the humanization of man when the latter are also 'naturalized'.[34] Therefore the long phase of the liberation of man from nature in his 'struggle for existence' must be replaced by a phase of the liberation of nature from inhumanity for the sake of 'peace in existence'. To the degree that the transition from an orientation on economic and ecological values and from an increase in the quantity of life to an appreciation of the quality of life, and thus from the possession of nature to the joy of existing in it can overcome the ecological crisis, *peace with nature is the symbol of the liberation of man from this vicious circle.*

(*e*) In the relationship of man, society and nature to the *meaning of life*, liberation means a significant life filled with the sense of the whole. A society which is oppressed with economic, political, cultural and industrial vicious circles is always also a 'disheartening society'.[35] In the background of personal and public awareness, perplexity, resignation and despair are widespread. This inner poisoning of life extends not only through poor societies but through rich societies as well. It cannot therefore be overcome simply by victory over economic need, political oppression, cultural alienation and the ecological crisis. Nor can it be reduced to these realms and dimensions. The crisis of meaning oppresses an unfilled life and a life filled in other ways, albeit in different manners. This wound remains open even in the best of all conceivable societies.[36] It can only be healed by the presence of meaning in all events and relationships of life.

The absence of meaning and the corresponding consequences of an ossified and absurd life are described in theological terms as godforsakenness; the presence of meaning is termed the presence and indwelling of God in a new creation. If God is all in all in it, man and nature then take part in God's fullness of meaning and potentiality. The freedom of the sons of God and the liberation of enslaved nature (Rom. 8.19ff.) are consummated in the arrival of the complete and universal indwelling of God. In a situation of godforsakenness and senselessness the knowledge of the hidden presence of God in the godforsaken Christ on the cross already gives 'courage to be', despite nothingness and all annihilating experiences.[37] Hell does not lie before men. It has been conquered in the cross. Here life and sacrifice for life against death gain their meaning amidst the general senselessness. Thus 'courage to be' becomes a 'key for being'. Faith becomes hope for significant fulfilment. Therefore in the situation of a 'disheartened society', Christian faith becomes 'counting on hope' and is demonstrated through freedom from panic and apathy, from escape and the death-wish. It then leads to courage to do what is necessary, resolutely and patiently, in the vicious circles mentioned above.

6. *The Transformations of God in the Liberations of Men*

If we begin to look at the relationships which condition the various processes of liberation, and attempt to make a counter test, we shall discover that socialism is impossible without democracy and democracy is impossible without socialism in the sense mentioned above.[38] Any attempt to establish social justice with the help of an élite dictatorship of the meritocracy or with the help of a nationalist dictatorship would only be to drive out one devil with another. As history shows, it would change democratic movements into socialist dictatorships. 'There is as little human dignity without the end of need, as there is good fortune for man without the end of old and new subservience.'[39] Conversely, if one were to try to set up political democracy at the cost of social justice, it would become incredible and lead to an aristocracy of those with economic privileges. As history shows, socialist movements would soon be established. Social justice and democracy are therefore reciprocally related. Human emancipation of man, indeed even racial identity, is impossible if economic and political relationships are overlooked.[40] Racism is too closely bound up with social injustice and political deprivation of rights. Conversely, social democracy or democratic socialism cannot come into play if they are not bound up with recognition of one another in racial, cultural and personal identity. There can be no social democracy without identity in recognition, and there can be no human emancipation without social and political democracy. Further, no human society worthy of the name can be constructed without peace with nature. And conversely, there will be no co-operative system of peace with nature as long as men do not organize themselves into a total human society. A technocratic solution of the problems of mankind without a solution of the ecological problem does not lead to life. Finally, there can hardly be peace between man and man and between mankind and nature without the overcoming of despair with hope for the indwelling of meaning in everything. Conversely, there can be no presence of meaning, no meaningful and fulfilled life without liberation from the needs outlined above. In every specific situation, these vicious circles are reciprocally interrelated, and as a result no way out of them can be seen. Therefore liberation must be sought in all these five dimensions simultaneously in every specific situation. Anyone who falls short here is courting death. Anyone who becomes too abstract and general here will achieve nothing. It is enough for liberating action that these five dimensions should constantly be remembered as guidelines.

It follows from this that in any *theology of liberations* the universal must be understood *in* the particular and the eschatological *in* the historical. Otherwise it is impossible to think concretely without becoming pragmatic, and impossible to think universally without becoming abstract. Hitherto we have allowed the concept of *liberation* to run through the dimensions of oppression and have found that in the vicious circle of poverty, liberation must be called social justice; in the vicious circle of force, it must be called democratic human rights; in the vicious circle of alienation, it must be called identity in recognition; in the vicious circle of ecology, it must be called peace with nature; and in the vicious circle of meaninglessness, it must be called courage to be, and faith. We have called these identifications *symbols*, because they both show liberation in real terms in various spheres and at the same time invite further thought. This thinking in particular symbols is thus capable of overcoming the general conceptual fetishism with which events in process are defined in order to establish them, while at the same time bringing the process to a standstill. In that way the word 'liberation', like the words 'revolution' and 'establishment', loses its evocative character. Symbolic thought which makes fast in negatives and takes matters further in positives is iconoclastic of language. It overcomes both the idolatry of ideological fixation and its counterpart, idolatry, with the normative force of what is factual. Thus the cause of liberation is not established, but is constantly in process and is only comprehended by participatory, dialectical thought.

The symbol in thought is matched by the conception of reality as a *sacrament*, that is, as a reality qualified by God's word and made the bearer of his presence. These realities are not another kingdom separate from God, nor are they just similes and equivalents of his kingdom. They are synecdochically, to take up Luther's language, real presences of his coming omnipresence. In this sense a theology of liberation cannot get by without corresponding materializations of the presence of God, unless it means to remain idealistic. For it, the identifications of the presence of God with the matter involved in liberation from vicious circles are real symbols, real ciphers and material anticipations of the physical presence of God. They are incarnations which point beyond themselves. They stand in parallel to the traditional real presence of God in the sacraments, and do not replace this. If we allow the theological language of the real presence of God to run through these dimensions of misery, we reach the following sequence of identifications. In the vicious circle of poverty it can be said: 'God is not dead. He is bread.' God is present as bread in that he is the unconditional which draws near, in the present sense. In the vicious circle of force God's presence is experienced as liberation for human dignity and responsibility. In the vicious circle of alienation his presence is perceived in the experience of human identity and recognition. In the vicious circle of the destruction of nature God is present in joy in existence and in peace between man and nature. In the vicious circle of meaninglessness and god-forsakenness, finally, he comes forward in the figure of the crucified Christ, who communicates courage to be.

In accordance with theological tradition it is possible to see this real presence of God, pointing beyond itself, as the history of the Shekinah wandering through the dust, as the history of the spirit which comes upon all flesh. We understand it here in the process of the trinitarian history of God. Thus the real presences of God acquire the character of a *'praesentia explosiva'*. Brotherhood with Christ means the suffering and active participation in the history of this God. Its criterion is the history of the crucified and risen Christ. Its power is the sighing and liberating spirit of God. Its consummation lies in the kingdom of the triune God which sets all things free and fills them with meaning.

NOTES

1. This chapter takes up the discussion of political theology again and connects it with the idea of a theology of liberation which has been developed especially in Latin America. Cf. J. B. Metz, *Theology of the World*, Burns and Oates 1969; J. Moltmann, 'Theologische Kritik der politischen Religion', in J. B. Metz/J. Moltmann/W. Oelmüller, *Kirche im Prozess der Aufklärung*, 1970, 11–52; J. M. Lochman, *Perspektiven politischer Theologie*, 1971; D. Sölle, *Politische Theologie. Auseinandersetzung mit R. Bultmann*, 1971; *Diskussion zur Theologie der Revolution*, ed. E. Feil and R. Weth, 1969; *Diskussion zur politischen Theologie*, ed. H. Peuckert, 1969; R. Alves, *A Theology of Human Hope*, Washington 1969; id., *Religion. Opio o Instrumento de Liberación?*, 1970; H. Assmann, *Opresión—Liberación. Desafio a los Christianos*, 1971; Gustavo Gutierrez, *Theology of Liberation*, SCM Press 1974. For a report see R. Frieling, 'Die lateinamerikanische Theologie der Befreiung', *Materialdienst des konfessionskundlichen Instituts Bensheim* 23, 1972, 21–39.

2. U. Duchrow, *Christenheit und Weltverantwortung. Traditionsgeschichte und systematische Struktur der Zweireichelehre*, 1970. G. Ebeling, 'The Necessity of the Doctrine of the Two Kingdoms', *Word and Faith*, SCM Press 1964, 386–406, has aptly drawn attention to the critical distinction.

3. Thus Karl Barth, 'Church and Culture' (1926), in *Theology and Church*, SCM Press 1962, 334–54; *Rechtfertigung und Recht*, 1938; 'The Christian Community and the Civil Community', in *Against the Stream*, SCM Press 1954; *Die Ordnung der Gemeinde*, 1955. See now F. W. Marquardt, *Theologie und Sozialismus. Das Beispiel Karl Barths*, 1972; H. Gollwitzer, *Reich Gottes und Sozialismus bei Karl Barth*, ThEx NF 169, 1972.

4. Karl Barth, *Church Dogmatics* III 4, T. & T. Clark 1961, 596.

5. Dietrich Bonhoeffer, *Ethics*, SCM Press 1955, 98ff.
6. H. Gollwitzer, op. cit., 9f.
7. Karl Barth, 'Der Christ in der Gesellschaft' (1919), in *Das Wort Gottes und die Theologie*, 1929, 33–69. Here Barth still understood the correspondences and likenesses in the historical movement of the life of God. They were not only reflections of the completed reconciliation but also signs and anticipations of the incomplete future of God in the world. They therefore had not only the character of images but also that of promise.
8. Here I am taking up the idea of a political hermeneutics of the gospel which I put forward in 1968. Cf. 'Existenzgeschichte und Weltgeschichte', in *Perspektiven der Theologie*, 1968, 128–48. Meanwhile Dorothee Sölle has also put forward 'Political theology as hermeneutics', op. cit., 71ff. The advantage in this is that differentiation and communication of the kingdom of God and the world need not be made in idealistic terms; the starting point is the particular history of Christ, which ends on earth with the cross and eschatologically with the liberation of all things.
9. For a historical survey see E. Peterson, 'Monotheismus als politisches Problem (1935)', in *Theologische Traktate*, 1951, 45–148; A. A. T. Ehrhardt, *Politische Metaphysik von Solon bis Augustin* I: *Die Gottesstadt der Grechen und Römer*, 1959; C. Schmitt, *Politische Theologie* I, 1922; II, 1970.
10. M. Pohlenz, *Die Stoa* I, ³1964, 198.
11. H. Arendt, *Über die Revolution*, 1963, 150.
12. See A. von Harnack, *Der Vorwurf des Atheismus in den drei ersten Jahrhunderten*, 1905, 10ff.
13. Cf. L. Reinisch (ed.), *Die deutsche Strafrechtsreform*, 1967.
14. K. E. Nipkow, 'Braucht unsere Bildung Religion? Zur gesellschaftlichen Verwendung religiöser Erziehung und zur Gesellschaftsferne der Religionspädagogik', in *Gedenkschrift für I. Robbelen*, ed. H. Horn, 1972.
15. J. J. Rousseau, *Du contrat social*, book 4, ch. 8.
16. P. Berger, *The Noise of Solemn Assemblies. Christian Commitment and the Religious Establishment in America*, New York 1961; R. Bellah, *Civil Religion in America*, New York 1967.
17. J. B. Metz, op. cit., 115ff.
18. H. Berkhof, *Kirche und Kaiser. Eine Untersuchung der Enstehung der byzantinischen und der theokratischen Staatsauffassung im vierten Jahrhundert*, 1947.
19. This is the closing sentence and the conclusion of E. Peterson's investigation of monotheism; against C. Schmitt, op. cit., 148.
20. J. B. Metz, op. cit., 113ff.; J. Moltmann, op. cit., 50ff.; J. M. Lochman, op. cit., 23ff.: 'The cross of faith and the faith of the cross are the prelude to a legitimate political theology and practice for the church.' D. Sölle, op. cit., 89ff., on the other hand, reflects more the historical Jesus, but in view of the historical trial of Jesus this represents no contradiction to the political theology of the cross.
21. G. W. F. Hegel, *Philosophy of Religion*, III, 89ff.
22. N. O. Brown, *Love's Body*, New York 1968, 122.

23. J. Q. Adams, quoted in N. O. Brown, op. cit., 114.

24. R. Smend has drawn attention to this in 'Das Problem der Institution und der Staat', *ZEE* 6, 1962, 66.

25. K. Wolzendorff, *Staatsrecht und Naturrecht in der Lehre vom Widerstandsrecht des Volkes gegen rechtswidrige Ausübung der Staatsgewalt*, 1916.

26. E. Eppler, 'Der Teufelskreis der Armut', *Neues Hochland* 64, 1972, 38–42.

27. D. Senghaas, *Abschreckung und Frieden. Studien zur Kritik organisierter Friedlosigkeit*, 1969; *Weltfrieden und Revolution*, ed. H. E. Bahr, 1968.

28. J. W. Forester, *Der teuflische Regelkreis*, 1970.

29. J. B. Wiesner, *Friedensforschung*, ed. E. Krippendorf, ²1970, 216.

30. J. H. Cone, *Black Theology. A Christian Interpretation of the Black Power Movement*, New York 1968; P. Freire, *Pedagogy of the Oppressed*, Penguin Books 1973.

31. E. Fromm, *Die Revolution der Hoffnung. Für eine humanisierte Technik*, 1971; *Texte zur Technokratiediskussion*, ed. C. Koch and D. Senghaas, 1970.

32. *Humanökologie und Umweltschutz*, Studien zur Friedenforschung 8, ed. E. von Weizsäcker, 1972.

33. D. Meadows, *The Limits to Growth*, Earth Island 1972.

34. K. Marx, *Frühschriften*, ed. Landshut, 235, 237: 'Thus society is the complete essential unity of man with nature, the true resurrection of nature, the accomplished naturalism of man and the accomplished humanization of nature.' This idea was taken up in a positive way in *Humanökologie und Umweltschutz*, op. cit., 53.

35. Cf. G. Picht, op. cit., 92.

36. E. Bloch, *Naturrecht und menschliche Würde*, 1961, 310f.: 'A society that is not antagonistic will not hold all the fate of the world in its hand; it produces economic and political disorientation and purposelessness, and for that very reason the unworthiness of existence emerges even more strongly, from the jaws of death to the ebbing away of life in tedium and satiation. The messengers from nothingness have lost their mere disguises from class society, and bear a new and now largely unimaginable face, but the sense of purpose which has been broken off in them now gnaws in a new way.' Bloch calls this 'the metaphysical question'. Paul Tillich, *The Courage to Be*, Fontana Books 1962, esp. 152ff. Here the justification for 'metaphysical theology' which is so much criticized today is made clear in a socio-political context. It is superficial and leads to apathy if for anti-religious feelings one overlooks the metaphysical evil that lies alongside physical and moral evil. Only the person who satisfies metaphysical need in a dogmatistic way, denies metaphysical evil.

38. Rosa Luxemburg, quoted in E. Bloch, *Naturrecht und menschliche Würde*, 13, where the struggle against an undemocratic socialism becomes as necessary as the struggle against an unsocial democracy.

39. E. Bloch, op. cit., 14.

40. The limitations of anti-racist liberation movements and theologies lie in the underestimation of these connections.

ABBREVIATIONS

BoA	Luthers Werke in Auswahl, Bonn edition
CR	Corpus Reformatorum
EMZ	*Evangelische Missionszeitschrift*
ESG	Evangelische Studentengemeinde
EvKomm	Evangelisches Kommentar
EvTh	*Evangelische Theologie*
KuD	*Kerygma und Dogma*
LThK	*Lexikon für Theologie und Kirche*
MPTh	*Monatsschrift für Pastoral Theologie*
NF	Neue Folge (New Series)
PhB	Philosophische Bücherei
RGG	*Die Religion in Geschichte und Gegenwart*
TDNT	*Theological Dictionary of the New Testament*, ed. G. Kittel
ThB	Theologische Bücherei
ThEx	Theologische Existenz Heute
ThLz	*Theologische Literaturzeitung*
VuF	*Verkündigung und Forschung*
WA	Weimarer Ausgabe (of Luther's works)
ZEE	*Zeitschrift für evangelische Ethik*
ZKG	*Zeitschrift für Kirchengeschichte*
ZNW	*Zeitschrift für die neutestamentliche Wissenschaft*
ZPMP	*Zeitschrift für psychosomatische Medizin und Psychoanalyse*
ZThK	*Zeitschrift für Theologie und Kirche*

INDEX OF NAMES

74 75 76 77 10 9 8 7 6 5 4 3 2 1